The Life and Times of Arthur Maloney

The Last of the Tribunes

CHARLES PULLEN

The Osgoode Society for Canadian Legal History

Printed and bound in Canada

The publisher wishes to acknowledge the generous assistance and ongoing support of the **Canada Council**, the **Book Publishing Industry Development Program** of the **Department of Canadian Heritage**, the **Ontario Arts Council**, the **Ontario Publishing Centre** of the **Ministry of Culture, Tourism and Recreation**, and the **Ontario Heritage Foundation**.

Care has been taken to trace the ownership of copyright material used in the text (including the illustrations). The author and publisher welcome any information enabling them to rectify any reference or credit in subsequent editions.

J. Kirk Howard, Publisher

Canadian Cataloguing in Publication Data

Pullen, Charles H., 1929–
The life and times of Arthur Maloney : the last of the tribunes

Co-published by the Osgoode Society for Canadian Legal History.
Includes bibliographical references and index.
ISBN 1-55002-224-5

1. Maloney, Arthur. 2. Lawyers – Canada – Biography. 3. Politicians – Canada – Biography. 4. Ombudsman – Ontario – Biography.
I. Osgoode Society for Canadian Legal History. II. Title.

KE416.M35P8 1994 345.71'0092 C94-932604-6

Dundurn Press Limited
2181 Queen Street East
Suite 301
Toronto, Canada
M4E 1E5

Dundurn Distribution
73 Lime Walk
Headington, Oxford
England
0X3 7AD

Dundurn Press Limited
1823 Maryland Avenue
P.O. Box 1000
Niagara Falls, N.Y.
U.S.A. 14302-1000

Contents

PUBLICATIONS OF THE OSGOODE SOCIETY FOR CANADIAN LEGAL HISTORY

1981 David H. Flaherty, ed., *Essays in the History of Canadian Law*, volume I

1982 Marion MacRae and Anthony Adamson, *Cornerstones of Order: Courthouses and Town Halls of Ontario, 1784–1914*

1983 David H. Flaherty, ed., *Essays in the History of Canadian Law*, volume II

1984 Patrick Brode, *Sir John Beverley Robinson: Bone and Sinew of the Compact*

1984 David Williams, *Duff: A Life in the Law*

1985 James Snell and Frederick Vaughan, *The Supreme Court of Canada: History of the Institution*

1986 Paul Romney, *Mr. Attorney: The Attorney General for Ontario in Court, Cabinet and Legislature, 1791–1899*

1986 Martin L. Friedland, *The Case of Valentine Shortis: A True Story of Crime and Politics in Canada*

1987 C. Ian Kyer and Jerome E. Bickenbach, *The Fiercest Debate: Cecil A. Wright, the Benchers and Legal Education in Ontario, 1923-1957*

1988 Robert J. Sharpe, *The Last Day, the Last Hour: The Currie Libel Trial*

1988 John D. Arnup, *Middleton: The Beloved Judge*

1989 Desmond Brown, *The Genesis of the Canadian Criminal Code of 1892*

1989 Patrick Brode, *The Odyssey of John Anderson*

1990 Jim Phillips and Philip Girard, eds., *Essays in the History of Canadian Law*, volume III, *Nova Scotia*

1990 Carol Wilton, ed., *Essays in the History of Canadian Law*, volume IV, *Beyond the Law, Lawyers and Business in Canada, 1830–1930*

1991 Constance Backhouse, *Petticoats and Prejudice: Women and Law in Nineteenth Century Canada*

1992 Brendan O'Brien, *Speedy Justice: The Tragic Last Voyage of His Majesty's Vessel Speedy*

1992 Robert Fraser, ed., *Provincial Justice: Upper Canadian Legal Portraits from the Dictionary of Canadian Biography*

1993 Greg Marquis, *Policing Canada's Century: A History of the Canadian Association of Chiefs of Police*

1993 Murray Greenwood, *Legacies of Fear: Law and Politics in Quebec in the Era of the French Revolution*

1994 Patrick Boyer, *A Passion for Justice: The Legacy of James Chalmers McRuer*

1994 Charles Pullen, *The Life and Times of Arthur Maloney: The Last of the Tribunes*

1994 Jim Phillips, Tina Loo, and Susan Lewthwaite, eds., *Essays in the History of Canadian Law*, volume V, *Crime and Criminal Justice*

1994 Brian Young, *The Politics of Codification: The Lower Canadian Civil Code of 1866*

PATRONS OF THE OSGOODE SOCIETY

Aird & Berlis
Blake, Cassels & Graydon
Davies, Ward & Beck
Holden Day Wilson
McCarthy Tétrault
Osler, Hoskin & Harcourt
The Harweg Foundation
Tory Tory DesLauriers & Binnington
Weir & Foulds

The Society also thanks The Law Foundation of Ontario and the Law Society of Upper Canada for their continuing support.

Foreword

THE OSGOODE SOCIETY FOR CANADIAN LEGAL HISTORY

The purpose of The Osgoode Society for Canadian Legal History is to encourage research and writing in the history of Canadian law. The Society, which was incorporated in 1979 and is registered as a charity, was founded at the initiative of the Honourable R. Roy McMurtry, former attorney-general for Ontario, and officials of the Law Society of Upper Canada. Its efforts to stimulate the study of legal history in Canada include a research support program, a graduate student research assistance program, and work in the fields of oral history and legal archives. The Society publishes (at the rate of about one a year) volumes of interest to the Society's members that contribute to legal-historical scholarship in Canada, including studies of the courts, the judiciary, and the legal profession, biographies, collections of documents, studies in criminology and penology, accounts of great trials, and work in the social and economic history of the law.

Current directors of The Osgoode Society for Canadian Legal History are Jane Banfield, Marion Boyd, Brian Bucknall, Archie Campbell, J. Douglas Ewart, Martin Friedland, John Honsberger, Kenneth Jarvis, Paul Lamek, Allen Linden, Colin McKinnon, Roy McMurtry, Brendan O'Brien, Peter Oliver, James Spence, and Richard Tinsley. The annual report and information about membership may be obtained by writing The Osgoode Society for Canadian Legal History, Osgoode Hall, 130 Queen Street West, Toronto, Ontario, Canada M5H 2N6. Members receive the annual volume published by the Society.

There are in Canada few good biographies of prominent lawyers and this regrettable circumstance has contributed largely to our failure to know and understand much about how our legal system developed and how it operates today. Few lawyers have written memoirs or produced autobiographies, and even fewer scholars have attempted to provide serious accounts of Canadian legal careers, in part a consequence of the frequent failure to preserve private legal papers.

The Osgoode Society believes that it is important to nurture and support a tradition of legal biography and it believes that its 1994 publications represent a significant step in that direction. Professor Pullen's biography of Arthur Maloney is a fascinating account of the life of a great criminal lawyer written in a manner which is equally accessible to lawyers, scholars, and the general reader. By providing a richly detailed account of the work of a superb trial lawyer, including a full analysis of four trials and reflections on Maloney's own sense of the role of the defence in the criminal trial, Professor Pullen has added significantly to our understanding of criminal law practice in Canada from the 1950s to the 1980s. We are delighted to be publishing *The Life and Times of Arthur Maloney: The Last of the Tribunes.*

R. Roy McMurtry
President

Peter N. Oliver
Editor-in-Chief

Preface and Acknowledgements

This book was written, in first draft, on five different second-hand, sometimes borrowed, well-worn portable typewriters, while I was following my wife about from one town to another as she pursued her career as a restorer of oil paintings. The research began in Toronto, and the first writing was done on the edge of the roaring Pacific in a little, old-fashioned motel (owned by a gentle old man, a former Canadian from Owen Sound who had served in the RCAF during the war) at Ocean Beach in San Diego, California. It continued in Kingston, Ontario, and in San Francisco, California; Great Chesterford, England; Kitchener, Ontario; Holland Park (just up the street from where the very great English novelist Ford Madox Ford lived years ago, which I thought might have some salutary influence on both the prose and the thought), in London, England; Newark, Delaware; and Ottawa. As a result, Peter Oliver, my editor, had to deal with manuscripts of dubious intellectual quality presented on scraps of paper, barely impressed by the feeble punch of old typewriter hammers. The greatest difficulty was finding ribbons, often faded and dry, for these tiny machines, fast on their way to becoming industrial antiques. Professor Oliver never complained, and has always been encouraging, constructive, and sweet-natured. Marilyn MacFarlane, his keeper of the Osgoode office flame, has been equally helpful, and always willing to listen to my concerns and complaints. She has also been responsible for dealing with the tedium and confusion of the texts, turning them into readable copy. Chris Kates, who has her own business to do for the Society, was also willing to give of her own experience as an interviewer, and generously handed over her file on Arthur Maloney for me to use as I thought fit. I will return it – it is in the pile – somewhere.

I would like to thank the Maloney and French families for the help they gave me in putting Arthur Maloney in the context of his childhood and family. They were generous with their time, even when months sometimes went by in silence while I worked on the study far away from Canada. I particularly appreciated the help of Mrs. Lillian Maloney, who not only was continually helpful in the obvious sense but, on more than one occasion, physically struggled at the bottom of the ladder while we dragged box after box of Arthur's files out of the loft in the old barn at the family farm on the Guelph line. My special thanks for help on that terrible snowy, icy day when my car bogged down on the thin ice outside the barn door, and Lillian, with some experience driving a tractor, got behind the wheel, and coaxed the vehicle, loaded with boxes of files, to slide along the ice to escape down the driveway. May she and her long line of stray cats have a long and happy life at "Malafield," the country home, near Rockwood on the Guelph line, where Arthur found such happiness in the later years of his life.

I would also thank all those friends, former students, and colleagues of Arthur who managed to see me (sometimes more than once) despite the fact that most of them are at the top of their careers and extremely busy. I apologize to the many friends of Arthur whom I could not, or did not reach, and who, I have no doubt, wanted to speak of his association with them. I could have gone on talking to members of the legal profession in Ontario for much longer, had the time and the expense money not finally run out. The truth is less callous, however, since it was simply a matter of having so much material that a stop had to be called. I apologize for not using all the marvellous stories I was told; we would otherwise have wound up with a very long book consisting entirely of well-remembered, cherished anecdotes, some of dubious propriety, but hypnotic charm. The men and women whom I did speak to were open, candid, patient, and a great pleasure to meet, and I enjoyed every moment with them, just as they enjoyed their memories of Arthur. It was often a touching experience.

I would also acknowledge the patience and generosity of my boyhood friend, Robert W. Stamp, who had been my Psi Upsilon roommate at the University of Toronto, and who allowed me to invade his apartment, often without notice, to sleep on his couch, when I made those dozens of trips from Kingston to Toronto to interview Maloney associates. Ken Jarvis deserves special thanks for accompanying me from his studio in Toronto to the Guelph line home for the purpose of photographing the bronze head, which he had created in 1975 for presentation at the dinner celebrating Maloney's appointment as Ombudsman. His offer to do so was generous – and who else was likely to concern himself with getting the best picture possible of that formidable representation of Arthur Maloney for the frontispiece?

When the time came to put the material in some civilized shape, I was at something of a loss since we found out that the publisher required the material to be IBM compatible, and I simply wasn't – until Professor Rudi Schnitzler, of Queen's University, offered to teach me how to use his lap-top computer and to do the printing for me so that the final hard copy would be presentable. I want to thank him for his generosity in allowing me to carry off and beat away at his expensive instrument, and his patience in working with me over a period of some months as we put the final copy together.

Finally my thanks to my wife who put up with piled boxes of musty Maloney material in small apartments in three different countries. God knows how I'm ever going to get all that stuff back from England, where Sue and Bob Moore are waiting patiently to retrieve their box room – just two of my friends who have put up with the making of this book for far too long.

And for extra effort: David C. Day, Jerry Wilk, Monte Harris, Paul, Frances, and John French, Anna Lyons, Nell Maloney, Hon. David G. Humphrey, Phil Patterson, Judith Turnbull of Dundurn Press, and, again, Marilyn MacFarlane.

Charles Pullen
The Montebello Apartment Hotel
Ottawa

To Sheila and My Father

THE LIFE AND TIMES OF ARTHUR MALONEY

The Last of the Tribunes

Portrait head in bronze of Arthur Maloney.
Sculptor and photographer, Kenneth Jarvis, RCA

1

The Figures in the Carpet

Their force was suited rather for opposition than for action. They were instituted to defend the oppressed, to pardon offences, to arraign the enemies of the people, and, when they judged it necessary, to stop, by a single word, the whole machine of government.

– Edward Gibbon, on the role of the Tribunes, *The History of the Decline and Fall of the Roman Empire*

This is a story of a man who was very lucky until the last years of his life. Knowing he was dying, he told Father Sean O'Sullivan, the former member of Parliament, as O'Sullivan records in his book, *Both My Houses*, "I cannot conceive of a God who is anything but merciful. He gives us so many chances, so many chances."[1] Arthur Maloney was quite right about those chances in relation to his own life. He was given many chances. Some he took and kept to, all his life; some he took for a little while – then he relinquished them; some he did not take, but seemed quite happy to acknowledge as possibilities to be ignored. This is a book about some of those chances, what they meant to Arthur Maloney, and to those who knew him.

Biography is a questionable practice. If less arrogant than autobiography, it still presumes the possibility of getting the subject not only true, but reasonably accurate. Arthur Maloney is, to a considerable extent, at the mercy of others. This book was begun some years after his death. He left no diary, and though the correspondence is considerable, most of it involves his professional life. There are a handful of letters to and from his mother, and a few notes to family members, but not much that could be called personal. There are surviving sisters, a wife, and two children; there are many who knew him professionally as a lawyer, a politician, and as a friend, most of whom were connected with him in his public life. There are the files from his law practice and from his career as Ontario's Ombudsman, and a very few political files. That is all.

But there is memory. There is, of course, in scholarly circles, some scepticism about that source of past action, despite the recent popularity of oral history. There is good reason for wry suspicion of a man such as Maloney who possessed the gift of instant charm. He was something of a minor celebrity, and people like to remember such figures in colourful ways. Perhaps more to the point, he had many close friends who remember him with anecdotal enthusiasm. He was well-liked, and if it is possible, without misunderstanding, given the present-day idea of male affection, to talk of personal feelings, Maloney was capable of engendering intense affection in men, principally engaged in the law, a confrontational and aggressive profession that would seem an unlikely place to find disinterested friendship. On three separate occasions, fully grown men, all of them case-hardened in the world of criminal law, surprised not only me, but themselves, by breaking into tears while talking about Arthur Maloney.

Arthur Maloney would qualify for a biography simply on the grounds of his skill as a trial lawyer, and that part of his life might well be satisfied by a simple cataloguing of his greatest successes in the courts. But that is not the whole story of what he was as a man. Sometimes what a man does is all that a man is, but Maloney was more than his high skill at the Bar. He was also a sometime politician, and a sometime civil servant (although "civil" would seem questionable to some of his critics). Perhaps more to the point, he was a kind of freelance humanist, not in the lettered sense, but in terms of personal conduct.

There is a further aspect of the Maloney history that has to be met. There is an accumulation of public, desultory memory of Maloney that is not flattering. From the beginning of this project, there has been some eye-shifting dubiety about the man. Indeed, within the Osgoode Society, and certainly within the legal profession, there are those who have a jaundiced view of him. Much of this opinion is confused, as well as vague, depending upon dim memories of newspaper reports and unsolicited word-of-mouth derision. Most of these people of opinion are innocent, unbiased spectators of the public scene who had heard enough about Maloney to presume to dislike him without much personal knowledge of the man. They were not intimates to the finer or grosser points of his life – they only know what they have heard.

The question then is who are to be the readers of this book? His friends, perhaps, all of whom possess sufficient anecdotal bits and pieces to satisfy them about their old acquaintance. Perhaps the members of the Law Society who are sufficiently interested in the history of the profession to welcome his life as a celebration of the skills of advocacy. These friends and fellow practitioners may be easily satisfied, and some of them hardly need a book at all, since they have their own, confident ideas about Maloney. Biographies, however, ought to be more than simple confirmations of what is already known, or presumed to be known, however strong and solid the basis for such knowledge may be. It is hoped that this work will add something to that which is already known by Arthur Maloney's intimates, and fellow practitioners, and that it will also be of some pleasure to those who know little or nothing, or to those who have ideas about the man which are not entirely correct, or quite wrong. It is also hoped that close discussion of a few of his trials may be of interest, and perhaps some scholarly value to present-day practitioners and law students.

Maloney was a great public character. Unwittingly (and that would be the word most appropriate in the minds of many), he accumulated, in the late 1970s, a reputation as a grand, preposterous poseur. He did it within a few months, despite the fact that in early 1975, he was the toast of Ontario. Nominated in the late spring of 1975 to be Ontario's first Ombudsman, he was swamped with congratulatory celebration by the government, the newspapers, the columnists, and anyone who cared to have an opinion on the matter. It was presumed that he would become the saviour of the public who would never again, at least in Ontario, have to fear or be intimidated or bewildered or abused by the behemoth of big government. It has been said that one of the greatest problems of late twentieth-century democracy is its inability to rid itself of the tyranny of the mutual self-interest of civil servants and politicians. In the late spring and early summer of 1975, Ontario fell in love with itself for having found in Arthur Maloney the man who would lead them out of the labyrinth of the government paper trail. He took the job with a flourish that enchanted everyone – but not for long. When he resigned in 1978, he was seen by many as an arrogant fool and a failure, and the public memory of him was forever tainted. However many Ontario citizens remember his skills, his charm, his generosity, his social and moral concern, what ultimately remains in the public memory is his failure as the Ombudsman, a failure that has been imprinted on the public mind as solely the responsibility of a man who made the mistake of foolishly taking himself at the world's estimation, misled, as he was, into thinking that governmental praise was a mandate for action, rather than political self-congratulation, which was nine parts public relations and one part social concern.

The book, therefore, is written not simply to praise, but to contemplate the nature of the ultimate Maloney reputation which is safe enough in the matter of his legal reputation, but considerably less so on the question of his skills as a civil servant. Is the mildly interested citizen right in thinking of Maloney as a fine chap to have in the courts, but a bungler on the larger public stage? It is not made any easier by the fact that many of his detractors willingly grant him his reputation not only as a lawyer, but as a great champion of social rights, yet hold tenaciously to the fact that his somewhat dandyish pose as a public figure was tinged with vanity and a sometime disrespect for social convention which marked him as a man who was not an innocent victim of celebrity. He knew well enough how to work a crowd, as well as enchant a single citizen who might meet him in an elevator. Dave Humphrey, the former criminal lawyer who is now on the Bench, and was in his time something of a skilled hand at attracting attention, suggested that the title of this book should be *Hi, My Name Is Arthur Maloney*, on the grounds that he never went anywhere with Arthur without the latter introducing himself to everyone who came within hand-shaking distance.

Maloney had a part in his moments of failure. What is interesting is the fact that he knew his limitations and excesses, and was not so pained by the contemplation of his flaws that he could not think of them, and often discuss them with his friends.

This book examines his strengths and his weaknesses in the context of his early life and character, as well as in the context not only of the somewhat hermetic world of the trial law and political adventurism, but of the world of social give-and-take in the Ontario of the middle decades of the twentieth century, a world in which the "mind set" of legal and political power often ignored the rules for expediency, sometimes benignly applied, but often with cruel indifference to the rights of the individual. Arthur Maloney began his career as a lawyer in a milieu of somewhat good-natured, but often mildly self-interested corruption and moral flexibility. The letter of the law was often less important than a kind of broad-stroke application of frontier justice, which was not confined to the far reaches of the province, but was a common element in criminal law in Toronto. He, like all criminal counsel, was obliged to live with this situation, and manipulate it as best he could, given his rigourist determination to give the little man and woman a chance in a society that in the main ignored them. It was a legal system that was often arbitrary, and sometimes unfair. It wasn't only police cruelty or judicial indifference. One of Arthur's students tells of being greeted with a happy laugh of derision when he informed a magistrate that he had been instructed by Arthur to speak to the sentence of a first offender who had sat in a car innocently while a shop robbery was perpetrated by his mates. The boy had subsequently been convicted of the robbery, despite the testimony of his friends that he knew nothing of what they were doing. The magistrate told the student to go right ahead, but the boy was getting five years whatever he said, and that he might try singing, as the magistrate put it, "The Spar-strangled Banner" [*sic*] while tap-dancing – the result would be the same – five years. The student, nevertheless, insisted on a twenty-minute plea to sentence, during which the magistrate leaned forward on one occasion to imitate a dance step on the lip of the Bench. He gave the boy five years. When the student told Arthur, he simply shook his head, and said, "He's always been a bastard." Arthur wasn't surprised, and did not presume to do anything about it. That was the way of the world.

Arthur disliked that kind of thing, but it could be an advantage to a counsel who could get along with the system. Police might lie, or they might not; they might even hold back if they felt so inclined, and it was possible to talk them out of charges if there seemed some reason for giving an accused the benefit of the doubt. The same flexibility was often seen in Crown counsel, who could be easy or they could be hard – it wasn't simply a matter of what was on paper. He was very good at dealing with police and Crowns, but he never forgot the inequities that were implicit in criminal law where most clients came from the lowest levels of the society and where they were often expected to come to court without benefit of any legal advice at all. He was not, however, so much of a sentimentalist to refuse the rewards that the same society gave to men with his talents – he aspired to the highest recognition of his own gifts in those centres of power that he had known from his childhood. He was a proud part of the Establishment that he often despised. He was also proud of his own work, and the work of those members of the Bar who were committed to the highest principles of legal practice, whether serving as defence counsel, prosecutors or judges. As a result, he was in and out of his society at one and the same time, possessed of a divided mind, at once conservative and deeply anarchic.

This peculiar double-mindedness was well-known to his friends and critics. It could manifest itself in such seemingly innocent gestures as his occasional habit of appearing before a judge with whom he was having difficulty, in a soft-collar shirt – wearing his tabs, but not the wing collar. It could be more seriously displayed in his standing up to a bullying judge, or chastising a police officer on the stand who had inadvertently revealed an indifference to the legal rights of an accused. It could lead him to take a case from some poor soul who approached him in the court corridors or on the street, knowing before he asked (which he usually didn't) that there was no fee to be had. It could be a matter of high principle or low mischief in the face of social *politesse*. Sometimes it looked like showing off. His friends and family, his students and colleagues all have stories of his changing moods and whims. The trouble is to call a stop to them, since most of his legal friends tell stories well, having had years of putting the best face on dubious facts in the courts. But they also have years of experience in paying close attention to detail, which may make them better witnesses to the past than untrained observers.

Certainly their skill as story tellers has much to do with the fact that some of the book relies upon quotation from taped interviews. It well may be that the testimony of friends is not always the best source of the truth about a man, but it well may be the best source of how they feel about him – since their memories of Arthur Maloney reveal deep, abiding affection, the highest respect for his work as a lawyer and as a social crusader, and an awareness that for many of them, he was the central influence in their lives, not only as lawyers, but as human beings. Then there is that other matter that Dave Humphrey speaks about with fervour – he was such great fun to be with! Perhaps the book will possess something of the aura of the man, which is one of the reasons why it occasionally wanders away from Arthur into his family life, or social surround, or seemingly peripheral detail about the time and places in which he lived. James Boswell, perhaps the greatest biographer of all time, learned from his subject, Samuel Johnson (who was also a very fine biographer), that it wasn't necessarily the grand moments of a man's life that told the truth, but the sometime intimate irrelevancies – the moments when no-one was looking, or nothing important seemed to be going on. The book is not simply, therefore, about Arthur, but about the life around him, first as a child, then as a student and a young lawyer, then as a counsel of growing reputation, not only at the Bar, but as a commentator upon social issues, as a politician, an active social reformer, and ultimately as a senior civil servant who saw a chance to bring his professional skills, his social idealism, and his concern for people in trouble together in a blazing moment of action before the realities of politics closed in on him in the late seventies. The close and measured examination of his work as the Ombudsman is an attempt to settle, if such is possible, the matter of why things seem to go so wrong for him. The material is also a public record of an unusual occurrence in Ontario politics in which a government for a moment let idealism get the better of political caution and expediency, and a human comedy of back-tracking and obfuscation was set in motion without much thought for the citizens who were supposed to be served by the experiment. It is also something of a personal tragedy for Maloney. It was his last chance to do something on a grand scale for the citizens of Ontario, in a manner consistent with his deeply held feelings for the common man. Some commentators, particularly at the Bar, would like to read the Ombudsman years as peripheral to his real business as a lawyer. It is hoped that the study of the same will show that everything he did in his public career was of a piece, and the Ombudsman incident was the largest portion of that idealistic construct that was to be his modest legacy as a public figure. The Ombudsman chapters, incidentally, are somewhat dense, in the scholarly sense, in order that the case for revaluation of what actually happened can be made adequately. If they prove too much of a burden for the general reader, one may skip through them without too much damage to the wider view of his life, so long as the first and last chapters on that subject are read with moderate attention.

Maloney was not a great legal thinker – he was not even the best criminal lawyer in the province of Ontario, although he was often called that, sometimes by fellow practitioners who well knew that in comparison with someone like G. Arthur Martin, he was the second-best man. But he was a great character who lived at an interesting time, and was deeply involved in the legal, social, and political incidents of that period. To see him in the context of his society over a period of several decades is to know something about what he was, about where he was, and what the experience of being there meant, in the existential sense, since Arthur was usually a participant, and rarely just a spectator. If there is any chance at catching the truth of Arthur Maloney's life, it isn't simply in what he did, but where and why he did it, and what was going on around him, given the fact that the dance of time was taking place with more characters in it than he, for all his intelligence and charm and skill, was able to control.

How can we know the dancer from the dance?
– W.B. Yeats

2

In the Valley

In the early seventies, Arthur Maloney and Dave Humphrey were involved in a bizarre murder-arson case, *R. v. Bencardino et al,* which went to jury trial three times (to appeal once), and was finally resolved in their clients' favour. It was necessary to interview two men who were implicated, but had fled to Italy, where they were held in custody. Maloney and Humphrey went on the trip. They flew into Rome, and took a train south to a town in Calabria to take part in the questioning. Humphrey remembers the following:

We arrived in Vibo Valentia, a small town. In the railway station there's a bar – right in the centre, and Maloney starts holding court, with Mary Apa, our interpreter, interpreting to all these people coming into town. Well, the word went out – there're all these Canadians who've come here – and we were curiosities anyways – just the appearance of us. And people started coming from all over. Well, Maloney is like the rich American. He has a ball of money, and he's pulling pieces off the ball, throwing it down, buying everybody a drink – two hours later, the party was well on its way. Maloney had announced that he was endowing the Arthur Maloney University On The Hill, just outside the town, that would specialize in Canadian studies or something like that. Somehow he got a cab driver who was a bit of an opera singer, too, and then we all wound up at the hotel in Maloney's suite of rooms with this opera singer singing Puccini or something – God! It was something? I miss him, you know. I tell you – I'd get a phone call from Arthur, saying, "Hey, Dave, what about lunch?" Or something like that. God, it was fun!

Arthur Maloney came from Eganville, Ontario, some seventy miles north-west of Ottawa. One local writer, determined to put some poetry in the landscape, described the town as sited in "the womb of the Valley." It is, in fact, quite handsomely placed on both sides of the Bonnechere River, which runs speedily through a narrow, deep, roaring cleft at this point, on its way south to Renfrew, cutting the town into almost equal halves. Unlike many small towns that suddenly pop up on the flat landscape of so much of rural Ontario, straggling along the sides of the highways, Eganville isn't there to the eye at all, though it is supposed to be, some ten miles north of Renfrew. Then, as the road curves, it is there – but not quite. As the road starts to dip sharply, the high spire of the Roman Catholic church, Saint James the Just, rises through the trees. Then the town begins to appear, reluctantly, a roof at a time, with the church shifting to the left as the road drops into a steep valley, and the streets, perhaps less than a quarter of a mile in length, appear, tiered some five lines high on both sides of the river gorge. The entire town can then be seen; each street rising clearly behind its lower companions, as the road slides down into the business centre of the town. If one looks to the left, into the second rank of the streets on the south-west side of the river, a large, square, two-storied, red-brick house, with an undersized white wood veranda can be seen, set apart from its neighbours. This is where Arthur Maloney was brought up. He wasn't the only one; nor does his accomplishment stand alone in his family, a family of considerable number and considerable endeavour with a close and important connection to the development of the town.

This part of the Ottawa Valley was lumbering country in the early nineteenth century, but by the 1840s a few settlers were struggling to survive as farmers; many of them were Irish Catholic immigrants. The Catholic church came into the area at the same time, conducting services in the farmers' homes, and later in a log-cabin church just outside of Eganville. By the 1860s, Eganville had established itself as the commercial centre for the settlers, and a new church was built in town, two miles away from the original log cabin. The land for the church was donated by two men involved in the lumber business. One, John Egan, gave his name to the town. The younger, James Bonfield, was to be the maternal grandfather of the Maloney family. Egan was well-established as the local timber baron long before James Bonfield arrived in the town, more by chance than intention. Egan, so the family story goes, met Bonfield in Ottawa at the old Russell hotel (located at Sparks and Elgin, but long since demolished). Bonfield was looking for a job. How he got to Ottawa is not known; the family believes that he had been sent from Ireland to the United States as a fund raiser for one of the Irish freedom groups. The family story is somewhat fragile at this stage but John French, the husband of Frances Maloney, Arthur's youngest sister, suggests that "there's a story that he came to America to raise money so the Irish could fight the English."[1] The Bonfield side of the family maintained a running aversion to the English. One of their cousins who was a priest during the "Black and Tan" troubles of the early 1920s, had been obliged to go into hiding, and there is a further fillip of indignation in the tale of the Tans deliberately damaging a beautiful piano owned by the priest's sister.

Long before that, however, James Bonfield had decided to give up the fight and find a new life in Canada. Egan was looking for an assistant with some education and Bonfield was just the man. The family thinks he might have been trained for the priesthood, and he may have taken part of his education at Louvain University in Belgium. He was certainly born in Tipperary, and he did not forget his allegiance to all things Irish, marrying Catherine Tracey, the daughter of Wicklow immigrants living in Ottawa. He soon became more than Egan's employee, and in 1867, after the death of Egan, he bought the business.

The Pembroke Observer of Friday, 15 March 1867, announced that "the entire [*sic*] of that large and valuable mill, village, and farm property situate in and around the rising village of Eganville, and formerly owned by the late John Egan, MPP, has just passed from the hands of the Trustees of the Egan Estate into those of James Bonfield, Esq., for the consideration of some $20,000, a sum which though large, is by no means in excess of that splendid property." At that time, as the newspaper went on to state, the town consisted of "six excellent stores, with some minor ones, three churches, grist saw, and carding mills, a tannery, town hall, and lock-up: good hotels, clergymen, physicians, and tradesmen of almost every craft – all of whom seem to be thriving and contented." Bonfield's purchase was obviously approved by the paper, who described him as "a man of great energy and public spirit, and possessing a clear head, he will be certain to assist industry and encourage every enterprise calculated to benefit the County generally and his own locality in particular." Bonfield's quick and steady rise to affluence was praised all the more since his starting out had been so modest. He had arrived in the area "with no other capital than a stout arm and a good character to commence life upon." As his first public act as the new owner of the Egan business he presented a piece of land to the St. James Episcopal Church, returning to them the $75 that they had recently paid to the Egan estate for the property. At a time when religious differences were often taken seriously, Bonfield's generosity was impressive. "This act of Mr. Bonfield is all the more kind and liberal, inasmuch as he is himself a Roman Catholic; but we think we can assure him that not only will the Protestants in his locality,[*sic*] be thankful to him for his gift, but that his liberality will be long and gratefully remembered by the Protestants throughout the County generally. We would be glad to see the good example which he has now set, largely imitated by proprietors of all denominations."

The family home of the Bonfields remained in the family long after

his death. There were seven children, one of whom, Margaret, was to be Arthur's mother. She was only six years old at the time of her father's death. Bonfield was serving as a Liberal MPP for South Renfrew under Sir Oliver Mowat at Queen's Park, when he came down with pneumonia. He was brought back to Eganville to recuperate, but died soon after. He was the first of the family to serve in Canadian politics, and he had much to do with establishing the Liberal hold on the Renfrew riding. However, the political tradition in the family was not to lie with the Liberals, since the Maloneys were always Conservatives. But Bonfield is still remembered as a politician of considerable colour and lively combativeness. Tom Edmondstone, a Renfrew lawyer and former partner of James Maloney, Arthur's brother, remembers the existence of a speech, which now seems to have gone missing, but which was a great favourite among political enthusiasts in the area. It was supposedly delivered by the reeve of the township of Head, on the occasion of Pembroke being made the county seat instead of the town of Douglas. It was, in part, an attack on James Bonfield. As Edmondstone tentatively recalls it, it went something like this: "and the back of me hand and the sole of me foot to you, James Bonfield, you scorpion of sedition. James Bonfield's mother will be pleased to see that her son what got run out of the old country for taking the King's money and stealing Paddy's broques was doing so well for himself in the new land."[2] With a grandfather who could incite such political venom, it is not surprising that the Maloney males were to be colourful additions to the world of politics.

The Bonfields were certainly the most important family in the area. Margaret had not been educated past high school, but that was not unusual at the time, even in families with money. Lillian Maloney, for instance, whose family situation was even more formidable, did not go on to university in the forties. What both these women possessed, however, was a good "finishing" education, and Margaret Bonfield was sensible, handsome, and cultured in that modest sense that served well in rural towns of limited pretension and opportunity in the early part of the century.

The Maloneys were farmers, living about ten miles outside the town. This, too, was a late nineteenth-century immigrant family; the grandparents had evidently met on the boat from Ireland. Patrick, the grandfather, died before any of his grandchildren were old enough to remember him, and the farm was run by two of his sons, Michael and Jack. If less financially successful, and without the substantial business interests of the Bonfields, the Maloneys were not without substance, and a university education for the boys, at a time when it was a rare achievement, was easily within their means. One brother, Timothy, went to law school for two years; he joined the civil service in Ottawa. Another brother, Simon, went to the western United States. Arthur's father, Martin, was born on 9 October 1875. He went to primary school in Eganville, and then went on to Pembroke High School, where he won a gold medal for mathematics. At eighteen, he went to McGill Medical School, where he graduated with some distinction, winning the gold medal for pathology. At the time of his graduation, he was still a few months short of his twenty-first birthday, and doctors had to be twenty-one to practice in Ontario. He was, therefore, obliged to wait, and he did so by working in the Eganville drug store. In the autumn of 1901, he began his long medical career in his home town.

One day, while he was still working at the pharmacy, Margaret Bonfield came upon him in the store, and returned home to announce to her sister that she had just seen the man she meant to marry. As Nell, one of her daughters tells it, "As often as she could, she would go into the drugstore; and when a Maloney aunt died, mother, who was not a particular friend of the deceased or of the Maloney family, went to the funeral service in the church, and on to the cemetery in her best hat and frock. She made a point of standing as close as she could to Martin."[3]

Martin was the son who made the most of his opportunities, not only as a doctor, but as a man interested in community service and politics. He was to become the model of the caring country physician, often working for nothing, or for a bagful of vegetables, and in his indifference to making sure that he was paid, he anticipated one of Arthur's common habits in his early years of practice. The area around Eganville was rugged, and the practice developed by Martin had an arduous country aspect; his children remember him travelling into the bush by horse and cutter in the deep of winter. If there was an emergency, and the roads were impassable, he would travel by train, and if no train was available, and the situation was very serious, he would take to a railroad hand-car, pumping his way across the frozen landscape to his patient. All his children remember him as constantly at work. The surgery was in the home, but he was often away on house calls until late at night. One family memory of "Pappa," as he is sometimes called by his children, is of him arriving in the front hall very late one evening in the middle of a snow storm, stomping the snow off his boots, brushing it off his eyebrows and announcing with a wry smile that he had worked all night for thirty-five cents.

He could be away for days in the lumber camps, and the children would often see him only at meals even when he was working at home. His regular absence from the home put a great deal of authority in the hands of his wife, and the children acknowledge her as the centre of the family in the homey scuffle of day-to-day life. This situation intensified when Martin became interested in politics; he started slowly, first in the town council, where he worked his way up to become reeve, but his real ambition was to become involved in provincial or federal politics. Although the riding was strongly Liberal, he was determined to make his way as a Conservative. In 1911, while reeve of Eganville, he fought the South Renfrew Federal election against the incumbent Liberal, the Hon. T.A. Low. As expected, he lost by some 600 votes, a significant rebuff in a rural riding. In 1912, Low retired, and a close lieutenant of Wilfrid Laurier, the Rt. Hon. George P. Graham, who had lost his own riding in 1911, came in to run for the Liberals.

Laurier badly wanted Graham in the House, and he came down from Ottawa to campaign for him. Robert Borden arrived to help the underdog Conservatives. Graham had been born in Eganville, the son of a popular local cleric, and he ran under the motto (which was equally applicable to his opponent, Martin Maloney): "An Eganville boy is good enough for South Renfrew." By 1912, Martin Maloney had a strong following as a doctor and as a local politician; so much so that Laurier warned his people to take some care, and not depend upon the past history of the riding to see them through. Graham won, but the majority was cut to 223 votes. The Conservatives read this as a sign of better things to come. The election, though lost, established Maloney as the most important Conservative politician in the area, with a chance of winning, sooner or later, if he was prepared to take on the bruising of further campaigns. In 1925, he ran again, and this time he won, and a further election in 1926, confirmed him as the district's choice in Ottawa, despite the fact that the Liberal nominee was a prominent Renfrew businessman, J.L. Murray. It was a near run thing – Martin Maloney only had a 221-vote majority; it looked as if his personal popularity was all that was keeping the riding from returning to the Liberals.

That first victory precipitated all the old-fashioned triumphalism that made politics a joyfully raucous combination of unvarnished self-interest and folk art in the early part of the century. Fifty years later, *The Eganville Leader* of 5 November 1975 reprinted an account of the celebration.

> Arnprior, like Eganville and Renfrew, accorded to Dr. Maloney a reception which will linger for years in the memory of the jubilant populace. On Friday night, at the request of his friends and admirers in Arnprior the member-elect visited the lumber town and feelingly expressed to them his appreciation and thanks for the honour they had in large measure helped to bestow on him. He assured them again that it would be his pleasure and duty to serve the riding to the utmost of his ability. Borne shoulder-high from his hotel to the town hall he was loudly acclaimed with much prolonged cheering and music by the crowd which packed the streets. With speech-making, music, song and dance the

citizens gave vent to pent-up joy and for universal rejoicing, the reception though orderly was unprecedented perhaps in force of demonstration. [*sic*]

It was probably the high point in Martin's political career, since the setting out was filled with high hopes that were not to be fulfilled. He became a respected back-bencher in Ottawa, with a sound reputation as an orator, and his skill as such was appreciated on both sides of the House. He was partly responsible for the bill that led to the building of the Ivy Lea bridge from Canada to the United States in the Thousand Islands area. Perhaps more to his inclination was his work on a bill that led eventually to pensions for the blind. But he never had a chance at higher office. John French remembers his skill on the campaign stump, shouting his way through the campaigns. "In those days, there were church picnics in the summer, and they were often the scene of political battles between the candidates, who were expected to provide the entertainment with their speeches. I can remember Dr. McCann, the Liberal candidate, and Dr. Maloney standing on the platforms which were roped off around the outside and looked something like a boxing ring. You had to have a healthy pair of lungs, and Dr. Maloney did. He was an orator in the old style, using colourful language and oratorical exaggeration."[4] The failure to go beyond the back-benches disappointed Martin Maloney. Nell knew that he had mixed feelings about his political life in his later years, sometimes suggesting that he ought to have stayed home, and paid more attention to his family and his practice. The family, if often left alone as Martin Maloney worked the district politically as well as professionally, enjoyed the battles – and the friendships, which sometimes paid little attention to party lines. Nell relished the encounters: "Politics were great in those days. Mr. Low, who was the Liberal candidate running against my father would come and sit on the veranda, and they would discuss the election. Anyone passing could certainly see them, side by side. There was no confrontation or nastiness; these two men, supposedly enemies, would be sitting on our veranda, and I, as a child, remember sitting on the step, listening to them talk."[5] John French believes that by the 1935 election, Dr. Maloney was ready to quit, and that like Arthur in 1962, he was not entirely unhappy when he lost his seat in 1935. He had hoped to be given a Senate seat by R.B. Bennett, but Bennett asked him to run just once more, since it was presumed that no one else could deny the Liberals their old hold on South Renfrew. But the swing away from the Conservatives was too strong, however much affection was held for him in the riding, and Dr. James McCann, a friend and fellow doctor, defeated him. Dr. Maloney had struggled to keep up a part-time practice in Eganville while he attended the House; now he was back at it full-time – but the Senate was gone forever.

However flamboyant Martin Maloney was on the stump, his children remember him as a quiet man about the house. If not out of town, he would always have his noon meal with his children, home from Catholic school just down the street. He would often appear at the table with any patient who might be at loose ends and in need of a meal. The office was in the house, in rooms that could be entered from the driveway side of the building. He had the house built just after he began practice, with the idea that he could combine his work with family life at close hand. Frances describes the building:

> It was a nice, big, red-brick house, sitting back about twenty-five feet from the street; there was a big flower bed running alongside the walk, right up to the steps; the veranda had a roofed balcony on it where some of us used to sleep on hot nights in the summer. It was on a double lot that ran right back to the next street, and there was, originally, a stable at the back where Pappa kept the horses and the cutter. We sometimes kept a cow. There was an iron fence at the edge of the street. Down the driveway, there was the veranda that led up to the office, and then a larger one that led into the kitchen. At the back there was another porch, roofed over, into the back kitchen, a kind of summer kitchen which was used for cooking in the summer.[6]

James Maloney came to the Bar some years before his much younger brother, Arthur. Soon after becoming a lawyer, James was called on by his father to prepare an unusual defence. A local boy, of limited intelligence, set the stable on fire, but had sufficient wit to warn Mrs. Maloney, terrified that she and the children might be harmed. He was charged with arson. Given the way the Maloney mind worked, it was not surprising that James was instructed by his father to defend the boy. Nell once asked James why he had done so (in a family variation of the favourite lay inquiry into how a lawyer can defend a guilty client), and James was unsentimentally laconic: "Well, what would you do if your father told you to do it?" James managed to get the boy off on mental grounds – a favourite defence for Arthur in years to come.

Margaret Mary Bonfield and Martin Maloney had married on 19 February 1901. Arthur, their last child, was born in 1919. Between those two events, ten other children were born, one of whom died within six months of her birth. Seven of the children were born before 1910, and the last three children, Henry, Frances, and Arthur, came after a few years respite – in 1915, 1916, and 1919 respectively. There is, as a result, a long, slowly changing memory of childhood still present in the family survivors of the present day. There are two sisters of the earlier group, Margaret and Anna, still alive, and one of the later group, Frances. In the best tradition of Roman Catholic family ambition, one child became a doctor, one a nurse (she also became a nun and a teacher), and the rest included a priest, two teachers, two lawyers (one of whom, James became an MPP and an Ontario Cabinet Minister; Arthur, the other, was an MP, and a parliamentary assistant to a federal Cabinet Minister). Two had long careers in the Ottawa civil service.

All the children were reared in the house on Queen Street, although they never all lived there at the same time. It was a crowded place, particularly through the first three decades of the century. The doctor was often absent, and more so during his parliamentary years; he never moved the family from Eganville, but kept an Ottawa apartment, sharing it with the children as some of them came up to the city to attend high school or begin their working lives. Long before the Ottawa period, it was obvious that Margaret needed help, which was easily obtained in a small town where there was not much work for young women past school age. Things were not made any easier by the serious health problems that Mary, the first daughter, had from early in her life. She was severely lamed by spinal meningitis, and later, scarlet fever was to leave her with grave hearing problems. She was, however, a bright, eager child, and she did not allow her physical liabilities to immobilize her completely.

The children remember that their mother always had help in the home. An English woman, Mrs. Long, a widow, was with them for thirty-five years. She lived with the family until old age. Anna remembers that she favoured the boys. She had come to Canada in search of her son who had, through family necessity, been put first in an English orphanage, and then, without her consent, sent to Canada. As soon as she could do so, she followed him, and ended up in Barrie's Bay as a hotel cook. "Dad was on a sick call up there when he and mother were looking for a housekeeper. "I think," says Anna, "she came when Pat was a baby. She used to get cross with us, of course, but she was very faithful, and Arthur became a great favourite of hers."[7]

Despite his busy life, Martin spent as much time as he could with his children. At dinner, he sat at the head of the table, serving the family; there were no "seconds" until Martin, who served himself last, had been through his first serving; the children were taught to wait patiently and quietly. On report card days, the child with the best marks sat at their father's right hand at the evening meal. "You could come to him at any time," says Margaret, "and he would put his hand on your shoulder and say, particularly if you had some problem,'Don't forget you've got a friend.'" This same restrained affection was displayed when Martin visited his mother, who lived out her life on the family farm. She was a tiny woman, who would sit in her big wicker rocking chair to receive her family. "They never hugged," says Margaret,"but Pappa would go over and put his hand on her shoulder and she would put her hand on his, and that was their way of expressing affection."[8]

In the evenings, Martin would help the children with their homework, and when the work was done, especially in the winter, as Nell recalled, "the boys would play hockey with father in the kitchen; if they couldn't find a puck, they would cut a piece of wood to the right shape; the girls would sit on the steps and Pappa and Jim and Pat, and later Henry and Arthur would push and slide around the room – and the noise? I don't know how my mother stood it; the puck striking the walls and the doors, and the girls screaming. But we had a good time. It was a great family."[9] The parents were deeply religious in that natural, unselfconscious way of Irish Catholics. The Church and the school were supposed to do most of the work, but the parents were also responsible for bringing up good Catholics. "Every evening father and mother and all the children would kneel in the living room to recite the family Rosary," said Nell. One of the girls remembers their father expressing wonder one evening when they were all down on their knees; he was suddenly in awe at what he and his wife had wrought in the form of the innumerable pairs of upturned shoe soles, ranked along the carpet. In its 5 May 1956 issue, *The Ensign*, a Catholic family magazine described the Maloney clan at prayers: "The living room became a little church where each evening, father, mother, and children knelt to recite the Family Rosary and the many 'Trimmin's on the Rosary' for which Mrs. Maloney has become famous in the Ottawa Valley." On the occasion of the Maloney golden wedding anniversary in 1951, it seemed appropriate that, as *The Ensign* reported, "Father Henry celebrated a thanksgiving mass in that very same living room."

Lillian Maloney, Arthur's wife, who only knew Martin Maloney in his old age, confirms the calm stillness of the man. His surviving daughters felt that James most resembled him, since both of them possessed a full, round, fleshy face, and wore their hair combed straight back like the American jazz trombonist Jack Teagarden, whom they both resembled, with a parting in their hair somewhat higher than was to be fashionable after the Second World War. It has been suggested by some that there might have been some American Indian blood in the family as evidenced in the looks of Martin, and James, but there doesn't seem to be any place to add such romantic intrusion. James was also the one who most resembled his father as a public speaker, prone to orotund, inflated dramatics. But James was a more outgoing, somewhat raffish personality, and it is Henry, whom the family take great pleasure in always calling "Father Henry" even amongst themselves, who was closest to his father temperamentally – a quiet, graver personality than James could be – or ever want to be.

Their mother, Margaret, lived long enough for Lillian to know her well, and her recollection of her mother-in-law is not unlike that of her children. Margaret Bonfield was bred to politics and there is a story that her first intuitive response to the hard and unforgiving world of elections occurred when she was only two weeks old and James Bonfield was elected the new member for South Renfrew; the baby Margaret, supposedly, squealed joyously in her crib while the festivities roared through the night. She was a strong, confident woman who ran the large, lively family, and was also a prominent leader in Catholic social life in Eganville. Nell spoke of her with great pride. "She was a remarkable woman; there was no high school in town in her day, but the Bonfields were certainly the most socially prominent family in town, and she was given the best of everything. She finished her education in Ottawa at the Sacred Heart; she was a good musician, and she made certain that all her children had music lessons." The family was often taken to Ottawa for musical or dramatic performances; the girls were once kept in Ottawa for a week to attend Sir Martin Harvey's Shakespearean season. The children were expected to graduate from high school, and to go further if they wished. "When it came time for one of the children to graduate from high school," said Nell, "there was never any discussion as to whether the child would go on: the only question was whether they would go to Loyola or St. Pat's or St. Mike's."[10]

Margaret Maloney could be very determined and very quick in defending her children, even from Martin's sometimes reasonable wrath. James, while still studying at Osgoode Hall, fell in love; obviously aware of how the news that he intended to marry would be received at home, he avoided the normal use of a letter or a telephone call, and sent a telegram, hoping, perhaps, that the novelty of the medium might distract from the implications of the message. Dr. Maloney, in the manner of fathers immemorial, beside himself with frustration at the silliness of what James proposed, announced to his wife that he was sending James two one-way tickets to Vancouver – and that would be the end of his support of his love-sick son. Mrs. Maloney's response was equally and just as succinctly to the point: "Martin, make that *three* one-way tickets. I'm going with them." Dr. Maloney, nonplussed, cooled down and relented, and his wife took herself off to Toronto to help James arrange his finances, and help him and his girl find a place to live. Lillian sensed Mrs. Maloney's strength from the start of their acquaintance. "I didn't know what to make of her when I first met her; she was really strong! On our way home from our honeymoon, we stopped over to have lunch with them, and she said, quite firmly to Arthur, 'Arthur, you're married now. Remember your wife comes first. The way you treat her, other people will also treat her.' Dr. Maloney was amused by her saying this, and he started to tease her (he called her 'Mug'), and he said, 'That's it! You tell him, Mug! You tell him! – You tell him, Mug!', laughing as he said it. She answered back, chiding him – 'Oh, Martin. Martin!'"[11]

She had a reputation as a storyteller, and as possessing a good sense of humour. Years of having kitchen help had dulled whatever prowess she had as a cook, and she was not known to be skilled in the kitchen; some women never know how their family feels about their food, but Margaret knew, and was amused by it. Nell remembers visiting from Ottawa and helping her mother make tea biscuits one afternoon. While they busied themselves with the preparation, her mother quietly informed her that, "If they turn out well, I'll say that I made them – and if not, I'll say that you did!" Her children knew how much she had sacrificed for them and her husband. Anna remembers how hard she worked.

Mom was alone so much as a result of Dad being a doctor, and being away later in politics, she more or less ruled the roost; she was always with us. I don't think her life could have been easy; there were so many children! Whenever she needed a doctor, Dad always seemed to be away, and she often had to call in someone else. It was probably easier then to bring up a big family; they were fairly common, and there was great unity with the Church and the school, and great respect for the authority of the priests and the nuns. She was very religious, but she wasn't awed by the Church. She would defend her children if she thought we were not being treated fairly. I remember I was in a concert, singing in the front row, and I hit a false note. The Sister who was conducting us had a kind of baton in her hand, and she hit me on the leg. When I was going to bed that night, I found a big bruise, and I was very proud of it, showing it to Margaret or Nell. Mom happened to go by the door, and she saw the bruise, and asked me what happened. The next day she was down at the school with me, complaining to the Mother Superior about her child being hit unnecessarily.[12]

In the summers the family moved immediately after school closed to a cottage at Golden Lake, ten miles west of town, on the route to Barrie's Bay. Anna admits that she never has wanted to own a cottage, having had quite enough of pastoral fastness as a child. They were kept there until the beginning of the school year in September, and it was, especially for the older children, somewhat constricting. All, however, admit it was a lovely place for a holiday. Anna remembers that it was quite big enough to handle the whole family: "It was a large cottage; the upstairs was like a big dormitory, and there were two more bedrooms downstairs, a couple of beds in the living room, and a veranda all around." There was enough room for Mrs. Long to go with them, and she had her own bedroom on the ground floor. It was not owned by the Maloneys, simply because it was on an Indian reservation, and the Indians rented the building to Dr. Maloney. The Indian children were the summer companions of the Maloney brood, and grew up with them. There was a row boat for the children to paddle about, and they could swim off the dock at the front of the cottage. Nell felt that her mother was not best pleased with the long summer stay up in the bush, but most evenings Martin would drive over from town, and spend the night. "We always knew when he was coming," says Frances. "You had to cross a bridge to come into the property, and he'd toot his horn four times, and we'd all run to meet him." There was a small, open motor boat as well and the boys were taught to run it. All the children were taught to swim by their father. Martin never took long summer holidays, contenting himself with short trips to medical or political meetings around the country, during the rest of the year. The summer time away from the house was used to advantage, given the wear and tear of so many children running about. "While we were away at the cottage, they would do the house over; the floors and the wallpaper were re-done, and when we got back in September, it would be spick and span."[13]

Golden Lake is still a popular summer cottage resort for Ottawa Valley residents; Frances's family still goes up there for several weeks each summer. The Maloney cottage was somewhat sequestered on the reservation, but it was not entirely a disadvantage. The children's association with the Indians, whom they knew were materially less fortunate than they were, may have had some influence on the way in which James and Arthur, in particular, responded to minorities in their professional and political careers. Their parents made it clear that the children were very fortunate to have so many chances in life; they also told them that they had the obligation to train themselves to serve others as well as provide for themselves. Such service was directly related to the lucky chance of being, in a sense, "chosen." "Mother felt that we were terribly blessed, and I think that she got that from her mother and father," said Nell.

> I remember that our grandmother on our mother's side, despite being crippled with arthritis, used to travel around in a trap, doing good work among the poor. She felt that was what the Lord meant her to do, and mother carried that on. God, according to mother, had showered us with wonderful things, and she really felt that she was descended from the kings of Ireland; she told us that she had cousins who came over from Ireland who also believed that. God was good to us; lots to eat and drink, and a good position in the town, and blessed with a mother and a father who love us dearly. We should share because there were so many people who didn't have that. She really felt that she was descended from the kings of Ireland![14]

Which may be the best clue to Arthur's occasional monarchical gestures. This family myth of kingship can be traced back to the Bonfield grandfather. It is harmless, and has some whimsical charm in its connection with the atavistic memory of Irish myth, and the Bonfield's determination to be identified with such stuff of Irish dreaming. Arthur would sometimes boast of it, jokingly.

The town itself can be seen as part of this pattern of education in civility and social concern. There were very few French Canadians in the area, although it is very close to the Quebec border. There was, however, a clear split in the town between Catholics and Protestants, living almost exclusively on opposite sides of the river, facing each other in what could be seen as a kind of physical opposition, the stepped streets mirroring each other over the deep divide of the river. Their children went to different schools, and although shopping was carried on by passing back and forth over the one bridge in the centre of town, there was an unspoken agreement that the two groups lived much of their lives separately. Pat, while in high school, had a minor attachment to a Protestant girl; his parents chose to say nothing to him about it, although it worried them, and his sisters knew that such associations were uncommon and not encouraged. There seems, however, to have been little serious rancour, even though the religious, and therefore sometime social differences, were openly acknowledged. Even "King Billy Day," that early summer celebration of the Protestant victory at the Battle of the Boyne, which was commonly celebrated throughout Ontario in the pre-Second World War period (Toronto used to have a parade which was second only in size and extravagance to its well-known Santa Claus parade), developed in Eganville into a kind of horse-play agreement to mock the old enmities. The Protestants would march in force on to the bridge, heading for the Catholic side of town. The Maloney girls remember how all the town children would gather to watch the good-natured scuffling that would go on as the Catholics youths sought to block the bridge. That kind of religious confrontation, with a tonal difference, partly racial, since many of the Protestants were of middle-European extraction, and the majority of the Catholics were Irish, may have something to do with Arthur's ease and awareness of difference that was to make him so receptive to the post-forties ethnic question in Parkdale when he entered politics.

In the 1990s, it is not much remembered that the social and religious structures of Ontario in the pre-Second World War period were considerably different than they are now. Now it is generally presumed that the mix of a multi-ethnic society is the ideal, however difficult it may be to achieve it without constant endeavour. In the first part of the century, it was taken for granted that there might be some lip-service paid to such enlightened ideas, but it was seldom practiced. Indeed, it often wasn't a problem. Toronto, where Arthur was to become one of the champions of ethnic understanding, had very few black citizens, for instance, and there were large sections of the city, particularly in the east end, in which continental Europeans were completely absent. It wasn't just a matter of the social structure being based upon money; that existed, and it was taken as obvious that the most successful members of the community lived in Rosedale or North Toronto. There was a Jewish enclave, as there is today, north of the Bloor-Bathurst area, but the working-class parts of town were, in the main, white Anglo-Saxon Protestant – first- or second-generation families from England and Scotland. East York, for instance, was almost entirely so; the architecture of the area, much of which is still intact, was a copy of English working-class "two-up and two-down." Fish-and-chip shops, with the ubiquitous sign of quality – "We fry halibut only" – flourished every two or three blocks. In East York, there were hardly any families with European connections, and Catholics were equally rare. It was only after the Second World War, and the influx of European immigrants, that this pattern changed – and not without some scepticism and derision being expressed by those who had got there first, and conveniently forgot that their grandfathers had only arrived with their cardboard suitcases a few decades previous.

The visceral hostility, which immigrants often evoke without doing anything but being present, was sensed by the newcomers, and they responded in the main by keeping their head down, which was one of the problems that Arthur was to confront when he entered Parkdale politics. Toronto was not quite the same as other places. European immigrants were common through the Prairies, as they were in many small Ontario towns where heavy, bruising industries absorbed them easily. But Toronto was different, and was to remain stubbornly so into the fifties.

It could be argued that Arthur was lucky, in a sense, to have been brought up outside of Toronto, where he could learn how to deal with ethnic and religious differences in the surround of small-town generosity. The problem was before the Maloney family every time they walked out the front door of their home – not a hundred yards away was a mirror image of their community with a difference – it looked the same, but it was not Irish, and it was not Catholic; it was educated differently, and it was presumed that it would keep itself to itself. But that proximity allowed both sides to recognize that despite the differences, there was no threat. That may have contributed quite as much to Arthur's instinctive ability to react to unfairness based on racial or religious or social difference as anything his parents or teachers said. There was nothing to be feared in Eganville, and a bit of jostling on the bridge on King Billy's

Day, or a bit of sophomoric jeering between teenage boys hurt no one – a sweet example of rural acceptance running well ahead of urban ignorance, and sometime suspicion.

But the family deepened such experience. All the sisters talk about a sense of obligation, and an awareness of being important. Anna remembers that it was "a very tight-knit family; with your father in politics, you learned diplomacy." Margaret put it this way: "We had a mission as Catholics to shine as Catholics; not in a bigoted way, but in a noble sort of way." Anna returned to the idea again, attempting to get it right, "I think that one of the things we were taught was diplomacy. I don't know how we were taught it, but whether someone was a French Canadian, and there were only a few of them, or a Catholic or a Protestant, you respected them." The fruit of that respect and caring was to be seen at the time of Dr. Maloney's death in November 1953. The local newspaper called him the "Crown Prince of the Ottawa Valley," and fondly remembered his years of service as the country doctor who didn't worry much about getting rich, or who his patients were. They paid what they could, when they could – often in kind, often fruit and vegetables from his rural patients. The old practice of barter among small-town merchants was commonly in play. Anna remembers being with her father in a local store when the shopkeeper presented the doctor with a long account. The doctor stood in the centre of the aisle, read the bill carefully, and put it down on the counter with the quiet comment that it seemed to be entirely correct, and that the total was "exactly what you owe me to date for medical services to your family." That was the end of the matter. He is remembered by his children with great affection, and there is an aura of deep love in their memories of him. Lillian recalls the day he was brought home, having died in an Ottawa hospital. "I was in the upstairs bedroom with Mrs. Maloney, looking out the window with her as they brought the casket into the house. The tears were running down her face as she cried, 'My darling Martin, what am I ever going to do without you? Why did you go and leave me? What am I going to do?'"[15] He left his wife the house, and a few investments, but not much more, and the boys helped to support their mother until her death. She was to survive Martin for less than three years, dying in October 1956, and evoked much of the same kind of public praise that had followed her husband's death, since she was well-known in the area for her social and religious activities?

Arthur's sisters, in old age, have a romantic memory of a family busy within itself and within the social life of the small town, rewarded with frequent visits to Ottawa. They have fond tales of their father hiring sleighs in the winter to take them out to their grandmother, or simply for the fun of a snowy ride. There were the common troubles of a growing family – the baby's death – Mary's serious illnesses – Arthur's hare lip, which he carried all his life, despite surgery as a child and later as an adult. He is remembered as a beautiful child with long curls and a sweet temperament. He was the last child, much celebrated by his parents and, especially, by his sisters. They think about him, without envy, as their mother's favourite child. Aside from the early operation on his lip, he had a serious bout of pneumonia that affected his lungs sufficiently to make it impossible for him to pass a medical during the war. Margaret was put in charge of him during that illness: "My mother told me not to let him do anything, not even pull the sheets up to cover himself. 'If he wants to turn, you turn him.' He was very sick for a while. I'm not sure, but I think that his life-long respiratory trouble started then; I remember when he tried to go into the army years later, he was turned down everywhere."[16]

The hare lip was to be a minor concern for him throughout his life. After his marriage, a plastic surgeon operated on it again, and managed to expose sufficient whisker for Arthur to grow a moustache to hide the scar, but Arthur didn't like the moustache, and shaved it off. Late in his life, when Kenneth Jarvis, the artist, who had spent most of his working life as an official of the Upper Canada Law Society, was commissioned to model a head for presentation to Arthur, Maloney suggested, on their first meeting to discuss the project, that, perhaps, it was inappropriate to make an artistic representation of a man with such an impediment. Jarvis, a courtly, sensitive man, argued gently that he saw nothing wrong with it – Arthur then, timidly asked if it was perhaps better to leave the scar off the head, but Jarvis told him that he would not do that, and Arthur was content to be modelled with the upper lip in its real state. He was sometimes sensitive about formal photographs, but there is no evidence that the scar had any serious effect on his personality.

Frances saw his tendency to leadership at an early age. "I always looked to Arthur, although I was older than him. I noticed, when we were in high school, that he was somehow more mature than others. If we went to a party, Arthur was always able to get over the shyness of the moment; at one party, when it became deathly quiet, and we were all shifting and shuffling about, trying to think of what to do, Arthur suddenly broke the stillness by asking one of the girls, Marie, to sing to us, and that just got the whole thing going again."[17] Margaret says that he used to write little plays, and put them on in the summer, staging them in the doorway of the barn, charging two cents a ticket. He was not always perfect; once he seized Frances's favourite doll from her and swung it about with such force that it hit the floor; the head was smashed. Frances remembered how remorseful he was – how upset he was about his foolish, thoughtless conduct. He was not entirely innocent of that uncontrollable greediness that sometimes affects a child, and which a child can hardly understand. When he was ill once, an uncle died. Family and friends, in town for the funeral, met at the Maloney home for the wake, and, as Frances remembers, "they all went up to see him, and everybody left him a little money." A few days after the funeral, when all the relatives had left, he suddenly asked, seemingly without intent, "'I wonder when there's going to be another wake?' And we all knew what he was thinking."[18]

If he was the darling of his mother's later years, he was not the only child in the family with natural gifts. It was, in the most obvious physical sense, a good-looking family of considerable intelligence. The sisters were all very pretty, and photographs of the family in early adulthood are formidable in their display of male and female beauty. Arthur was the least handsome of the boys in early manhood, although he was to pass from a kind of thin-faced foxiness as he put on weight and attained the full-faced Irish good looks of his brothers. The sisters had a fine-featured, high-cheek-bone beauty that has lasted into old age. Arthur looked least like his father, resembling the girls in the finer moulding of his features.

There is a small collection of letters from his childhood years, contained in one small envelope. In 1928, his parents travelled to the west coast, and a card from his mother, posted in Cochrane, Ontario, shows her concern: "Don't miss school like a dear and I will bring you a present." A card from Jasper hints at how she missed him: "I saw a little boy on the train that looked like you, [*sic*] Love, Mamma." Her strong religious faith, which shows up in much of her correspondence, comes out in a card from Kitwanga, B.C. with a picture of totem poles on the front: "I am very anxious to see you and will be glad to get home ... These poles are what folks used to adore before they were converted to God. I was at mass at Edmonton this morning." His mother was sometimes slow in mailing the cards at the appropriate location, but it was unlikely that Arthur would have noticed, in his excitement in hearing from his mother.

In 1930, he was off to Montreal without the family, and the sanctity and the taste for night life, which were to be common elements in his adult life, show up: "Dear Mamma: I had a lovely trip on the Parlor Car coming and have seen quite a few things so far. I was at Notre Dame Church and Brother Andrew's [*sic*] Shrine and I think Montreal is very nice. I am going to a show, *One Embarrassing Night*. Love to all, Arthur."[19] He did not forget the family; there are two other cards from this trip: one to Mrs. Long, the housekeeper, and one to Henry, whom he wants to impress with his high life: "Montreal is a nice place, isn't it? I am going to see *One Embarrassing Night* at the Princess. Arthur."

What comes next in the small pile of personal papers from his childhood is a letter from Sister St. Dorothy, the Principal of the Roman Catholic Continuation School in Eganville, dated 31 March 1937: "Arthur Maloney, a student in this school during the 1933–34 term, passed the examinations required, and was granted a certificate by the Ontario Department of Education in the following subjects: British History, Art, Geography, Zoology." In 1936, he was living, during the school year, with his older sisters in Ottawa, taking Grade XIII at Lisgar Collegiate. In 1937, he entered St. Michael's in the three-year pass arts course. In 1938, a letter from his mother suggests that he was having a busy time outside class: "You will have a lot of fun, now that you belong to so many clubs. You will meet many nice people, and, I think you were wise to join. A later comment in the same letter brings up a Maloney family enthusiasm: "Dad is delighted you joined the Young Conservative Club. Says it will help you *a lot*. Don't let it interfere with your studies."[20] His mother knew her son: "You can hold your own with your liberal friends. Dont [*sic*] let them get away with anything." But politics was not to take all his extra-curricular time; among the few papers collected by him during this period, is a *Toronto Star* clipping, undated, encased in plastic, and accompanied by the following typewritten comment: "This is a clipping from the Toronto Star circa 1938 or 1939 in the Fall referring to my appearance in the St. Michael's College production of the entire First Act of *Hamlet* in which I played the role of Hamlet? Not quite up to the whole play, but clearly proud of being able to handle the "entire" first act.

The English custom of serving refreshments at a play will be introduced at the Royal Alexandra theatre next week when Maurice Evans comes to play "Hamlet." The curtains rise at the early hour of 7:30, to give time for the four-hour play, suggested refreshments, and so St. George's chapter, I.O.D.E., is to have buffet tables in the foyer downstairs, upstairs and in the gallery promenade. Proceeds will be in aid of war work. Maurice Evans, one of the finest actors of all time, first earned his living as a clerk in a Bond St. music store and recalls that once he was sent out to buy a pair of suspenders for the composer, Jerome Kern. Nights he spent in amateur theatricals which led to his professional debut at the Cambridge Festival Theatre. A Toronto Hamlet in embryo is Arthur Malloney [*sic*] of St. Michael's College, says Sam Pearce, speaking in Toronto in advance of Hamlet. He saw an act of the play in which the boy played the title role.

The report wanders in its anecdotal excesses about Maurice Evans, but it must have thrilled Maloney, the boy, to get into the same paragraph with the popular actor, even if Sam Pearce was not prepared to comment on the quality of his performance, and his name was incorrectly spelled. If Arthur had read the paragraph closely he might have guessed that it could not have happened in 1938, given the reference to "war work." Theatre was not his only interest. He was a member of the Varsity Students' Administrative Council, and in his last year, he was President of the St. Michael's Student's Administrative Council. A letter from P. M. Dewan, the Ontario Minister of Agriculture, dated 12 April 1940, shows him, for the first time, at one of his favourite activities, chairing a public dinner: "May I again offer my sincere congratulations to you upon the very efficient manner in which you presided at the Arts Banquet on Wednesday evening of this week. It was obvious that you prepared for the task which you were to carry out, and for this you deserve special credit."

These were busy days for Arthur. On the back of the envelope containing the above letter he had marked the following: "April 26: Military Studies, April 29: Ethics, May 3: French Authors, May 4: French Composition, May 6: Pol Sci, May 8: Phil, May 9: History. In June 1940, he graduated. James did not forget him, adding some money to the envelope: "So sorry we cannot be with you to participate in your cup of joy which must be full to overflowing as it should be. The enclosed is but a slight token of the high esteem in which you are held by the Mrs, Kids, & self. Sincere congratulations. Jim."[21]

Pat, if never to achieve the public reputation of Arthur or James, became one of the best known and most popular pediatricians in Ottawa. He was a Queen's University graduate in 1931, and went on to do postgraduate work in the States. In 1936, he set up practice in Ottawa. He was the only Maloney male to serve in the Second World War, becoming a lieutenant-colonel; he served with distinction as a commander of a casualty station in the bloody battles in Holland, and was mentioned in dispatches; he received a decoration from the Dutch Underground for his work during the liberation of Amsterdam. He was interested in politics, and he became the first president of the Ottawa West Progressive Conservative Association. His sisters felt that he might have done well in politics, and he wanted to run, but his practice made him hesitate and he never found the right time to try. Like his father, he had the abrupt, casual air of a country doctor. He and Henry were the serious boys. "Pat was very serious about his homework," says Frances, "and he wouldn't let us talk at the dining room table where we all worked together." He and several other Ottawa and Montreal doctors developed a health programme for the Indian children in the far north. He died at sixty-five of a heart attack; his father had died of the same. John Diefenbaker was one of his honorary pall bearers.

At the time, a letter in the *Ottawa Citizen* put the matter of his rough-hewn public persona into context: "But there was another side to Dr. Maloney, known well to mothers like me, who gladly handed over their little ones to him. Under a sometimes (necessarily) brusque manner was a heart as big as the world, and a deep personal concern for individuals ... Children adored him. For them, he combined the magic of a large-as-life leprechaun with the fascination of the Pied Piper, making his rounds with a bottomless pocket full of lollipops."[22] Jake Dunlap's wife, Neda, whose children he cared for, had another tale of the lollipops: "He would never give the children a needle. The nurse would do that, and he would then come back into the office with a lollipop in his hand, and soothe the crying child, consoling them about his nurse, whispering to them, 'Isn't she a mean lady!'"[23]

According to Jake Dunlap, the lawyer and former professional athlete, Pat had a restrained streak of wildness in him, but kept his penchant for a good party under better control than either James or Arthur. He was, as were all the Maloney males, a mix of overt toughness and charming tact. As the *Citizen* reported at his death: "Dr. Maloney was an incomparable and paradoxical composite of up-to-the-minute expertise and warm folksiness. Legions of little hearts belonged to Dr. Maloney. For some mothers, he was a hard taskmaster. His passion for ensuring that you followed his order sometimes had humorous overtones. 'Madame!' I once heard him saying over the telephone, 'I am your child's doctor, not the next-door neighbour lady!' He will be missed."[24]

The naming of John Diefenbaker as an honorary pall bearer might be explained by Pat's prominence in Ottawa Conservative organizations, but Diefenbaker also shows up in Father Henry's career. Henry was the quietest of the boys. Ken Godin, Margaret's husband, and John French were his school mates at Eganville, and they remember how solemnly quiet he was. Jake Dunlap describes him as "more like the girls in the family." All the children took music lessons, but Henry was the best musician. At university he decided to become a priest. He studied philosophy at St. Michael's and went on to St. Peter's Seminary in London, Ontario. Most of his life was spent as a parish priest in north-eastern Ontario; he began his service in Bancroft, and then moved on to Calabogie, Combermere, and Pembroke. He was next in Renfrew, and in 1949, he got home to Eganville. In 1957, he was appointed pastor of Our Lady of Mercy in Bancroft and he remained there until he became seriously ill in the autumn of 1986. When he first went to Bancroft, there was considerable unease between Protestants and Catholics. There is a story that the old priest who had preceded Henry, was shunned on the streets by Protestants, who would pointedly cross the street to avoid greeting him. One of Henry's first acts as a priest was to appear, without invitation, at a bazaar put on by one of the Protestant churches. He continued throughout his time there to attempt to rid the community of religious bias, and years later, at the time of the burning of the Catholic church mortgage, a group of Protestant women supplied the banquet. He had much to do with the building of a new Separate School there, and with the building of a new church in Haliburton. In 1966, at the celebration of his twenty-fifth anniversary as a priest, he was addressed by one of the speakers as "Father Bancroft," a title he had earned in 1962 when it was announced by the federal government that the last four uranium mines in the area were to be closed down. A committee went to Ottawa with Father Henry as their spokesman. John Diefenbaker and Father Henry discussed the problem over lunch. As a result, the contract was extended for a further year-and-a-half, and Father Henry and Diefenbaker became friends. On his death, Bishop Windle spoke of Henry's service: "We honour Father Henry and all the members of the Maloney family. You have brought glory to the valley, brought glory and honour to all of us and the good Lord blesses you and rewards you sincerely."

In the previous year, 1961, James had died. Like Arthur, if to a lesser extent, James had achieved some public notice, and had been involved in some public controversy during a lively career as a politician at the provincial level. James was the child most remembered as robustly mischievous, and he was something of a cheeky blusterer in political encounter. As a child he was a rough-and-tumble creature, and that reputation was never lost. He played football and baseball at Loyola College, and went on to Osgoode Hall, the first of the Maloneys to enter the law. He practised first in Perth, then Eganville for a time, but finally settled on Renfrew, where he ran an office with as much emphasis on criminal law as was possible in a country practice.

James became rudely coarsened as he grew older. One of Arthur's students, in the late fifties, had a sudden collision with this lively man. "When I first met him, I mistook him for a criminal client (which amused Arthur). He burst into the office, beefy and ebullient, with a banged-up look of an old prize fighter. I tried, as was my duty, to block him, since he was clearly on his way right into Arthur's office. He hit me like a ton of bricks, and broke into a loud laugh, announcing that he was 'Jimmy! I'm Jimmy! – Arthur's brother!'" Once the student stood back, it made perfect sense. He was a somewhat older, abused copy of the same bone structure, flushed and less finely made, sturdy and weighty, looking like an athlete who had, in late middle age, been obliged to pay for the hard battles he had imposed on his flesh. Which was, in James's case, partly true, since he had been a fine sportsman in college. "Fine" may not be quite the right word – as a football player he had a fearsome reputation for going through the line in full flight, feet first.

He had been old enough to aid his father in his political campaigns and from early on in his law career, he made himself available as an active supporter and organizer for Conservative candidates. In 1945, he ran for the first time, against Dr. McCann, the federal Liberal who had defeated his father in 1935. He did not win, but he did very well, despite the fact that McCann had years of experience and had the added authority of being a Cabinet Minister. James, like his father, was prepared to come back again and again. As John French says of him, "He was a controversial character and a consummate politician. He was very intelligent and nimble-witted – a powerful speaker, more in the line of his father than Arthur was. Arthur was able to bring Shakespeare into his speeches; I don't think Jim could or would do that; he was just an old-fashioned stump speaker. But he knew everybody, and he would drive around the county, and very much like his father and Arthur he would have people coming up to him for favours. Because he did favours. He didn't have to know someone to help them, if he could; particularly if they were from Eganville."[25] Charles Lynch, the Ottawa columnist, in comparing him once to Arthur, suggested that he confined himself to doing favours for proven Conservatives, but he had a local reputation for breaking the rules of patronage. "He would often ignore strict political rules, and support Liberals if it took his fancy to do so," says John French. "He seemed to believe that one of the functions of political power was to help those who asked for it, and in his own peculiar way of judging, deserved it. He was very good at little things; getting the small favour done. Somebody up in Barrie's Bay area had a cottage lot on a lake, and the access was through Crown Land. He spoke to Jim about getting permanent access to the cottage and Jim made a note of it. About a month after Jim's funeral, this man got a note from the ministry in charge, granting the right-of-way 'at the request of the late James A. Maloney.'" John French laughs at this, "That was James for you! – He was still operating after death!"

Always politically busy, he was not necessarily tidy about how he practised the trade, which often requires considerable obedience to party discipline. He was an active worker for James Dempsey, the local provincial Member, who got into trouble in 1955 with the Progressive Conservative head office over unreported political contributions. The Party disowned him. Dempsey was not a smart man, but he was a wily politician, particularly on his home ground, and he possessed the same kind of hand-hewn friendliness that James had. As John French saw them, "They were tough men. Dempsey was as much a character as

James, coming out of the experience of the early days of lumbering; they were big men, handy with their fists, and not easily rejected or discouraged. Leslie Frost might refuse to have Dempsey as a candidate in the 1955 election, but Dempsey ran anyway, as an Independent Conservative – and Jimmy was his campaign manager. I don't know for certain if this was Frost's introduction to Jim or not, but from then on, Frost paid attention to him." Dempsey won the 9 July election, and honour satisfied, he died in October. "When Dempsey died in office," said French, "a bunch of his old Conservative enemies, those who had rejected him, wanted the chance to run for the nomination in his place, but Jimmy said, 'A pox on your houses. You wouldn't support Dempsey – I supported him! I'm going to run!' And he did and got elected. Not long after that, Frost put him in the Cabinet."

James didn't take the nomination as a repentant, returning to the fold. He was determined to make his run as a still-unconverted supporter of Dempsey, the man the party couldn't stomach. The Toronto *Telegram* of 8 December 1955, reported his defiance: "It was made very clear yesterday that the ghost of Jim Dempsey will stalk the Renfrew South by-election on January 12. James A. Maloney, Renfrew lawyer, nominated as the Progressive Conservative candidate, said he would fight his campaign under the Dempsey mantle. 'I'm going to succeed the great Jim Dempsey,' he said." The Liberals, sensing a chance in possible party disunity, put on a special effort. "Liberal headquarters," continued the *Tely*, "is sending special speakers from Toronto in an effort to gain some prestige by a victory in Renfrew South, now the most famous riding in Ontario." James saw them all off, and took his rustic gifts to Queen's Park. Tom Edmondstone recognized his peculiar talent: "Jim was really the only Tory who could talk the language of the northern ridings; the miners, the lumbermen, the rough-neck communities all liked him. Frost personally liked him, surprisingly, and he was reputed to be the man to listen to if you were going to play any attention at all to what the boondocks had to say."[26]

As in Arthur's case, there was a strong line of obvious affection in James's mix of personal and political connections, and he was often reluctant to separate them or to plead political prohibitions in order to avoid compromising situations. When he joined the Frost Cabinet, he might have looked awkward, but he rapidly established himself as a lively speaker. While some other members of the Frost entourage were *de haut en bas* about James's excesses, Frost seemed to find him amusing – and useful. But he could be perverse. When his friend Frank Dunlap ran for the provincial Liberals in Ottawa, the Conservative candidate specifically asked James to appear with him and speak on his behalf. James, although he seemed perfectly at liberty to appear for other

Conservative candidates throughout the province, was, maddeningly, unavailable in the riding where his old friend was the enemy. He simply would not appear, however much he was coaxed and cajoled. Dunlap did not win, but the picture in the Renfrew *Mercury* of the following day, of the defeated candidate in his riding headquarters seemed to belie that with its general air of hilarity and high spirits – standing proudly beside the unbowed, defeated candidate, beaming happily, was his old friend, James Maloney.

He was off the back benches very quickly, first as the Chairman of the Private Bills Committee, and then into the Cabinet as the Minister of Mines. On his appointment to the Cabinet, there was a dinner in his honour at the Hotel Renfrew, of which the *Ottawa Journal* reported on 9 February 1956: "Only 365 sat down to eat, one organizer apologized, but that was because it was all the hotel's dining facilities could stand. Many others went without dinner, some sat on the stairs, some even waited in the outside vestibule, but none went home. They were there to pay their respects to one of the most passionately-supported and equally passionately-opposed politicians in Ottawa Valley history and they all saw it through." If he was a charmer with the rural voters, he was a bruiser in the Legislature, with a reputation as an agile, short sharp stick in the eyes of the Opposition. Not for him the sly edge of Arthur's rhetoric; he once turned on the CCF leader, Donald MacDonald, for indulging in what James called "dirty, swill-pail, pigpen tactics," which gives some short suggestion of why he was popular in the back country. In a letter sent to Arthur at the time of James's death, his gifts were extolled: "I shall always remember him as the man who gave the best goddam tub-thumping political speech I ever heard – when he nominated Fleming five years ago. I told him that at the time – I repeat it now."[27] This at the time of the PC convention of 1956, when Diefenbaker took the leadership over Donald Fleming. As Dalton Camp put it, "James Maloney of Ontario moves Fleming's nomination, vigorously perspiring, loudly emphatic – giving a near-perfect parody of the ritual performance. But it develops into a cruel and cunning speech."[28]

Tom Edmondstone, who started practice in his home town of St. Catharines and moved to the north-eastern townships early in his career, joined James in the late fifties, and was with him until James died:

> Jimmy had probably more natural ability than any lawyer I knew; he had a great "trial" memory, and an intuitive knowledge of the law. I don't think he read much law, but I never saw a lawyer with a better memory; on a three-day trial, some little, seemingly unimportant point would come out on day "one," and on day "three," Jimmy would spot a discrepancy that would lead right back to the

point. It was hard to believe that Arthur and Jimmy were brothers; they were so different. Of course, they looked alike, but they also looked different. Jim had that pugged-nose, flat-faced look of his father, but it was more than looks. Jim wasn't a scholar, and he was much rougher than Arthur in cross- examination. He didn't use honeyed words. Once he was cross-examining a woman, and she got so upset that she threw a shoe at him. The judge simply commented that "I don't know, Mr. Maloney, which is going to happen first: whether you're going to lose your right to cross-examine this witness or lose your left eye." He was larger than life around Renfrew, with a legendary reputation. He didn't pay well, but that was partly because we didn't have a very lucrative practice, but if he got a windfall, he would suddenly give me a bonus. Once he bought me a car. It was a criminal practice in the main, and it spread all over the area, as far north as North Bay and south to Brockville and west to Belleville, with much of it coming in bits and pieces from the area north of Highway 7. He could be very rough, and could make life miserable for timid Crowns. Once while a Crown was addressing a jury, he told him, under his breath, to sit down, and the Crown, before he knew what he was doing, did just that. He would stomp all over Graham Walsh, the Renfrew Crown, who once told me, "You know, Jimmy isn't such a bad fellow as long as you're not standing where he wants to be walking."[29]

He might well have been a successful commercial solicitor, given his intelligence, charm, and political contacts, but he was cursed with a love for criminal law, and like Arthur, he frequently spoke of his affection for the courtroom and his boredom with office work. There was, however, nothing like the general poise and gentility of Arthur about him, and he often felt that Arthur piled on the honey too thickly. Edmondstone remembers that they had a client applying for a liquor licence in the late fifties, at a time when such applications had to be dressed with a fine gloss of respectability (and some Conservative connections, if possible). James was in the Ontario Cabinet so it was decided that Arthur, who, not surprisingly, given his PC connections, did quite a lot of this work, should make the submission for the Renfrew client. A delegation of temperance women appeared at the hearing and made their opposition to the licence known. After the session was over, Arthur approached the group, and praised the "lovely ladies" for their civic spirit, although he had been arguing for the other side moments before. "I guess that Jimmy and I must have been lurking in the back, because on the way back from Ottawa, Jimmy kept grumbling, 'That Arthur? Arthur! How could he stand there and do that? Lovely ladies? Old bitches!!'" Jimmy was not much good at oleaginous waffle.

Frank Dunlap, an early student of Arthur's, liked Jimmy better. It may have something to do with the fact that they were both athletes, but

Frank thinks it was something more than that. Years after James's death, Frank, who was an Irish word-spinner of some reputation, was patently lyrical about James. "I don't think he ever read a book of law after Osgoode, but he knew the book of life. He reminds me of that old song 'Maggie'." Dunlap broke into a cracked *arco* at that moment: "'I wandered today to the hills, Maggie ...' There's a line in that song – 'My face is a well-written page, Maggie/And time all alone has the pen ...' Well, Jimmy had lived every aspect of life. He was a modern-day Robin Hood with a poor distribution service. He was one of the all-time greats in speaking to people. The law meant nothing to him; he was the direct opposite to everything Arthur stood for in the profession. Arthur had a tremendous ability to cross-examine, but Jimmy blustered and pushed – and he knew human nature, even more so than Arthur."[30] Dunlap knew that Arthur did much more for him than James, but he could not resist James's vigour, his child-like boisterousness, and unpolished enthusiasm for life.

James never resented Arthur's grander reputation. At one time in the late fifties, and early sixties, they were in politics in tandem; Arthur was a Member in Ottawa, and James had the far more powerful position as a minister in the Ontario Cabinet; but it made no difference – Arthur was still the Maloney whom the public admired. On at least one occasion, James had the opportunity to outshine him – surprisingly at the law. A Renfrew family had been in a motor accident in Hamilton, and two of the family members were killed. James called Arthur in to help him with the civil trial. Arthur took the cross-examinations; James took the jury address, and Edmondstone took the trial notes.

> It was the only time that I know of when they worked together. [They did, in fact, work together on other, rare occasions.] Jimmy became very emotional in his address: "Picture this little family coming from the Ottawa Valley. Little did they know that only three of them would return from the big city of Hamilton!" It seemed to be working, and when the jury went out, the defence counsel objected to Mr. Justice Dan Kelly about Jimmy stirring up the jury. Kelly said, "I'm inclined to agree with you. He went pretty far, but he didn't go far enough." We won, and after, one of the old court attendants came up to Jimmy and said, "I haven't heard an address like that since the days of Charlie Bell!" Bell had been a great criminal lawyer around Hamilton. We went back to the hotel. Jimmy wasn't drinking at the time, but Arthur and I were, and all night long, Jimmy walked about the hotel room, intoning: "Since the days of Charlie Bell!!"[31]

Inevitably, the old Maloney male curse arrived, and James died, age fifty-six, in October 1961 – of a heart attack. He had been in ill health for a long time, and his death brought out the excesses of newspaper sentimentality. *The Renfrew Advance* set the tone in its 5 October 1961 editorial: "The Hon James A. Maloney who died Sunday night was in the tradition of a century of Canadian political speakers and he came by this fluency and forcefulness and platform power through both inheritance and exposure in his birth place of Eganville where the art of politics is ingrained ... There is no one around that will take Jim Maloney's colorful place in the history of this riding." James was a great dispenser of political spoils and favours, and particularly effective in dealing with the problems of a poor riding. Lillian remembers the crowd at the funeral and the constant murmurings of regret and appreciation: "People kept coming up and sayings things like – 'My children could not have gone to school if Jim hadn't bought them snow suits and boots.'"[32] Edmondstone found one moment of the funeral service eerie. James had been generous in defending the Indians from the local reservation, and at the last moment, in the hush just before the service began, a long, silent file of Indians slipped into the back row of the pews.

He was as gifted as any of the children, but gripped early in his life by alcohol, which wore him down by his early fifties. Without that impediment he might well have done important things since he not only had the Maloney desire to help people, the ability to make public declamations of considerable rough-hewn attractiveness and humour, but a public presence – a florid personality, and a taste for fighting for what he wanted. The *Advance* knew his gifts: "He had an instinctive love of people, and with that an instinctive generosity. The human qualities, the strong, out-going personality, his presence at an Irish wake, at a Polish or German wedding, these are the things for which James A. Maloney, QC, Minister of Mines for Ontario, will be remembered in Renfrew South." Unfortunately, that was not to be the last word. Arthur said that he had lost his greatest friend – and Arthur had many friends. He was, almost immediately on James's death, to be called on to defend his brother, not for the first time, and not, sadly, with much success. But more on that problem later.

There were quieter, substantial lives among the other children. Catherine, who trained as a nurse in Ogdensburg, New York, became a nun. Her mother was not happy with that choice, initially, but the child was determined and never seemed to regret her decision. She became Sister Martin of the Sacred Heart with the Grey Nuns, an American order. She spent some of her service in Alaska, and then came back to teach in New York state. Mary had a career in the civil service, but her physical difficulties became too much for her. In a letter from Pat to Arthur on 25 August 1959, her predicament was outlined: "Mary apparently is going to quit her job because it is impossible for her to carry on with the crutches. She is going to give up her apartment and intends, I would judge, to stay in Eganville for the time being." The boys helped her financially while she maintained the family home. Arthur kept a close eye on her, but he had to be careful, as did the others who worried about her, since she was strong-willed and hated to be patronized. She could be very difficult if she suspected any attempt to protect her from her inclination to do for herself, and Lillian has affectionate memories of Mary putting Arthur in his place when he tried to help her too overtly. She could shout him down, and she would. She and Nell were the women with the strongest sense of independence. Nell trained as a teacher, and worked at it for two years in a one-room school in Pine Valley. Then she went into the civil service in Ottawa, in the Customs division of National Revenue, and stayed for over thirty years. Late in her career, she tried for a promotion, and was denied in favour of a male. She officially protested, claiming that she was a victim of sexual discrimination. She was informed that she could certainly object if she wished, but that the claim of sexual discrimination was irrelevant. She was so disgusted by this that she soon left the service, and returned to teaching, at the age of sixty-two. She found out that she loved teaching, and was sorry she hadn't returned years before. She, Mary, and Catherine were the unmarried daughters.

Margaret married Ken Godin while very young, and Frances who married John French, had a short career as a high school teacher. Anna worked for a time in the Ottawa civil service, but also married early; she became the wife of James Lyons, one of James Maloney's Osgoode friends. In the early 1990s as this book was being developed, only Nell, Frances, Anna, and Margaret were alive. Nell died in 1993, but not before she contributed to this book. There was little contradiction in their memories of their parents, and of their sisters and brothers. There was considerable agreement about the manner in which their parents prepared them for life, seemingly without harassment or nagging. Arthur was not alone in being trained for a life of service through the possession of a high skill; it was common practice for the Maloney children to be prepared to make their mark, and they all did, in different ways.

3

Early Years

One of the first law students who came to Arthur under articles was Frank Dunlap, an Ottawa boy. In 1942, he had visited Arthur at St. Michael's, hoping to get some idea of whether or not he should enrol at the college. Arthur was going into his last year at Osgoode, but he still lived at St. Mike's, and most of his social connections were centred on the school. Arthur took Dunlap up and sought to guide him when the younger man entered the university in the autumn of 1942.

Mr. Justice Frank Dunlap, who died in 1993, cheerfully admitted that he needed help. He was an athlete of considerable skill and promising reputation, both as a football and a hockey player; the professional scouts were watching him. He had been scheduled to go to Notre Dame in the States, but the war stopped that. Instead, he came to St. Mike's on a Toronto Maple Leaf hockey scholarship, and he was still playing football for Ottawa on the weekends when the term began. He should have been something of a celebrity on campus, but Arthur and his friend, Bill Quigley, who was studying dentistry, made it plain that they were doing Frank a favour by including him in their social life. They spent a lot of time, as many University of Toronto students did, in the King Cole Room of the Park Plaza Hotel at the corner of Bloor Street and Avenue Road, drinking beer and talking nonsense – and sometimes, more substantial topics.

Arthur knew where he was going, even in those days. He made no pretext of being a student. He wasn't interested in great marks, but he knew then where he was going, and how he was going to get there. He had a tremendous interest in the arts. It used to appal me when he'd spend Saturday afternoon listening to the opera on the radio. But he was also impressed by the fact that his father knew who I was, because Dr. Maloney was interested in sport, and I had some reputation. He couldn't understand that his father was impressed by me, simply because I was an athlete. He was like his mother rather than his father. He was a Bonfield. Jimmy and Pat had the same looks and some of the rougher temperament of their father, with the flat faces and high cheek-bones. They were a rugged kind of animal. Arthur was much gentler, much less roughly masculine.[1]

Frank Dunlap looked back on Arthur as a major influence on his life, since it was Arthur who convinced him that he could be better than a professional athlete, with all the liabilities and limitations of that life. "Arthur wasn't interested in sport; he thought it was a waste of my time. He used to say, 'Read the Classics, my boy. They'll make you learned.'" What Arthur did for Dunlap, while still but a student himself, was to be repeated with other young men throughout his career. But Frank Dunlap continued to play two sports, and in the 1943–44 season, he went up to the Toronto Maple Leafs for a nine-game try-out. Hap Day, the Toronto coach, and the Leafs' management wanted him to go professional; Day believed that he had, at least, a ten-year career ahead of him, which in hockey is better than average. Dunlap's father was cautious, but it was Arthur who made the real difference. He was against Dunlap leaving his studies, and Dunlap paid attention.

Frank, and his younger brother, Jake, also an athlete of promise, and also to become a close friend of Arthur, were bemused by him. They had reputation; their names were in the newspapers; and they came from Ottawa. Arthur was no-one from the hick town of Eganville. "It's strange – he, coming from Eganville, up the Valley – it never bothered him. In fact, he used to boast in that mock grand voice,'I'm Arthur Maloney from Eganville!'" Frank had no hope for himself beyond athletics. Later he was to realize that he was something of a psychological victim of the Depression years, just hoping for a steady, simple job. For Arthur, it was different – he presumed that he would do well, and he convinced Frank that he, too, could make something of himself.

If I hadn't met him – well! Of course, it undermined my hockey career, but it opened up vast vistas of what life could be. Arthur used to sit and talk to me, and he was something! He was the centre of his own little group. He took part in debates, and was good at them, and he did other things that now, you can see, were a help. Not only the interest in drama, and the opera, but other things. For a while, he used to broadcast the Sunday noon Mass from St. Michael's. Oh, just to hear him say "And now the priest approaches the altar; he has in his hand the unleavened bread" – just to hear him say it was fantastic! Particularly if you knew he'd had three or four belts in him, which was not uncommon at the time at the school. I'm sure that it was at St. Mike's that he developed that colour in his address that Arthur Martin and Charlie Dubin didn't have, although they were intellectually his superior. I remember one time, he had gone out to make a recruiting speech, sometime in 1942 – he was a Saturday night soldier at the university; and he and I and Quigley met afterwards for a

> drink, and he was full of himself. "Dunlap, you should have heard me speaking to that multitude!!" He loved all that kind of thing, and he would make fun of himself doing it.[2]

Lillian remembers a story that he told her about this playful misuse of his oratorical gifts during his Osgoode years. He was living on St. George Street, near the Newman Club. Walking by one night, he heard sounds of revelry, so he went in to find that they were holding elections for the club presidency. The candidates were expected to speak, and Arthur somehow got himself in among them. He spoke so eloquently that with the help of a friend, who was in on the joke, he got himself nominated. He might well have won, had not another candidate, suspicious of this seeming newcomer (although Arthur had been an active member of Newman in his undergraduate years), taken time to discover that he was neither a member any longer of the university or the Newman Club. But there were limits to his youthful confidence. Dunlap had a unpromising first year at St. Mike's, but Arthur kept urging him to put it behind him and come back again. Arthur came up to Eganville in the summer, and invited Dunlap over to see him, in order to convince him to give the university another try. When Dunlap got there, he saw a side of Arthur that surprised him.

> I hitch-hiked up there. As I was passing the Foy Hotel, there was a man watering the grass, and the hose was snarled, so I jumped up to help him, and while we were struggling with the hose, I saw Arthur driving by, with his mother. He saw me, out of the corner of his eye and I called to him, but he never made any sign of seeing me, and drove on. I went over to the house, but no one was there, so I went back to the hotel, and he finally came back. I said, "You bugger! Why didn't you stop?" And he said, "I thought you were tight! I was afraid to stop and pick you up! – With my mother!"[3]

It was the only time Frank saw Arthur Maloney afraid of anyone.

Arthur always looked back on his St. Michael's days ruefully; he was pleased with what he had made of his undergraduate years, but sorry that he hadn't done more. He told Lillian that it was the time when he felt closest to his religious faith, and for a time he thought of entering the priesthood. He might have had some trouble doing that, given his marks. In his first year he had a B average, based on a wide mix of marks. He had an A in French, a B in history, and Cs in Latin, economics, and philosophy. His second year was better balanced; he kept his B average, with an A in one philosophy course, and Bs in French, economics, history, and a second philosophy. (That year, a student named Paul Hess won the Carswell Prize in English constitutional law at the university; he was to show up later in Arthur's legal career.) In his final year, Arthur was obviously thinking of other things. He had a C average, with a D in French and in one of his two philosophy courses, and Bs in economics, history, and the other philosophy. He didn't take English, and he was always to regret that, and used to urge students to get as much literature in their studies as they could manage. Otherwise, he had a good college career. He had an active student council life, and had done some debating, drama, and broadcasting. He had impressed everyone, student and staff alike, with his confidence, and his social and political skills. He got himself into the Students' Administrative Council (SAC) offices as an employee in the first summer after graduation, and he kept that job through his first two years at Osgoode.

He wanted to join the armed forces, and he tried on more than one occasion to get past the medicals, but the doctors always detected his respiratory weaknesses. He did, however, serve in the university Canadian Officer Training Corps (COTC), both at Varsity and Osgoode Hall. Getting a job with the SAC office was a help, since he was trying to be as independent as possible, but the Osgoode programme required students to be articled to a lawyer as of the autumn of the first school term, and that meant that although he could work out of the profession in his first summer out of university, he would be required to work in a law office in the subsequent vacations. James took up Arthur's articles, however, and Arthur was excited about going to law school. His mother's letter of the 20 September 1940 shows her understanding of his high hopes. "You always wanted to go. So you have your wish and I know you will do well there, as you did every place else. God love you." The letter was full of war news, seen from the perspective of the Valley; the girls, for instance, were having difficulty finding a place to live in Ottawa. "The girls didn't have an apartment when I left. You have no idea how hard it is to get one. They tell me there are 6 or 8000 more people in Ottawa doing war work and that accounts for the shortage of apts. I'm afraid it's going to be hard to get a suitable place. Anna and I looked at every thing we saw advertized [*sic*] and the rents are gone sky high." Worrying about where her daughters were to live didn't take all her time; she had some concern over family members falling away from the church. "This morning we had a visit from Pat and Basil Maloney and their wives from Timmins; two nice women – and a dear little girl, Coreen, – but they are all protestants, desperate, isn't it. I spoke to Pat & Basil when I got the ladies upstairs. They said they knew it was very wrong, but found it hard now to go back. I asked them to go and see their parish priest. They didn't promise, so please pray for them Art. Their mother and father (both dead) were very fine Catholics."

On a Valentine's Day card from his mother in 1941, his enthusiasm for Churchill is noted: "How did you like Mr. Churchill's speech – We were saying you would remember it word for word. It was very good, and encouraging. I hope and pray, they don't take our boys. I will send some cash soon." Money seemed to be short and there is constant apology for not being able to do better for him. His mother's birthday letter of 25 November 1942, enclosed "this small amount to buy a gift for yourself, as I really don't know what you need." But mother really does know best and she suggests a possibility of some diplomatic value: "Why don't you take Father Sullivan out to a show or dinner to celebrate the occasion. [*sic*] He is so good to you."

Arthur might, indeed, remember Churchill's words. Aside from his general admiration for the British Prime Minister, he had, in fact, a minor confrontation with him in early January 1942. Churchill was scheduled to speak to the House of Commons in Ottawa, and Arthur learned that the *Eganville Leader* had no plans to send a representative to report on the speech. He offered his services to Paddy McHugh, the editor, and McHugh arranged to have the young law student accredited as the paper's correspondent. Arthur, however, was not content to report the speech, but was determined to take part in the question period after the same. Evidently he came up with a question that did not please Churchill, who gave the young man a very hard look indeed, which Arthur remembered with some sensitivity, but with the satisfaction of having spoken, if across a crowded room, to his hero. The question that piqued Churchill has been forgotten by the family.

There are only a few of these letters from his mother during the Osgoode years (there are none from his father), and they are something of a microcosm of the Eganville world, only intruded upon vaguely by the war. The worry about Dr. Maloney's health starts at this time; it is first mentioned in the letter of 6 July 1940, and probably has something to do with Arthur's determination to pay his own way.

> Dad is still in Ottawa, and will have an X Ray starting Sunday night; it takes about three days. I hope to our dear Lord and His Blessed Mother that the X Ray [*sic*] will not show anything serious. So pray hard Art. Jim and Henry came up from the city last night ... I hate going to Ottawa as it makes me so sad to see Dad sick. Gen says he seemed very much better and more like himself. Poor dear was never sick before and he seemed so weak ... Margaret has taken her holidays and is staying with Dad. The house and office seems strange without him, and so many come to ask for him. He has a great many friends. He never had a holiday, and he must be very tired.

Mrs. Long (who was always called "Mrs. Long"), the old housekeeper, had retired but she always remembered the boys. "Mrs. Long missed you. She isn't having a good time she expected with you and Henry." Arthur may have understood that last sentence; it seems to mean that Mrs. Long was not having the good time in her retirement that she had when she was looking after the Maloney boys, years previous.

Nor was domestic help so dependable as Mrs. Long had been. Maids came and went, and were becoming hard to find in 1940 as the young women left the small towns for work in the defence plants down south. With all the children gone, things were quieter; Father Henry managed to come to town regularly. Frances was working in Ottawa. "Frances is well. She likes her boarding house and also her school. She is good child."

Mrs. Maloney's letter of 25 November 1942, begins with news of Dr. Maloney's health. "Dad is well, and has been quite busy and he likes that. Pray for him to get completely cured, and to have a good office practice. Its easier than going to the country." Mrs. Long shows up again: "Mrs. Long is quite happy in the St. Patricks. Nell says she is always saying – 'You know Nellie, your Mother told me I could go home any time I like.' Nell says that is a great joy to her, to know she can leave at any time. I will always be good to her as she was a faithful old soul." A new maid, Jetty, is discussed in a manner that might be considered patronizing now (if, indeed, families in the Maloney economic bracket could afford such a luxury), but Mrs. Maloney's comments would be normal for a woman who had managed servants much of her married life.

> My new maid, that Fr. Henry got me is a very nice girl. Never runs the streets at night. Will make a nice cook, always in good humour. Has a lot to learn about things. For instance, she goes to the door. She loves that. This is how she greets the patients. "Good day. Come in. Sit down. Yes, he's in." Then she bangs the office door and locates Dad. She says, pointing with her finger. "It's a man (or 'It's a woman') and it's for you." She likes to go to the door, and loves the show. She reads a lot. I gave her Pecks bad boy [*sic*] to read, and she laughed out loud at Peck's clowning. She is 18. Clean, and I hope she stays a long time. Pat McGrath still makes the fires, and brings in the wood. Fr. Henry thinks it was better to keep him on the job. It's so hard to get maids.

This particular letter makes the first mention of Arthur's broadcasting: "You will be on the Radio this Sunday. We will be watching for your dear voice." It was a family event to listen to him, and her letter of 13 December 1942, reveals that it wasn't simply a matter of turning on the radio; the kindness of others was involved. "We sat and listened very attentively to you today, and your voice and pronunciation was perfect. So clear, and your articulation was, as I said, perfect." In 1942, electric power wasn't always available in Eganville. "I asked Mr Deagle, the man who owns the electric lights hire to please leave the lights on till 12:20 and he did. Said he would love to have a son speaking over the air himself and understood how I felt. Wasn't he nice to change the hour for me? Frances and John, Nora McNamara and I sat here, listening to every word. John said that your voice was excellent." By this time, John French was courting Frances. He had graduated from dental college, and was in the Army Dental Corp. "Frances is well and is a sweet child. She and John are still very much in love. John looks well in his uniform." The approach of Christmas was causing a minor problem: "My maid wants to go home for Christmas. I suppose I cant [*sic*] blame her, but I was wishing she wouldn't go. She is a nice girl, has a lot to learn, but she is alright, and always in a good humor. Mrs Long is quite happy at St Patricks. She is better there in cold weather. We got her an increase in her pension. She gets 20.00 [*sic*] now and she is pleased, but she pays 18 at St. P's ... She was a good old soul in many ways."

The war continually worried her. Pat was already in the service; Jim was too old to be drafted, even if he had been fit, but there was still the possibility of Arthur being taken, particularly since he kept trying to enlist. She seems to think that if he failed his Christmas exams, he would not have to go into the service. It would seem that quite the opposite would have been the case, but her reasoning may have something to do with the fact that Arthur was trying to get in as an officer candidate. "I pray for you to get all your exams. Perhaps if you didn't, you wouldn't have to go to the Army. I guess I'm not patriotic when it comes to you and my own family." She may, of course, have presumed that if he failed, he would be allowed to stay on at Osgoode to finish up before joining the army. What she did not know was that Arthur was having some difficulty getting out of Osgoode, whether or not he passed his exams. The scheduled graduation was in the early summer, but Arthur was not to get his call to the Bar until the following October. He used to console himself by recalling that John Wintermeyer, who was to go on to become the leader of the provincial Liberal party, graduated with him.

Arthur had problems with the administrators at Osgoode from early on, caused in part by his determination to support himself at law school. Although he was officially articled to James in June 1940, he had spent the summer before coming to Osgoode in the employ of the SAC. As a result, he had no office experience, and his oral exams at the end of the first year had been judged unsatisfactory; he was given a "no rating" grade. He was, in fact, a poor student all round. He failed two of his first seven exams. His highest mark, perhaps significantly, was in Criminal Procedure, but that was only a 68, and on his supplemental exams in Contracts, and Torts, he could only manage a 63 and a 60 respectively.

He stood sixty-first in a class of seventy-seven. Second year was no better. He stood fifty-three out of sixty at Christmas and failed one of three exams, although on his supplemental, he managed miraculously to take Sale of Goods from a 42 to an 86, the highest mark of his Osgoode career. In the second year finals, he failed two out of five, but again retrieved them in supplementals, one with a 60 and one with a respectable 76. He stood forty-fifth out of fifty-six. In his final year, he got the hang of it, and he passed everything first time, but he had two subjects in the low 50s, three in the low 60s, one in the high 60s, a 75 in evidence, and an 80 in a subject that would surprise all who knew his inept way with office finance – Bookkeeping. His final standing was twenty-third out of forty-eight.

They were not impressed at Osgoode, especially when his final oral examinations were so mediocre. The notes taken by his examiners, all practising members of the Bar, were peppered with unfavourable comments: "Some short periods in summer with brother," "but not sure" on real estate questions, "only in lectures," "fair only," "sketchy," "not sure," "guessing and not very happy," "very vague."[4] The only thing in his favour was the fact that by luck more than design or personal worth he had spent his final year in the law office of John Cartwright and Colonel Dick Greer, both of whom were leaders at the Bar. For some odd reason, the examiners gave him a B rating, which Arthur fastened on when the trouble started.

At the end of his second year at Osgoode, the Law Society was after Arthur about the unsatisfactory state of his articles. He was still articled to James, back in the Valley, but he was, in fact, living in Toronto. He had never attempted to have his articles transferred to a Toronto lawyer, claiming that he was obliged to work outside the law in order to pay his way. In his letter, written from Teefy Hall at St. Michael's, where he was in residence, he put the best face on the situation, "I have during my first and second years at Osgoode Hall been engaged as Assistant to the General Secretary-Treasurer of the Students' Administrative Council of the University of Toronto. As a result of this position, it was possible for me to completely finance myself as a student without having to call upon my father to bear the burden that he otherwise would have had to undertake." He claims to have intended to work with James in the summer of 1941, the summer following his first year at Osgoode, "but by reason of the serious illness of my father, Doctor M.J. Maloney of Eganville, Ontario, this was made quite impossible." He had, however, promised to spend his final year at Osgoode, articled to a Toronto firm, and unfazed by his mediocre record, and his lack of attendance in a law firm, he faced them down again. "I will for my final year in Osgoode Hall be engaged in that way [*i.e.* work in a law office] rather than in the manner I have been for the first two years of my course. The sudden change in my status as a law student will undoubtedly require that I augment my income considerably more during the coming summer than I have had to do in the past by reason of my position with the Students' Administrative Council of the University of Toronto. For that reason I shall submit also a petition to be allowed to be engaged in employment for the coming summer vacation."[5] The "sudden change" that he was talking about was complying with the rules as every other law student was obliged to do. If they were going to make him to do that, he would need to do one more summer of outside work. Arthur, in short, was determined to blind the Osgoode's Legal Education Committee with more foot work if he could – never apologizing, and demanding to do at least one more summer of what they were complaining about. "I trust this explanation will be given your careful consideration, and that you will understand that it was a financial necessity that I should have been employed as I have been during the past two years."[6] Osgoode was not happy with this display of arrogance, and their "in-house" memo concluded with the opinion that he ought to be put into a law office in the summer of 1942, and that his request to continue in outside employment should be denied. Despite this, they reluctantly accepted his plea of financial hardship, and let him have another summer to pursue the outside work, but only on the condition that he *might* have to make up the time in the following summer of 1943 – which meant, of course, that he would not graduate with his class. In the autumn of 1942, as Arthur was beginning his last year, James got a very stiff letter from the Society, complaining about his conduct in the matter, and reminding him that he had an obligation as Arthur's principal to educate him, in part. "This student entered into certain important covenants from your point of view and the articles of clerkship contain the time-honoured covenant that you will to the best of your ability 'teach or instruct the clerk in the practice or profession of a solicitor' ... in fitting the student to practice law like a gentleman, and as a well-trained member of our profession ... This is a matter of the greatest importance to the student, and the purpose of this somewhat lengthy letter is to appeal to you to help the student as much as you can."[7]

In the late summer of 1943, Arthur was still not called; the rest of his class had graduated in the late spring. The Society was thinking of keeping him in articles for a further period in the autumn, and in a letter of 21 August 1943, they so informed him. Arthur struck back from the Knights of Columbus Canadian army huts at Petawawa. Those who were later to find his voluminous annual reports as Ombudsman examples of "lily gilding" would see the same gift at work in his long letter of rationalization. The Society obviously did not frighten him, and he was not prepared to suppress his natural gift for irony. Addressing the fact that he had been allowed to work outside the law in the summer of 1942, with the unpleasant possibility of having to make up the time at the end of his last school year, he steelily put the position: "I am, however, fully mindful of the fact that when that leave was given to me, it was made clear – as you have pointed out in your letter that I might be required to serve longer under articles than I would otherwise have been required to do. As I see it, it is the effect of these instructions that I may now be made to feel."[8] That last sentence is Arthur Maloney at his sandily, succinct best, suggesting his displeasure, despite the fact that he is the one who has failed to fulfil his obligation. He piles on the agony, claiming that, despite the permission to do outside work in the summer of 1942, he had only used the privilege for three weeks. "As it happened, I developed a slight sickness from which I recovered around the end of July of that year. Then, instead of carrying on with the employment I had been given leave to take I went into the law office of my brother – Mr. James A. Maloney of Renfrew, Ontario – and remained with him until my return to Toronto." And if that wasn't enough to get the Society to back off (despite the fact that even if Arthur had spent the last month of the summer of 1942 in James's office, his oral exams in the next spring were still unsatisfactory), Arthur had an even more compelling song to sing. Having spent his last year at Osgoode, quite properly in articles with Smith, Rae, Greer, he wrote:

> In June of this year I made application to join the Royal Canadian Navy. My application was accepted but I was subsequently rejected by the Medical Examiner who found me unfit for service at sea. During this last month I was accepted into the Auxiliary Services with the Knights of Columbus ... being trained for an overseas posting. I have just been informed that it will not be possible for me to go Overseas [*sic*] and I have therefore decided to leave this organization and to enlist in the ranks of the Active Army. My enlistment should be accomplished before the end of this month. I point all of this out to you merely to show that if I am required to serve for a longer period of time under articles I could not possibly do so until after the war. It has always been my ambition to be a lawyer and I – sir – should feel sincerely distressed if the fulfilment of that ambition were to be postponed for so uncertain and so indefinite a time.

It was a shameless performance, and a quite remarkable one, given that Arthur was still a mere law student with not much in the way of academic credentials to merit consideration of any kind. But what could they do after such heartfelt argument? In October 1943, the Law Society gave in, and called him to the Bar. The letter seemed to do the trick. But was the letter the real basis for their change of position? On 11

September, J. Shirley Denison, K.C., Chairman of the Legal Education Committee had received a letter from Colonel Greer, Arthur's Toronto principal:

> This young man probably was as good a student as we ever had in this office, being not only extremely industrious but also intelligent, and for a student, seemed to have an unusually keen appreciation of legal matters. He is not physically too strong, and had an attack of illness about a year ago, during the summer months, while he was in this office, and I understand that during part of his law term he was compelled to work in order to pay his way, and he seems to have lost time in consequence. Having had close contact with the young man, I can speak in high terms of him and am glad to do so, and if you could extend him some consideration in his call I should be grateful, as I think he is worthy of every help which might be given to him.[9]

If that is what his principal thought of him, and his skills, who was to quarrel, particularly about a boy on his way to fight for King and Country? Which, of course, he did not do, and probably, given his physical condition, could not have done. Whatever or whoever turned the Committee around (it may well have been a combination of Arthur's lament and Colonel Greer's letter), one of the significant elements in the battle is an early example of something that both J.J. Robinette and G. Arthur Martin were to remark on: Arthur's fearlessness in the face of authority.

The Law Society of Upper Canada at Osgoode Hall makes and breaks Ontario lawyers. The handsome sprawl of Victorian buildings set back on its long, deep lawn, separated from the curb-hugging concrete facades of Queen Street by its high, wrought-iron fence, is imposing, particularly in this age of minimalist architectural decoration. In its labyrinth of administrative offices, chambers for the judges of both the trial and the appeal divisions of the Supreme Court of Ontario, the Court of Appeal, the Great Library, the huge, two-storied dining hall, and the inner sanctum of the Benchers, glimpsed in its Victorian opulence down the long, carpeted halls, it represents long-entrenched power. It stands against the intrusion of high slabs of glass-and-metal Mies-imitations that have become the centre of architectural banality in downtown Toronto, and is a memorial to a more elegant age, and a repository of gentlemanly professional conduct that reaches back into the earliest years of Ontario history in the nineteenth century. It can make a young man mind his manners if he chooses to step inside, and the Society that exists within is not to be gainsayed.

In that last letter of rejoinder, however, Arthur was unmoved by the disapproval of the Society, and addressed the Secretary with an icy, laconic *hauteur* that must have astonished the Committee. Who was this fellow, with his accumulation of exams and orals in intellectual tatters who would strike back so tersely: "As I see it, it is the effect of these instructions that I may now be made to feel." As if it was the lash he was to meet. There could not have been a Bencher who would not have wished to swing that sentence in the face of a surly judge. "As I see it" has the disdainful smartness of a man addressing the lower orders, and the significant placing of "now," as a kind of death knell, is potently redolent with disgust. Most writers would have placed it at the end of the sentence where it would possess little force. The rest of the letter is a foretaste of how Arthur would, later, marshall evidence – taking it one way, then another, until the reader or juror would be insecure about what, in fact, was really the truth of the matter.

He had been given permission in his penultimate summer (1942) to work outside the law, albeit with the warning that he might have to make up the time later. He did work, but only for a short time – then he was sick – then he did work in August, but in his brother's law office (as they wanted him to do). Why didn't he inform the Society that he was working for James? The letter suggests that they ought to have known, somehow – yet it was only for a very short time before he returned to Toronto and began his last year, finally, properly fulfilling his articles with Colonel Greer. He had then told the Society of the time he spent with James in August, and that information was put in his file. Why, he seems to suggest, wasn't he given any credit for that? He is going into the Navy; then he's off with the Knights of Columbus, and then he isn't. But he is going into the army (cannily called the "Active Army"). By the end of the month he will be gone, perhaps forever, and at least until "after the war." Suddenly, he addresses the Secretary directly: "it has always been my ambition to be a lawyer and I – sir – should feel sincerely distressed if the fulfilment of that ambition were to be postponed for so uncertain and so indefinite a time." The dashes, before and after "sir" are examples of Arthur's use of an oral style to make intimate that which the Society is trying to keep on a formal level. The final touch is "uncertain" with its implication of "never," given the military surround of the time. If the Committee had turned stubborn and looked closely at the comments made by the examiners at his orals, his claim of respectability, based on the B that they had foolishly given him, might well have been diminished. But he got away with it, and it may well be the sheer audacity of the performance that had, somehow, melted their hearts. It was not the last time that he was to get the better of his betters.

The common idea of the leading counsel presumes a distinguished academic career both as an university undergraduate and as a law student. That was not necessarily the case in the early forties, when there were lawyers with various backgrounds at the Bar. There were many in mid-career who had never gone to university, but who had articled with practitioners for a period of years, and then gone on to Osgoode Hall to study and take their call. There were some who had taken honour programmes in law at university, and then gone on to Osgoode. The most common pattern was to take a three-year "pass" degree at university in any combination of subjects, and then come on. Some students, with particularly interest in a discipline other than the law might take a four-year "honour" degree before Osgoode. Arthur and James had settled for the easy, three-year "pass" option. Nevertheless, Arthur had a reputation at the Bar as "a man of letters," and he had some skill in using apposite quotations, usually from Shakespeare, or his other favourite, G.K. Chesterton. Yet his favourite jury addresses show no such literary allusions. In fact, he does not seem to have been deeply read. Lillian does not remember him reading much of anything save his briefs, and there was no serious accumulation of literature in his possession at his death. He simply seemed "lettered," and that was sufficient to give him the reputation, since the Bar, despite its obvious connection with oratory and the printed word, is like any complicated and difficult profession with intellectual proportion and pretension – only sparsely inhabited with thoughtful readers of the great authors. In fact, most of the lawyers who were closely associated with Arthur, although they expressed admiration for his interest in literature as they saw it, were quite uninterested in it, as is the case with most normal university graduates, however surprising that may seem. Arthur obviously wished it was otherwise, but there is no evidence of any serious attempt on his part to find time to read literature, although he did spend a lot of time teaching his children an appreciation of Shakespeare. What he had, which impressed, was a store of apt quotations, and he could deliver these with an offhand panache that distinguished him from others – with the exception of the florid, older practitioner, Joe Sedgwick, who was one of the great Osgoode masters of the literary allusion.

The young Arthur Maloney would have needed more than a gift for literary asides to suggest that he had much future in the law, even if the matter of his questionable, limited experience as an articled student was put aside. He simply showed little natural talent for the law when it came to examinations, and his school career, both as an undergraduate and as a law student, must be some consolation to those members of the Bar who did little to make their mark in their studies, but went on to have good careers. When Arthur came out in 1943, his record suggested, at best, a modest life as an office-bound solicitor. No leading counsel ever started with a less promising *c.v.* Indeed, given his obvious mediocrity, it would have been a lucky chance for Arthur to have articled with a first-class firm in his final year. It was James who finally did something to help his brother's career, after failing as his principal. James had lost a murder trial in Renfrew, and had taken it to appeal through the Smith, Rae, and Greer office.

So when I was looking around for a law office to article with, I got my brother Jim to help. Now, if Col. Greer had been a great corporation lawyer or a real estate lawyer, my career would have taken a different turn, I am sure. But I went in with Col. Greer and John Cartwright. Col. Greer was, I suppose, in those days, the leading criminal trial lawyer in Canada ... It was a great experience to go to court with Col. Greer and John Cartwright, and to see Col. Greer cross-examine ... John Cartwright, as Lord Denning had suggested in his book, *The Discipline of Law*, was able to articulate his thoughts and feelings in an attractive manner. He had committed to memory every line that I think had been written by Gilbert Keith Chesterton. His library contained every one of his books and essays. He had also committed to memory hundreds of lines from the English poets, and the same is true of Joe Sedgwick.[10]

Arthur never lost his admiration for John Cartwright. He was certainly an influence upon Arthur as a lawyer, and his conduct as a public figure (he became the Chief Justice of the Supreme Court of Canada) was to be an example to Arthur.

John Cartwright was the greatest human being I ever met. He was the one closest to perfection. He, at no time, in any of the years I knew him, ever lost his composure; I never saw him speak or act in anger. I never heard him say a single unkind word about anybody, and he was really idolized by the members of the profession when he was in practice. He never lost that sense of humility even when he became chief justice. When you appeared in the Supreme Court of Canada and he was on the Bench, you knew you were going to get a courteous hearing from a distinguished gentleman.[11]

Arthur was, like Cartwright, generally a courteous man, but he was not without a public ego, and he could be angry and often critical. He was a gentleman, but not in anything like the same unruffled mode of John Cartwright. It was through the Greer-Cartwright firm that Arthur was to meet another young lawyer more akin to Cartwright in demeanour and personality.

Col. Greer was developing an association with a young lawyer whose office was also in the Canada Permanent Building, just out some five years, deeply involved in criminal law. I am talking of Arthur Martin; he and the Colonel formed a very close friendship, and Arthur Martin was in our office almost every day, accepting briefs that the Colonel would send him, advising the Colonel of problems that he had, and mutually discussing their problems with each other, and the cases that they had. And to sit in on those discussions and to remember them and to see the friendship grow and flourish and to see the mutual advantage that each derived was an incredible experience.[12]

G. Arthur Martin had been called in 1938, and had been involved in criminal practice, as much as it was possible so to be, from the beginning of his career. It was a determined or fool-hardy (or a combination of both) lawyer who started out with the ambition to be a criminal counsel in the late thirties. There really wasn't anything that could be called a "criminal bar" in Toronto, although a few men tried to make something out of it. Martin was really the only lawyer of first-class talent who was determined to hold himself out exclusively as a criminal advocate, and he found it very hard going, despite having an excellent reputation from the moment of his entrance into the profession. He had been educated in the four-year Honour Law course at the University of Toronto, graduating in 1935 with the gold medal. He graduated from Osgoode with the same honour. He articled, somewhat inappropriately, with A.B. Mortimer, who was an authority on land titles, in a firm specializing in property, estate, and corporation law. Martin stayed with the Mortimer firm until 1940, when he decided to try to practice criminal law on his own, however perilous that might be financially. It certainly was that. There was no legal aid, as we know it, for indigent accused. That was not to come until the late 1960s, so most accused, particularly petty criminals, and the unfortunates of foolish encounter and silly conduct (usually under the influence of alcohol), simply did not have counsel and did not expect any support in their encounter with the magistrates or judges. For more serious charges, the Crown Attorney's office kept a list of lawyers who would take cases without fee; those listed were usually young lawyers, eager to get some experience. There was no money provided in most of these cases, either for the counsel or for expenses. In a murder trial, however, there was an *ex gratia* payment of forty dollars a day, but that would only run for ten days. There was no fund for appeals. There wasn't the enormous volume of criminal activity that is common in the last decades of the century, in the main, simply because the drug trade was much more circumscribed in its social appeal. In the forties, Toronto or Montreal, and to a lesser extent, Hamilton and Windsor were the towns to work in the criminal law. But it was very chancy to base a law practice on it, and the fees were very low. If anything proves that crime does not pay, it is the generally impecunious state of most criminals – occasionally alleviated by periods of ill-gotten gain. That hasn't changed much over the years.

Arthur Martin was so skilled that he was appearing in the Court of Appeal at the age of twenty-six. In his first appearance before that court, in the well-known Mickey MacDonald murder appeal (1939 O.R.), he was praised by the Bench – and that was most unusual. It made the newspapers. Mr. Justice Martin still remembers that case with pride. Frank Regan had taken the trial, and Martin took the appeal, somewhat to the surprise of the Court, who were not used to counsel of Martin's age appearing before them. Mr. Justice Fisher, who had questioned Martin sharply during the presentation of the arguments, astonished everyone – Martin, the other lawyers, and the newspaper reporters, with his comment at the end of the hearing, which Mr. Justice Martin can still quote: "Mr. Martin, it is not the custom of this Court to praise the argument of counsel, but in the case of a man so young, we feel we should depart from this rule. Your argument was at all times brilliant, although I did not always agree with you."[13]

I thought that I would be besieged by clients, but I still only got the penniless. Occasionally, I was paid, but I never made much money. My sister was my secretary, and we had a tiny office at the Canada Permanent Building. Smith, Rae, and Greer, Arthur's firm, was in the same building. Fees for criminal work were very small in those days. I remember that I took two Court of Appeal cases in 1942, both of which were reported, and I got fifty dollars for one and forty dollars for the other. Criminal law wasn't considered important; it wasn't stressed at Osgoode. There was a course, but the emphasis in courses was placed on other subjects. Fortunately, I was appointed as a lecturer in criminal law in 1942. At eight hundred dollars a year, it was a great help in keeping my office solvent. I was helped further by the appointment as Associate Editor of the *Canadian Criminal Cases;* that gave me another five hundred dollars.[14]

Martin is still considered by many to be the best scholar of the criminal law of his time in Canada, and his reputation is not confined to Ontario. Bob Barr, a former Crown, later a criminal counsel in Brockville until his death, told the story of Martin visiting with the Chief Justice of the United States and being driven to the airport in Washington by him. The Chief Justice took care of Martin's luggage; this was remarked upon by a watching porter, "I know who you are – you're the Chief Justice!" Turning to Arthur Martin, he said, "You must be really important if he's carrying your bag!"

While he was still at Osgoode, Arthur Martin had followed the practice of most students interested in trial work, and hung around the courts between classes, watching the few men who did most of the major criminal trials in Toronto. Arthur Slaght impressed him, although he was not to follow Slaght's obvious theatricality in his own courtroom style.

His eloquence would be dated and ineffective today. He, often, in his closing address to the jury asked them to send his client back to his little, aged mother who was waiting with outstretched arms to receive her child. At one trial, Colonel Lennox, who was acting for the Crown, opened his argument to the jury by noticing that Slaght had made such a request. "What about the mother of the girl, whose daughter was returned to her in a casket?" Slaght took the conviction to appeal, asserting that, in fact, the mother of the deceased had been dead for over twenty years. The Court was unsympathetic, accepting the Crown's argument that Slaght had provoked the comment. I always thought that Mr. Slaght would have done well on the stage.

Joe Sedgwick, proud of his reputation as the best "lettered" man at the Bar, once corrected Slaght, who had offered a quotation to a jury with the information that it was by Shakespeare. Sedgwick claimed that it wasn't Shakespeare, but Byron. "Arthur thought about it for a minute and he said, 'Joe, for all I know, you may be right. But I shall continue to tell juries it was Shakespeare. They have heard of him; they have never heard of Byron.' He was a realist. He was a character!"

Charles W. Bell, a Hamilton lawyer, also had theatrical skills; he had written a moderately successful play that was later made into a Buster Keaton movie. He also wrote a book about the law, *Who Said Murder?* He, like Slaght, was a counsel of considerable elegance and eloquence. But Slaght was the real master of feelings in the courtroom, and he could sometimes make a jury weep. Arthur's principal, Colonel R.H. Greer (the use of a military rank after leaving the Service was a common habit at the time), was entirely different. Arthur Martin remembers him as slightly tedious and plodding, "but he was often very effective in eliciting facts in cross-examination. He had a man-to-man manner. Don't forget – in those days, we didn't have ladies on the jury. Greer was a man's man; he talked simply, and was very brusque sometimes. But his forte, nevertheless, was handling juries." Arthur Martin has seen the art from top to bottom through the last seven decades, and he thinks that Slaght and Bell might be forced to repress their impassioned style in late twentieth-century courts. Colonel Greer would be at home, however. Martin believes that jurors are now less impressed by lawyers, less inclined to expect theatrical performances, and more seriously inclined to make up their own minds, and do their duty. It is not, in his opinion, quite as easy today to charm a jury out of the evidence.

In the thirties, forties, and fifties, there was a further group of capable lawyers, not all of them young, who practised a hand-to-mouth form of criminal law in the magistrates' courts. Some of these would go into the County Court, but rarely into the Supreme Court, where the most serious criminal offences were adjudicated. They were, perforce, considered good enough in the rough, chaotic scrum of the magistrates' court, and it was common for some of them to pick up their cases in the halls of the old City Hall – in a sense, soliciting for business on the spot. It was not uncommon to hear these practitioners characterized derisively as willing to take a case for an accused's watch.

Robinette and Martin recall Maloney's early years – somewhat out of the corner of their eyes. "I think I met him at the Cartwright firm," says Arthur Martin. "He used to junior for John Cartwright, and I think he learned a lot from him as far as style – the use of his voice, and particularly his courtesy. Mr. Cartwright had little criminal work, mind you. Dick Greer did the trial criminal work, and Arthur was, in fact, articled to him, but Cartwright took the civil trial list and did most of the appeals, civil and criminal. John had a delightful manner, and like Arthur, he had an interest in literature and the ability to use it in court."

Both men remember how Arthur quickly fitted himself in with the small group of senior trial lawyers, always deferential to his superiors, and not shy to ask them for help with difficult problems. He was, from the start, obviously capable of taking care of himself in the intense world of the courts in which a timid soul can be easily intimidated by an experienced Crown or a sceptical judge. "Arthur," said Arthur Martin,"was a courageous person. He was not afraid of judges, and certainly not of Crowns, and he was an absolutely fearless defender of his clients. But he had a pleasant way about him, and he was never gratuitously aggressive." People liked him, and he soon established himself as one of the two "coming" counsel of the early forties – the other one was Charles Dubin.

Charles (or "Charlie," as he is usually called) Dubin had taken the same route as G. Arthur Martin, through four years of Honour Law at the University of Toronto, and then Osgoode. He was a brilliant student, and articled with R.L. Kellock, one of the best counsel in the city. "I used to watch Kellock and Cartwright regularly," says Chief Justice Charles Dubin of the Ontario Court of Appeal, "since they had most of the civil appeals, and often appeared on opposite sides. Arthur, of course, would be in attendance with Cartwright, and I would be with Kellock."[15] Dubin graduated during the war, and worked in Ottawa in the Wartime Prices and Trade Board, returning to Toronto in 1945 to open a practice with his law school friend, Jack Kimber. He was interested in general trial work, and had the same problem as others in making any money out of criminal clients. He remembers Arthur as "just being always there. By the late forties, Arthur was already being thought of as one of the leading members of the criminal bar; there was an aura about him – a kind of presence." As J.J. Robinette recalls:

> First of all, he was very courteous. He delivered his arguments with a mellifluous voice, and the arguments were always carefully articulated. He was respect-

ed immediately, which was odd for someone so young at the Bar – which doesn't mean he didn't have difficulties; the judges could give him a bad time, especially Chief Justice McRuer, who, at the same time, developed a quite formidable respect for him. He prepared well; he didn't argue ridiculous points, and he concentrated on those few strong points that supported his comments. It was a logical mind, and a very pleasant one. He knew I was always available to help him, and later on, as he became more experienced, I didn't hesitate to ask his opinion. We became good friends. At first, it was a relation of senior to junior, but we often met and had lunch together. I would say that his strength lay in his loyalty to his clients, his friends, to the profession, to John Diefenbaker [Mr. Robinette broke into a laugh here], and especially to his family. He often spoke of his father and his mother, and he was always loyal to Jim, who was so often a bit of a wild man.[16]

G. Arthur Martin has a similar memory of him, and he also saw the way in which younger lawyers were drawn to Arthur. "He was idolized by younger lawyers; it was a very warm personality. We were to become very good friends. It started out with Arthur asking for occasional help, but we often met for lunch, and it became more than that. His real strength was, of course, his eloquence, but he was a good, all-round counsel. He argued law well from early on. He wasn't a profound student. There was a theatrical turn to his jury work, but he would tone that down at appeal, and he was a formidable counsel at the appeal level." (Dubin says that "Arthur Martin was superior to everyone as far as knowledge of the law was concerned, but Art was first-rate.")

The practice of taking cases without fee went on throughout the fifties and early sixties. Indeed, as late as Arthur's last months in the House of Commons, Arthur Martin remembers them getting involved in a case that took them to the Supreme Court of Canada – neither of them had a fee. It was the one time that Arthur Martin actually led Arthur Maloney in court. The matter in question would seem trivial now, but until recently, a criminal record, however slight, was a serious matter, and could follow a person through life with serious consequences.

A college boy, working for the summer at a resort, became emotionally involved with one of the female employees, and they fell in love – given the nature of that age-old experience, they also had a serious quarrel, and the girl decided to leave. The boy, in order to stop her, hid her luggage, and she called the police, presuming that she had been robbed. The police charged the boy, and he was convicted of theft. The magistrate, fully aware of the facts, but not sufficiently intelligent to reason himself to the obvious and proper conclusion that the boy had no intent to steal, fined him one dollar. But the conviction was registered. Maloney somehow got involved, although the boy had no money for an appeal. Surprisingly, the conviction was upheld. Arthur Martin says, "I remember joking with him about the case, and telling him that 'You better win this appeal because the Court of Appeal has set the law back a hundred years with that judgment.' Arthur came right back at me, and said, 'Well, you better argue this with me. I'll prepare the appeal.'There was no money; we paid our own expenses. Arthur, of course, was already up in Ottawa in the House, and he paid for the necessary paper work to perfect the appeal." Arthur Martin, however, prepared the factum, the written plan of argument supported by the list of cases that would confirm the same. On speaking of the matter, Arthur Martin was particularly emphatic about having prepared the factum, which is one of the nicer skills in appeal. There was no question that he was the best man to do the job. He remembers that particular factum with considerable satisfaction; it was to have a life of its own, after the case, since it went the way of many of his finest works of legal preparation – into the hands of the legal fraternity who often passed it on, eager to make use of Arthur Martin's ideas and arguments.

> I came up to Ottawa, at my expense, and I simply recited the facts to the Court. When I got to the part of the boy's feeling for the girl, the Chief Justice, Taschereau, asked me if it was reciprocated, and I said, "Oh, yes, it was!" It was the only question he asked me. The Court allowed the appeal from the Bench. There was no report; no written judgment. It was rather unusual to allow an appeal from the Bench, since the Court usually reserved judgment. But we didn't get paid for it, and it cost us more than our time. But Arthur didn't worry much about money; nor did I.[17]

Arthur Martin admired Maloney's instinctive generosity, not only with clients, but sometimes with friends. When a fellow lawyer died suddenly, the widow was in some financial trouble, which was compounded by her late husband's sorry office finances. "When he died, he had a number of files in the office, and it was either a case of his widow giving back the money already put down, or getting them processed. So Arthur parcelled out the cases to people in that group of his, and they, in turn, defended the clients." He says, jokingly, that it was dangerous to be Arthur Maloney's friend, since the younger man had no compunction about asking for all sorts of help. In the mid-sixties, when Maloney was deeply involved in the abolishment of capital punishment movement, he phoned Martin, asking him to stand in for him that very evening at a west Toronto meeting since he could not get back to town in time to address the group. Arthur Martin supported the movement, so he went along to the hall, and discovered that although Arthur had been thoughtful enough to recruit him as a surrogate speaker, he had forgotten to inform the organizers. Sitting modestly on the stage, he found himself being introduced as the famous social reformer, politician, and champion of the abolitionist movement – Arthur Maloney!

Mr. Justice Martin, who speaks of his profession with fastidious propriety, made it clear that however much Maloney demanded of him, he knew that Arthur was prepared to make the same sort of sacrifices if called upon to do so. He remembers that Arthur, however, was not easily put off by the niceties of conduct in asking for favours. If he needed help, particularly on a point of law, he was not likely to wait his turn – he didn't seem to worry about what Martin might be doing – he needed help, and he wanted it right away! Arthur Martin remembers that on one occasion he got an importunate phone call from Arthur who was in the middle of an important appeal up in Osgoode Hall. Martin listened carefully, and pointed out just one thing – Maloney won the appeal on that single point. Arthur Martin, generous and careful in his comments, has his limits of magnanimity however – he differs with Robinette on the strength of Maloney's legal mind. He acknowledges his skill in court, but was less impressed by his legal reasoning.

Maloney was, however, sufficiently skilled at legal argument by the mid-forties to make him a respectable figure in the Court of Appeal. His first reported appearance there was, appropriately, for a client who had appealed to the court on his own, and for whom the Court had found counsel to argue the law. In short, the appellant had no lawyer and no money. *R. v. Quon* (1947) 47 *Ontario Reports* 856, may not, however, have been Arthur's first appearance in the Court of Appeal, since only cases with some substantial legal interest are published in the law reports. Appropriately, it was a case in which the justice system had failed to protect the accused, who was convicted not only of an armed robbery, committed on 30 March 1947 (to which he pleaded guilty), but also under s. 122 of the Criminal Code: "that at the City of Toronto, on or about the 30th of March, 1947, he had upon his person a pistol, revolver or firearm capable of being concealed upon the person while committing a criminal offence." The judge thought that it was proper to convict him of both charges, and it was Arthur's position that the possession of the gun was part of the first offence, and could not be used to punish the accused twice. In the forties, the judiciary handed out sharp sentences, and in this case it was truly a double punishment, since the man was sentenced to two years on each charge, and the sentences were not to run concurrently, which is usually the case now, but consecutively.

Arthur argued that it was a case of *res judicata* since the first charge encompassed the second. He won the appeal, but not quite on the specific ground he argued. Mr. Justice W.D. Roach put the matter succinctly: "In my opinion, it is clear that the appellant has a complete defence to the second charge but it is not the defence of *res judicata*. It is simply this, that the facts do not come within the offence created by s. 122 ... If a thief should use a revolver in order to commit the theft, he should be guilty of armed robbery and there would be no need for s. 122 because he could be adequately punished for that offence, an essential element of which is the possession of the weapon." (pp. 859–64)

His second reported case was in the same year. Again it was as a court-appointed counsel, and this time he had Paul Hess, the student who had done so well at St. Mike's while he was doing so poorly, with him. They argued against a murder conviction on the ground that the body of the supposed victim had not been found. It was an attempt to use the old *corpus delicti* defence, but the Court found that the rule was not as invulnerable as most laymen think, and that there was sufficient evidence, aside from the missing corpse, to convict. He had a further reported case in early 1948; again he had been appointed by the Court.

At the same time, Charlie Dubin starts appearing in cases, and he, too, was dealing with appeals referred to him by the Court; but through the late forties the difference in their careers reveals itself as Maloney's reported cases are, in the main, on criminal matters, while Dubin begins to show up arguing not only criminal, but civil matters. Maloney, by this time, was getting some agency work, and this was to become a strong element in his appeal practice. In the *Ontario Reports* of 1948, he argued for a new trial in *R. v. Pawlyna* for Donohue and Maher of Sarnia, and won with his argument that a judge erred in presuming that a child witness should be allowed to give evidence unsworn, without taking the time to question the child as to its understanding of the oath. One of his few civil cases of note came down from the Valley, and on this occasion, he appeared with his brother James on a timber lease matter. They failed to convince the Court that their client was in the right.

When Bert J. MacKinnon was named to the Court of Appeal, the *Toronto Star* recalled his first triumph, in an article of 21 December 1974: "Fresh out of law school in the late forties, MacKinnon won a case against the formidable Arthur Maloney which led to a Supreme Court of Canada decision strengthening the rights of the natural mother in cases where illegitimate children are given up for adoption. 'Maloney got all the publicity but I got the baby,' MacKinnon reflected yesterday." This is a case that Maloney used later in his political pamphlets as an example of his social concerns. It became an addition to the law of child adoption, and was referred to as "The Baby Duffell case." An unwed mother gave her consent for the adoption of her child, but later changed her mind before the official adoption order was made. Arthur represented the adopting parents. It went, finally, to the Privy Council, and Maloney did not, in fact, quite win the case, since it was ruled that the natural mother had not lost her right to change her mind before the official adoption order was made. On the other hand, she could not simply change her mind and take the child back. The Court ruled that ultimately the "paramount question, and the consideration upon which all such matters must be decided, is the welfare of the child." (1950, *Supreme Court Reports*, 737) The question of who was to have the child was sent back to the county Surrogate Court, where the natural mother won custody. Whatever the outcome, both Maloney and MacKinnon looked upon the case as something of a victory, and in an odd ways of the law, both of them were correct. MacKinnon got the child, and Maloney had managed to get the waiting period for the final order for adoption down from two years to one, giving some protection to all future adopting parents from the arbitrary loss of a child to a natural parent with second thoughts, come to unconscionably late.

An examination of the newspapers of the forties, shows nothing of his career until late in the decade. One of the first appearances in print has nothing to do with the law, but with his developing relationship with Lillian LaBine. The *Star*, on 1 February 1947, reported the guest list at a dinner honouring Gilbert LaBine at the Royal York Hotel, and included, in this order, "Lillian LaBine, Arthur Maloney ..." But as Lillian has said, commenting on that entry, "You must remember that until Suchan and Jackson, Arthur didn't do that much criminal law. He was trying to be a general counsel." Whatever he was trying, the inexorable push of his own skills was obviously leading him into criminal work, and despite Lillian's suggestion to the contrary, it is as a criminal counsel that he is best remembered even in his earliest days at the Bar. It was not, of course, easy to get important cases that might make the newspapers, and there are times when nothing seems to go well, particularly in trial work. There were even times when Arthur, noted for his confidence, doubted himself. In 1947, having lost an important case at appeal, he was met by George Walsh, a senior practitioner, who had, by chance, listened to his argument, and praised him for such a good try. Arthur remembers that he said, "'Well, I don't deserve to be congratulated. I lost the case.' George replied, 'Nonsense, young man, I built the roof of my house losing cases.' So that gave me great consolation for the future." If he wasn't getting the best cases, he certainly was establishing himself as one of the better counsel, and during the forties, he took his place as one of the trusted, younger members of the Bar who were asked to help out in the Osgoode Law School, which must have given him some wry satisfaction. He worked in the Osgoode Practice group in the 1946–47 year, and marked papers in criminal law in 1948.

Criminal lawyers are not quite like the rest of the Bar. B. Clive Bynoe, a student with Arthur in the mid-fifties, is fiercely proud of being a criminal counsel, in part because it can be argued that the practice is more difficult in some ways at trial than civil work, and the consequences for many clients are infinitely more serious, since they involve a loss of liberty (and until the mid-seventies a possible loss of life for murderers). Civil counsel, of course, will argue, often with cool disdain, that their cases are often much more complicated, and require extremely fine reasoning in the details of the law, and in the organization of the materials thereof, while most criminal cases rest on the simple consideration of the facts. It should be remembered, however, that the same kind of legal skill is often practised by criminal lawyers in those cases of alleged criminal conduct that come out of the business community, in which the piling up of boxes of evidence is equally as formidable as that accumulated in civil cases.

Criminal counsel often act, in a sense, without a net, or, it might be suggested without all their equipment, in many cases. Their clients are usually accused of socially offensive conduct that rarely elicits sympathy from a judge or a jury, and they are rarely arrested without being somewhere in the vicinity, in fact or otherwise, of a criminal act. Most criminal acts are morally unambiguous and are accepted by laymen as reprehensible – some more so than others. The clients are often the unashamed possessors of criminal records, which makes it dangerous to put them on the stand since the records can be revealed, and usually are, by the Crown. The rationale behind that right to reveal past, punished conduct is simple – indeed, it might be argued that it is simplistic, since it is argued that a person with a criminal record is likely to lie even under oath. Yet many kinds of criminal conduct have no connection at all with a weakness for telling fibs, big or little. A man who has a record as a thief does not necessarily have a weakness for lying. A fraud artist is a liar, but a stick-up man is hardly trying to deceive anybody. Nevertheless, if an accused with a criminal record is put on the witness stand, the Crown has a right to ask about that record. It is true that a trial judge has the power to exclude evidence of the accused's prior record if it seems to him that it would be likely to prejudice the accused unduly, but that discretion is rarely exercised, and it is pedantic hairsplitting to suggest that it is really a serious possibility. Maloney often complained about the liability of a criminal record keeping his accused off the stand. Whatever presumption might exist in the cloud-cuckoo land of legal ideality which argues that the revelation of a previous conviction to a jury will only be thought on as to whether the accused is telling the truth, most lawyers are of the opinion that juries, whatever the judge may tell them to the contrary, are influenced adversely by being told that the accused has a criminal record.

Monte Harris, one of Maloney's young followers of the early sixties, was confronted with an unusual example of its use when he took an injury case against the Toronto Transit Commission (TTC). Under cross-examination his client was asked if he had a criminal record – he, in fact, did. Harris was astonished to see the question raised in a civil case, and as soon as he could, he phoned Arthur, who advised him that it was certainly unusual and a bit mean-spirited of the defence, but not prohibited. He gave Harris a bit of advice. In his address to the jury, Harris brought up the matter of his client's record, and then launched into an appropriate version of the Shylock's speech in Act III, Scene I of *The Merchant of Venice*: "If you prick us, do we not bleed?" Admitting his client's criminal past, he put it to the jury that despite that liability, he still felt pain as other men did, still bled as they did, and his injury on a TTC streetcar was as damaging to him as it would have been to anyone on the jury. Harris won the case, although he had to fight it through the appeal process since the TTC felt the judgment was too high. It was, however, one of those rare times in which Arthur's knowledge of Shakespeare shows up in his legal thinking.

Criminal counsel fear such revelation so much that an accused is often kept off the witness stand, and a criminal counsel is left with only two weapons – his ability to cross-examine and his final address to the judge and jury or to the judge alone. He may retain the right to address the jury after the prosecutor has summed up his case, but this privilege is lost if he brings in a defence. The criminal counsel always loses more cases than are won. J.J. Robinette saved Evelyn Dick on one serious charge, but she went to jail on another. He lost Steve Suchan, and all of Harold Ballard's money could not keep him out of jail. Arthur certainly lost considerably more cases than he ever won.

By the time Frank Dunlap joined him as his articled student in 1948, Arthur was well established, if not yet in the first rank of the criminal counsel in the city. Frank came to town with a wife and a child; he had no place to live, so Arthur, who was sharing an apartment with another man, moved out to give Frank a place to settle his small family. Frank found little change in Arthur; he still was playfully genial, and despite the fact that he was on the point of marrying, he was still hopeless about money. Lillian LaBine knew he was undependable, if good-heartedly so, when it came to finances: "Money wasn't important to him. He liked to spend it; he liked the good life, but money itself wasn't important. If I looked in my purse after we were married, and I asked him for some change, he would give me whatever was in his pocket." From the beginning of his business life, keeping track of fees was a mystery to him. Frank Dunlap saw it as his one weakness as a lawyer. "Arthur never made big money. Jake and I made five times what he did most years. He wasn't a businessman; he wanted to live well, but he didn't really understand the commercial aspect of running a law practice." It was a common problem until, at least, the seventies. As late as 1957, in his first year as a Member of Parliament, when he was well established as a leading counsel, his taxable income was only $7000 and he was still carrying a small overdraft in his office account in the early sixties. Part of this was sheer indifference to collecting fees, and part of it was caused by the fact that he would take clients who had no capacity to pay. But he was happy with his career, and was accumulating a reputation that went beyond the practice into the public domain.

In 1947 he was appointed to the Ontario Board of Parole. More to the point, he resigned from the same three months later. He had quickly become dissatisfied with the Board's refusal to change some of its methods and rules. In defence, the Board suggested that Arthur was a bit too full of himself, something of a young whipper-snapper telling his elders what to do. The Department of Reform Institutions was put on the defensive because Arthur had quickly learned that the press could be useful, and he released his 5 May resignation letter to the papers. Even at this stage of his career, barely five years out of Osgoode, he was prepared to take on the established order, and demand that they think creatively about criminals. He fell out with the Board over the way in which first offenders were automatically granted parole in most cases, while prisoners with records or previously paroled recidivists had a harder time getting out at all. One would have thought that this practice made sense, but to Arthur it was unfair. It is an early example of his peculiar refusal to presume that past conduct is the best proof of how a person may act in the future. He was always optimistic about criminals, always determined to give them another chance. It wasn't a question of sentimental idealism. Arthur was fully aware of the fact that many of his clients were rogues with very little social conscience. That did not, however, mean that they shouldn't be allowed to try again. In his opinion the automatic response of the Board to convicts as less dependable than first offenders was being made too much of by the Board.

Arthur also claimed that the Board lacked credibility with the prison population, who, in the main, despised the organization. Instead of considering why such might be the case, the Board spokesman admitted that he was right, significantly confusing the function of the Board with that of the courts: "To the claim that a substantial number of the prisoners hold the board in disrepute, this official remarked that it would be unusual for a prisoner to have any affection for the judge or magistrate who sentenced him."[18] Which, in part, seemed to prove Arthur's point that the Board was not acting out of a desire to help the prisoners get started on a new life, but saw their function as part of the system of punishment.

The final defence of the Board was, perhaps, to be expected. One of the Department officials pointed out the comparative youth of Mr. Maloney, "as compared to the other members of the five-man board, and the fact that he was appointed only three months ago. These other men have experience and mature judgment in the matters that come before them, and apparently Mr. Maloney is 'peeved' because he was unable to dominate them with his opinions, said this official." The headline in the *Star* – "'Peeve' Blamed for Maloney Resignation" – might well have been used years later when the Ombudsman job fell apart. It was certainly a precursor of things to come, and might well have been thought on when the Ombudsman office was being considered for Arthur. Who was right or wrong is perhaps less important than the nature of the argument. Arthur wanted to change things, and was not content to play the junior for the older men, one a cleric, one a judge with juvenile court experience, and one a high-ranking Salvation Army officer. Nor did he think it was necessarily a fair procedure to presume that certain prisoners should be dealt with in a way that prejudiced their chances – he wanted each prisoner to be treated as an individual. He also wanted the Board to see itself as separate and apart from the judicial system – a source of remedy, not punishment. So there he was, the odd man out, simply because he would not respect his elders – but when was Arthur ever respectful if he felt something was unfair.

By this time, Arthur had become part of a new firm, Edmonds, Maloney, and Edmonds, with offices in the Toronto Star building. The two Edmonds, father and son (both named George), were commercial attorneys, and Arthur's association with them was always to be somewhat strained, since the older Edmonds, a serious, hard-working, commercial solicitor, nervously watched the mercurial antics of this promising young lawyer who was getting too much into the public eye with his criminal practice. The headline of the *Star* of 24 April 1947 was the kind of publicity that Mr. Edmonds did not like to have associated with his firm: "Sentenced to Hang May 8/Hamilton Execution Stayed." The accompanying story related the problems that two young lawyers, Frank D. Nasso and Arthur Maloney, had in appealing a murder case. Their first obstacle lay in the fact that the Notice of Appeal had not been filed on time, and it was necessary to obtain a special order from the Minister of Justice in Ottawa to overcome the error – it was the first time such an order had been obtained in Ontario. On 12 May 1947, the *Star* reported on the case again, this time on page two, and the hierarchy was established: "Arthur Maloney, appellant's counsel, assisted by Frank Nasso ..." It had some of the common elements of a typical Maloney case, with a defendant who was a mental defective. Arthur argued that he was incapable of forming the intent to kill, and that the trial judge should have put the question of his ability to do so to the jury. On 29 May, the case was back on the *Star* front page: "Hamilton Man Won't Hang/Gets Jail For Life." The Cabinet had commuted the death penalty, so the story went, as a result of the jury's recommendation for mercy, as well as that of the Court of Appeal. Arthur and Nasso didn't get quite what they wanted, but they saved the man's life. However, they weren't quite celebrities yet. They were not important enough to be mentioned in this final story. Frankie Nasso was one of the natural survivors of the criminal law, who was to spend most of his career in the lower courts; he was never to reach the reputation that seemingly came so easily to Arthur Maloney. Nasso worked a full day nevertheless between the magistrate and country court criminal list. He and Arthur, the latter on his way to the heights of the profession, and the other plugging away among the small fees and the promises of payment never seen, were good friends.

By the late forties Arthur had become something of a young man of promise in the Roman Catholic society of the town. He was still very thin, standing six feet tall, weighing less than 130 pounds, with dark brown hair that tended to curl in humid weather. He still had that sharp-featured, foxy Bonfield look about him that he was only to lose after his marriage to Lillian LaBine, the daughter of Gilbert LaBine, the Canadian mining genius. Lillian had, by chance, some training from childhood that was to help her in living with Arthur, who was often away from home because of trials in county towns, and rarely got home when he was in Toronto until late in the evening. When she was a child, her father, a self-educated prospector and mining engineer, used to spend several months each year in the Canadian north, alone with his pack of provisions, pushing his way through the wilderness in search of ore of any kind. "I didn't really know my father until I was about ten. He was away so much. He was like Santa Claus when he came home; he used to bring us lovely white, soft leather moccasins, all hand-done by the Indians, decorated with fine, beaded embroidery." But even a generous father could sometimes get things wrong:

> Once he brought me a muskrat coat with a little round collar; just a plain, little girl's coat. And the first Sunday was a cold, winter Sunday. Mother said, "Wear your fur coat; it's cold." I can still remember hiding behind the door. There was no way I was going to wear a fur coat! Nobody else I knew of my age had a fur

coat! So I didn't go to church and I would not wear that fur coat. Poor Dad! It was the very best skins. I can still remember it – the little brown collar. Just a plain little coat. I don't know what they did with it, but Lillian didn't wear it. [Laughs][19]

It was not simply in his frequent absences that Arthur resembled his father-in-law. Gilbert LaBine, like Arthur, was a man of adamantine determination, professional prowess, and, eventually, outstanding success. They were both natives of the Valley. LaBine was born and brought up on the family farm at Westmeath, near Pembroke. Born in 1890, he dreamed from early childhood of being a prospector. At the age of fifteen, he left home and went to Cobalt, Ontario, where several rich strikes had been recently made. He got a job in one of the mines as a boiler fireman, but within months he had made his first silver find, which he sold for $5000. At seventeen, he was lucky once more, establishing his reputation as a boy wonder with a "natural nose" for hidden ores. But finding ore was one thing; making the best of the find was another. He turned down $25,000 for the claim, only to discover that it was too low in grade to merit extraction. He knew, then, that luck and instinct weren't enough – that he needed to know more if he was to survive in a business that was a mix of hard work, luck, instinct, guile, and special knowledge. From that time forward, he read everything on mining that he could find, took courses at the Ontario School of Mines in Haileybury, attended any lecture that might help, and continually went over the maps of northern Canada, looking for clues to the riches he instinctively knew were there to be found. When he was home, resting after months in the bush, he was still at it, honing his skills for the needle-in-the-haystack world of prospecting. "He started as a simple prospector, but he never stopped learning. He'd take every chance he could get to learn something; he used to go to the Archives in Ottawa to search for information on the north, and I can still remember my father to this day – reading, reading, reading, and he ended up, a boy who had never gone to university, on the Board of the University of Toronto!" Lillian Maloney was, in fact, to be associated with two important men, and she is very proud of both of them.

No-one could have guessed that Gilbert LaBine was to be so important in the first decade of the century, although he, working with his brother Charles, managed to survive, and gradually accumulate not only reputation, but some financial substance. By the late twenties, the brothers, with some associates, had founded the Eldorado Gold Mines, and Gilbert LaBine started to look closely at the Great Bear Lake, despite the fact that it was quite impossible to reach the area overland. But it was there that LaBine's great find was to be made, putting the years of gold and silver finds far behind in importance. What LaBine knew was something everyone who was scuffling about in prospecting knew: what pitchblende ore looked like, though no-one had been lucky enough to see enough to make anything out of it. Pitchblende – which meant "radium" – was selling in 1929 for $75,000 a gram, and no-one quite knew where to look for it, save for the Belgians, who had found it in their Congo colony, and were charging whatever they wanted for it.

There had been hints of its existence in Canada as early as the middle of the nineteenth century, with vague sightings around Lake Superior, and in Quebec. There was a small, uneconomic find in eastern Ontario. In 1914, Ontario and British Columbia offered substantial cash awards for any discoveries, but none were made.

Gilbert LaBine had made a serious study of pitchblende, but he was not in fact looking specifically for it in 1929; he had been sent north on a general search, and he staked four claims that looked as if they might yield some copper, bismuth, and cobalt. LaBine had a theory that there might be a line of ore sweeping as far north as the Arctic Ocean, and stories from Indian trappers, who described cliff formations around Great Bear Lake, suggested the possibility of mineral outcroppings. The only way in was by aircraft, and he convinced his partners that the expense of such a trip, if only by one man, was worth the money. He found the outcrops, and signs of several minerals, but nothing of quantity. When "Punch" Dickens, one of the veteran bush pilots, came to pick him up, weeks later, LaBine was still unsatisfied with what he had found, and the eastern shore of the lake, which he had no hope of reaching by land, tantalized him. He asked his pilot to fly past the area, and there it was – a rocky outcrop displaying the combination of colours which LaBine had read about hundreds of times, but had never seen before: green, yellow, orange, and black! If that outcrop was as LaBine suspected, his company and all of the partners were on their way to personal fortunes, and fame.

The next spring, he was back; this time with another prospector, Charles St. Paul, and they confirmed the find. There it was, about 1400 miles northwest of Winnipeg, and 1000 miles northeast of Edmonton, and not a road in sight, but it was so valuable that there was no question that it had to be developed! With the discovery, the price dropped by $50,000 a gram – which meant that the Canadian find was still worth $25,000 a gram. That was the making of the LaBine family fortune. It completely changed their lives. They moved, with ease, into the social world of North Toronto, and became particularly active in Roman Catholic social circles. Lillian went to St. Anne de Bellevue College in Montreal, but did not go on to university. She took her place in the busy social life of the family. "I was the eldest of the family. I worked during the later war years, for a while, with the Red Cross, and then I did some other social work. But most of my time was taken up with the family. My parents often travelled, and when they went away, I was expected to take care of the family, and I could never do anything in the way of work permanently. Mother's mother lived with us, and she was quite old. We had help in the house, but I had a younger sister in her teens. Arthur was very good about it. Even after we were married, we would move back into my parent's house in the winter while they were down south."[20]

Lillian was happily in the full swing of her own social life in 1947, when she first met Arthur:

I remember my best friend, Dorothy Byrne, talking about this Arthur Maloney, whom she had met with a group she was out with, and how he was something important at Newman Club. Some months later, a friend of Arthur's, Donny MacDonald, who was also a lawyer, had a group get together for a dinner party at the Royal York for a friend who was getting married. So I came with a male friend of mine, home on leave from the Services. Arthur was sitting across from me at the table, and we chatted normally. Next day, Dorothy asked me what I thought of him, and I said, "I guess he seemed all right." I hadn't known him when he was at law school; he was already a lawyer when I met him. We didn't have much in common. I loved sports, and had been a champion fencer and broad jumper at school. I was very sports-minded. I played badminton, basketball, and all sorts of games, and Arthur had no interest in any of them. He liked to swim, but just a little swim would do him, and that's all the physical activity he was likely to do. Dad had a box at Maple Leaf Gardens for the Leafs' games, and we would go there, but Arthur was never a real fan.[21]

Nevertheless, Arthur had found something in Lillian that interested him, and a few weeks after the Royal York meeting, he called and invited her to a concert at Massey Hall.

He wanted to hear Beethoven's *Fifth*. At first, I didn't see that much of him. I dated other people for a while. Especially if anyone was a good dancer.Arthur wasn't and he didn't much like dancing, but he would push me around the floor for a dance, as he did all our lives together, and then he thought he had done his duty. Being the eldest daughter, I was brought up to do what my parents expected of me, and when Arthur would phone for a date, particularly early on, I would ask my parents if I could go. About a year before we got married, it got serious. I had liked him, you know, from the beginning. Arthur was really fun to be with and I was in my mid-twenties, so I had no doubts about him. But I was close to my parents. When it looked as if it was going to come to something, I told Mom, "You know, Arthur is going to come up and ask Dad one of these days ..." I think this was about a month before he did just that. I don't know whether my younger sister, Trish, heard Mother telling Dad, but the three last times Arthur came to the house, before he got nerve enough to do it, she was apparently hiding behind the door. She was afraid that I was going to be an old maid!!

The LaBine family had planned to spend August 1948 at Jasper, with the wedding to take place in late September, but Arthur's trial schedule made it necessary to bring the marriage forward, cancelling the family vacation. "My sister," laughs Lillian, "to this day remembers my wedding year. She always says, 'We missed that nice month at Jasper because of you!'" They were married at the Blessed Sacrament on Yonge Street. They flew to New York for the shows, and then on to Montreal, where they picked up the new Pontiac that the LaBines had given them as a wedding present. In Montreal, Arthur's professional enthusiasms broke out, somewhat lugubriously. "I'll never forget one day when we were still in Montreal, Arthur got up early. He knew somebody there, of course, and he went to see an autopsy, and he came back – I was still in bed, and he wanted to tell me all about it! I remember saying, 'Arthur, how can we go down now and have breakfast!'"

In the early post-war years, housing in Toronto was scarce, and the Maloneys wanted something that they could afford, but in North Toronto, one of the most expensive parts of the city. They lived with the LaBines while they looked around, and then took a small apartment. Finally they found a small bungalow at the corner of Lawrence and Otter Crescent. Gilbert LaBine paid for it, but he put a small mortgage on it, "just to make sure that things were going to work out," as Lillian delicately puts it. "It had the nicest kitchen I ever had. It was built by a man for his mistress, but she never lived in it. It was brand new, and we had six years there."

The physical change in Arthur to respectable girth and full-faced Irish handsomeness started two years after the marriage, when he decided to quit smoking. He tried over and over to stop through the years, and each time he gained weight. On his first serious attempt he put on thirty pounds, but he hardly gave himself much chance to do otherwise. "He decided to quit. I can remember him coming home with a great big box of Laura Secords. I thought he was bringing them home for me, because he knew the ones I liked. I didn't have one! He ate the whole box! 'I hand-picked every single one of them,' he said, with a big grin, and he got a big kick out of eating them."

Lillian wanted to learn to play bridge, but Arthur would not cooperate, claiming that he had quite enough hard thinking in his profession without bringing it into his pleasures. They liked the same kind of classical music, and regularly attended Massey Hall; their taste was unexceptionable, and they were unimpressed by the more adventurous twentieth-century composers. "I can remember walking out of Massey Hall one night; Arthur was so upset by some modern work! We always loved dining at the Royal York with family or friends." Arthur, of course, knew the maître d' there, and was treated as a special customer. He was, for all his zest for travelling and enthusiasm for good restaurants, a simple meat-and-potatoes man at home. "He always praised me for whatever I put before him, but he was usually quite satisfied with roast beef or lamb. When we were first married, he didn't like fish, or pasta, and he never became a wine buff, although he liked a good bottle of wine with dinner."

They were serious Catholics, and expected to have a family. They tried and failed. "We had two children but they didn't live. I was just beginning the sixth month of pregnancy with the first, and that little boy was born dead. The next one, a couple of years later, I held a little over six months, but she died after three days. Today, I'm sure that child would have lived." It seemed that Lillian could not have children, and she tentatively suggested to Arthur that they should think of adopting. He was very shy about the idea. "I had mentioned it to him once, and he said, 'You know, Lillian, if one of your sisters died or one of mine and we took their child to bring up, we would know the background, and that would be different.' I just mentioned it, and let it drop." One day in the mid-fifties, they were, by chance, faced with a choice. Lillian was offered a child yet to be born to an unwed mother – at a time when it was common practice for girls in respectable families (as the moral and social standards of the time went), for the sake of their reputations and those of their parents, to give away such children. The family histories were known, and the baby would, in all likelihood, be both healthy and intelligent. Lillian phoned Arthur at the office; Arthur, who was obviously with a client, given his guarded answers, seemed unenthusiastic. He was prepared, however, to talk about it, and suggested that the person offering the child should phone him at home that evening after dinner. "So finally he got home, and the doctor called and talked to Arthur, and Arthur got off the phone, and said, 'We're having a baby in May.'"[22] In May 1956, their daughter Martha was born.

They were delighted with the child and made it known that they would be interested in another if the chance arose again. A year-and-a-half later, the same doctor came up with another young unwed mother willing to allow her child to be adopted, and it too had a background which suggested a healthy, bright child. Matthew joined the family. "Here was Arthur," says Lillian, "who didn't know whether he wanted to adopt a child. I don't know how you could love anybody more than he loved his children!" By the time of Matthew's arrival in March 1958, the family had moved to a larger house on Cortleigh Blvd., still in the north end of the city. It was to be the family home until 1981, when, in the last years of Arthur's illness, he and Lillian, with their university-educated children off in the world in interesting careers, moved into their handsome condominium at the Oaklands, on Avenue Road, just south of St. Clair. Years before that, however, they had purchased an old stone farm house on the Guelph line, which Arthur felt was necessary for the children as they came into their early teen years, and it was here, at "Malafield" (Roy McMurtry's oil painting of the house was used on one of the Maloney family Christmas cards), near Campbellville, Ontario, that the family spent most of the summer months, and where Lillian lives now. It was her hope that one of their children might, eventually, take over the house, but that seems unlikely. Matthew works in Colorado, and Martha, originally interested in the theatre, has gone into language studies, and lives in Quebec City.

Lillian Maloney is a tall, slim, lively woman, something of an old-fashioned chain-smoker. She is enormously loyal to the memory of Arthur, and talks freely of his problems in politics, and particularly of his frustrations at the Ombudsman's office, which were constant topics of conversation at the dinner table – when he managed to get there. She was hardly supine in their relationship, and could lose her temper with him when he made too much of a nuisance of himself with his gregarious absenteeism. Students, who were often ordered to phone to inform her that he would be late for dinner, could be treated to a curt dismissal, and a slammed-down telephone receiver. It has been said that Arthur's occasional habit of inviting cab drivers in for a drink was prompted as much by the chance to avert Lillian's wrath as by natural kindness. His favourite name for her among his colleagues was "Diamond Lil," which was delivered with a mixture of affection and implied wariness. Although he discussed his political problems with her, he kept his law practice very much to himself, and surprisingly, she never saw him in court; they discussed it on occasion, but he felt that he might be inhibited by her presence, and he made it clear that he did not want her to see him in the full flight of his highest skill. Of course, she saw him dozens of times at public meetings, charming the public, but now, in her early old age, she speaks wistfully of never having heard him address a jury. As a result, she seems somewhat mystified by the deep enthusiasm for his memory that is still held by so many of his colleagues, since that part of his life is the least familiar to her.

4

Serious Business: Suchan and Jackson

Arthur Maloney became an attentive father and a good family man, but he never lost his love for drinking with his pals, who were often, in and out of their cups, as colourful (and sometimes more so) as Arthur himself. He possessed a cheerful, sometimes mischievous inclination to hang around with the boys, long after most of them were past the first blush of youth. The hard business of criminal law often leads to raucous behaviour on the part of its practitioners; it certainly did with the group of young lawyers with whom Arthur was associating on his call to the Bar, many of whom he had known at St. Mike's and at Osgoode. It was to develop into an after-hours, extended family that included students, former students, and anyone else with a tenuous connection to the law, as long as they were prepared to pass their free time in drink and accompanying nonsense. There is, partly as a result of the constant losses and very occasional wins in the criminal law, a tendency for counsel to have, often, a whimsical whistling-in-the-dark attitude and an anarchic playfulness that is expressed in long, joshing, raffish foolishness. Not all criminal lawyers are so inclined, but Arthur certainly was. One might suspect that he would not have been so different had he wound up doing real estate, but his chosen specialty nurtured it, given its tensions, its continual defeats and sometimes eccentric victories. Many of his closest friends had the same taste for innocent, alcoholic vulgarity, and he brought his students into that atmosphere of laughing it off as much as possible in the company, regularly, of adversaries – the Crowns, the police, and the occasional judge. One student recalls that Arthur, somehow, usually had the last case on the court list, and at the adjournment, seemingly by chance, the whole Dickensian cast of legal characters would troop down Bay Street from the courts in the old City Hall, at Queen and Bay, to the Metropole Hotel, located on King Street, near the *Toronto Star* building.

Arthur loved to report back to the Metropole after the day in court, and he'd drink there as long as anybody would stay with him. He was always generous in buying for anyone, and often everyone; and he, in a sense, held court. Ralph Cooper was the piano player there, and he always greeted Arthur's entrance with some musical crack. One of his favourite numbers was "Our Mailman Has the Longest Route in Town." We had more fun there! By the early fifties, Arthur was becoming a celebrity; he was on "Fighting Words," an early popular TV show, and everybody knew him. He was really starting to blossom![1]

There was a Direct Winters Transport depot nearby, as well as the newspapers, so the customers at the Metropole were a motley crew. Sid Strauss, the owner, and Eddie Adananc, the manager, were adept at handling the crowds of sometimes volatile drinkers. Doug Crane, who was a student with Arthur in the early sixties, and has gone on to a substantial career in Toronto, enjoyed the way in which the groups got along: "It was a mixed bag of working men, printers, lawyers, brokers. There were a lot of Direct Winters drivers, and Arthur mixed with everyone. He had an act of arm wrestling with me to prove to the drivers how tough he was!"[2] Added to the group were the newspaper reporters, many of whom were following Arthur's exploits in the courts. In the forties, there were three papers that were to dominate communications until the middle fifties. As Bob Johnstone, now with the CBC, remembers it, "The *Globe* was on the corner and the *Star* was down the street, and the *Tely* a block south of that, and they were all in the Metropole, often drinking with Arthur."[3] Frank Dunlap saw Arthur in his still-youthful glory at the Metropole, admired, talented, full of life, and often silly with the joy of being with his friends: "He had a personality alien to the Valley. He was a naturally sophisticated, city boy. I always envied the fact that he didn't seem to care about the consequences of our wild drinking. And he didn't give a shit if he had a dime. Money meant nothing; something would come up." All of his associates of the forties and fifties and sixties have vivid, happy memories of romping about in the Metropole (and various other bars), with the piano player, Ralph Cooper, quite often as drunk as the patrons, responding to jibes from the audience, and answering in insultingly cheerful song. Sometimes the Maloney gang would take a room on the second floor, on the King Street side of the hotel, and there they would loll away the evening in private, if a constant coming-and-going of intimates could be called such. The room was called "the snug," as small drinking rooms are sometimes called in English pubs, and here Arthur would proclaim his relief in getting away "from the riff-raff," which was hardly accurate since it was an odd group of roisterers who accompanied him to that higher place. He was always careful about not driving while drinking, and he had a favourite cab driver called Switzi on whom he depended. If Switzi was not available when Arthur's student phoned, Arthur was content to wait until he was free. Switzi, in turn, was prepared to wait until Arthur made his goodbyes, which could take some time. It was at the Metropole and in the courts that Arthur developed his good relations with the press. "I watched him court the press," says Frank Dunlap,"but he was the real thing; he always delivered. He was little short of brilliant, even if he had been drinking late the night before. He knew where the real issue was in a case, and no judge could challenge him, and if they did, he was almost lethal in the way in which he would destroy their arguments."[4] Arthur took good care of Frank, and Frank has never forgotten it, but Frank could do something for Arthur, since he, too, had important connections: "I introduced him to the football crowd; he loved that. He loved to be where the spotlight was."

All his friends remember that he had a playful, mock pomposity in his informal moments that was expressed in a plummy, W.C. Fields-like voice – a teasing, ironic celebration of his eminence among friends. He was enormously skilled, possessed considerable political aura, and had proven, from early in his career, to be possessed by an instinctive interest in people, particularly people in trouble, often to his financial detriment. He was sometimes vain, and did puff himself up when he saw a crowd, but he was aware of the weakness, and the young men with whom he surrounded himself were allowed considerable leeway in puncturing any extremes of personal preening. He was not a difficult man. One student remembers joining his office with some apprehension about how to act in his presence, but the problem never came up, since Maloney treated him as if he had always been there; there was no need for formality. Associates such as Bynoe and Humphrey took no hints of pomposity without immediate derision.

The immediate social surround of his law practice was a private world of horseplay, often relieved by high wit and sophisticated legal allusion – but it was never very respectful. Nor did he expect it to be. He expected hard work, long hours, skill, dependability, and sometimes obedience, but in the social group, he was one of the gang. Clive Bynoe, shortly after he joined him as his student, was taken to one of the drinking parties in a hotel suite, where, in the presence of less humble associates, he continued to call him, "Mr. Maloney." Arthur suddenly stopped the alcoholic hubbub to instruct Bynoe, "Don't call me Mr. Maloney. You can call me Arthur, or Art, or Fuck Face, but not Mr. Maloney." Bynoe, who was a quick study, and of sternly raucous Toronto-East-End lineage, immediately leapt from deference to intimacy with the scatological energy that is part of his character, "Okay, Fuck Face, pass the scotch!"

There is no point in being delicate about Arthur's "little" language. He did swear, as did many of his associates, but it would be calvinistic pusillanimity to think it had much to do with his character. There was a pervading air of benign vulgarity about their meetings. As the English journalist, Peregrine Worsthorne said in defence of London's Garrick Club, in the *Sunday Telegraph* of 12 July 1992, when it resisted the attempt to bring women into its membership, men sometimes want to be left alone with their own sex, given "the enormous pleasure men – or, at any rate Englishmen – get from teasing each other, to the point where the borderline between irony and sarcasm is often crossed."

J.J. Robinette and G. Arthur Martin might command unquestioned respect, although Martin, especially in his earlier years, had a slightly theatrical air about him, a modest swish in his tailoring, and he could relax in good-natured raillery. But Maloney's world was a wilder mix, including would-be hangers-on (who were often despised by the inner circle who actually worked with him). Something needs to be said about these outsiders, who will know who they are. It was one thing for Arthur to take care of his own students, whom he had hand-picked, and who more often than not possessed considerable intelligence, and confidence. They were, in retrospect, a handsome lot of young men, lively, gregarious, and suitable companions for a leading counsel. What was peculiar to him, however, was his kindness to young members of the Bar of less promise. He was often very open to the importunities of lawyers who showed little natural skill, and he would spend hours helping these men, if they had enough nerve to search him out, teaching them how to prepare cases, correcting their briefs, and sometimes their diction in an odd, fatherly, abusive manner that sometimes frightened them with its intensity, but ultimately aided them in overcoming their obvious shyness and mediocrity. They are sometimes forgotten, but they remember him with great affection, as well they might, since they did not, for a moment, possess the high promise that most of his students revealed immediately, and they were not naturally part of his tough, yea-saying group of revellers.

In his later years, after the Ombudsman office with its crowd of satellite retainers, he liked to travel with two students. But even Jonathan Swift, when he became the Dean of St. Patrick's Cathedral in Dublin, used to travel with two outriders as a mark of his importance – and he was a cleric. In the law, it is common for senior counsel to be supported by juniors. When Arthur became ill, it was a matter of physical necessity for him to be accompanied wherever he went. Partly, however, it was the harmless vanity of the old counsel – like an old actor – living on his reputation – innocently remembering the old Metropole days. Doug Crane, who kept in contact with Arthur until the end, suspected that Arthur, even at his portentous worst, realized his own vanities: "There were some young lawyers who liked to hang around with him, almost like little sycophants, and Arthur would like to have them fawning about him. That would have been, maybe, one of his weaknesses. I'm sure he saw through them, but he seemed to like it, particularly in his later years, but that was the later Arthur, not the Arthur of the sixties, when he would travel to the Supreme Court of Canada with only one junior or a student."

In the fifties and sixties, it was all just good-natured nonsense. Frankie Nasso threw a pre-nuptial party for Arthur, and Frank Dunlap managed to get into a quarrel with a young lawyer. "Next morning, I told Arthur that I wasn't too impressed by his friends." Arthur turned to his student in seeming astonishment, and in mock dignity, roared, "Well, Mr. Dunlap, we'll see what lustre you add to the profession!!" Dunlap had, for a moment, been serious, but Arthur would simply not be so, and it taught Dunlap a lesson in not taking himself or his own opinions or, for that matter, anything about their social world to heart. Arthur was a great deflater of egos, while often strutting his own in a mutually undermining gesture. Tom Edmondstone thought of him as more of a Bonfield than a Maloney in his demeanour. "The Maloneys were down to earth; Arthur was a bit more dignified, a bit of a Bonfield." But even Edmondstone could not resist Arthur's playful, swaggering hot air; there was the time in a hotel room, for instance, when Arthur, on the phone to the bar, in his plummiest voice, ordered "Twenty-four cold beers on a silver salver."

When Clive Bynoe came into the Maloney office in the mid-fifties, the party was still going on.

If he'd been in court in the morning, and had a good battle, he found it very difficult to go back and sit in the office. And I'd say that is very common among trial lawyers. It's a release. After you've fought your case in the morning, you get hyped-up obviously; then to just walk in and sit down at your desk and have a sandwich or something, – it just doesn't work that way. Some of us used to go to the Town Tavern for lunch, and we all used to have "Steak O'Brians" as I recall. Sammy Berger was running the place at the time, in the late fifties and early sixties, at the time of the Bluestein-Johnny Pappalia thing [a case in which a Mafia enforcer beat a gambler senseless in the lobby of the Town Tavern without, seemingly, anybody seeing him do it. Bynoe defended one of the accused]. We all used to go there. Malcolm Robb, Wally Rose, Harry Rose, Dave Rose ... none of the last three, related. Of course, once Arthur got going, he didn't want to stop; he was having such a great time. And then he'd go to the Metropole, particularly on Saturday. During the elections, we'd walk in and Ralph Cooper would immediately break into song with the lyric, "Don't be a phoney, vote for Maloney."[5]

Doug Crane remembers the Cooper lyric somewhat more fully: "He had a song when we came in that went, 'If you're a queer son, vote for Pearson/Don't be a phoney, vote for Maloney.'" Cooper's price for a song was a vodka and orange juice. Crane remembers that he kept a close eye on the customers, looking for ideas for his musical asides. "If he saw a prostitute working the tables, and a detective came in, he would immediately break into 'Mack the Knife.' Once when I was in there with my wife, he leaned over and said to me, 'Doug, I don't know why you're buying all the drinks; I'm getting all the looks!'"[6] Cooper was to come to an appropriate end. An alcoholic, he sometimes needed to be restrained. Monte Harris tells of the night that they locked him in his room when he was in particularly bad shape. "He defeated them. They wouldn't let him out of his room, so he connected a whole pile of bed sheets, and went out the window. Naturally the bed sheets tore and he dropped to the street and was killed."[7]

Unlike James, who became a victim of drink, and had gone long past social drinking in his last years, Arthur liked to consume in company, telling Roy McMurtry one happy evening, "Brother McMurtry, I do love to get pissed!" It seems to have had no influence on his courtroom skills, though there were harmless occasions when the alcoholic spell would be on him in court. Dave Humphrey tells of the time when he, Arthur, the Crown and a judge were passing time in the judge's chambers, waiting for a verdict. Arthur had brought in a bottle, and they were sharing it "with Arthur taking the largest equal share." There seemed little chance of an acquittal, but the jury fooled them, and the foreman proclaimed the accused not guilty. Arthur, sitting next to Humphrey at the counsel table, was so delightfully surprised, that in his alcoholic ease, he blurted out, supposedly *sotto voce,* but more *voce* than *sotto,* to Humphrey – "It's a miracle!!" Everyone in the court heard his religious response to the verdict. If he was working at the Toronto City Hall courts, and a jury deliberation was likely to be lengthy, he would slip down to the Metropole, and wait for the court bailiffs to phone down for him to return. On more than one occasion, students remember having to ever-so-slightly prop him up to hear a verdict. But, in the main, he was well able to pick the time and place for his serious drinking, and there were times, when he simply stopped drinking for long periods.

Jake Dunlap, Frank's brother, who was an Osgoode student in the late forties and early fifties, was not Arthur's student, but he was taken into the Maloney gang, nevertheless. He needed a place to read, and he knew that Arthur had an office close to Osgoode.

I used to study up there on the eighteenth floor of the *Star* building. I had a key to the office. We used to hang out at the Metropole, and he would let me know when he was going to be there, even when I was in class at Osgoode. Without anyone else knowing, we used to put our names backwards. He was "Ruhtra Yenolam" and I was "E. Kaj Palnud." I'd be sitting in class and a note would be announced, something like, "Mr. Yenolam will meet you for lunch at the Metropolitan Club." Meaning the Metropole. Pat Galligan was the same; he was "Tap Nagillag."[8]

His comparatively rapid ascent to prominence at the criminal bar, alongside Charlie Dubin, completed the group who were seen to be the best criminal counsel in the fifties and sixties. Robinette, when he consented to so act, and G. Arthur Martin were to continue to be the two major figures. Joe Sedgwick with his bow ties and rubato air was on the edge of the old-fashioned oratory, and Arthur was closest in style to him, and like him, had a dramatic swagger, only barely restrained by an air of sly dignity. Arthur Martin traces the changes back to the late thirties, when a plainer, less patronizing style was coming into the bar to satisfy juries less impressed by oratory. Sedgwick's success, and Arthur's developing reputation might suggest that there was still room for panache in the courtroom, and the arrival in the late forties of Dave Humphrey, the American naval veteran, who came to Canada to be educated, and never went home, showed a new way of bringing personality into play. Humphrey, a sleek, twinkling rogue, who never pretended to be anything but a sophisticated rough-neck, spent his spare time hanging about with athletes, and, sometimes, sportsmen of more questionable intent. He made it clear, first as a Crown, and then as a defence counsel that he thought courts ought to be fun, and he teased and winked his way nervelessly into a reputation as a criminal counsel with improvisational zeal, and the charm of a snake-oil salesman; he could tempt juries into decisions that often went against their best instincts, and he was one of the very few counsel confident enough and gifted enough to make jokes as he danced his way through difficult trials. He was to become a perfect foil for Arthur, and they worked in tandem for years, with Arthur playing the man of feeling, with dignity, and Humphrey playing the wise fool. It was often irresistible. The plain style might have been the standard, used with great skill by most of the counsel, but personality still had a place – presuming one had any personality – and Maloney and Humphrey often depended very heavily upon that gift – it cannot be learned; it comes from the gods.

But Arthur Martin knew that Maloney had more than style. He also knew how to use it. "One of the best things about Arthur Maloney was that he retained much of the eloquence of the former times, but was able to adapt it to the changing social conditions. The eloquence remained, but he was able to convey a sense of a wonderfully warm personality. He was very much in awe of the eloquence of Winston Churchill, and he would, sometimes, in our moments of informality, imitate him – his voice, and his style. J.J. Robinette, Charlie Dubin, Joe Sedgwick, Arthur and I did most of the important cases, and the senior criminal bar was very small throughout the fifties. We were all good friends, and we often met for lunch. Rivals for work, but we'd often discuss our cases, and give each other advice."[9]

What finally established him as part of the inner circle of major criminal counsel was the Suchan-Jackson murder trial. J.J. Robinette was the other defence counsel, and both of them were to be deeply affected, personally and professionally, by a disaster that happened just by the chance of automobiles passing on the street. There was more to it than that, of course, but it was, in fact, the most serious chance culmination of a series of rather commonplace bank robberies. Guns had been waved about, and occasionally fired, but not with much serious intent; no one had been hurt. But as the gang of robbers kept at it, something was bound to go wrong, and, eventually, a police officer was killed, though not at the scene of any robbery. The fatality was ultimately to rivet the moral sensibility of both Robinette and Maloney to the hard facts of capital punishment, bringing them face-to-face with the existential fact that murder, in the early fifties, could lead to further death. What looked like motion-picture fun as a gang of young men cavorted through the banks of Toronto waving guns, led to two men having their necks clinically broken in the grimy surroundings of the Don Jail on Broadview Avenue, a few feet from the passing traffic and within view of the skyline of downtown Toronto. Life for a split moment imitated cheap entertainment, but it was not quite so well-shaped as it was in the movies, which then, as now, had a facile way of making an amusing few minutes out of criminal irresponsibility, and half-baked courage.

What made the matter dramatic and thus attractive titillation for the press and public, hungry for sensation, was in part its hapless, accumulated minutiae. There was the cocky daring of Edwin Alonzo Boyd, the gang leader, a Second World War, Canadian army veteran, with the slight, chiselled features of Jimmy Cagney, sometimes complemented by a smart hairline moustache. He, more than any of his followers, caught the public fancy. Newspaper photos caught him in insouciant saunter in and out of police vans, on those occasions when the authorities were able to keep track of him. His smiling nonchalance in the face of capture hid a fertile mind, and a refusal to sit quietly in his cell, which resulted in two jail breaks, and a near-miss on a third, and, in the long run, the death of three men.

If this wasn't enough, there was a violin-playing killer, a distraught mother who made her living as a charlady in the offices of a great criminal lawyer, an accomplice with an artificial foot, who was obliged, given the arrested sensibility of the officials at the Don Jail to hobble to his hanging sans his prosthesis, supposedly to prevent him running away again, a last-minute conversion to Roman Catholicism brought about by a priest who was actually trying to console a convict in an adjoining cell to the convert, and two reluctant counsel who could never contemplate what had happened without coming close to tears. If there was anything constructive about the whole mess it was that Boyd, who might be most responsible for what happened, went on his way, finally, to Kingston Penitentiary, did his time, and on release, disappeared into western Canada, never to be seen again. He was one of the lucky ones. Two of his associates, Steve Suchan and Leonard Jackson, were executed.

Three things made a capital trial in the fifties a much more immediate experience than it might seem in retrospect. There was the death penalty. It was usually carried out, and without much delay, within weeks of the trial decision. Even if an appeal was to be heard, it usually occurred in a short time after the trial, and executions followed quickly on a failed appeal. Most of Ontario was still parochial in its social and political interests, and Toronto was the centre of its attention. What happened in Toronto is what most mattered. Added to that was the uncomfortable fact that murder was punished on the spot. Unlike the U.S. system, where the condemned is executed in a penitentiary often very far from the scene of the crime, executions in Canada took place in the jail in the county in which the homicide occurred. This had a peculiarly macabre effect in small county towns, where the county jail was usually part of the county administrative offices. In Welland, for instance, at that time, the courts, both of County and Supreme Court jurisdiction, the jail, the sheriff's office, the county administration, and the land registry office were all in the same building, right in the centre of town. It was possible for a lawyer with a general practice to search a title, deal with any county business, and visit a criminal client without leaving the building, and he might throw in a jury trial before a Supreme Court judge if he had the time. If he had bad luck, he might have a client hung in the small room that housed the noose and a collapsing floor. When someone was executed, it was known to everyone, and anyone could stand outside on the sidewalk, not a hundred yards away while the terrible act took place.

Even Toronto, for all its size, had a small-town intimacy in the fifties that made any important news interesting to the entire city. Toronto's Don Jail, while not quite in the centre of the town, is close enough to be well-known to everyone – on the east side of the Don Valley, set back from Queen Street, the central east-and-west artery of downtown

Toronto. When a man was executed in Toronto, it was no hole-in-the-corner affair. Everybody knew when and everybody knew where – across the street from one of the largest working-class districts in the city, just at the west edge of the east end of the city. It was hard to give an execution much mystery or dignity in such mundane surroundings.

What intensified the matter was the hold that newspapers had on the city in the early fifties. The newspaper may be the second-class communicator in the presence of television, but in the early fifties, television was just beginning to be the flickering blue light in the living room window; the local newspapers still ruled, with several editions a day, and with considerable attention paid to local matters, especially of the more sensational side of city life. The Suchan-Jackson case was part of a gift to the newspapers that had been going on for several months. It was certainly the longest running story in the province at the time. The two unfortunates were part of a loosely disorganized gang of bank robbers, led, if anyone could really be said to be leading, by Edwin Alonzo Boyd, who planned the robberies and hired one or two men at a time to help him rob Toronto banks in broad-daylight hold-ups. In the initial stages of this eventually joyless farrago, the public interest lay in what was called, by the newspapers, the "Boyd Gang." There has been much written about this group – articles, a book; and there was a lame attempt at a motion picture. The gang, although somewhat inaccurate in name, has taken a modest place in that odd social mythology of criminal romanticism that every society seems to need, and with which society has an ambiguous, innocently hypocritical love-hate relationship. America has dozens of these idealized outlaws; Australia has Ned Kelly and Britain has Dick Turpin, and in the twentieth century, the unsavory Kray brothers, and the Great Train Robbers. The Boyd gang has barely sufficient qualifications in criminal mischief for inclusion in such portentous company, but they had some skill at bank robbery, a night escape from the Don Jail, a few sieges with firearms in play, and finally a botched attempt to elude police that ended in murder. Then they were done. Well, not quite. After the murder, they escaped from the Don Jail once again, adding to their reputation as the most elusive of the Don's tenants – then they were rounded up once more with suitable gunplay, and were settled down for the grim task of having themselves sorted out for suitable punishment.

Boyd was the only constant in the gang. He, in fact, was the gang, and certainly the most intelligent and most ingenious member thereof. In late autumn of 1951, however, he was down on his luck, sitting in the Don Jail, waiting trial for a series of bank robberies in which he had been involved on the outer fringes of Toronto. Two of his co-accused were with him, housed in the same range of cells. One was Leonard Jackson, who can be distinguished from the second man, also named Jackson, by the fact that he had lost part of one foot while hopping freights, and wore an artificial limb. He was, also, somewhat less obstreperous than his fellow prisoner, Willie, whose loud, risible nature had earned him the name of Willie "the Clown" Jackson. They were not related.

Boyd was not a man inclined to sit still or give up; he never stopped thinking about how to keep on keeping on. He managed to get a hacksaw smuggled into the jail, and set about sawing his way out of the cells and out a window that faced on the exercise yard, forty feet below. Bedding was used to make a rope, and the three men slipped down into the yard, over the sixteen-foot outside wall, and they were away in the night. Soon after, a fellow part-time thief, Steve Suchan, collected them by car from a pre-arranged hiding place near the jail, and drove them further away to a hide-out in the city. On 4 November 1951, the Boyd gang was back in the papers, and the robberies started again. In early 1952, $46,207 were taken in the largest bank robbery in the history of Toronto to that time. Steve Suchan was now working as a member of the group. He should have been an unlikely criminal. He was a violin player, of sufficient skill to occasionally play as a substitute in the orchestra at the King Edward Hotel, where he also worked as a part-time doorman, off and on. He was the youngest of the Boyd associates, a dark, handsome, good-natured man, quiet and well-mannered. But steady work was sometimes difficult for unskilled labourers in the early fifties, and he had a sweet tooth for high living. So he pawned his violin for a .45 pistol (the pawnbroker was to testified to this romantic fact at the murder trial), and became a full-time robber.

The gang seemed impossible to catch in the winter months of 1952, but the police were keeping an eye on all the professional and social contacts of the guilty parties. On the evening of March 5, Arthur Maloney was having a late meal at the Metropole when two detectives, Sergeants Edmund Tong and Roy Perry passed his table. In the desultory badinage common to their mutual trade, Maloney asked them what they were planning for the evening. Whatever was the reply, it had something of that style and content of male braggadocio familiar in encounters of policemen and lawyers, locked in oral confrontations barely civilized by low-grade wit. The detectives may have said something about sometime tomorrow picking up a couple of thugs, or more pointedly, boasted of planning to arrest a couple of those guys "who keep you lawyers in business." Jack Batten reports it one way in his book *In Court,* and the other way in his book on J.J. Robinette. Whatever the exact words, Maloney was to remember the encounter, having by chance been involved in what might be called a "coincidence before the fact." But that was only to be a matter of idle contemplation several months later.

The next day, Tong and Perry were out in their unmarked car, looking for the gang, in the west end of the city. They suspected that Suchan and the fugitive Jackson were hiding in that area. The detectives had been given a tip, probably by an irate girl friend, of what kind of car to look for; they also had a licence number. They saw the car, driven by Suchan, followed it for a few blocks, and when it stopped at a red light on College Street West, Tong, who was riding as the passenger, yelled to Suchan to stay where he was. Perry parked behind the Suchan vehicle, and Tong got out, and walked towards the first car. He got around to the driver's side, and was slightly back of the car, when Suchan fired his gun. He struck Tong in the chest, and continued firing back at the second car. The car was struck several times, and Perry, still sitting, was also wounded. Leonard Jackson leapt out, waving his gun, and suddenly realizing what they had gotten into, urged Suchan to get in and drive away – and they did, leaving two policemen wounded, one of them close to death. Suchan and Jackson both fled to Montreal, where they had separate flats in which they hid. A few days later, they were both caught in separate police raids, in which they were seriously wounded. They were in the Don once again, on more serious charges than ever before. They were not alone, however, since Boyd and Willie the Clown had also been re-captured. Boyd and Willie at least had the consolation of facing the old charges – Suchan and Jackson weren't quite sure how serious was the trouble they were in, but on March 23, Edmund Tong died. If there was any consolation, all four were housed together in the death row at the Don Jail; that surely focussed the minds of all of them. Boyd and Willie were bound to have years of imprisonment ahead of them, but Suchan and Jackson, charged with murder, might well be dead before the year was out.

Some weeks later, working late in the richly caparisoned offices of McCarthy and McCarthy in the Imperial Life Building, across from Osgoode Hall on University Avenue, J.J. Robinette looked up to see a cleaning lady, whom he knew only by the nod, approaching his desk. Her son was in trouble and needed a lawyer. Would Mr. Robinette take the case? He asked for details and discovered that he, in a sense, knew the son – one of the men whose picture was all over the front pages of the papers – Steve Suchan, the sometime violinist. Robinette took the brief, and the cleaning lady paid him a modest fee for the service. This lucky chance of a mother being able to walk right into the office of one of the best lawyers in the country gave Suchan a bit of a chance. But Jackson was not so fortunate. He had no money, and no mother cleaning floors in the right place at the right time. In short, he had no lawyer, and nobody seemed to care. Edwin Boyd, however, had an idea that might have made that liability irrelevant. He decided to leave the Don Jail once again, and take his friends with him. Again, he got his hands on a hacksaw blade and again the group went out the window, and legging it down the Don Valley, on 8 September, the quartet got clean away, despite the fact that Leonard Jackson was severely impeded by the foresight of the prison staff, who had taken his artificial limb, with the foolish hope that it would keep him off the streets. He was slowed down, but Jackson was a man running for his life, and he stumbled along, deep into the suburbs of North Toronto. They had done it again, and J.J. Robinette's client was among the missing. The men hid out in a barn, but they were finally seen coming and going as they collected provisions, as well as weapons, and an artificial limb for Jackson. This time they were only out for just over a week, and then, they were back in the Don Jail once more.

The day after their return to jail, Suchan and Jackson were before Chief Justice James McRuer for arraignment. The trial date had been set previously for 22 September. Robinette asked for an adjournment on the grounds that he had not had sufficient time to prepare for trial. McRuer, who was not known to dally where his trial list was concerned, rejected the request, suggesting that if Robinette had wanted more time, he should have asked for it at the time of the escape. Robinette, who knew when he was flogging a dead horse, got some dry satisfaction out of talking back, respectfully, by suggesting that at that time, he wasn't sure there was ever going to be a trial. The judge was not dissuaded by this smart talk. The trial would go on the 22nd of September.

McRuer was, however, bothered by the fact that Jackson still did not have a lawyer, and he was determined, if no one else did, to find someone who could expect to be paid badly for taking a case that he stood an almost absolute certainty of losing. Immediately after the arraignment the Chief Justice returned to Osgoode, where Arthur Maloney was on his way to lunch in the Great Hall. They came together in the elevator – the young lawyer just barely nine years out of law school, and the judge. What Arthur didn't know, at that moment, was that the snatch of conversation that he had with Tong and Perry months ago was to accumulate wry piquancy. Moments later, Arthur Maloney was to go on to lunch, with a new client – he had been chosen to be Jackson's counsel. The casually peremptory way of the choice may seem impossible now, but that was the way it was done. Jackson was not consulted before Arthur was directed to take up the case. Indeed, it may seem quite as odd that the judge who was to hear the case, however distinguished, should presume to find counsel for a man whom he might be obliged to sentence to death. Jackson, on being informed, was slightly taken aback, but he was assured that if the Chief Justice chose someone to defend him, he could depend on the man.

There was even a chance that Jackson might be saved, if not from prison, at least from execution, and if that went the right way, it might also save Suchan. The right way was simple enough: the two men had to be pushed as far apart as possible at the moment of the shooting. In a sense, they had to disclaim each other, but not in the usual way of co-accused, by doing harm to each other by pushing all the blame on their opposite number. There was no question that Suchan had to be the admitted killer of Tong. Jackson had waved his gun about, but there was no evidence that he had fired it, and Tong had already been wounded when Jackson jumped out of the car. If, however, the jury believed that Suchan, firing wildly, had not meant to hit Tong, it might be manslaughter. But in this case, there was a catch to it, and it hinged on the presence of Leonard Jackson in the car. Jackson was an escaped criminal, and it is a criminal offence to aid and abet such. So, even if Suchan had not meant to hit Tong, but did it to scare whomever had ordered them to stop, with the intention to protect Jackson from capture – it would be murder, since the wounding would have occurred during the commission of a criminal offence that, by definition, was of a kind that designated any fatality occasioned by the same as murder.

Suchan's story, which he put with some skill on the stand and which he held to tenaciously through cross-examination was that he did not know who the man was who ordered him to say put, but thought it might have been someone with whom he had a quarrel in traffic shortly before. He thought the man might have wanted a face-to-face fight. He wanted to avoid that, particularly since he was sensitive to the fact that he had a well-publicized criminal, Leonard Jackson, in the car with him. He just wanted to get away, and as the man walked up, he rolled down his window, and fired several shots over his shoulder to disable the following car. He had no intention of shooting the man – he was shooting the car, and then meant to drive off. He had no arrangement with Jackson to defend him or protect him. If the jury were to believe all that (and they had to believe all of it), Suchan might get away with manslaughter. Since the men were jointly charged with murder arising out of a criminal conspiracy, if Suchan was believed, Jackson could not be convicted of a charge higher than manslaughter. They both would go to prison, for a long time, but they would not hang.

It would not have been easy for the jury to stomach that story, particularly since they had, in the prosecution case, been given two pieces of evidence guaranteed to make them uneasy. Perry, the surviving officer, had testified that Suchan had, in fact, opened the door, put his legs outside the car, and then turned to fire at Tong; if so, it was not an aimless shooting that had gone wrong. Secondly, all the bullet holes in the car were in the windshield. If Suchan wanted to disable the car, why hadn't he fired at the motor? Of course, it might be argued that those shots, obviously in the wrong place to stop the vehicle, were proof of Suchan's argument that he fired without much aim, over his shoulder. Or that he wasn't much of a shot anyway – which would support his argument that hitting Tong was just an accident, irresponsible, yes, but not intentional. There was, however, another piece of evidence that Robinette and Maloney fought desperately to keep out, arguing that it would inflame the jury. The judge let it in: a simple tailor's dummy, found in the basement of their hide-out. Someone had used it for target practice, and the head and the heart had been blasted to shreds by spot-on firing. Someone knew how to shoot to kill.

Suchan had not wanted to testify, and Robinette originally agreed with him, but it became clear that his intentions – what was in his mind at the time, and how he viewed his relationship to Leonard Jackson – had to be explained. He was a good witness not only for himself but for Jackson, holding steadily to the argument that he had not fired to protect Jackson. Nor to stop any police officer (although there were rumours floating around the legal community that he had, in fact, recognized Tong, and frightened by Tong's reputation as a rough man to deal with, had fired with intent), since he had no idea who the man was. He just wanted to get away from anyone! It might just catch the jury's fancy, but it would be a near run thing. Robinette was as satisfied as he could be with this slender defence, and he presumed it would all depend, from that moment on, on legal argument. But someone else wanted to have his say. Robinette presumed that Jackson would not take the stand, and so did Maloney, but Jackson insisted on doing so.

All he had to do was corroborate Suchan's testimony; that he didn't know Suchan was armed, and that he had no arrangement with Suchan to protect him from arrest. This was the way he started, and it looked as if the two stories might help each other. But the cross-examination was yet to come. If Jackson could hold to the proposition that Suchan had presented, that he fired to protect himself, and not to protect Jackson, they were still on the tight-rope, but might make it. If not, he could hang both of them. Bill Gibson, the Crown, a stolid, serious cross-examiner, picked Jackson apart with the help of the judge, who also got into the cross-examination with devastating effect. Maloney sat helpless as Jackson seemed to simply give up, leaving the stand with the jury under the impression, if not the certainty, that he knew Suchan was armed and could be depended upon to use his gun if there was any danger of Jackson being captured. Jackson apologized later to Maloney, arguing that he had lost control of himself under the pressure of the questioning: if they wanted to convict him that badly, then so be it.

It was one of the most damaging incidents in Arthur Maloney's career. He knew that he had made a mistake in letting Jackson on to the stand, although in theory he could not have refused him the right to speak in his own defence. In practice, it was one of the very few times that Arthur let a client run the defence, and it was doubly damaging since it not only harmed Jackson, but also sank Suchan. Years later, Robinette, a man of magnanimity and reserve, always reluctant to criticize another counsel, still spoke of it as a mistake. His comment upon Jackson's performance was succinct: "He was simply awful." It would never happen to Maloney again; he was much admired for handling clients well, and sometimes, when necessary, roughly. One student remembers him working with a client, going over possible cross-examination questions that might be asked. Maloney's voice rose higher and higher in the empty office on a Sunday afternoon, "Listen to the question! Listen! Now I'll ask you again. Think about what you are saying! Listen to the bloody question!" His clients belonged to him and did as he told them, however important they might be in their own right.

It is unlikely, however, that anything Maloney had told Jackson would have made much difference once Jackson got into the hands of the Crown. The mistake was allowing him to testify. Talking to Roy McMurtry years after, Arthur revealed that Jackson obviously did not quite understand what was going on. He told Arthur that he thought that Suchan had no chance on the basis of his performance on the stand, and that he determined not to let Suchan take all the blame on himself. It was part of the accumulation of half-formed opinion, ignorance, and bad luck that befell the defence in the trial. Robinette believed that Suchan only fired his gun because he wanted to show how tough he was, needing in some weak-minded way to impress Jackson. Maloney believed that Jackson, on the other hand, admired Suchan, and that his explanation for his failure on the stand, and his determination to go where Eddie was doomed to go, was part of that affection.

Robinette and Maloney had little time for rueful "what-ifs." Jackson, whether intentionally or not, had dropped himself and Suchan into an impossible position. Their counsel in addressing the jury were determined to pull the jury back to the narrow line of the defence that they had agreed upon from the beginning. Robinette argued that the killing was accidental – that Suchan had no idea who had accosted him, and only meant to disable the automobile in order to avoid being found in the company of a celebrated bank robber and prison escapee. He had no interest in helping Jackson; he was simply helping himself. Arthur insisted that Jackson was not depending upon Suchan to protect him, and was as surprised as anyone when the shooting started. He conceded that Jackson could not walk away from the disaster; a death had occurred, and Jackson was somehow involved, but hanging was not the correct legal punishment for what, at the worst, was manslaughter.

If Maloney had made a big mistake in loosing his client to cross-examination, Robinette admitted that he made a little one in his address to the jury. He had been impressed by the fact that Suchan, when he was cornered in his Montreal hide-out, had not attempted to defend himself, despite the fact that he was well-armed, was fired upon, and badly wounded. Robinette, who usually eschewed emotion in his addresses, indulged himself in his summing-up in suggesting that the fact that Suchan had survived, had supernatural overtones. "Something intervened. He could have died there, but he didn't."

Bill Gibson, a dour man, not given to frivolity, and capable of expressing moral indignation without the piousness that flaws the performance of many Crowns, was not going to let Robinette take the trial to a higher level. He immediately deflated any romantic afflatus that Robinette may had caused, by beginning his address to the jury in descendent common sense. He had been working on this case for months, he told the jury, and this was the first time he had heard of the possibility of Divine Intervention. His laconic scepticism captured the jury and from then on, he had them back to the facts of the case, which he placed before them stolidly – there was nothing mysterious, and certainly nothing spiritual about what had happened. It was just another murder. In less than two hours deliberation, the jury agreed with him, and McRuer sentenced both men to be executed on the 16 December 1952. Robinette and Maloney were shattered; neither of them had ever had a client sentenced to death. Robinette told Maloney that despite his long career at the Bar, he had never heard the sentence of death pronounced by a judge. They took the case to the Court of Appeal, requesting a new trial on the grounds that the dressmaker's dummy should not have been allowed in evidence, and that the evidence in total was insufficient to suggest that the men had been intent on protecting Jackson from arrest. They were turned down. In early December they went to the Supreme Court of Canada, seeking leave to appeal. They appeared before Mr. Justice Estey who was sufficiently impressed with their argument to reserve his decision, an unusual occurrence in such hearings. On 12 December, he issued a twelve-page judgment, but refused their request to argue the case before the full court. That was the end of it – four days later the men were to die.

Paul French, Frances's son, who served as Arthur's student in the early seventies, and was later his associate in practice, often heard of the case.

Suchan and Jackson had a profound influence on Arthur's life. He often spoke of the case. Whenever he did, it was always very direct, very personal, and you could hear a pin drop in any audience when he spoke of it. He obviously drew on it for his pursuit of the abolishment of the death penalty, and he carried it further. He was able to be very movingly subjective. He always focussed on the last days of their lives. He never complained about the case or the disposition of it, and he always focussed on it for the contemplation of the value of every human life. He would talk about how these men were so foul, and had committed such a horrible crime, and how they redeemed themselves, and how in the last days of their lives, his client, Jackson, when asked what he wanted for his last meal, asked what Jesus Christ wanted. Jackson went off to his death, saying, "Mr. Maloney, I'll be your lawyer in heaven." Utterly at peace! The way Arthur would tell that – you could just feel the tears welling up in the audiences![10]

In most criminal cases, once the trial is over, the connection between counsel and their clients is finished. Arthur, however, sometimes developed continuing connections with his former clients, sending them newspapers, arranging for magazine subscriptions, doing modest jobs to get them settled in. In the Suchan-Jackson case, both counsel kept in close contact with their clients until the end, and formed a moving relationship with them. It was not simply a matter of keeping them in touch with the appeal battle. There was also a bit of drama at the jail. Suchan was a lapsed Catholic; his mother had wanted him, in fact, to become a priest. Now she felt he ought to see one, but Suchan didn't like the priest who visited the Don, and surly and uninterested, he rebuffed the poor man, who was a thoroughly respectable cleric, but didn't strike Suchan's fancy. Lillian remembers that Arthur, who was in and out of the jail during this time, heard of Suchan's stubborn refusal to see the priest. Arthur had always kept up his connections with St. Michael's College, and he thought that Father John Kelly, an old friend, might be just the man to settle Suchan. He asked Robinette if he would mind, since Suchan was, in fact, still Robinette's client; Robinette gave his consent. Maloney had properly followed protocol by asking Robinette first, but he almost didn't get the second step in correct order. He tried to contact Father Kelly, but could not find him. So he called Father Shook, a Medieval English scholar, who was Kelly's superior, and as such should have called in the first place. He told the Father of his idea, and Shook, and later Father Kelly, agreed to the intrusion of the college priest into the matter. Kelly had exactly the kind of personality that Maloney thought would attract Suchan. He loved sports, and had a bluff, out-going informality and lack of piousness that made him popular with the St. Michael's students. Suchan reluctantly agreed to see him, but was still very stubborn about paying attention to Kelly's attempts to talk to him seriously about his plight. Jackson, housed in an adjoining cell, exposed to Kelly's cajoling, lost patience and told Suchan to listen to the priest, who was only trying to help him. Suchan, who respected Jackson's opinions on everything, did as he was told, and so did Jackson, who suddenly decided that he too wanted to be counselled, to the point that he decided to become a Catholic. He did so under Father Kelly's instruction. In the tradition of converts, he became so enthusiastic that he caused a problem over his last meal, insisting that he wanted exactly what Christ had consumed at the Last Supper. The warders didn't know what to do. Aside from the fact that prisoners were not allowed alcohol (in Ontario at the time, hardly any diners in public, in prison or out, could get alcohol with their meals), there was the simple matter of Biblical scholarship to be considered – what was the menu at the Last Supper? Father Kelly was called in to deal with Jackson's adamant determination to live out his life to the letter of his Redeemer. Kelly managed to convince Jackson that such devotion was unnecessary, and that his last communion was, in fact, a lay celebration of the Last Supper. Jackson, satisfied with this, asked what Suchan was having. It was fried chicken, apple pie, and cigars. Jackson had the same. Early the next morning, the men, with Father Kelly's assistance, walked down the corridor to the gallows. Jackson stumbled along, forbidden the use of his small leg support. The execution chamber was so cold that Suchan, still in some control of himself, urged Jackson to hurry up, since he was of the opinion that he was to hang, not be frozen to death.

All in all it seems too colourful in a lugubrious way to be the real thing. Robinette remembers that "Arthur was terribly upset. We went out to see them two or three days before the hanging and we talked to our clients. I was so upset that I was crying, and Suchan said, 'Don't cry, Mr. Robinette. I will have an afterlife, and my main regret is that my brother is marked by my name.'" The lawyers attempted to console each other. Arthur came to the conclusion, as he told Robinette, that it was the ultimate test of a criminal lawyer's character to lose a client to the hangman. It was a kind of negative moment of truth for both of them, and fixed inexorably their hatred of capital punishment, which Arthur, in particular, was to take to himself as a personal crusade.

The Suchan and Jackson case firmly placed Maloney as a leader at the criminal bar and as a celebrity, but it also gave him a chance at cases for which he might not have been considered previously. He acknowledged this in a speech that he made at one of the many testimonial dinners, which his colleagues visited upon him in the later years of his career. At a Royal York dinner in 1979, he recalled the first case of serious proportion that came his way after Suchan and Jackson. The Goodrich Rubber Company and the Kaufman Rubber Company were charged with price fixing. J.D. Pickup was to be one of the counsel, but immediately prior to the trial, Mr. Pickup was asked to succeed Chief

Justice Robertson as the Chief Justice of Ontario. "So John Robinette very kindly recommended my name to those two corporations, which was a pretty important appointment to me at that stage." When Robinette phoned Arthur with the good news that he was to join the defence team, he could not resist a bit of in-house teasing: "For God's sake, Maloney, concentrate on the bloody law in this case because even the Catholic Church can't get a rubber company into heaven!" Leonard Jackson's conversion might have impressed Robinette, but not sufficiently for him to lose perspective when it came to defending corporations.

5

Brown Eggs and Murder

Maloney was often asked by young counsel for advice on trial procedure, and on jury addresses, and he was always happy to send them copies of his best work, as he saw it. The cases which he thought best exemplified his work are, in fact, the cases that are analysed, in their proper chronological position, in this book, save for the McCorkell case, which was chosen by the author for other reasons. The *Esposito* case is an early example of his skills, and is discussed with two kinds of readers in mind – the legal profession, and the general public. It is hoped that it does not patronize the latter, nor prove too simplistic for the former.

For all the talk about the sensational talent Maloney had for criminal trial work, he was not a flamboyant counsel. He tended to take his duties seriously in court, with only occasional flashes of very modest wit, although he could be very stubborn and sometimes exercised if he thought himself abused by a tough judge. He was generally courteous, good-natured, and frank in his presentation, and he rarely attacked a witness.

When it came to the jury address, he imposed a sense of serious business, stressing the solemn duty of the jury, and the importance of their decision not only to the accused, but to society in general. He always took extreme care at the outset of his address to define the rights and duties of the judge, the prosecution, the defence counsel, and particularly those of the jury. Those passages varied little from trial to trial. He was particularly careful to advise the jury on the limitations of the powers of the legal participants, and on the rights of the jury to make up their own minds, whatever the prosecution or the judge might say. When addressing the jury, he stood very still, behind a lectern, with his notes, spoke slowly and firmly, and gestured sparingly. His notes, which are still extant for most of his cases, were not a full expression of what he planned to say, and he used them, in the main, to keep the argument straight while he pursued the matter informally, extemporaneously, and with modest feeling which could, on occasion, become quietly impassioned, and sometimes deeply moving. He tended to economy in his argument, and to brevity rather than long-winded repetitions. Surprisingly, given his reputation, he rarely used literary allusion. The occasional grammatical errors, which are an indication of the improvisational manner of his address, were rarely corrected, and he would, sometimes, quite deliberately, drop into the language of the street, to get past the barrier of respect and deference that a jury usually throws up in its natural uncertainty and insecurity. He would, occasionally, speak directly to a juror, by name, as if by chance, and he made a point of having a chart of the jury box, with the jurors named in their respective seats, to facilitate this sudden, flattering intimacy. The final aim of all this was to present the jury with an argument that was organized, informed, easily understood, and offered not by a man who knew better than they, not by a well-known celebrity counsel, but by a fellow citizen, gifted perhaps, and trained, but still just a citizen speaking to other citizens engaged in one of the most serious duties of a civilized society.

If the Suchan and Jackson case displayed the limits of a criminal defence in the face of overwhelming evidence and a recalcitrant client, Arthur Maloney's real skills are well illustrated in the *Esposito* case, which was tried before Mr. Justice R.W. Treleaven at Port Arthur, beginning on 26 October 1954. This was one of several cases that Arthur did in tandem with Alf Petrone, a Lakehead lawyer, who knew Arthur well and is one of his greatest admirers. The facts are simple enough on their face, and it is an example of Maloney's talents that their seeming simplicity was systematically and successfully riddled by a mass of detail that undermined the straight-forwardness of the Crown's evidence. Arthur always weighed the two approaches to defence carefully before coming down on one side or the other. (There was, of course, a third line of defence, which Maloney often used, in which the argument was made that the accused was not mentally capable of forming the intent to do the act, but that is another matter.) It was often a fine line that divided the alternatives: whether to defend on the grounds that the accused could not have done the act, or, in the alternative, whether there was any possibility of suggesting, persuasively, that there could be *some doubt* that the accused had done the act. A conviction in a criminal case must be based beyond a reasonable doubt on the perception that the accused did do it – any doubt sets the accused free – and Arthur Maloney was a natural master at creating doubt, sometimes without anyone quite knowing what he was doing until it all fell into place in his address to the jury. The *Esposito* case is that sort of trial.

Raffaele Esposito, an Italian immigrant, with a limited grasp on the

English language, was charged with the murder of a German immigrant woman, Hedwig Kopplin. Her two children were killed in the same attack. Hedwig Kopplin lived with her husband and children on a remote CNR railway line seventy miles northwest of Port Arthur. No other family lived near them, but a section foreman for the railroad lived in a station across from the house that Mr. Kopplin had built for his family, and a crew of section men lived in a bunk house, adjoining the station. Horst Kopplin, the husband, worked as a CNR labourer. His wife had followed him from Germany with their young son, and a daughter had been born in Canada. Kopplin had recently asked for, and had been given a transfer to another section, Mine Centre, some 100 miles away, and was already working there at the time of the murder. He intended to move his family as soon as he could house them. Kelly Siding, as the little settlement was called, could not be reached by road, but there was access east and west by rail, and paths and bush roads – most of which were very primitive.

On Saturday, 19 June 1954, the crew of a light train, consisting of an engine and a caboose, travelling east, in the very late afternoon, saw smoke rising from Kelly Siding, and found the Kopplin house on fire. Mrs. Kopplin was found outside, behind the house, her hands tied with a rope, and with a further rope around her neck. Her head was bashed in, and her body and clothing partially burned; she was dead. So were her children, found in the house. The crew who were stationed at the site had been absent since late afternoon of the previous day, Friday, having all gone to Port Arthur for the weekend, leaving the Kopplin family alone at the site.

Raffaele Esposito was living and working as a section hand at station some six miles further east, and he had been seen near Kelly Siding in the mid-morning, Saturday, travelling on a velocipede. At the time he was seen, the Kopplin house was untouched; later in the morning, the five-year-old son had been seen playing with his dog outside the house. Evidence was presented that strongly suggested that the killings must have taken place late in the afternoon, and that the fire had been set sometime around five o'clock p.m. Esposito was seen at his home station, Larson, around noon, and later, around seven o'clock in the evening. No one had any evidence that could place him at the murder scene in the afternoon. It was claimed that he had said that while his fellow labourers were off in Port Arthur on the weekend, he intended to visit Kelly Station and sexually service Mrs. Kopplin. Esposito admitted being near the site on Saturday morning on his way to order some groceries further down the line, but he had turned around before passing Kelly Station because he was having some serious stomach trouble, and had returned to Larson.

He was taken into custody by the Ontario Provincial Police on a vagrancy charge, a convenient way to hold a man while further charges were contemplated; in Esposito's case, the detention on that charge was dubious, since he was simply not a vagrant. He had a job, a place of residence, was not destitute, and certainly was not acting in any way that suggested vagrancy. It was a common device used by the police at the time to give them time to collect evidence, although it was not, in fact, strictly legal. He was held for a week before being charged with murder.

There was evidence that some of his clothing had been recently washed, but his boots did not show that thc soil on them came from Kelly Station, and the tests for blood, though displaying minor responses, were inconclusive at best. Mrs. Kopplin had bled profusely. Lengths of rope, similar to those found on Mrs. Kopplin's body, were found in his locker and in the bunkhouse where he lived with other workers. He claimed that he had spent the afternoon in a boat on a nearby lake – the rope used to tie up the boat was the same kind as that found on the body.

The first preliminary hearing was so unsatisfactory that Mr. Justice Wells, on being asked to review its worth by the defence, had made it clear that he found it untenable, and suggested that unless further evidence could be found, Esposito must needs be released. At the second preliminary, the evidence pertaining to the rope was presented, and it was claimed that Esposito, when arrested, had a scratch on his lip. That additional evidence satisfied the court, and the case was sent for trial. At the trial, one further piece of evidence was offered by the Crown – it was claimed, by one of his fellow workers, that Esposito was seen cooking brown-shelled eggs on the Saturday night or Sunday morning; brown eggs were not available at the retail outlets serving the labourers. The Kopplins, however, had a small group of laying hens, and they produced brown eggs. Some time following the murder, bits of brown egg shells were found by the police in the refuse dump at Larson.

What the evidence amounted to in total was (1) a remark of salacious possibility that Esposito may have made about visiting Mrs. Kopplin on the Saturday when his fellow workers were absent, and when the Kelly Station workers were also away, (2) a siting of Esposito on a railway handcar close to Kelly Station on Saturday morning (several hours before the murder), (3) the possession by him, or at least a finding, of rope in his locker, in the bunkhouse, and on the boat which he admitted he had used. These various pieces matched the rope on the body, (4) some apprehension on his part when he was questioned by the police, (5) some very minor, inconclusive blood tests on his boots, (6) some recently washed clothing, and (7) a claim that he was cooking brown eggs. This bit of evidence was put forward by a man who admitted that he and Esposito had quarrelled, and (8) confirmed by the finding of brown egg shells in a communal dump several days after Esposito was arrested. The final evidence (9) was the lack of any proof that anyone else had been near the station at any time during that Saturday. So there was Esposito – he had the inclination, given the comment he supposedly made – he had the opportunity. The Crown claimed that his early morning visit was to plan his attack. There was also a small amount of male sperm found in the deceased body, but the coroner could not be sure how long it had been there. No further evidence of sexual contact was found. There was no evidence of sexual forcing, and no sign of sperm on Esposito's clothing.

During the trial, Maloney made much of two lines of argument that the judge and the Crown found otiose and irrelevant. The first of these was centred on Mr. Justice Wells's finding that the original preliminary hearing was too short of evidence to charge Esposito, and Wells's comment that it was shocking to hold a man on so little evidence. Maloney tried to get Sergeant Eric Erickson to admit that Wells's characterization of the case had some serious influence on his introduction, at the second preliminary, of further evidence – that he had, in fact, been so determined to press the case against Esposito that evidence was conveniently discovered. It has to be remembered that the Crown, at a preliminary, does not have to put in all its evidence, but only sufficient to satisfy the Judge that there is a *prima facie* case to be answered. This was Erickson's position on the matter – the evidence of the rope and the scratch had been known, but he had not been asked to reveal it by the Crown. There was some skirmishing between Maloney, the Crown, and the judge about Maloney's determination to hang on doggedly to Erickson on this matter, as he attempted to get the officer to admit that the later evidence was only dug up as a result of Wells's warning. Erickson would not budge, but Maloney had managed to get the idea before the jury that Erickson was determined to prosecute Esposito. Maloney had laid the basis for that suggestion in another example of Erickson's conduct, which he had introduced prior to the battle over the added evidence. That confrontation rested on the vagrancy charge that had kept Esposito in jail while the police investigated the murder. Erickson, with the bland confidence that often marks police testimony, claimed that Esposito was properly charged, despite his obvious ability to take care of himself financially. This line of arrogant indifference to the legal meaning of "vagrancy" was also taken by another officer, who bare-facedly claimed the charge could be used as a general "hold-all," until the police could figure out a proper charge. The vagrancy charge no longer exists, but at the time of *Esposito*, it was not unusual for the police to misuse it in this manner. Inspector John Craig, the OPP criminal investigation expert, brought up from Toronto to aid in the investigation, was asked by Maloney what he thought constituted a vagrancy arrest.

Craig: Vagrancy to me in a case of this nature is a holding charge only used in a case of this nature.
Maloney: Do you realize that there is no such thing as a holding charge in this country?
C: That is the charge that is used ...
M: He was not a vagrant?
C: He was unable to give a good account of himself.

That seemed to bring out the best in Maloney – his indignation over what he saw as unfair and abusive power.

M: He was unable to give a good account of himself? You mean that he was unable to give a good account of himself that satisfied you. Do you think you are entitled to arrest everyone who cannot give himself an accounting to you, and hold him in custody; do you think you are entitled to do that?
C: I am entitled to do that in any case of this nature.
M: You are not entitled to do it at all ...
HIS LORDSHIP: Now, Mr. Maloney, you can ask the questions, but you cannot tell him what he can do or not do.
M: I think this is relevant ...
HL: Your questions are all right, but I am objecting to you saying that he is not entitled to do any such thing, because he is the one who is giving the evidence.

Arthur could be stubborn when he was aroused:

M: I submit it is relevant for the jury to know that he is completely wrong.
HL: Are you giving evidence?
M: No, but it is a matter of law ...
HL: Well, you are when you make a statement like that.
M: Well, it is a matter of law ... and you know that as well as I do ...
HL: You know you cannot purport to give statements like that to a witness. There is a proper way of putting in what the law is and it is not. Will you proceed, please?[1]

On the face of it, this exchange, first with the witness and then with the judge seems to be a bit of a loss for Maloney, caused in part by his anger over an officer using the charge for the convenience of a criminal investigation; it leads him into an attempt to chastise the officer, and legitimately precipitates the intrusion of the judge, who is quite right in his ruling. If the aim in questioning a witness is to elicit facts pertinent to the case, little seems to have been accomplished. But Maloney's idea of cross-examination often has wider intention than simply establishing facts. Maloney's claim that "I think this is relevant," and the tenacity with which he holds on are really doing something else – establishing implicitly an attitude towards the accused that goes beyond simply pointing out the common tendency of policemen to be ignorant of the law, or, more to the point, deliberately manipulative in how they use the law. It will be used later, in the jury address as a line of the defence – the idea that the police from the very beginning had closed minds on the matter, were convinced that Esposito was their man, and that they needed to look no further. Maloney appears at the time of this exchange to be simply incensed by the misuse of the vagrancy charge – and he probably was – but more to the point, he had established an attitude of stubborn indifference and unapologetic smugness among the officers, convinced, as they were, that they had the right man, and could hold him until they found the evidence to back up their opinion. If that was true, it meant that they were close-minded and did not consider alternative possibilities, which, perhaps, should have been thought on – and ruled out – before charging Esposito. Maloney loved police work that was unfinished. He feasted on alternative possibilities. The other aspect of the case that Maloney was determined to undermine was the argument that it had to be Esposito, since no one else was around. Maloney spent a good deal of time establishing the possibility of quite a few people being about. There was, in fact, a genuine vagrant walking the track. Both sides agreed that he was an old man unlikely to be a reasonable candidate for the murder, but Maloney kept the fact of his presence continually before the jury, and used him to buttress his argument about the misuse of the vagrancy charge in Esposito's case.

Maloney: You questioned Mr. Beatty?
Craig: I did.
M: Mr. Beatty was questioned by you very carefully?
C: Yes.
M: And for some considerable time?
C: Yes.
M: And on more than one occasion?
C: I believe so, yes.
M: He was a man who was obviously a mental case?
C: No, definitely not.
M: You do not agree to that. Was it you who told the newspapers that he looked like a half-crazed man?
C: No, sir.
M: And that he was a man of a very eccentric appearance?
C: He was rough in dress, but he knew what it was all about.
M: Did you not think it was eccentric for a man to walk down the railway track between Sioux Lookout and Port Arthur?

C: Very odd.
M: He was brought into jail here?
C: Yes.
M: And pleaded guilty to vagrancy?
C: Yes.
M: And was such vagrancy the inability to give a good account of himself?
C: Yes.
M: And you let him plead guilty?
C: Yes.
M: You could have stopped it – there was nothing wrong with him in your estimation?
C: He had to be charged to be held.
M: Why let him plead guilty to something that he did not commit ...
C: He did not have any money or any visible means of support.
M: Is that why you arrested Esposito – because he did not have any money or any visible means of support?
C: No.[2]

If the tramp was some help to Maloney in proving that Craig knew how a vagrancy charge should be properly used, even if, in the case of Mr. Beatty he seemed to be using it in two ways, there was never any question of pinning the charge on him. It was, however, a question of discrediting the Crown's contention that Esposito was the only man about in the area. If Beatty was there – why wouldn't it be possible for others to be there? True, Beatty was coming right down the track, and was easily seen but – perhaps – there were other ways to come and go in the area, where a man could move without much danger of being detected.

When a Maloney address to the jury is read, it often looks so seamless, so easy, and reasonable that the art behind it can be missed, and there is a tendency to see him as some kind of "natural," who was lucky enough to have a kind of divine sense of how to put a defence together. But if his addresses are taken apart carefully, and the component parts traced back to their support in the cross-examination, it will be seen that he depended very heavily on two rather mundane elements, hard work and enormous patience, and a third, less common – an ability to see evidence not only in terms of its main intent, but also to see the possibilities of using it in other ways – a kind of peripheral vision, sometimes instantaneously put into play, to expand the number of ways in which the testimony could be presented to the jury. It is probably his patience that was his finest gift – he was quite prepared, in a sense, to wait a witness out. He doesn't usually rag them, and he rarely attacks, but he keeps them on the point, sometimes maddeningly so, and sometimes with a judge hanging over him, telling him to get on – which may be his fourth gift – a deaf ear to the importunities of judges who want him to move off a point when he still has things to do. In this case, Arthur saw the points that could cause trouble and those that might help, and he concentrated, in the main, on them: the rope, the eggs, and the local trails, and he dragged this little bag of tokens from witness to witness, looking for help.

The rope was the easiest, despite the fact that pieces of the same seemed to surround Esposito. Dante Rossi, a fellow worker, had helped the police get much of their evidence together, and in examination-in-chief, he did some of the work to diminish the importance of the rope.

Question: And what kind of rope was it?
Rossi: It was made of that rope that you wrap a parcel with.
Q: Did you take any person down to where the boat was tied and show him the boat?
R: Yes.
Q: Who did you take down?
R: I took the inspector – I don't know the names.
Q: You took the police?
R: Yes. ...
Q: Would you look at this piece of rope and tell me if that is the piece?
R: Yes, I think this is that piece, because there are lots of pieces he take from the bunk house.
Q: That who took from the bunk house.
R: Him.
Q: Esposito?
R: Yes. ...
Q: Where did Esposito get the rope in the bunk house, do you know?
R: In his place.
Q: In his place. Did he have much rope there?
R: Yes.

Then the Crown did some of Arthur's work for him, corroborating a point which Arthur had been exploring with previous witnesses.

Q: Did you have any kind of rope like that there?
R: Yes, I have some.
Q: Do you keep your rope there?
R: Yes.
Q: Where does the rope come from?
R: From the groceries.
Q: From Brosnett's groceries?
R: Yes.[3]

Arthur did not pursue the matter further. He had what he wanted, an admission that Rossi also had some of the rope, and that it came on the groceries. But Arthur knew that juries are not to be depended upon to remember evidence heard only once, and so he pursued the point with other witnesses.

Maloney: How often would you get an order for groceries?
Vincenzo Tiano: Every time there was a need.
M: When you got delivery, were your groceries parcelled with rope like this, and I am showing you exhibit nine?
T: Sometimes it was something like that.[4]

He also discussed it with another labourer:

Maloney: And arrangements would be made to ship your food out to you regularly?
Walter Koczkur: Yes.
M: How often would you get a delivery a week?
K: Well, in the summer months every week and sometimes two times a week.
M: And when they came, were your parcels tied up with binder twine or small rope?
K: Well, not very often binder twine – I don't know what you call it – It is a quarter inch rope.
M: Was it this type of rope (indicating)[*sic*]
K: Well, sometimes this kind and sometimes heavier – it just depends what kind of a bundle of rope they buy.
M: It was sometimes this type of rope that I hold in my hand?
K: Yes.
M: And sometimes another type?
K: Yes.
M: And how would you describe the other type?
K: Well, it was heavier, and a double strand.
M: But otherwise like this?
K: Yes, and this kind too.[5]

Further help was given in the testimony of Peter Kuryliw, who had years of experience in the railway camps.

Maloney: But you have worked at a great many of these sections?
Kuryliw: Yes.
M: And in your experience as a railway man and a section foreman, where do all these section hands get their groceries and foodstuffs from?
K: Well, they send in for them.

M: They send where?
K: To anywhere they like.
M: I understand a lot of them send to Kakabeka Falls?
K: Yes, and I used to get mine from Fort William.
M: When they get them from Kakabeka Falls they go to Mr. Dekvikio or Mr. Liderman?
K: Yes.
M: And delivery is made around three times a week?
K: Yes.
M: And these parcels of groceries when they are delivered to the section man are invariably tied with rope?
K: Yes.
M: And this type of rope? (producing)
K: Well, some like that, and some just twine, and most of it like that.
...
M: And in your experience as section foreman you have noticed that the railway workers save the rope?
K: Yes, lots of them save it because if they move away they need it to tie their boxes.
M: And is it common practice to save it?
K: Yes, because they have to move.[6]

What the railroad labourers didn't do, the police officials did, in helping Maloney to diminish the importance of the rope. Maloney's examination of Dr. Ward Smith, from the Attorney General's crime lab in Toronto, took on odd turn when he revealed that he was a specialist on ropes – but not quite the right kind of specialist.

Maloney: Now, in regard to the rope, you not being a specialist in that field, turned them back to Inspector Craig ...
Smith: I am a specialist in the fibre content, but being such a very common type of cordage, I thought the knots would have some special significance, in that they were the sort that they were ...
M: I suppose you did not know, and it might have assisted you to know, that the section men at all these various sections from Kakabeka Falls to Graham used to get their groceries from grocery-men in Kakabeka Falls, and in Fort William, and who, according to many of the witnesses, invariably wrapped their grocery parcels in this type of rope – and there was nothing unusual about the rope?
S: No, it is binder twine, and you find it on farms and everywhere – the knots should have been interesting ...

This return to the knots, which Maloney had pushed aside in Smith's first answer, might have been trouble, but had they been so, Maloney reasoned that it would have come up in the examination-in-chief. It was one of those rare occasions when a lawyer could ask a question of which the answer was not known – presuming that the Crown has not left it unasked to trap counsel. Maloney decided to let the man have his say about the knots; he immediately was able to take the answer and proceed to give it generalized irrelevance.

M: While you are not an expert [on knots], they suggested to you that they might have been tied by the same source?
S: As a layman [Smith knew his place and was prepared to play it on the matter of knots], the knots seemed to be involved and of similar type, from the various samples of rope submitted.

The rope in the courtroom had not come from one source, but was part of the collection of bits and pieces found on the body, in Esposito's locker, on the boat, and in the bunkhouse generally. What Maloney wanted to do was to make Smith's finding of similarity in the knots work for the defence – it was a question of how one used the word "source."

M: And that would be consistent with the rope having come from the same original source of supply?
S: Yes – for all I knew, that was a common type of tie.
M: And may have come from the Liderman store or the Vedekio store in Kakabeka Falls?

The doctor had been trapped and gave in gracefully.

S: Well, I don't know – they may all have tied their knots in that way for all I know.
M: That is all, thank you.[7]

It was getting something for nothing. Smith had noticed the knots, and found a consistency in them, which might have led to something if it had been looked into. What if only the pieces of rope found on the body, in the locker, and on the boat showed that kind of knot? Maloney seems, here, to be working on the spot, instantly coming to the conclusion that the knots would have been in the examination-in-chief if anything was to be made of them. And if that was not the case, or in the alternative, if the police had not thought to make such comparison, he could presume that similar knots were on all the bits of rope, or, at the very least, the investigation had stopped short of determining whether they were so. Their presence could be used to argue for a generalized practice in the grocery store of tying knots thusly, diminishing further the significance of the bits of rope that could be traced to the accused. Maloney was often a great scavenger. He seemed to have a theory of "waste not, want not" when it came to evidence.

Most lawyers would have stopped there, but Arthur had a tenacious way of getting a point absolutely settled before he went to the jury. Craig, the officer whom he battled with over arresting Esposito on the vagrancy charge, got a thorough going-over about the rope.

Maloney: Do you remember when I questioned you in the magistrate's court at Fort William on October 7th and 8th, you were asked these questions, at page fifty-four: "**Question**: The ropes which have been filed in your evidence taken from the lady and boat and of the accused were they examined by anyone else other than yourself? **Answer**: No. **Q**. No expert examination made of them. **A**: No."
Craig: That is right.
M: You said you brought them down to Doctor Smith?
C: They were not examined – I turned them over to him, and he returned them to me on the 22nd, and told me that he was not qualified to make any examination.
M: He told us the other day that he examined them and felt that he was not qualified – he told us the other day that he examined them?
C: He did not tell me that.
M: Why did you swear in the magistrate's court that no one else other than yourself had examined the rope?
C: Because I did not know that he had examined them. They were taken to him for that purpose, but they were returned to me, and he told me that he had not examined them.
M: You brought them down to him for examination?
C: Yes, I did.
M: And did you have them examined by any official of the Mounted Police out west?
C: No.
M: Was it suggested that you should?
C: Yes.
M: And that there is only one expert on ropes in Canada?
C: Yes.
M: And that is a gentleman connected with the Mounted Police.
C: Yes.

Maloney took that line no further, leaving it in the air with the implicit suggestion that Craig, consistent with his determination to convict Esposito, might have tried to mislead Maloney at the preliminary; at any rate, Craig had seemingly lost interest in the ropes, and refrained from carrying out the examination of the same with the only man in the country who might have made something of them. If Craig wasn't deliberately misleading, he seemed at least to be puzzlingly incompetent – and more to the point, he proved that the Crown had no expert evidence to back up their claims for the ropes. Maloney went off on another question for a few minutes, and then he swung back to the ropes again:

M: Was any attempt made to examine any items or objects in the case for finger prints.
C: There was nothing suitable.
M: Did you inquire at any of the grocery stores at Kakabeka Falls or Fort William?
C: Yes.
M: Did you speak to the grocery people there?
C: Yes.
M: Did you ascertain that they sent out parcels with rope?
C: Yes.
M: Are they similar to the kind you found here?
C: Yes.
M: You did not bring that out before, did you?
C: I was not asked.[8]

Maloney left it at that, having established that the officer knew before the preliminary that the ropes were in common use – and perhaps more to the point of his line of police prejudice – that Craig had not offered that information to the defence.

Each witness added a bit to Maloney's accumulation of doubt about the rope, while at the same time, adding incremental weight to the major point that the rope was all around them, and that nothing before the court could distinguish the rope involved in the crime and the rope connected to Esposito as any different. Here, he makes use of the testimony in the address to the jury.

Now, let us come to the rope. Let us come to the rope. I mention that piece of evidence for one very good reason – it is to invite you to disregard it. On the hands and around the neck of this poor lady is found rope that corresponds with rope that can be found and that admittedly is kept in every bunk house from the Lakehead to Sioux Lookout. What does that prove? Nothing. But here is something very, very sinister about the evidence of the rope. Here is something that you, charged with the proper administration of justice in the Lakehead, should not forget – we were not told that the police had investigated the grocery store in the Lakehead and Kakabeka Falls. We were not told that the police had found out that this was a common type of rope. We were not told that the police had found out that this rope was kept by every section hand from the Lakehead all the way up the line. We dragged that out. If this man had been before you without a lawyer, you would have been left with the impression clearly that rope was found on her body that corresponded and was similar to rope in his possession. Think of the damaging effect that would have had on your minds, and yet the investigating officers knew all the time when they tried to create that impression – they knew nothing whatever of any importance attached to the rope. That is a sinister piece of business indeed. I hope I never see anything like that happen, never in the experience I will have as a lawyer. Nothing turns on the rope. Shown to Doctor Ward Smith, he said, "Show them to an expert." There is only one expert in Canada, and we are told it was not shown to him at all.[9]

Maloney took a similar tack in dealing with the allegations about the brown eggs. Anybody who had anything to do with those eggs was carefully handled, in part, because the egg clue had not been mentioned at either the first or second preliminary. It came at the trial, and Maloney was not quite sure how to meet it. The information came from Dante Rossi, who reluctantly admitted to Maloney that he and Esposito were, at the time of the murder, not on the best terms. The quarrel was not serious, but it might explain why Rossi had been so busy in pointing the police at bits of evidence they might not otherwise have seen.

Maloney: Now, Mr. Rossi, you and Raffaele Esposito were mad at each other around this time, weren't you?
Rossi: We had a few words, but nothing extraordinary.
M: Were you mad at him this particular day?
R: No.
M: Were you friendly with him?
R: Not very much, because we were talking a few days before. [meaning they quarreled at that time][10]

Maloney got little more than that, but had, at least, established that Rossi was not much amused by Esposito at the time, and his eager co-operation with the police seemed to confirm that. It was Rossi who claimed to have seen Esposito using brown-shelled eggs, and it was Rossi who pointed out that this was an oddity, since all the eggs they purchased were white; it was also Rossi who pointed out that the hens at the murder site laid brown eggs.

Rossi: Saturday or Sunday I saw him eat some eggs.
Crown: In the bunk house?
R: Yes.

C: Do you know where he got the eggs.
R: No.
C: Did you have any eggs there?
R: Yes.
C: What kind of eggs did you have?
R: White eggs.
C: What kind of eggs were they that Esposito was eating?
R: Kind of brown eggs.[11]

But Rossi, under cross-examination was not entirely certain what came first – not the chicken or the egg – but a variation thereof: whether he told Inspector Craig about them or Craig told him.

Maloney: Then you gave evidence again at the second preliminary hearing on October 7th or 8th, and you never told us anything about the eggs, did you?
Rossi: They never asked me anything about it or anything like that.
M: You were asked to tell what Esposito did when he came back to the bunk house, weren't you?
R: They asked me questions, and I answered them.
M: And on that occasion you did not tell anything about the eggs?
R: I think not.
M: Who did you first tell about the eggs?
R: The Inspector? [*sic*]
M: Inspector Craig?
R: Yes.
M: Was that after the second preliminary hearing?
R: I don't remember.
M: Do you think it probably was?
R: I can't say.
M: Did he come up and ask you about it?
R: He tell me in the bunk house, and before that he did not have any eggs.
M: Did Inspector Craig come up and ask you about the eggs?
R: Yes, he asked me there for sure.
M: Was that after the preliminary hearing last October 7th or 8th?
R: I think not, but I don't know for sure.
M: Was it Inspector Craig who told you that they were brown eggs?
R: Yes – I saw myself that.

It was inconclusive and confusing. It didn't exactly prove that Inspector Craig had withheld the evidence from the second preliminary, or that he had put the idea into Rossi's head, and Rossi's slender hold on the English language could be excused for adding to the ambiguity of the situation, but Arthur left it that way – uncertainty as to what actually happened is no bad thing in a criminal defence. What Inspector Craig handed the Court was a bag full of eggs shells and an egg – the shells and the egg were brown.

Craig: On the 29th we returned to Larson, and at that time we searched a small dump to the southwest of the bunk house at Larson, and retrieved some brown egg shells. Further investigation was made in the area, and we returned to Kelly, and in the long grass just opposite the Kopplin house I retrieved a brown egg in the grass.[12]

There was never any question that the Kopplins kept chickens, and that those chickens laid brown eggs. It took Maloney's cross-examination to put them into a context that suggested either that Craig was incompetent or too crafty by half.

Maloney: You say that you found the egg shells on what date?
Craig: The 29th.
M: Ten days after the commission of this terrible crime?
C: Yes.
M: Eight days after the accused was taken into custody?
C: That is right.
M: And found where?
C: In the dump on the southwest corner of the bunk house at Larson.
M: A dump or a garbage tin?
C: No, it is a small dump.
M: A hole in the ground?
C: Yes.
M: And on the top of the pile?
C: Yes.
M: And freshly put there?
C: No, mixed in.
M: At the top of the pile?
C: Yes, at the top, and mixed in.
M: And recently put there?
C: It had not been there too long ...
M: The accused had not been there for a week?
C: No.
M: And he could not have put those egg shells there?
C: He could have.
M: And after finding the egg shells you went down to the scene of the crime and you say you found the egg in the grass?
C: I did.
M: And those are the egg and egg shells you did not tell us anything about until now?
C: That is right.[13]

Just previous to this exchange, Maloney had suggested to Craig that the continuing appearances of bits of rope that had turned up after the initial investigation might have led him to ask Rossi if he was adding richness to the stew Esposito was in. Craig dismissed the suggestion tersely. Something of the same must have crossed his mind on the matter of the eggs, but he restrained himself, choosing to do his damage in the matter with the help of the experts. Dr. Smith was to be the first to be found wanting, although Maloney commenced modestly enough:

Maloney: The egg itself is marked as having come from the Kopplin chickens – is there any other word there that is obliterated? – By the way, what are your particular qualifications about eggs and egg shells?
Smith: My particular qualifications would be those of being able to examine from the point of view of markings and comparing the colour and range of colours under identical conditions, and those of any investigator ...

Here enters Arthur Maloney, *naif* and innocently curious:

M: I do not have any qualifications at all as a layman. Do you have some special training about eggs and their development?
S: Yes – not their development – from courses in comparative biology.
M: Are you more qualified to express an opinion of the similarity between this egg and these egg shells than any member of the jury panel?
S: No, only that I have examined the irregularities in the surface of the shell which I know from my experience grow out of the way in which the egg shell is laid down, and I have satisfied myself about having come from a given source, but not necessarily having come from the given source. [Whatever that might mean. Arthur seemed prepared to leave it for the moment.]
M: There are different types of birds lay eggs?
S: Yes.
M: Are you in a position to say whether a particular egg came from a particular type of bird?
S: I know little more than the average man about that particular topic.
M: So you could not really tell us whether the egg involved in or forming part of exhibit eighteen came from a chicken at all?
S: I could indicate the high probability that it came from a chicken.
M: But you could not swear to it?
S: Well, if you wanted to postulate some strange type of bird, I would have to agree it might be possible.

There was more of the same with Maloney gently knocking the poor doctor about in the box without actually deriding him; it was a very mild, cat-and-mouse exhibition, which led from question to question, leading inevitably down hill for the witness:

M: But having regard to the points of dissimilarity, it is equally consistent that it did not come from that source?
S: No, I could not – I could not make an identification ...
M: You do not know, in other words, what source the egg shells came from?
S: No, nor the egg.
M: And you are not in a position to say whether the egg shells all came from the same source?
S: No, nor the egg. ...
M: And you are not in a position to say whether they all came from the same source originally?
S: No – they are similar in size – and there is a range of colours. ...
M: You are not in a position to say whether the egg shells forming part of the exhibit were chickens' eggs?
S: No, no more than with respect to the egg itself.

Then he chose to put the poor fellow out of his misery:

M: So, really, your evidence in regard to the eggs, apart your qualifications, does not add much to the case?
S: No, only that it could be from the same source and it could be from different sources.[14]

Exactly. Well, not quite. Arthur moved on to other less painful things.

The Crown, however, seemed to have a yearning for punishment in the case, and later on Dr. Albert E. Allin, the pathologist, was dragged into the matter of the eggs, despite the previous virtuoso performance that Arthur had performed on the hapless Dr. Smith.

Crown: Doctor Allin, in addition to you being a pathologist I believe you are also an ornithologist, is that right?
Allin: I believe so. [Which should have warned the Crown that all was not going to be well.]
C: Perhaps you could tell the jury what that is?
A: Well, first of all, I should say that my avocation or my hobby is that of a naturalist or conservationist, and it goes back to your original question of what my qualifications are, and I stated I was a graduate in biology and medicine from the University of Toronto in 1929, so I had two years in honour biology as well as my medical, and subsequently I have continued my hobby of natural history,

and particularly birds or ornithology, and belong to most of the leading bird societies of Eastern North America, and I hold a permit from the Federal Government to collect birds and their eggs for this area.

After much brandishing of his years of note-taking, the doctor came to the conclusion that the egg in the whole state, found at the murder scene and the bits of shell did not come from the same hen, but that the shells were likely to be the product of a chicken. Maloney was prepared to accept the first conclusion, but thought he might just be able to undermine the second, and cast doubt upon the proposition that Esposito was necessarily cooking chicken eggs. This seems to be a case, again, of Maloney picking up an idea on the fly from the prosecution. Very late in the examination-in-chief, the Crown, seemingly to buttress Allin's qualifications to talk about eggs, had led him into padding his background experience.

C: Of course, in dealing with your hobby, have you made a collection of eggs?
A: I have.
C: And what kind of birds did you get them from?
A: I have not a complete collection of the local birds' eggs, but between my colleague whom I am usually out with and myself we have almost the complete collection of the eggs of birds which occur in this area, and my colleague's collection I have examined almost as many times. I have looked at my own, so I am familiar with both my own and his.
C: Do you know a partridge egg?
A: I do – we have three kinds of partridge or prairie chickens in this area, and of which the ordinary partridge is most common, but this year is extremely rare. It lays a brown egg, in colour not too different from the egg here, but in contrast to this, one which measures two and a half – slightly under two and a half inches in length, – the maximum size of partridge eggs is one and a half to one and three-fifths, and they have a shorter and rounder tendency than the oval shape of the hen's egg.[15]

Every trial lawyer knows, sometimes to his grief and sometimes to his advantage, to be wary of the expert who comes bearing a too eager opinion of his knowledge – he is likely to talk too much, and Maloney was particularly good at responding immediately to the gift of informed fulsomeness. The cross-examination began with some back-and-forth skirmishing over the exact colour of the shattered egg shells, but Maloney managed to get the doctor to admit that there were several shades of brown in the pile, and that he believed, "it is most likely that they came from different hens." Maloney started, ever so gently, to lay on the irony:

Maloney: And then in your expert capacity as an egg man, we can come to this conclusion, that the whole egg forming part of exhibit eighteen and the egg shells certainly did not come from the same source?
Allin: I do not think they came from the same hen.

But Maloney wanted more than that from the "egg man" – he wanted to get him to admit that the source of the fragments might not be a chicken. And the witness had given him the birds to try it on.

M: Did they come necessarily from the same type of hen?
A: I believe they came from the same major type of hen which lays a brown egg rather than that large group of hens which lays a white egg.
M: Are you familiar with the ruffled grouse.
A: That is our common partridge of the north which I said this year is uncommon.
M: What is the time of the year that it is normal to find eggs of the ruffled grouse in this district?
A: From late April until early June, and with the great preponderance in the latter part of May, but with overlapping into June and into April.
M: I understand you had a very late spring in this area?
A: Yes.
M: And the effect of the lateness of the spring would delay the egg-laying process?
A: We come to the same result. I do not think it delayed the original laying, but I believe there was a tendency for lost broods to later nest.
M: So there would be nothing unusual this year finding grouse eggs in this general area around the end of June?
A: In this year?
M: Yes.
A: It would not be particularly unusual.
M: It would not be unusual at all having regard to the lateness of the spring?
A: It is unusual to find them because they are so rare, but not so unusual in this year – it is not unusual this year because it is late to find them towards the end of the month.
M: And their eggs are brown?
A: Their eggs are brown.
M: Is there any difference between the ruffled grouse and the young partridge?
A: The ruffled grouse is the so-called birch partridge in this area.
M: What about the prairie chicken: what colour are its eggs?
A: The eggs of the prairie chicken are also a shade of brown, and usually somewhat lighter than this, and of the same size, and that bird is extremely rare in this area.
M: I understand it had been seen from time to time in the Kelly area?

A: That is perfectly correct. I said it was rare; I did not say it was non-extant. I have seen one set of eggs in twenty years, and that was in the Kelly area – I am speaking of the sharp-tailed grouse.
M: And it has been seen in the Kelly area?
A: On one occasion there was one dead bird found on the railway track.
M: And it lays a brown egg?
A: Yes, a very small brown egg; it is spherical to slightly elongated or ovate.
M: And what other kind of bird lays brown eggs?
A: Spruce partridge, only its eggs are mottled and splotched with dark red or purple, and it is a small egg – approximately one to one and three-fifths inches in diameter.
M: And another type of bird?
A: The American bittern – I think some people call it a mud hen. It lays a brown egg, oval in shape, but rather an olive brown ...
M: And anything else that lays a brown egg?
A: Well, still using brown in a rather general sense – there are certain ducks – the pin tail and the mallard and black, which lays an egg which would be considered a very light shade of brown.
M: And anything else?
A: I do not think so. I cannot think of any.[16]

In the jury address, Maloney goes about pulling all this testimony together in a manner similar to his work with the rope, not only to discredit the value of the same, but also to add to the suspicion that the police were determined, despite the facts, to pile this evidence on, however thin it might seem.

Now, let us come to the egg shells. Remember the first preliminary hearing in August; remember the judge in Toronto; remember the second preliminary hearing in October. I never once heard that egg shells had the slightest connection with the case. What are you entitled to think? When you hear about egg shells for the first time after a judge at Toronto says, "Produce more evidence against this man or let him go." What are you entitled to think? You and I know and think it. What is the evidence about the egg shells? It is alleged, first of all, that on Saturday or Sunday, the accused man was seen to cook some eggs for his lunch. Rossi says that. Bear in mind, it is always Rossi who strives to tell the strongest tale against us, and do not forget the significance of that. On Saturday or Sunday he says the accused man cooked himself some eggs. On June 21st, the accused man is arrested. June 22nd goes by, and so does the 23rd, the 24th, the 25th, and so on, all the way down the line to the 29th, when Rossi brings Inspector Craig to the dump, and on the top of the dump he finds some egg shells – eight days later – ten days after the 19th – at a time when the accused man was in the custody of the law, at a time when Rossi was the only one who occupied that bunk house, at a time when everyone in Larson had access to that dump, and if I had known what the evidence of the eggs was going to be, I would have asked his Lordship not to have allowed you to hear it, and I will ask him to tell you to disregard it now. That is the least suspicious piece of evidence I have ever heard in a criminal case of any kind; and lo and behold, they fly up Doctor Smith all the way from Toronto to hold up an egg and to hold up the egg shells, and say, "In my opinion, gentlemen, they are similar," and he does not know any more about eggs than you do. The only man who knows less about chickens than Doctor Smith is myself, because he never accused a rooster of laying an egg. Suppose he did have brown eggs, if you call them brown. I don't; they are white to me. Suppose he was seen to cook the eggs. We have the evidence of Doctor Allin, who is also an ornithologist, who tells us of three or four different types of birds that lay eggs up in this type of community, and would have been laying eggs around the time that this happened – brown eggs. Rossi did not take out a ruler like Doctor Allin did, and measure the eggs shells. Even if Rossi is telling the truth, all he can say is "I saw a man with egg shells that were brown."[17]

Maloney worked his way through the rope and egg evidence without too much trouble with the judge, but he got on his nerves when he started to work out the topography surrounding the murder site. Arthur wanted, in fact, to bring two things together – the fact, as he saw it, that although there were not any roads to the site, there were still plenty of ways of getting there, through the bush, and he also wanted to suggest that, despite the fact that only one eccentric old man had been seen anywhere near the site, save for Esposito, there were plenty of men who might have got there if they had the mind to do so. He knew, as every good criminal counsel knows, that he didn't have to prove that anyone had done so, but only to convince the jury that others might have done so. But to do that, he had to get them some way to get around, and the original idea put to the jury was that the railway line, which Esposito had used on the handcar, was the only way to go. One of the CNR draughtsmen helped him to attack that theory.

Maloney: I have one more question I forgot – what about roads into Kelly, ordinary roads?

R. MacKinnon: Well, there is no road that is accessible to any vehicular traffic.

M: Do you know of any trails?

R.M.: There is – I understand there is a trail from Savanne, but I have never actually travelled on it myself.

...

M: You said you were familiar with the topography of the land at the rear of the Kopplin property?

R.M.: Well, I would not say – I have been through there doing ditching work. We have done a considerable amount of ditching work all through the Graham sub-division, and I have been in there with our engineers, but the general idea is that it is wet ground and it is not too passable.
M: How far south of the Kopplin property are you talking about when you say that?
R.M.: Well, in that area I have been back in there about a quarter of a mile.
M: And have you ever walked any distance once you got to that point – have you ever walked any distance east or west through the bush?
R.M.: Yes, we have walked back and forth in there, to some extent.
M: And what do you say about that?
R.M.: It is not easily accessible to walk through. It is swampy, and muskeg.
M: What distance did you walk east and west?
R.M.: Well, I would not like to say immediately in the vicinity of that residence, but back in behind there, between Larson and in through that area, I guess I have been about a mile away from the track.

The witness made it clear that the area was a mess of water, rock and dead-fall trees, but he also admitted that it was passable – if slow work.

R.M.: ... you could walk through it – it is wet in places, and there have been logging operations carried on there several years ago, and unless you had a purpose in being there, you would not go there – unless there was some reason for being there, like making a ditching survey, or hunting ...
M: Supposing you were to walk one hundred yards south into the bush behind the Kopplin dwelling and then turn to the west and try to walk a mile in a westerly direction, have you any estimate of how long a time it would take?
R.M.: I would not like to say definitely on that, how long it would take. That would depend pretty much on who was walking there and all the other circumstances.
M: Well, supposing you were walking it?
R.M.: Well, it would take you probably three-quarters of an hour.

Maloney had coaxed an admission from this witness that it could be walked, and he had also got a time on the possibility of how long it might take to walk from Kelly to Larson or vice versa. But he wanted more.

M: Have you ever seen any of the bush camps located in the bush between Kelly and Larson?
R.M.: No, I have never seen any of them. They are not in operation at the present time, to the best of my knowledge.
M: Have you any knowledge of the trappers who carry on their business in that area?

R.M.: No.
M: Are you aware of the fact that there are trappers there?
R.M.: I understand there are trappers in there.[18]

It might be dense, and it might be dirty, and damp, but there were trails back in there, and they were passable, and there were trappers back there – somewhere. Closer to home, there were others who had been wandering around in the back country off the tracks between Larson and Kelly. Rossi, the ubiquitous taleteller, and another labourer, Johnny Lylak, went for a little walk.

Maloney: And when you went out on your trip with Lylak did you walk along the track.
Rossi: Yes.
M: So you started to walk east towards Kelly?
R: Yes.
...
M: And how many miles did you walk on the track proceeding east from Larson towards Kelly?
R: I don't know for sure – about two miles.
M: Could it have been more?
R: Maybe.
M: And when you turned off the track, where did you go?
R: In the camp.
M: How far was the camp from the track?
R: Maybe two or three miles.
...
M: And when you left the track was there a path or a trail?
R: Yes, there was a slight road, but there was growth and trees ...
M: Could you tell me how many miles on the road or trail you walked?
R: Two or three – I don't know how many miles.
M: How long did it take you to walk from Larson down the track to the point where you turned off the track?[19]

Rossi guessed that it took them an hour to walk down the track, and a couple of hours to get to the camp, where they spent about an hour, where the two men wandered about, rowed a boat on the lake, and got lost for a short time. His companion had a somewhat different idea of the distances, and the times, but otherwise, their stories coincided. The point was simple – two other men from Larson had started out in the direction of Kelly prior to the time of the murder, and claimed to have branched off into the woods.

Constable Douglas Forbes added something further to the mix of trails and men that Arthur Maloney was slowly putting together.

Maloney: There is a paper mill in this vicinity, is there – aren't there big piles of lumber and things like that between Linco and Kelly?
Forbes: Yes, that is the road where the Great Lakes camp used to be located, and a few hundred yards west of that, on the CNR Sioux Lookout line, there are in the neighbourhood of a thousand cords of wood piled there.

...

I believe there are jobbers in there working.
M: How far east of Kelly is it located?
F: That would be about twelve and a half or twelve and three-quarters miles east.

...

M: You do not know where the men live who work on that lumber?
F: I don't know – I think they were making living quarters there for them.
M: You do not know whether they were younger or older men?
F: No, the only person I saw there were two caretakers, and they were cleaning up the place.[20]

The judge was becoming restless with all this searching out of trails, but Maloney tried it on two further witnesses. One, a trapper, estimated that there were at least four other trappers working in the bush behind the railway line in the vicinity of the murder site at Kelly. The second, Frank Henry Kailik, a section foreman, was not much help; he had denied seeing anybody using the trails, save for hunters in the autumn. Maloney squeezed him to admit that there were possibly further trails in the area, and got him to do so, if tepidly – and then the judge stepped in.

Maloney: There is maybe another trail?
Kailik: Yes, it may be.
HIS LORDSHIP: Why waste any more time on this trail.

The judge may not have known what Maloney was up to, but Arthur let him know that he did:

M: Trails are a pretty important item in this case.
H.L.: I think we have heard enough evidence about the trails. However, go on.
M: Well, I am finished, as a matter of fact.[21]

And as a matter of fact, he was – he had enough for what he wanted to do in the jury address, since he had also managed to ascertain that there was a crew working the railway line on the afternoon in question, and though the foremen insisted that they never lost sight of a man, there was some uncertainty about how true that could be for the entire time, given the manner in which they were spread out along the line. Once again he had it all there – it was simply a matter of putting it together persuasively.

I want to address myself to this so-called process of elimination that the Crown used, allegedly to establish this man's complicity in this most terrible crime. The Crown says, we will find out every one who might have done it, and we will eliminate them, and that will prove by the process of elimination that the accused must have done it, so they take all the possible suspects. They take Rossi, first of all, and Lylak, and the Crown says, "Well, they did not do it"; they told you they went down the track to an abandoned bush camp. Who says so? Did you see them go there? Did I? Did my friend? They said so; what else do you think they would say? Do not forget what I mentioned briefly a little while ago – in giving you various people as possible suspects, I am not for a moment suggesting that they are guilty. I have no right to do that, because I have nothing but suspicion against them, but all I ask is that I be given the same consideration. Do not forget that at three o'clock Rossi and Lylak, having suddenly formed the intention to go to an abandoned bush camp, set out east towards Kelly. How long did it take as they travelled down the track? Rossi says an hour, and Lylak says half an hour. How long did it take once you got into the bush? An hour says Rossi; an hour, says Lylak. How long from the track back to Larson? One hour, says Rossi; half an hour, says Lylak – seven hours in all, says Rossi ... Do not forget that when you are considering whether or not the Crown has eliminated all possible suspects. Once you establish that this lady was alive at eleven-thirty, as I submit she clearly was, Esposito is less suspect than anyone else in the vicinity, because he is the only one seen to walk away to Larson. Two other men are seen to walk right down in the direction of the lady's house.

It was obvious by now that Maloney was working on the idea of reasonable doubt, bringing into play, as was a common mark of his defence work, the possibility of alternatives that the police had not chosen to investigate. In order to make it work, of course, the possibilities have to be credible, and Maloney was exceptionally talented in developing other worlds of action outside that which the police had chosen to take.

What search was made by the investigating officers for the abandoned camp? None. What search was made for the lake? None. What search for a boat? None. What search to show they had fired their guns? None. When Dante Rossi and Lylak told them that version of their conduct, why was an investigation not made to prove its truth or falsity? When Esposito told them that he had gone out in a boat in the lake, what did they do? They went to find out if there was a lake, – and there was. They went to find out if there was a boat – and there was. They did not tell that evidence until I dragged it out of them ... You may think when you consider the nature of the perfectly horrible injuries to this poor lady, that

> one man could not have done it ... How could he tie her if he was alone ... Who held her while the ropes were tied? Examine the injuries to her head – two different types of instruments – I do not know whether two men did it. That rather suggests to me that two men might well have done it ... they were a matter of only a few miles from the scene of the crime once they get into that bush, if they did go into the bush.

The same sort of ruminative doubt was used on another worker, Tiano, whom the dead woman had complained about to her husband in a letter, but so ambiguously that it wasn't quite clear what was bothering her. Tiano explained that it was simply a matter of a language difficulty, and that when she thought he was making an improper suggestion, he was really trying to buy a rooster. But Tiano was not in the area at the time of the murder. That did not deter Arthur, who was a master of making bricks of suspicion from the straw of ignorance.

> Do you believe for one single moment that is the reason why Mrs. Kopplin wanted to confide some secret to her husband? ... What had Tiano done? You do not know; I do not know; my friend does not know; we will never know. This is important in considering this possibility – the husband's original plan was to return to Kelly on June 19th. That plan was changed. ... I am going to come instead on the 25th – six days later – the following Friday. Anyone who had a single solitary reason for getting rid of Mrs. Kopplin before her husband returned, this was his last chance ... But we are told he [Tiano] is not a suspect. He went to town. He stayed at the Princess Hotel. He did not come back until Sunday. Who said so? Did you see him in town? Did I? Did my friend? He said so; Borrelli said so; and Kuryliw said so. Where is the register from the hotel, and even if that is produced, why did they check out at eight o'clock in the morning? ... He is not a suspect. Why? That is what I would like to know. Why isn't he a suspect?

Maloney often used this technique of spreading the choices in his defences, searching for suspects, evidence. Not to prove them. He never took a step out of the way to find the answer to his questions. Where some counsel would have gone out to find out the truth about these other men, Arthur used his ignorance – and everyone else's, not to prove that his client could not have done the criminal act, but to suggest that he was not the only one who could, pushing the Crown's case into a dog's dinner of choices. In this case, it seemed particularly appropriate to wonder why the police did not check these stories more closely – and the answer had been developed from early on in the defence. Craig and company had made up their minds that Esposito was the man, and had ignored, in their pigheadedness, the surrounding terrain of conduct, sufficiently so for Maloney to use it to create doubt, not only as to the fairness of their investigation, but as to the conclusion they had reached, which could only obtain, perhaps, if they looked no further.

I am not accusing anyone of the murder here. I have no right to. I have not got enough evidence against them, but I have more reason to be suspicious of the three men I have mentioned so far than of the accused.

He piled on the possibilities:

What about the Indian trappers. They called one, who says that he did not do it, but adds to the confusion by saying that there are four or five others in the area. Who are they? What did they look like? ... Where were they on June 19th? What about the lumber project just twelve miles east. How many men were working there? We do not know. A lot of men – I cannot tell you. Old men? ... Young men? ... Men with criminal records? – I do not know – nor do you. Where were they on Saturday June 19th? ... what about all those male passengers on the local that went through Kelly that afternoon ... all the men on the extra gang ... There are perhaps hundreds of others who have not been eliminated, and some of them are men against whom greater suspicion attaches for the reason I have already suggested than against this accused man. Having mentioned these additional suspects whose movements have not been accounted for, let me remind you again – I am entitled to the benefit of the doubt.[22]

Of course, this kind of thrashing about for other villains can be self-defeating and sometimes ridiculous; what saves the Maloney musings from such fate is the careful way in which he built up the whole picture – the landscape, the trails, the distances, the back woods camps, the presence of a few men who testified to their wandering about in the bush, and the presence of dozens of others, railroad gangs, trappers, itinerants who did not. The case started with Esposito on his own, pumping his way back from Kelly in the morning, and emerging from the bush close to Larson in the early evening, but by the time Maloney got through with the testimony of several witnesses, it was possible to presume that the place might well have been crawling with other men, most of whom were like Esposito, far away from female companionship, at loose ends on a pleasant Saturday afternoon, and well able to slip through the bushes into the Kelly compound.

There were other matters to be spoken to, such as the claim that Esposito had spoken of sexually accosting Mrs. Kopplin, but Maloney simply put that into the context of the kind of common dirty talk that men indulge in, particularly when they are deprived of female company. But he also made further use of it. Some of the men claimed that no such talk ever occurred in the bunkhouses, but they seemed to help Maloney rather than hinder him with their lame, shame-faced replies. "Bear in mind that they lied when they told me that they never talked about women or sex ..."

He was so confident that he had made his case out of the mouths of the Crown witnesses that he asked for a non-suit – a dismissal of the charge by the judge on the grounds that there was not a sufficient case to be met by the defence. He was denied that way out of the matter, but was still sufficiently confident that he refused to put in any evidence, thus gaining the opportunity to speak to the jury after the Crown. The jury were out for just over half an hour, and the verdict of not guilty was returned.

It was a masterful example of how a criminal lawyer can live off the evidence of the Crown, and how he could establish the basis for the address to the jury by, in a sense, not simply cross-examining for the purpose of undermining the case, but for the more difficult purpose of building the defence. Not a word of evidence was heard from the defence – it all came from the prosecution.

6

The Fifties and Politics

One of Maloney's longest and most typical associations with other lawyers occurred during the fifties; it began while he was still with the Edmonds firm, and continued for several years. John O'Driscoll came from Sault Ste. Marie first to St. Michael's and then to Osgoode, and returned there to article in the year 1953–54, but he needed an office in Toronto for his final year at Osgoode. He knew no Toronto lawyer, but his principal in the Sault, Terence Murphy, had used Arthur for agency work and offered to speak to him. O'Driscoll was interviewed by Arthur in May 1953 and was engaged, but instead of coming in the autumn as the Osgoode term started, he came earlier since Stanton Hogg, the student in residence, who was to go on to a career as a spirited, pugnacious Crown in the late fifties, was leaving. "I arrived in June 1954. Next door, Pat Galligan [who was to wind up on the Ontario Court of Appeal] was starting to article with G. Arthur Martin. I had planned to return to the Sault on graduating, but that spring [1954], the firm of Edmonds, Maloney, Nelligan, and Edmonds needed someone since Nelligan was going to Ottawa. They asked me to stay, at least for a year. Arthur suggested that it was easy to go out of Toronto, but very difficult to come in, and I should give it a try." The Edmonds firm was a very loose arrangement: "It was really two firms in one," says Mr. Justice John O'Driscoll, "on the eighteenth floor of the Star building. In the next suite of offices Carrick, O'Connor, Coutts and Rogers had something of the same arrangement." O'Driscoll worked exclusively for Arthur, and proved, very quickly, to be a lawyer of considerable intelligence and scholarship. Arthur made full use of his ability to read law, but he did not sequester him in the library.

Within twelve months I had been in every court in the province, including the Supreme Court of Canada. He was very good in that way. We did a lot of agency work from the north country, both civil and criminal, and a lot of appeal work. I learned what a super lawyer Arthur was. Of course, everyone knew he had a great gift with a jury, but he was great in the Court of Appeal, and in the

> Supreme Court of Canada. Up until he got into politics, it was just organized pandemonium. He would show up and listen, and bang, bang – he made decisions – one of the things about Arthur was that if he got into something he was either fascinated or totally bored, and if the details were not interesting, he would ignore them. If he was interested, he would work night and day, even if it was for free. He didn't like the drudgery; not that he couldn't do it, if he had to. He could handle people, juries, judges, publicity, but if he was bored, he would lose interest no matter how much money was involved.

O'Driscoll does not remember if there was any particular reason for the cooling relation with the older Edmonds, but suspects that Arthur's personal involvement in Federal politics, which began 1955, might have brought to an end the mildly uneasy connection between the two men. The new burden of political whisperings might have been enough. Arthur was not, as he was to be generally from that time forward, simply sharing office space, but was part of the firm, and as such, he was responsible for bringing fees into the practice. His tendency to ignore this obligation may have irritated Edmonds (as it was later to irritate O'Driscoll), and O'Driscoll feels that Edmonds's natural primness was offended by the unsavoury characters who often turned up as Arthur's clients. His son, who is still in practice in Toronto, cannot remember any particular quarrel between the two men, but does admit that Arthur's type of practice discomfited his father.

Late in 1957, Arthur and John O'Driscoll left, and moved to 320 Bay Street, the Canada Permanent Building, sharing office space with the Carrick, O'Connor firm, which had also moved over from the Star building. G. Arthur Martin was just down the hall. By this time, Arthur was in the House of Commons, and things were even more frenetic for O'Driscoll, who was expected to run the office, keep Arthur's cases organized and prepared for trial, and also carry his own case load. Unlike many MPs, Arthur was determined to practice while serving in Ottawa, and it made office life extremely difficult. John O'Driscoll remembers one case, *Sagan v. the Town of Hawkesbury,* when they almost didn't get to the court on time. Mr. Sagan's house had caught on fire; the Hawkesbury fire department arrived, but there was no water pressure in the hydrant; the house burned down. Sagan had no insurance, and sued the town. Mr. Justice Kelly found that the town, even if it had a fire department, had no obligation to attend the fire, and even if they did come, they had no obligation to attempt to put the fire out. Their only obligation, according to the judge's reading of the Municipal Act, was to refrain from making things worse than they found them. If that was so, it was parliamentary draughting at its most ludicrous, but O'Driscoll, preparing the appeal, was convinced that Mr. Justice Kelly's reading was correct.

Arthur was up in Ottawa, but he had to argue it. They wanted him. I'll never forget it. I tried to get him to discuss it. I tried to corner him and sit him down to talk about this thing. I was petrified because Andy Brewin was on the other side, and that meant trouble. Finally I got him on the Sunday night on the phone and said, 'Arthur, this thing is on tomorrow morning!' So we agreed to meet at Osgoode outside the Appeal court on Monday morning. It was to be heard first thing at eleven o'clock. We met on the second floor of the rotunda at Osgoode at 9:00 a.m., and we just walked around the upper passage of the rotunda. I don't know how long – probably until we had to go in. I told him all the facts [laughs], all the law, and we went in, and both Andy and Arthur put their case. When Arthur was called and got up – well, if you hadn't known, as I did, you would have thought that he had written several books on Municipal law, and I sat there with my mouth open. How could somebody grasp all this detail in such a short time? I was fascinated; his mind was so quick, so sharp, and so fast. Anyway, I suppose to rub salt into the wounds, the Court of Appeal dismissed our appeal, but congratulated Arthur for the fine factum he had offered!

O'Driscoll had more to contend with than simply catching Arthur on the fly. They did a lot of work in the fifties, but didn't make much money. O'Driscoll was not a partner, and had no control over the finances. From the beginning, he was ill paid, and worried about Arthur's penchant for taking cases off the street that did not and could not pay. His disapproval of this unbusinesslike conduct is still tempered by an admiration for the same, and is, perhaps, the most telling comment upon the Maloney career at the law.

I often thought, without any adverse reflection on Arthur Martin or John Robinette, that there was no lawyer I ever knew who would put as much blood, sweat, and tears into hopeless cases as he did. The worse the odds, the harder he fought, but beyond that, he would take anything on. Lots of times I would get an order from on high, and I would say that there's no money in it, and he would say, "Do it!" You have to look at it from that point of view. We put a lot of free days in. He would look at a case, and see an injustice going on. Not just sensational cases, or important cases. Arthur was at home with anyone; he took cases because they intrigued him, and anyone could reach him. He was the same with a cab driver as he was with a judge or a jury. We'd get into a cab, and we'd have a client when we got out. He didn't chase ambulances, but he got an awful lot of clients off the street.

Maloney was, in many ways, the link between the dignified bar of pin-striped counsel, kept at a distance behind a barrier of mahogany doors and glassed-in receptionists, and the Runyonesque practitioners of the magistrate's courts, taking cases for whatever the clients, shuffling their feet on the butt-littered floors of the basement courtrooms in City Hall, had in their pockets. The criminal law was just getting some respectability, thanks to the distinguished work of men like Martin and Dubin and the dignity they brought to the practice – but here was their contemporary and companion practitioner, still flirting with the old idea of the criminal mouthpiece, rubbing shoulders with the unwashed and destitute. As O'Driscoll remembers him, "His strength was in the criminal work because he was exasperated with civil paper chase. He practiced by word of mouth; he dropped in to see the Crown – to kid around. No-one had any files or notes to speak of; he was a maverick and it suited him. He wasn't purely altruistic; he knew if he did a good job on an interesting case, it would be noticed, but money didn't drive him at all."

Arthur had learned, early on, the trick of simplifying a case, of channelling it into a persuasive point of view that was readily understandable not only to the judge, but, particularly, to a jury. O'Driscoll watched Maloney perfect this technical skill:

> In most cases, if you can find some catch phrase and keep repeating it, they will remember it, and Arthur was a master of this. As far as oratory, I never heard addresses to the jury from the simple standpoint of oratory that would touch his. Some counsel might make better arguments on a legal basis, but for spellbinding, I never heard better. And he had a good sense of how to run a trial with one eye on the judge and jury, and one on the Court of Appeal. And this was despite the fact that he had a tendency to bore easily. Sometimes that would happen with a case; he would give you the instruction to show up at the court with the law prepared, and feed it to him as he needed it. Sometimes he would be unnerving because he would feel he had enough to keep him going, and he just wouldn't listen. It's not that he would go in unprepared, but he would go in less prepared than most counsel, and he would ask me to hold off any more information until he needed it. If you look through the Reports of the fifties, we did an awful lot of work that was important enough to get recorded.[1]

He rarely prosecuted, although trial lawyers sometimes get very lucrative cases from the provincial or federal governments if their political credentials are correct. Bob Johnstone remembers Arthur telling him that he never had much interest in taking those cases, and that those he did take often turned out badly. Johnstone once watched him prosecute a complicated combines case. Maloney was obviously ill-at-ease, and bored; he wasn't making mistakes, but he wasn't doing much of anything. "At the break, he came over and looked at me and gave a sheepish little grin. We walked out together and he put his arm around my shoulder, and pulled me over close as if he didn't want anyone to hear,

'I told you years ago that I couldn't work with any enthusiasm for the prosecution.' I didn't say anything – just laughed."[2]

John O'Driscoll's business relation with Arthur was as close as Arthur ever got to running a law firm. He felt most comfortable with other lawyers at hand, particularly if they were former students, or men he liked personally, but he never made any attempt to build a firm, although there were plenty of lawyers who would have been happy to join him. O'Driscoll was less of a drinker than many of Arthur's students; they had a candid, easy-going relationship. But it wasn't the start of a dignified structure of legal moment. Although Maloney liked to adorn his own office with mementos and photographs of his family (he had, for instance, a mural of a country scene stretching around three walls of his office at 320 Bay that appeared suddenly in early 1958, and was probably painted by a Parkdale admirer of limited skill), he seemed to have no desire to possess grandiose office surroundings. He was practising very modestly during the time with O'Driscoll; not exactly, as is sometimes said of criminal lawyers – "out of his hat," but not far from it. His share of the office consisted of two rooms right at the front of the Carrick suite, facing each other across the reception area. O'Driscoll and later Paul Hess, his old St. Michael's schoolmate, who replaced O'Driscoll, had the second office. The one secretary shared a very tiny office just inside the hall door with Clive Bynoe's secretary, and Bynoe had the facing office on the other side of the door.

Arthur was very fortunate in his choice of secretaries, who often stayed with him for years, at low pay, and long hours. They were given a good deal of responsibility, and were often fiercely loyal to him, even when he was driving them unconscionably. The secretary at that time of the break with Edmonds was Marjorie Dickson, a tiny, lively, bird-like woman in early middle age, from London, Ontario. She had been John Nelligan's secretary at Edmonds, and came with O'Driscoll, but served both men in the new firm. Students with him in the late fifties remember it was very hectic in the confined quarters. Arthur was commuting regularly to Ottawa – making flying visits to Toronto to meet court appearances or to appear at political meetings. Although he had a lively riding organization in Parkdale, the politics still came through the office, and Marjorie Dickson was responsible for dealing with them, as well as all the office paper work. It was a job of considerable tension and responsibility, since she also ran the books, attempted to collect fees, and keep track of the student. She was a cheerful, slightly rattled, scatty woman who was enormously capable, and kind. Most law offices have a senior secretary who knows everything and can make life miserable for a student if they have any inclination to do so, particularly if they know, as they usually do, more about law, and specifically, more about the maddening art of preparing and filing court documents. Often in non-trial offices, the secretaries know considerably more about real estate, corporation law, and estate matters than their employers, and they teach, or don't teach, as the spirit moves them, the students how to produce the paper needed to facilitate the complicated processes of the law. Marjorie Dickson took on that role with care and considerable patience. She was continually harassed by always importunate and sometimes irrelevant phone calls. She rarely got much help from Arthur when it came to getting fees from a client. She would often scuttle into his office as a new client left, and would return just as quickly, admitting irritably that he hadn't discussed money – again. She was to leave at the end of the fifties, worn out by Arthur's easy way about financing the office, and by the general pressure of the practice, complicated as it was by political demands. She was not the first to go.

By early 1958, John O'Driscoll was doing most of the work in the office, with Arthur coming down from Ottawa to take cases that demanded his services. They made a good team; both graduates of St. Mike's, and serious Catholics – the resemblance stopped there. John O'Driscoll in the nineties is not unlike the young lawyer of the fifties, a diminutive, fair-haired man, whose nickname is "Archie" (picked up at St. Mike's since his studious conduct suggested the possibility that he might well become an Archbishop if he chose to join the Church), with a thin, high voice, and a quiet, unassuming demeanour, whose stern Catholicism sometimes shows up in his judgments – not always to his advantage. He learned much from Arthur, but he never imitated him, and given his low-keyed personality, it is unlikely that he would have been a success had he tried to model his work on that of his principal. He is similar to Arthur Martin and Charlie Dubin in his deliberate absence of colour, his natural *gravitas,* and matter-of-fact particularity. He prepared well (which is one of the best compliments that a counsel can receive), and that preparation and a good legal mind was to be the basis for his early success. He had his own air of muted confidence and wit, and an instinct for putting his cases together persuasively that was much admired in the courts, and he became a very busy counsel before his early ascent to the Ontario Supreme Court. Being with Arthur had given him the chance at serious cases, and within a surprisingly short time, he was a thoroughly competent trial lawyer. But the firm made little real money. Like James, Arthur was tight with his juniors, in part because the money simply was not there; his income tax returns at this time show he was making surprisingly little for a major counsel. His bank was continually, tactfully, reminding him of his overdraft.

O'Driscoll had married and had begun a family, but Arthur did not increase his salary. O'Driscoll asked for a raise. "I left because he would not pay any more. We didn't quarrel about it. I asked for a raise, and he said 'no,' so I left to go out on my own with Bernie Kelly [who had been a school mate of O'Driscoll at St. Mike's and was later to become the Regional Senior Judge for Metropolitan Toronto in the Provincial Court Division. Another St. Mike's friend, Nick McRae, was to come out of the Crown's office to join them, and later follow O'Driscoll to the Supreme Court.] Poor Marjorie was also unhappy; she was getting a hundred calls a day, and seventy-five percent of them were political, and, as you know, she finally got tired of it and went back to London. And then Paul Hess came in [in early 1959]." Mr. Justice O'Driscoll remembers Arthur with affection and respect, but he is not, as many of his former students are, besotted by him. One student who was with them, near the end, saw the strain in their relationship when John would complain about cases being taken without financial support; it is fair to say that there were moments when the steel of Arthur's personality would emerge, and he would simply make it clear that he was the boss. That, however, was consistent with his general conduct. All who associated with him knew him to be, generally, good-natured – but if crossed, he could be momentarily abusive, and what was good for a difficult judge or opposing counsel was good for his students and staff. As O'Driscoll puts it, "He was a one-man operation. He was a great guy as long as you agreed with him, but not such a great guy if you didn't. He had an ego, and he didn't take kindly to people disagreeing with him – lawyers, judges, jurors."

This rigorous defence of his superiority sometimes went beyond himself. Even the most exclusive specialist law office has odd jobs that are taken care of by the students. Usually it is a simple will or a small real estate deal for a friend or a major client, done as a favour. One student who had come to Arthur after extensive training with a real estate solicitor, remembers doing one of those deals. It went modestly astray just before closing, and the solicitor on the other side, phoned to complain, although the error had been made by the real estate agent, not by either law office. It was only a minor problem, causing a short delay, which the real estate agent had fixed up amicably between the buyer and the seller. Arthur's student had been informed, and had passed the information on to the other solicitor, who, obviously upset that someone had been tampering with his client, took it out on Arthur's student on the telephone. He was (and still is) a senior member of the Bar, and the student took the abuse, which was very raw (surprisingly, the real estate lawyers in Toronto were often discourteous and quarrelsome and the Registry Office on closing days had the decorum of an all-in pub brawl), without talking back, save to say that he was sorry, and not responsible for what had happened. While he was spluttering away, Arthur walked into his office, which, given the shortage of space at 320 Bay, was always used by his students in his absence. The bad-tempered solicitor hung up just as Arthur got his coat off, and Arthur wanted to know what was going on. His student explained, and Arthur asked one question, "Are we at fault?" On being told the story, he picked up the phone, rung the solicitor and at high speed, in a sheet of cold derision, told the man off. "This is Arthur Maloney. You've been talking to my student. In fact, you have been attacking my student, who has assured me that we are not at fault, and you are not at fault. I want you to know that when you speak to my student, you are speaking to me, and you will conduct yourself accordingly. If you ever abuse him again, I'll take this matter to the Law Society." He rung off, instantly calmed and cheerful, and said, "Now what's been happening?" It was worth a week's pay to the student, who had, in fact, taken a five-dollar reduction in pay when he joined Maloney, who at the job interview had said to him, "How much are you getting with Ed Hyde [a real-estate solicitor in the Percy Hermant Building on Dundas Square]?" The student said, "I'm getting thirty dollars a week." "I'll give you twenty-five." "I'll take it." "I thought you would." It was that fast. Arthur knew his value.

He was, as all his students and friends affirm, a generous man in a bar or a restaurant, who didn't like to pay his employees well. This has to be put into the context of his limitations as a businessman. Clients who had money paid handsomely, but there were too many clients who simply could not pay, and often had serious cases to be dealt with, often into the appeal courts.

Arthur's entrance into politics was much less planned than might have seem inevitable, given his family history. Lillian was told, with some pleasure by Arthur, of his memory of sitting in the gallery of the House of Commons, listening to the speeches when his father was a Member in the thirties. In the fifties, James's erratic lunge towards Queen's Park was cheered on and given modest financial support by his younger brother, but Arthur seemed happy enough to be a loyal supporter of the Conservatives, rather than a participant. He made no effort to get involved in Toronto ward politics, and showed no sign of being interested in either a provincial or a federal nomination. According to Lillian, it was George Drew who phoned him, without previous warning, asking him to have a look at the Parkdale riding, which was in Liberal hands and considered a safe Liberal seat. Lillian was not enthusiastic, recognizing that it would mean that Arthur would spend even less time at home. The other problem was money. Arthur was later to tell Glenn Hainey, a student of the seventies, that "unless you were independently wealthy or had some means of financial support, you just couldn't do it."[3] There is some evidence that Lillian's family could be called on for some help, but it was still a serious drain on Arthur's finances, which was one of the reasons why he insisted on trying to run his practice, and he never gave it up through his five years in parliament. As Mike Starr put it, "Don't forget when I got in, and later when Arthur got in, we were getting $6000. You had to pay for accommodation, for meals – for everything!"[4]

Bob Johnstone advised him against running. "When he told me he wanted to run, I told him he was nuts. I said to him, 'It's the dullest sport invented by man. You'll die of boredom, Art.' But he wanted to be Minister of Justice, and he thought he had a chance. I said,'It's my duty as a friend to talk you out of it.'" Johnstone knew there was more to it than the possibility of capping his law career with the highest elected legal office. "Arthur went into politics with great, great hopes; the sort of naivety that you find in people who are running for the school board for the first time. Of course, capital punishment was not only on the books, but being actively practised, and for Arthur that was a lure; getting rid of that was really a passion with him – it really was! I was kind of pro-capital punishment. I won't say Art converted me, but he was probably, in the long run, the greatest single factor in my change of mind – Arthur guided me; he and I had long talks. ... he was a religious man, and he believed it was wrong to kill any man made in God's image."[5]

Peter Oliver's book on Allan Grossman, *Unlikely Tory: The Life and Politics of Allan Grossman*, explores the phenomenon of post-Second World War Toronto politics and the influence of European immigration on the same: "Between 1946 and 1971, 3,536,757 immigrants entered Canada. Of these, 1,864,529 came to Ontario, and more than half settled in Toronto. The 1961 census indicated that 385,000 persons had migrated to Metropolitan Toronto in the previous nine years, and only 128,000 of these were British in origin. Between 1951 and 1960, Torontonians of British descent declined from 70 to 40 per cent of the population."[6] Oliver follows the development of the Ontario Progressive Conservative party's interest in this new group of voters, and its interest in encouraging them to settle in Ontario. "Persuaded that Ontario's economic growth depended on an expanded population and more skilled and unskilled workers, George Drew's Conservatives developed an aggressive and active immigration policy."[7] Politicians such as Allan Grossman and John Yaremko were naturals for such new voters. Grossman was the son on a Jewish immigrant, and Yaremko was an immigrant. Arthur, a third-generation Canadian with some political and social connections to the established power structure of the country, but with no connection to the working class or the working-class areas of Toronto, might have seemed, at first glance, a dubious candidate. His Roman Catholicism, however, was attractive to Ukrainian and Polish immigrants, and his distaste for the ungodly world of communism, as he saw it, which he spoke about regularly, made him at one with many of these people, delighted as they were in being able to practice their religion openly and safely. His Irish parentage also helped; he was not quite British, however much he espoused affection for the Empire connection. There was about him a strong aura of being an outsider – as they all were down in Parkdale, and he had never been identified with the inner circle of Toronto Tories. As a result, the new Canadians, of several racial strains, were prepared to accept a Roman Catholic Irishman to protect their interests in a city that still seemed to be an Anglo-Saxon Protestant stronghold in the mid-fifties.

Parkdale was, unlike its eastern counterpart East York, a mix of housing and industry. East York was almost all working-class housing, with the bulk of its population flowing west, down the Danforth to employment in the downtown area. Parkdale, however, was an undistinguished mess of small homes, often semi-detached, in the East York mode, but also of small rooming houses, meat packing plants, food processors, and factories. It was the cheapest part of town for an immigrant to live and find his first job, an entirely self-sufficient and somewhat self-enclosed area of the city, more in the tradition of an American immigrant neighbourhood in the fifties, than any other part of town. Its basic population was still working-class Anglo-Saxon, but it was rapidly changing. What no-one knew was how far that old pre-and-post-war racial purity had been eroded in the early stages of what was later to be named "multiculturalism." No-one knew the consequences of this new ethnic mix; nor did it yet have a name, but it was coming. Those in power welcomed the burgeoning population, seeing in it a new economic richness for Ontario. The immigrants themselves saw Canada in general as a kind of Eden, if often physically and economically harsh. They had put up with much worse. Canada was socially, politically, and spiritually a safe haven after years of terror in and out of two world wars. Many Canadians saw their arrival with disquiet and alarm, and sought to push it out of arm's length by mutterings and jokes about "D.P.s" and "Hunkies." For Arthur, who had been brought up with immigrants from several European nations, they were a natural audience for his ideas about social fairness and equality. He was used to defending the socially despised in his profession, and personally had no sense of them as a lesser breed, which didn't stop him from occasionally referring to his ethnic Parkdale constituents with affectionate mockery as "his Hunkies." But then Arthur was not a man with much concern for propriety *per se*; he was more interested in real equality, and damn the language, however demotic.

Arthur was never able to get all of his political work out of the office. Aside from the language problems, there was a further difficulty in explaining the various obligations of the different governmental levels to many of his constituents, determined to get some action. One student remembers a particularly irate Ukrainian woman insisting that something be done about her drains that were blocked by a large tree on city property in the front of her house. The woman, angry, confused, and not a little hampered by her inability to speak or understand English, seemed to have no idea that there were three different levels of government, and that she was barking up the wrong tree in calling Maloney. Arthur had promised to take care of her, and she expected him to do so.

She was, in some ways, quite right – Arthur did promise to help these people, and what the Parkdale voters often presumed was that meant help with everything. If the post-Second World War immigrants were timid and reluctant at first, they were, once they got over that, enthusiastic consumers of democratic government, and much more demanding than native Canadian voters in hunting down their elected representatives. They had a genuine thirst for politics and they practised their relation with Arthur in a way that is best characterized in F.S. Oliver's book on eighteenth-century English politics, *The Endless Adventure*, which sums up the whole aim of politics as an exercise in self-interest. Arthur's riding was a hotbed of demands, some modestly put, but most of them presented with a unselfconscious brashness that made it clear that they knew what they were entitled to receive from their representative: service, action, and reward. Not for Arthur the quiet withdrawal of the voters between elections, resigned to the fact that politicians make promises, but rarely do anything. The pretty fiction that obtains with most Anglo-Saxon Canadian voters that politicians say, but do not do, was not understood, if, indeed, it was even contemplated down in Parkdale. Parkdale expected something for its loyalty, and Arthur revelled in its vulgar, lively ferment, much of which he was responsible for encouraging from the start of his intrusion into a part of town that he knew nothing about before 1955.

Not that he really knew anything about what he was getting into, despite his family history in politics, which was so parochially neat and easy to deal with in terms of local, simplistic demands. But he learned as quickly as he could. He was particularly responsive to the sensitivities of the various ethnic groups and made a point of having most of his speeches translated and in the hands of the newspaper editors in Parkdale on the morning after, if not the afternoon previous. It was not an easy business: in 1957, there were twenty-five ethnic papers in the Toronto area, many of them located in the Parkdale riding, including five Ukrainian publications, two Estonian, two Hungarian, two

Slovenian, two German, two Polish, and one each of Bulgarian, Czechoslovakian, Finnish, Italian, Latvian, Lithuanian, Russian, and Serbian content. It was a new world for politicians, and Arthur responded with great enthusiasm.

He didn't even seem to know how to choose a campaign manager. Ralph McCreath, a young lawyer, primarily involved in civil work, knew Arthur through their wives who were friends before their respective marriages. The two couples were part of the same North Toronto social set. Arthur decided that McCreath, a bluff, good-looking charmer in his own right, would make the perfect campaign manager. Ralph thought otherwise, but was no match for Arthur's cavalier insistence.

He came to me and said, "You're going to manage my campaign." I said, "Arthur, in the first place, I'm a Liberal. In the second place, I don't like politics, and I won't be any good at it. Anyway, I don't know how to manage a campaign." Well, it was a lot of fun, I must say. I was practising on my own, and business was pretty good, but not so good that I could take off as much time as I wanted. I asked a lot of dumb questions about what I was supposed to do, and we just went; by absolutely sheer luck Arthur was in Parkdale, an absolute hive of the ethnic population of Canada. It held the largest group of Polish and German people, and hordes of Ukrainians, and, of course, they loved Arthur. He didn't care what nationality they were; he would just joke and laugh with them. We had three campaigns. The first was an absolute fluke; everybody got elected. The second was a landslide. The people who came out to be campaign workers were fabulous. The Europeans were far more politically oriented and enthusiastic from a working point of view. They all belonged to little, politically centred clubs – and I'm still working for some of them forty years later. Arthur was perfect; he just always said the right thing.[8]

Michael Starr, no mean ethnic politician himself, was impressed by Arthur's support: "the ethnic groups worshipped him; he was a household word with them."[9]

If Arthur charmed the ethnic voters, he also gave them something that they yearned for – credibility as Canadian citizens. Jerry Wilk, one of the colourful Ukrainians who landed on the Maloney shore of hopes and promises, puts the gift thusly: "he came to us and told us that we were needed." It was a plea beyond the legalism of their right to vote. He made it clear that they not only had the vote, but the obligation as Canadian citizens to use it. No-one had told them that. No-one, in a sense, had made them welcome. Arthur did that. It made a tremendous impression on the Parkdale voters, particularly the ethnic voters who were not quite sure how other Canadians took them, sensing the coldness of the welcome on all sides. Arthur simply waded in, as McCreath suggests, and made them feel, not only by what he said, but by his easy, open friendliness that it was not even crossing his mind that they were newcomers. They were, to him, as good as anyone else.

He might not know how to choose a campaign manager, but he did know how to prepare for an election, and in early 1955, he was down in Parkdale, looking around carefully. The Parkdale Progressive Conservative association was a small group of forty to fifty people, most of them Canadian-born, Anglo-Saxon businessmen. Wilk, one of the first immigrants whom Arthur contacted, saw what happened when Arthur showed up: "Arthur was advanced, thinking a bit ahead; he started with the idea of organizing the ethnic communities because Parkdale was about fifty-fifty at the time. It was a Liberal riding, but once Arthur said he was going to try for the nomination, he took it seriously. He saw the mistake that the riding association was making in ignoring us. They were living in the past; he wanted to create something that was true at that time, taking in the ethnics."[10] Wilk had been active in politics in the Ukraine, and had narrowly missed being killed during the war for his anti-Communist activities. When he came to Canada he decided to pay attention to making a living. He arrived in Toronto in 1947, married, and opened a butcher shop, despite the fact that neither he nor his wife knew anything about meat or about business. "I couldn't see the difference between pork, lamb, or beef!" Two years later, he helped two friends set up butcher shops, and not long after he went into the wholesale grocery business. "I'm just lucky to come to Canada. We lived quietly. We didn't know what else to do with ourselves." He was still sufficiently interested in public life to help set up a Ukrainian youth association, and he gradually became involved in other social clubs intent on bringing the Ukrainian immigrants together. "See, they left us alone to do whatever we wanted, and so we worked." But Wilk was restless, and began to look at the politics of this new home; he was not the only one, but few of them knew what to do about it.

Arthur phoned me, since I was the secretary of the Ukrainian Youth Association; it was 1955. "Why don't you join the Progressive Conservative association? Why don't you belong to the Albany Club, the Canadian Club?" I had never met him, and we got together with a few friends from the ethnic community. He asked me, "Why didn't you get involved in politics before?" And I said, "Because I didn't know I was welcome here." I didn't know what to do, where to go before. We put a choir together; we celebrated Ukrainian holidays, put the youth association together, but we kept to ourselves. Arthur told us to do more, to get involved in politics. I went with Arthur Maloney to every Ukrainian club in Toronto – to every club. I introduced him to other Ukrainians, and he got me and some other Ukrainians into the Albany Club. And we started working for him then, even though he was not yet nominated. I was so active! Because I loved politics. I spent all my free time working on his campaign.

Wilk managed to get over one hundred of his friends into the local Conservative association by 1957, and the membership, including representatives of all the ethnic groups, rose to over two hundred and fifty. "He worked very hard for the two years before the election with several of us covering all the various ethnic groups." A full year before the election, Maloney took a leading role in organizing the Young Progressive Conservatives Association in the riding, where emphasis was not put simply upon their youthful enthusiasm for politics, but upon their ethnic diversity. "I cannot tell you how much it impresses me to know that we have active workers among the Hungarian, Estonian, German, Latvian, Lithuanian, Polish, Ukrainian, and Slovak people."[11]

Maloney's idea of the way in which Parkdale might be taken from the Liberals did not rest solely in his wooing of ethnic voters, although such was at the centre of his appeal. He also knew that the kind of campaign he was to carry on down there, on the western edge of the downtown area, could not be quite the same as might be legitimate in North Toronto, since the electorate was not, economically or socially, legitimate Progressive Conservative material. It was a working class and small business district – as it still is years later – and the Conservative message, even with the developing enthusiasm for Diefenbaker, needed to be carefully tuned. His speeches are unremarkable from any literary standpoint, but that is not unusual. For all his reputation as an orator, Arthur's political material is hardly Churchillian. What his speeches cover is significant; they show a subtle understanding of what he has in his favour – and what he hasn't, given his party allegiance. A pattern is used in the speeches that is similar to his jury addresses – he seeks to use the assertions of the opposition to prove his points. Here, for instance, is his way of dismissing the Liberal self-congratulation over its immigration policy: "Among the myths that the Liberal propagandists have succeeded in creating and have attempted to perpetuate is the one they seek to use most effectively on those courageous people [characterized earlier as 'the enslaved nations of Europe who will exercise the franchise here – many for the first time']." Unaccustomed as many of them were to our way of life, our language, our culture and our method of doing things, efforts have been made to lead them to believe that they would not be here if it were not because of the present Liberal administration. This is a myth that it is our plain duty to dispel." Arthur claims that the Conservatives are quite as aware of the value of the immigrants and are committed to further immigration, a serious enthusiasm for many of the groups who wished to bring their families out of the mess of eastern Europe in the late fifties.

There is even an early anticipation of "multiculturalism" in his claim that "the contribution made to the social, economic and cultural life of our country by these worthy people is something none of us should fail to recognize. It is Conservative policy to encourage them to retain what is best of the traditions and the cultures that they brought with them from their respective countries – cultures that are centuries older than anything we have ever known. In other words, the Conservative party has never felt that the immigrant to this country should so completely assimilate himself into our way of life as to shake off all the bonds that attach him to the way of life to which he was accustomed in the country of his birth."[12]

He knew that the immigrants were often split personalities emotionally and politically, with one eye on their future in Canada, and the other on their European past, which was often also their present because of relatives and friends left behind. Arthur was sensitive, from the beginning, to the wide peripheral vision of the immigrants, especially those from the Communist countries, where families and friends were still enmeshed in sometimes dangerous situations. It could be argued that his party affiliation was the least valuable element in his campaign, and he seemed to know it. Despite his North Toronto address, his marriage into a family with money, and his social and professional position, he was an ideal candidate, not simply because of his anti-Red Catholicism, but because of his reputation as a defender of the common man, and often the uncommon man – the outcast of society. His publicity folders did not describe him simply as a celebrated criminal lawyer, but went on to make much of Suchan and Jackson and the Coffin appeal. Arthur suspected that at the working-class level of society there was a silent sense of identification with all unfortunates, including murderers – and he knew how to put his work in the best light:

> Up until his nomination as the Progressive Conservative candidate, Maloney was best known as a lawyer. When the poor and the friendless were in need, he was never known to refuse his help. He was never known to turn down a case because he thought it was "a loser" or simply because it was an unpopular cause if, to him, it was deserving ... When the Coffin case which originated in the Province of Quebec reached the Supreme Court of Canada, he was called in as counsel and pleaded the case of the famous prospector before that tribunal and was a central figure in the controversy that the case created. It was as a direct result of this case that the law was amended to facilitate appeals in all criminal cases to the Supreme Court of Canada.

It may look to be pretty rough stuff, particularly in the reference to the accused Coffin as "the famous prospector," when one considers the nature of that fame. Coffin was no Gilbert LaBine. Arthur sometimes fell into lapses of taste when it came to publicity, and he allowed another, more sentimental claim to be used.

> Among the civil cases in which he figured was the famous "Baby Duffel" case, the celebrated adoption case that Maloney took directly to the Privy Council in England in 1950. It was one of the last cases from Canada to be argued before that tribunal and he is probably the youngest Canadian lawyer ever to appear before the Privy Council. As a result of this case the law was changed again. The period of residence before foster parents could get final adoption papers was reduced from two years to one.

This kind of material was not available to most candidates, and however baldly it was expressed, it gave Maloney the kind of distinction that allowed him to distance himself from the taint of social and economic elitism that might have resulted from his party connection, in a riding that had long repulsed Conservative candidates. If his record as a lawyer wasn't enough, he was willing to put an ad *hominem* spin on his sentimental paean to the working man:

> It has been my experience with the working man in my professional career that whatever be his faults, he has one unfailing virtue ... I have always found him to be notoriously fair. He hates unfairness in others and feels no sympathy and has no gratitude for the man, the group or even the party who, in order to woo his favour or curry his support, would take an unjust position supposedly on labour's behalf.

Arthur, or his speech writer, seemed not to know what "notoriously" means; given his profession, it was an odd lapse. Much of what he says would have been considered arrogant bosh had it not been coming from a man well known for his generosity in dealing with the troubles of undistinguished unfortunates. It is hardly party politics at all that he speaks much of the time, but sentimental, populist pleading from a man whom they knew had defended the poor, the abused, and the despised, often without making a dime out of them – had they had such to give him. His speeches, on the page, look like rather loosely rambling parodies of the most flatulent kind of political balderdash. But Arthur Maloney had a right to use such language without blushing – he had been involved in public service for a long time.

7

Waiting for Diefenbaker

Maloney went to Ottawa in 1957, determined to do something, and his easy re-election in 1958 confirmed his constituents' belief in him – but nothing came of it. He was to be remembered as an electrifying speaker on the few occasions when he did speak in the House, and as late as 1969, seven years after he was defeated, Charles Lynch, the prominent Hill columnist, was to say that his speech on capital punishment of 18 February 1960 was one of the most powerful pieces of advocacy ever heard in the House of Commons. That speech was to be his best piece of parliamentary business and was always quoted when the matter of capital punishment was discussed – but the problem was not resolved until long after Arthur left Federal politics. He was also to be remembered as the Parliamentary Assistant to the Minister of Labour, Michael Starr, but not in any particularly constructive way. Yet when he went to Ottawa in 1957, and again in 1958, he was recognized as one of the most promising of the new Conservatives. In the eyes of quite a few observers, he was the best of them. Michael Starr, who got to know him in Ottawa, immediately liked him, and saw him as Cabinet material. But, in all fairness, Diefenbaker had problems, initially, in coming to power with so many senior men, long on the Opposition benches, who were entitled to Cabinet posts. His appointment of Davie Fulton as Minister of Justice, the post that Maloney wanted, was valid, both in terms of Fulton's service to the party and his qualifications for the job. Arthur could expect to wait, and could afford to do so, but not for too long in the quickly deteriorating Diefenbaker reign.

Michael Starr is of the opinion that Diefenbaker was too reluctant to weed his Cabinet to satisfy high-flyers like Arthur. "He was a marvellous parliamentarian, and everybody listened when he spoke, but he was never given a chance. It was John Diefenbaker's poor management; he frustrated them all." If Arthur was at fault, according to Starr, it was in his reluctance to put himself forward, a rather surprising observation, given Arthur's ego. "He was frustrated; I think that he thought that he could do so many things as a Cabinet Minister, and I think he would have brought the Party to a higher level. Maybe he could have been more forceful; people liked him, and he was very helpful. Everybody went to him with problems. But there was a reluctance on his part, which finally became a kind of indifference."[1]

His appointment as Starr's Parliamentary Assistant in the summer of 1957 was something of a sop for Arthur, and nobody took it seriously, least of all Starr and Maloney. Arthur told his friends that he did not want to take it, determined to wait until he could get into the Cabinet. Diefenbaker, determined to pin him down for future use, phoned Leslie Frost, the Ontario Premier, asking for advice. Frost suggested that the only way to get Maloney in a malleable position was to play on his religion. He suggested that the cardinal be asked to speak to him, and he was. The cardinal advised Arthur to go in, arguing that Toronto Catholics were unrepresented at the centre of things in Ottawa.

That is the story Arthur told, but the problem and the solution were probably more complicated. The Cabinet had a full complement of Toronto Tories, and there was some resistance to taking in any more – although Arthur was never really a member of the inner core of Toronto Tory politics. Ralph McCreath saw the problem in another way: "I think there was a group of people advising Dief who didn't want him in the Cabinet – a group who thought they had enough Irish Catholics, and on top of that, too many Toronto lawyers. There were others who were trying to get him in, but nothing came of it."[2]

Bob Johnstone helped Arthur get elected, despite his advice to Arthur to desist, and he looked for Arthur to do well in Ottawa. But Arthur and Jimmy, or both of them may have queered the pitch early on, according to Johnstone. When nothing seemed to fall to Arthur some time after the election, Johnstone asked Arthur what was going on. Arthur told him that, as Johnstone puts it, "it wasn't going to happen" – and why. Evidently he and Jimmy (by then a Minister at Queen's Park) had arrived late and somewhat liquored up at a Toronto hotel where the Prime Minister was speaking. "With the elaborate caution of the drunk, they came to a service door, got the door open and in their effort to be quiet, one of them knocked something over, and everybody stopped and looked at them. One of them – Arthur didn't remember which one – said in a hoarse, stage whisper, 'Has the old bugger done talking yet?' Years later, when we were talking about it, he said, 'I now know I shouldn't have even concerned myself with it. Davie Fulton had the job.'"[3]

Certainly the appointment of Fulton made sense, and probably was not influenced by any minor peccadillo of Arthur and James in alcoholic knockabout. However the question persisted throughout his short political career. A number of alternative theories float around, complicated by the fact that Arthur often talked about it to friends, and seemed to enjoy improvising on the theme. On one occasion, in the early days of his Ottawa service, he told a friend, who had picked him up at the Toronto airport, that he should watch the papers since the Cabinet appointment was imminent. But nothing happened. Some put his exclusion down to Arthur's habit of wandering about the bars of Ottawa as he had done in Toronto. However, there were problems beyond his control. As Michael Starr says, "It was a good Cabinet to start with for six months or a year, and then Diefenbaker threw it away. You know people worshipped him in '57. They looked at him as some kind of Messiah, but he wasn't a good manager, and he blew it all – always blaming someone else, and all the time, these good men, like Arthur, were hanging around – waiting – waiting."

Who promised what to whom is difficult to ascertain over thirty years later, particularly when the people who remember anything were often not directly engaged in the matter, and were getting their information second-hand on someone else's career. What seems to be certain is that the Cabinet question came up at least twice during Maloney's parliamentary stay. In the first instance, Arthur seems to have hoped that he might just get into the Cabinet soon after he was first elected. That would make sense of the conversation with Bob Johnstone about the *faux pas* of the two happy brothers arriving late for the Diefenbaker speech.

The second stage of the matter seems to fall into two parts: (1) in which Arthur informs a few people that he is definitely in, and (2) a later state in which Arthur ponders aloud, with several separate friends, what Diefenbaker might have against him, or, in the alternative, who had Diefenbaker's ear and was holding Arthur back. Sometimes it was suggested that it was the Toronto Tories who were keeping him out, since he was considered too radically liberal for them. Davie Fulton, for instance, was more to their taste because of his conservative views on capital punishment. "Capital punishment was the issue we talked about most. [In Davie Fulton's Justice Committee] Fulton was a strong believer in retention. Diefenbaker was an abolitionist."[4] Doug Crane and Fred Stinson (who was in the House at the time) felt that he was kept out simply because of his support for Fleming in the leadership battle.

Mr. Justice Pat LeSage, who is not a man inclined to fiction, was the source of the story about Maloney being dragged reluctantly into the assistantship with Michael Starr – and he got it from Arthur.

> Arthur wanted to be a Cabinet Minister; he expected to be one; and he probably was entitled to be one. I suspect that Diefenbaker's intelligence was such that he thought that Arthur would be a risk because of his personal conduct. Alcohol

was the principal risk, but there may well have been concerns beyond that. Arthur told me the story; he's the one who told me that information supplied obviously caused Diefenbaker to think twice. He only told me the story once, but he definitely told me that he had been considered and turned down, and he either told me directly or indirectly that it was the information supplied Diefenbaker that had caused him to be concerned. He didn't tell me the particulars.[5]

Frank McGee, who was one of the young promising members of the victories late fifties, thought that Arthur's drinking might have been the problem, although drinking was not a rarity in Cabinet. "Arthur was, by any objective standard, the brightest of the new men, but Diefenbaker had this thing about drinking. I'm reasonably sure that it was part of it. Arthur was a long, long way from being a drunk, but he was a *bon vivant*. He liked a good party and he liked to drink and to Diefenbaker's eye that was a problem."[6]

Whatever information the Prime Minister was getting about Maloney, it was sufficient in the salad days of his victories that Arthur was some kind of public risk. McGee, however, sees it as something more complicated, possibly influenced by Diefenbaker's own personality. "Arthur used to throw some pretty good parties up there. He had lots of friends in and around Ottawa, and up the Valley, and relatives as well. Diefenbaker was a strange man – always suspicious. I often thought that Arthur and John Pratt, the man who sang 'You'll Get Used to It' in the old Navy shows, had the same attitude – a kind of bemused attitude to an odd fellow."

The job with Mike Starr led nowhere. Starr admits that he made little use of him, more out of inexperience than intent.

Don't forget we were all novices in '57; I didn't know where to park my car! I was learning. How was I to know what to tell Arthur in those days what he should be doing? When I didn't know what I should be doing. I know we never discussed policy – that was Cabinet business, and he was never really privy to what was going on. He was only there in name only; but he never came to me and said, 'Mike, what part do you want me to play in your department?' He wasn't there in full spirit. He was just there in name only, to be honest with you. With all due respect, I would have loved him to do more.

There was a lot more that he could have done, and Starr, years later, knew how the office could have been used, if only he and Arthur had put some thought into it. Starr now admits that "Parliamentary Secretaries can take on certain responsibilities in the department, and they can answer on behalf of the Minister in the House; can speak with him in the presentation of his estimates, in the details of the office." But they were not the only pair who made little use of the appointment. Peter Stursberg, in his studies of the Diefenbaker years, comments upon the feckless way in which the appointments were used. "The status of the parliamentary assistants was as obscure then as it is now. The appointment of these so-called 'junior ministers' carried with it a small extra stipend but no power. There could be a great deal of work or nothing to do – the job depended on the minister. It is significant that Gowan Guest could not recall the parliamentary assistants to Diefenbaker."[7] Starr may have recognized the potential of a superlative parliamentarian in Maloney, but he has to admit that he made nothing of Maloney's abilities, and Maloney did not press him for work: "He did some minor comment in the House on behalf of the ministry, but I don't recall anything that he did of substance." Starr thought it was up to Diefenbaker to do something for Arthur:

> It was obvious that he was someday going to be a Cabinet Minister, and in the not-too-distant future. Now the Cabinet was made up of a lot of old fellows who'd been there for years, and many didn't like Diefenbaker, and didn't support him for the leadership. Diefenbaker kept most of them for six goddam years with all these young guys frustrated. He could have put the older ones off in the Senate, or in the judiciary, and bring in those young fellows who would have worshipped the ground he walked on. But no – he kept them waiting, and they were later to stab him in the back – they were hanging around, waiting and waiting.

Starr and Maloney became and remained good friends, so much so that in 1966, when Dalton Camp was attempting to drive Diefenbaker out of the party, it was Starr who thought of bringing Maloney in to attack Camp. (There are several versions of who thought of Arthur first, but Michael Starr claims that he did, and he was the one sent to Toronto to discuss it with Maloney.)

The point is, however, that whatever Diefenbaker thought he was doing in pressing Arthur to take a parliamentary assistantship that he clearly did not want, it did not work – Arthur was still the golden odd man out, and at loose ends. Jake Dunlap was regularly drawn away from his busy practice to keep Arthur company. He was surprised how often Arthur called upon him to come over for a steam bath, and an evening of drinking. He saw that the longer Arthur was in Ottawa, the less time seemed to be spent on politics, as Arthur began to realize that he was to be nothing more than a backbencher. "If he had some place of importance, he would have done the job, but as it was, he just lost interest. I got the distinct impression that he, eventually, was fed up."[8]

There was no problem back in Parkdale for Maloney, and the second election in 1958 was even more successful than the first. He was from a family of politicians who knew how to keep constituents happy, even if it ran his office staff ragged. It was not an easy riding to satisfy, since the ethnic groups needed constant help with immigration problems. Like James, he believed in politicians using what power they had, and was always available for consultation on minor patronage appointments. The immigrant Canadians loved to have banquets, and Arthur tried to attend them all. It was, in many ways, similar to a rural riding in its constant demand for attendance by its elected representatives, and wedding and anniversary invitations were expected to be taken as seriously as legitimate political functions. It made a mess of his family life, just at a time when he wanted to be at home with the two babies, but he had a natural enthusiasm for social occasions that carried him through a hectic scheduled. They adored him in Parkdale. He understood how anxious many of them were about the old countries, and what was going on there, particularly if they were under Communist regimes. It gave him a touchstone identification with their worries, and he was always ready to voice their international concerns in the House. It might have been more appropriate if he had been allowed to serve as the parliamentary assistant to the Secretary of State for External Affairs, if he was not to go to Justice. There is no mystery about his parliamentary career, once the Cabinet question is put aside. He was a good constituency member, always attentive, concerned, understanding, and easy to get to at any time. In the June 1957 election, he had a majority of 2200. In March 1958, it went to over 5000. The party organization was excellent, and cannily balanced, with over 50 percent of the members representing the new Canadians.

By early 1959, however, he was obviously restless. Jerry Wilk tells a story of Arthur going to Diefenbaker with a proposal to take over the presidency of the national party organization in order to stop the slippage that he saw occurring.

> Maloney was aware that the party wasn't progressive enough; that it was still in the hands of the old establishment. That it needed to be shook up and re-organized. He said to me, "Jaroslaw, I offered to take on the job of rebuilding the Conservative party from coast to coast, but only if he would appoint me to the Senate. At least that would provide me with a position and a few cents to throw about." That was Arthur's idea; that was in 1959. It was Arthur's idea, and Diefenbaker said, "Okay, okay." He was going to think about it, but nothing more was said to Arthur about it.[9]

Wilk seems to be the only one who knows this story. He was certain that it was not later, as it might have been, in the early sixties. Whether he is right or not, there was no question that Arthur was becoming unhappy with his role and with Diefenbaker's conduct by the end of the decade. Starr remembers him whiling away his time in the member's dining room: "He was drinking I think out of frustration. He used to gather a gang in his office in the evenings and they would eat and drink together." However frustrated he became, he rarely showed any bitterness. George Karmanin, who had been a loyal Parkdale supporter from the beginning, once asked him what was going on. "I told him once – I said to him, 'Arthur, I am surprised that you are not yet a minister. We don't have many Maloneys there.' He looked at me – if you recall his smile – you know – and he said, 'George, sometimes you have to accept life as it is, and you realize you can't do very much against it.' I felt the pain he had, but he was still proud, too proud to make any explanations."[10]

By the time of the 1962 election, his personal frustrations were of lesser moment than possible defeat in Parkdale. He had, for the first time, in Dr. Stanley Haidasz, a serious Liberal contender, a candidate who could surpass him, if not in celebrity and accomplishment, at least in one way that mattered down there – he was Polish. He was also a Catholic. On top of that, the riding was quickly changing, and Arthur's older, more successful supporters were now following the Anglo-Saxon Protestants to the suburbs. George Nagy, the Hungarian journalist, who was with Arthur from the start, recognized the trouble:

> Parkdale was changing; it was still an area of cheap housing where people came from the old countries to get a start, but they went on to something better. A lot of my Hungarian friends were moving out, and that included many of Arthur's original supporters; that was one of the main reasons for the loss. Arthur had tremendous authority at the time of the second election in '57. He took part in all our ethnic and inter- ethnic activities. He was – how can I say it – he was our spokesman. Diefenbaker was also sympathetic, and during the Hungarian revolution, he saw us and was sensitive to our problems as Hungarians, but Arthur was our voice in Ottawa.[11]

But no one believes that he lost in 1962 because of a simple shift of ethnic and religious loyalties. It was the failure of Diefenbaker, and his retreat into bunker spleen and indecision. Yet there was some feeling that Arthur was not quite as sharp in 1961. McCreath served again as the campaign manager, and was optimistic. "He was still very conscientious. The fact that he hadn't got into the Cabinet meant that he had lost a bit of interest; but the election he lost, he was just as keen as ever. I still thought we were unbeatable." Monte Harris, who was to go on to a career in Toronto municipal politics, and eventually became a Provincial

Court judge, was involved for the first time in a Maloney campaign, and felt that Arthur wasn't nearly as focussed and energetic as he should have been. Harris had some experience, having worked at the provincial level for Allan Grossman. "Arthur took it for granted. He was running against an inferior candidate intellectually, and one of the reasons he lost is he didn't take the thing seriously enough. He'd be out there, having a few beers with the boys, but that was all. I suppose he felt that despite Diefenbaker's problems, he, himself, was a popular Canadian.[12]

McCreath was relatively satisfied that all was well, and that Arthur was still a viable candidate despite the Diefenbaker problem, but he, in part, agrees with Harris that it hadn't quite the same night-and-day urgency of the previous elections. "He wasn't doing the things he needed to do to win the election. He was playing with the people he knew and liked and avoiding those he thought would cause him trouble. I was often frustrated. I'd line up meetings and he wouldn't show up, and that's the worst thing that you can do, particularly with ethnic supporters, who are very sensitive. He'd gotten pretty nonchalant."[13]

Doug Crane was the articled student, and Arthur had him out on the streets with him. He saw another side of the problem of getting elected in a riding where there were no rules of gentlemanly conduct. Campaign posters were continually being pulled down, or surrounded by Liberal advertisements, and on one occasion, while he and Arthur were handing out emery boards at a street-car stop, they were informed by a youth that Arthur Maloney had just been carried out of a store down the street, dead drunk. "We had several ethnic rallies, and Arthur brought in Walter Dinsdale and Howard Green and Davie Fulton. We had a giant ethnic rally for Diefenbaker at the Queen Elizabeth Building. We spent a lot of time organizing that; and I can tell you, I spent a lot of time getting grandmothers over from Poland or the Ukraine, and Arthur would never take money for any costs we had in dealing with immigration matters."[14]

Some of his old supporters felt that if the Liberal candidate had been an Anglo-Saxon Protestant, the Diefenbaker curse would not have been strong enough to stop Maloney. Henry Hodowany, a young real estate agent at the time, born in Canada, but a Catholic of Polish parentage, joined the Conservatives because of Arthur, and was involved politically with him from the time of the 1958 election.

> I can't pinpoint Arthur's fault in the election of 1962. He worked hard; he stood on the street with me, handing out leaflets to people getting on the Queen streetcars. There was, before him, an impression that the Conservative party was a "Wasp" party, and the ethnics were welcome to run messages, but Arthur changed that. He said, "No, no, no! You belong to the Party! You are part of

Canada!" But in 1962, the Liberals had a candidate who had a very high profile in the Polish community. Arthur had a lot of Polish people who supported him before, but some of them now had one of their own to vote for. We thought, at first, that he might get in, but not with his old, big majority. To my knowledge, there were no complaints about his service as a member. Everybody liked him, but this was the Diefenbaker election, and the Liberals gave us an ethnic, and we all began to sense that we were in trouble; that we were not going to make it unless we worked hard. But the Liberal candidate was attractive, and our own son. We were dissatisfied with Diefenbaker, disappointed that Arthur had not been made a Cabinet Minister, and the voters started to drift away. If Diefenbaker hadn't gone wrong, Maloney would have had a distinguished career in politics. We were all hurt by his defeat. We had lost a high-profile candidate, but it wasn't his fault. You go down there, and they still remember him as a great individual.[15]

He took the loss graciously. Everyone connected with him had the impression that he was relieved to be out of it. It had cost a lot of money, and there was a considerable debt. Bob Johnstone tried to console him by suggesting that it wasn't so bad, but Arthur was not to be fooled, "It was awful. I got clobbered."[16] Lillian was relieved, if sorry for him. Yet they were both happy that it was all over. He felt that he had done enough, had enjoyed giving it a try, and had got out the honourable way, by being defeated. "On the night of the defeat, there was a big party down in Parkdale, and he was very happy, and had a few drinks and he had hired a taxi driver who told him not to worry. Arthur could have some drinks and the cabby would drive us home. Well, you know what happened – I ended up driving both of them home. The cabby told us where he lived and I took him home first, and we had the taxi in the driveway overnight!"[17]

He told Clive Bynoe that the defeat had some compensations; at least he could spend some time with the family again, and get back to practising law in a sane manner. He had nothing to say about Diefenbaker, and, in fact, had never complained of him to Bynoe through the years of waiting for the Prime Minister to do something for him. In a letter to his sister Catherine, who was at D'Youville College in Buffalo, he showed no sign of self-pity:

I worked hard to win the election, but I must confess that I did not feel any great regrets when I realized I was being defeated. The attempt to carry on both the practice of law and the duties of an MP was becoming increasingly difficult. If I had been elected this time, in view of the fact that it is a minority government, I would really have had to give up my practice completely because it would be impossible to be absent from the House of Commons in the event of a surprise vote being called. Pat flew up from Ottawa and Father Henry drove down from Bancroft to be with me as the returns came in. I think Pat was more disappointed than I was. Margaret joined us also to watch the results and to join the party we held afterwards. I think we had a bigger and better party losing than we would have had winning.[18]

The dead hand of defeat was on him quickly. The Clerk of the House got in touch: "It is my duty to inform you that, as you have ceased to be a Member of the House of Commons, your right as such to free transportation on Canadian railways has expired and your pass has been cancelled." But just in case old habits prevailed: "At your earliest convenience, would you be good enough to return to me the pass you were issued for the current year." It wasn't all civil service cold shoulder. Senator Joseph A. Sullivan brought up the idea of the Senate: "I am very pleased to hear that you will not lose interest and as a Catholic man to dissociate yourself from the party." The syntax might be confusing, but the next sentence was more to the point: "I do not know whether you wish to be a Senator or not, and if that is the case please let me know and you can rest assured I will do everything in my power."[19]

Paul French, who was too young to quite understand why his Uncle Arthur was spending so much time in Ottawa during the late fifties, was instructed later in the more complicated aspects of a political career. Maloney told him that it was a grand experience, but hardly a bed of roses. "But he would also say 'You never know who your friends are.' He thought it was most difficult to hold a metropolitan riding. He would never discourage anyone; he always encouraged, but when asked he would always suggest, 'Why don't you go to a rural area if you want to pursue politics – a rural area where you can hold your base?'" His father and brother had done just that; Arthur had tried a city riding, and he ended up dissatisfied and unfulfilled as a politician, although he was the most promising of the three. Glenn Hainey, one of the law students who was to follow him into the Ombudsman's office, remembers a further *caveat* that Arthur held to in later years: "When it came to discussing politics, he had a great love for his Parkdale days, and he had wonderful memories of it, but whenever you got on to the subject with him, the bottom line was money."[20]

Perhaps it was all for the best. Had Diefenbaker taken him in, it might well have ended in tears. Eric Murray, the trial lawyer, who was to be employed by him in running fights with Queen's Park in the last days of the Ombudsman battle, thought that had he got into the Cabinet, he would have been out of it very quickly. "He'd have gotten into trouble because he certainly was outspoken."[21]

But was it simply a matter of too many Torontonians or too much drink or wild parties that kept Maloney out of the Cabinet? There are some who saw him, in the long run, as a possible threat to Diefenbaker, who, given his vanity and aggrieved personality, did not take easily to the idea of someone who might be seen as a kind of crown prince. Frank Dunlap, who was not alone in the suggestion, believed that Maloney had too much personality, and was too particularly gifted in those areas which the Prime Minister claimed as his own. He was, for instance, a criminal lawyer of far greater accomplishment and experience than Diefenbaker, whose reputation as a criminal counsel was sound, but nothing like that of Maloney. Maloney also had a proven reputation as the defender of the common man, and, perhaps, more damaging than anything else, he had an outgoing personality that was effective in any social group. Taken all in all, as political animals, starting on the square, Diefenbaker had length and strength even if his gifts were less obvious than those of Maloney. He had done it the hard way, absorbing defeat after defeat on his way up, and he may have seen Maloney as too much of a golden boy, having come to Ottawa on his first try at public office, eager, expecting (and expected) to be rewarded for his manifest talents. In politics, it is not necessarily the best who win, but the one who is determined to win in the long run, however limited in talent. It is a business in which perfect attendance has its rewards, and Arthur was neither mediocre enough to have nothing else to do but wait, nor determined enough to wait for better days. Diefenbaker was known not to suffer men of too much overt ambition near him, and Arthur was ambitious. What is more to the point, everyone saw Arthur as a natural choice for high office. The Prime Minister, not a magnanimous man, may have decided, given the difficulties and the possible dangers, that no-one would tell him who was entitled as of right to join the Cabinet. He would decide, and Arthur would wait until he was called – but there was a problem – Arthur was indeed ambitious, but only so short-term, as he so often displayed in his career.

Diefenbaker, in serious trouble, called for him in 1963, but it was too late. "Mr. Diefenbaker phoned him and promised him a Cabinet post right then, before the election," says Lillian, fearful of Arthur's response. But "Arthur said 'no'; he'd given five years and that was enough." It was general knowledge that if Arthur had come back, he would have gone into the Cabinet. Diefenbaker knew how much he needed him: "Although we had some fine candidates (such as Joel Aldred, D.F.C., in Toronto St. Paul's), many good prospective candidates were discouraged from seeking nomination, and it seemed little I could do to convince them of their duty. To take a case in point, had Arthur Maloney agreed to run again in Toronto Parkdale, where in 1962, the Liberal candidate had beaten him by less than two thousand votes, I would have appointed him to the Cabinet. As it was, I appointed Frank McGee to the Cabinet as Minister without Portfolio."[22] It wasn't a difficult decision for Arthur to make; it wasn't even a self-interested, cold-blooded reading of the PC's failing powers. It was based on an accumulation of experience and frustration. He hadn't, as he saw it, been given the chance he deserved. His advice about the party had been ignored. He had lost a great deal of money, spent a good deal more, missed the earliest years of his childrens' lives, and he never managed to really do anything in Ottawa. He was liked, admired, and respected – he had made a stirring speech on capital punishment – and that was all. True, he had done what he could for his constituents, despite the mannered inertia of the parliamentary process and civil service stone-walling. As Lillian says, "A lot of them owed their jobs to Arthur." Or as Dave Humphrey likes to put it: "He got so goddam many people jobs in liquor stores and other government jobs that he could have formed his own labour union." He told Lillian, "'I got out at a good time.' I think he would not have run again even if he had run in '62. One of the things he was mad about was that he couldn't get all that he wanted to help his constituents. Even as a member, he was always waiting around, being fobbed off with promises by people who didn't care who he was."[23]

The five years in politics had got him nowhere, but as several men who were with him in Ottawa said, he did not push himself. Perhaps he made the mistake of being too confident that the gift would fall into his hands without forelock tugging and genuflection that is a common exercise on the way to power. Perhaps the years of legal success and public adulation, based as it was on genuinely first-class work, had spoiled him into thinking that quality without the gloss of servility would draw him to a higher place. But what of his reputation as a drinker and a party-goer? For Arthur, and most of his friends and family, drink, often to excess, among males was common. The "drink" in the family did serious public and political damage in his generation and in the generation after his, in the political career of Pat's son, Mark, who served with great distinction in Ottawa politics until alcohol got him into trouble and forced his resignation in early 1994. It goes farther back than that. Paul French, on a visit to Ireland, learned that the respiratory problems that Arthur had, which were common in the family, and which French also has, have always been a weakness in the Bonfields, but he also discovered that the Maloneys are well-remembered back into the nineteenth century as heavy drinkers. But liquor was also a common element in the society from which Arthur came in the back reaches of the small towns, the farms, and the lumber camps of the Ottawa Valley.

What concerned his friends was his tendency to go on too long and too far. While everybody drank a bit too much, Arthur had a taste for drinking long into the night, even if he had started in the early afternoon. He would sometimes be drunk, late in the evenings. The problem was not really so much the alcohol, but the danger of the same leading him into situations and associations that might be embarrassing if made public – simply because he had become something of a celebrity. The later it got, as is the way of the world of alcoholic excess, the more questionable the company would become, as his legal associates withdrew, slipping away one by one. Arthur was a happy, sociable drunk, and his natural curiosity about people, his charm, and his generosity expanded to include all as the night went on. Many of his bar acquaintances were simply not fit company for a man in his position. When he was a young criminal lawyer, much of his social life in close connection with the subfusc side of the city was just barely acceptable, sustained by the public's romantic ideas of how a criminal "mouthpiece" would comport himself. Even then, however, there was the danger of a lawyer getting too close to his dubious clients. Bynoe, who had close connections with the police department that went beyond his professional life, had an arrangement with some senior detectives to keep an eye on Arthur as he roamed the clubs late at night. (On one celebratory occasion, Arthur was asked who had been his best student, and he named Bynoe, on the grounds that he was the only one who always was able to locate him somewhere in the demi-monde of downtown Toronto.) When Arthur became a politician, the need for discretion increased, since society presumes instinctively that some kinds of conduct are not to be countenanced of public figures. If something more was to be added to the responsibility of public respectability – such as a Cabinet position – the standard changed again, and that is where, perhaps, it was presumed that Arthur would not take instruction. That may have been true. Or it may, sadly, have been wrong. Perhaps the elevation to Cabinet would have kept him sufficiently busy to take up his spare time. Whether it would have made any difference ultimately to the Diefenbaker government, if Arthur and other young men had been brought in earlier, it is impossible to guess. It might, however, have made for a more flexible, imaginative way of doing the business, and to a sense of public connection and openness that might have helped to dissolve the fortress surliness of the later Diefenbaker years. But that would have depended upon Diefenbaker changing at the behest of those new men who might have brought him round to some kind of civility as their paternal mentor. Of course, the Diefenbaker failure is more complicated than the choice or lack of choice in his Cabinet appointments, but it is true that most of those who were denied did little to help him ultimately, and some were involved in bringing him down. It is some indication of Maloney's character that he was not among the latter, and when called upon he did otherwise.

It is difficult to imagine that Arthur's drinking, which had never been an embarrassment or impediment in his work, could, of itself, explain Diefenbaker's reluctance to take him into Cabinet. Certainly, drink was a common element in the House. These were men of a normal stripe of coarse manliness; they were often far from home, with a good deal of time on their hands, especially if they were backbenchers with nothing much to do. Yet Maloney should have know better, given Diefenbaker's reputation for eccentric pickiness. In fact, he did know. Much of what is known of why Arthur was rejected comes from Arthur himself. He did believe that Diefenbaker had seriously considered him early on, and rejected him. He thought it might well have had something to do with his social habits, and his inclination to hang about with anybody, however questionable. Of course, Diefenbaker was politician enough to swallow such concern in the early sixties, when he needed all the help he could get. If his early rejection of Maloney was based upon distaste for his wild ways, it did not prove to be a deep-seated moral judgment, and the political expediency of the later years led him to promise Arthur high office if he would only return to politics. Arthur, by that time, had shifted into that peculiar state of mind that so often marked his career – he chose not to serve any longer.

When he came out of politics in 1962, he was still a relatively young man. Paul Hess, the taciturn, somewhat colourless, scholarly replacement for John O'Driscoll, had been holding the practice together while Arthur made his last election run, and they were relieved to settle down to a sensible sharing of the work. If the last five years had been an interesting experience that had led to nothing substantial, it had done no damage to Arthur's reputation at the Bar, in part because he had always kept his hand in as much as possible. But it was not an entirely seamless transition, in part because of problems over which he had no control, and which could not have anticipated. It started while he was still a Member of Parliament. He was in Toronto in March 1961 when he received a note from his Commons secretary: "Am enclosing part of the front page of *Citizen* – you are the talk of the House – the guy who slashed his wrists has taken a back seat to yours. Hope you get this all straightened out." The unfortunate with the slashed wrists has disappeared, but it is of no matter. What was important was that Arthur Maloney, the hardly used back-bencher was in the headlines. It was to take him considerable time to get out of them, and the final resolution of the problem hung on into 1963. The end of the matter was to be only in part a happy one for Arthur and his brother James, and an example of the way in which lawyers, particularly criminal lawyers, and politicians, can sometimes find themselves in questionable postures, subject to public scrutiny. What happened proved how fragile was the varnish of reputation in the face of unfounded rumour, and how easily the political world could be infiltrated by determined crooks. Beyond that it displayed the loose, easy-going morality of both the legal, and the political world of the time in Ontario. On the personal level, it was a last display of the close relationship that Arthur had with his older brother James, who was not to outlive the scandal.

In a preliminary hearing on the question of whether two gamblers, Joseph McDermott and Vincent Feeley had managed to infiltrate the gambling unit of the Ontario Provincial Police, it was alleged, among many other things, that the "Two Thieves" (as they were called by the police), had arranged to provide the Ontario Provincial Police anti-gambling unit with a do-it-yourself manual on how to close down a rival gambling club in Niagara Falls, which they (the Two Thieves) had ambitions to take over. The Ramsay Club had been, as a result, successfully prosecuted, but had risen again – under the management of the two men. An officer claimed that he had been told that the brief had been prepared by David Humphrey, at the instruction of McDermott, and that it had been passed on to Arthur Maloney, MP to vet it, who sent it on to his brother, James Maloney, MPP, the provincial Minister of Mines – who had also contemplated it and then passed it on to the police. A document with such distinguished provenance – prepared by Humphrey, who was a former Crown prosecutor and a leading criminal lawyer, deeply experienced in gambling cases, then considered by an even better criminal lawyer (and an MP to boot), and then delivered to the police by a provincial Cabinet Minister – had to have some purchase with the police, and it certainly did.

That was the story told on the stand under oath. The magistrate, Joseph Addison, mused innocently aloud as to the journey this shaggy-dog document made on its way into the OPP gambling squad: "Why did it go through so many hands?" he asked – of nobody in particular, since it was obvious that the qualifications of the various handlers supplied the answer. By the following day of trial, Thursday, 23 March 1961, the protests and howls of innocence were pouring in, since the officer had named not only Humphrey and the Maloneys, but several others as aiders and abettors of the gamblers. The magistrate tried to stop the nonsense by stating that what the officer had said was not necessarily true, since there was no real evidence to back up his allegations; but the damage was done. So much so that Ross Whicher, a Liberal MPP, demanded that the Ontario government strike a Royal Commission.

The officer who had received the brief tried to clear up the matter, by claiming that although he had got a phone call from a man who said he was David Humphrey, who offered him the brief, he knew nothing of any involvement of the Maloney brothers. Humphrey, who was conveniently on hand as one of the lawyers for the defendants, denied that he wrote the brief, or made the phone call, or sent the brief on to anyone, including Arthur Maloney. But it didn't seem to do much good, and the Maloneys kept coming up in the newspaper reports. On the fourth day of the trial Arthur arrived in the courtroom, unannounced, and did one of those unusual things that were a mark of his personality. He demanded to be allowed to speak to the matter. It was certainly unusual – he was not a party to the proceedings, and he was not counsel to any of the parties. G. Arthur Martin, who was representing one of the accused, presented Maloney to the Court, and His Worship, Joseph Addison, who obviously sensed that he was on the edge of opening his proceedings to a line-up of self-proclaiming innocents, allowed Arthur to deny the allegations, but only just, since he made it clear that no-one else would be allowed the privilege. After that dramatic moment, Arthur took on the newspapers, and both he and James made formal denials in their respective Houses of Parliament, federal and provincial. They seemed to be well out of it, and eventually the case went on, without them, to ultimate conviction of the gamblers and one of the police officers.

But Arthur kept his eye nervously on the proceedings, and his file on the matter is full of newspaper clippings as the trial proceeded, and later, and more ominously, as the Attorney-General and Premier Leslie Frost reluctantly struck a Royal Commission almost a year later under Mr. Justice W.D. Roach to investigate the extent of corruption involved in the matter. Many of the same witnesses told their stories once again, and the Maloneys, again, were named. The newspapers seemed not to remember that the pair had been cleared. *The Hamilton Spectator* of Tuesday, 17 April 1962, showed no memory of Maloney's impassioned pleas of innocence: "A brief which passed through the hands of Arthur Maloney, a Toronto MP and his brother, the late James Maloney, Ontario mines minister, outlining how the old Ramsay Club in Niagara Falls could be successfully prosecuted, was referred to at the royal commission probe on crime here yesterday." B.J. MacKinnon, the Liberal party counsel, in questioning the head of the OPP anti-gambling squad, brought up the old story, and was quoted by the *Spectator*: "The brief was prepared by David Humphrey (a Toronto lawyer), constable George Wright (since convicted with Feeley and McDermott for seeking illegal information from an OPP undercover agent) and others and forwarded to Mr. Maloney who gave it to district Inspector Allan Stringer, who in turn gave it to you?" Answer: "Yes."

Again Humphrey denied everything, but admitted that Arthur

Maloney had, on occasion, worked for McDermott and Feeley – which was perfectly legitimate, given his skills. But Humphrey was obliged to admit that although he had no memory of discussing the brief with James Maloney: "There is a remote possibility that I did, but I doubt it." It was the first indication that James was the real target. Then MacKinnon struck – suddenly asking Humphrey if he had any knowledge of an attempt to influence the magistrate Fred Thompson in a gaming trial against the Finnish Club, a Feeley-McDermott enterprise in Toronto. Humphrey admitted that he was told that James Maloney had phoned the magistrate, asking him to take things easy – Arthur Maloney was representing one of the accused. Humphrey also admitted that he had asked McDermott and Feeley about it, but they denied any involvement, and James, when asked, had done the same.

A further element was added in the revelation that the Two Thieves owned a small mining company, and that on one occasion, Humphrey, and his clients – Feeley and McDermott – had met with James Maloney, in his role as Minister of Mines, to discuss a minor problem that they had with the business. Humphrey got the impression at that meeting that James had met his clients previously.

Arthur again came to defend himself, the family name, and particularly James, who had nothing to say for himself, having died the previous October. James, however, had denied making any calls to Thompson, or doing anything untoward for the gamblers in their mining enterprises. In the process of defending James, Arthur was obliged to admit that he had appeared as counsel for Feeley-McDermott enterprises on a few occasions, but had done nothing unethical. He had questioned James and had been assured that his conduct was also proper.

Sadly, the matter was taken out of his hands. Witnesses started turning up who claimed that James was often more than zealous in intruding behind the scenes. Thompson was certain it was James who had called him, not once, but three times, and the Deputy Attorney-General admitted that James "had been in the department's hair before." A former Renfrew Crown, H. Graham Walsh came down to claim that James "sometimes asked the impossible." An OPP Inspector testified that James had threatened to have him transferred for prosecuting Renfrew truckers. Added to that was the revelation that James had supported an application by Feeley and McDermott to set up a small loans company.

In fairness, it should be said that attempts to get charges reduced or dropped is common practice, particularly so in small town and rural jurisdictions where the lawyers, the police, the Crowns, and the judges – and often the clients – are well-known to each other. The law officers often haggle, good-naturedly, over charges without there being any sense in which any one is attempting to obstruct justice. Tom

Edmondstone feels that Walsh's complaints were excessive, but he also admits that James had a long-practised tendency to mock Walsh, often in the middle of a trial. Now it was Walsh's turn to have the last word. Edmondstone, though not a native of the Valley, has accumulated some of its folksy mannerisms through the years, and his final, laconic comment upon the matter is telling: "There were a lot of big men born the day Jimmy died."

The final blows were struck at Jimmy in a wider context. Kelso Roberts, the sometimes comically bellicose Attorney-General reluctantly appeared, and admitted that Jimmy, like a lot of MPPs, tried to influence his department. He went on to admit that Thompson's claim might have been true, but that he wasn't concerned about it – it was for Thompson to do something about it, if he felt James had attempted to influence him improperly. Which seemed to be exactly what Thompson was doing in informing his superiors. On the matter of whether or not James might have been drunk at the time, Kelso Roberts allowed as such was possible, but he bristled on that matter: "The health situation of Mr. Maloney was nothing to you, sir, and I. I don't think it should be brought out in public unless it's relevant."

What it comes to ultimately is an open question. James's conduct as a criminal counsel – wheedling, and attempting to deal for lesser charges or withdrawals was a common aspect of the old-style magistrates' courts, and was carried on without any serious damage to the justice system. It saved time, often satisfied the need for justice tempered with a kind of parochial mercy, and would surprise no-one familiar with those courts. It probably still works today in the smaller provincial courts, which are the old magistrates' courts under an inflated name. The appearance of a Crown at the Roach commission, complaining about the conduct of a criminal counsel, seems pusillanimous, if not vindictive.

On the other hand, the question of James, on more than one occasion, using his position as an MPP, and as a Cabinet Minister to nudge the judiciary, if true, is somewhat more disturbing, but there was evidence before Mr. Justice Roach that he was not alone in so doing, and government officers, such as Kelso Roberts, admitted that they were flexible in dealing with gambling charges in ways that might well lead old-style politicians like James to think that there was no harm in trying – after all, what were politicians elected for, if not, in small part, to help their friends?

Mr. Justice Roach delivered his report on 15 March 1963 in which he expressed his contempt for the gamblers. On the matter of James's association with them, he could find no direct evidence that James had been corrupted, although he suspected that the two might well have put it about that they had James in their pocket. "An association the extent and effect of which these two men in the course of their illegal operations in my opinion exaggerated in order to further their own evil purposes."[24] Mr. Justice Roach was particularly unhappy because James had also endorsed the good character of the pair in writing when they attempted to obtain a provincial patent for a loan business, and it was in discussing that act that the worst damage was done:

> I cannot avoid the impression that what he knew about them should have repelled him from certifying to their good character. Mr. Maloney is not here to defend himself; he died on October 1, 1961. In possible amelioration for what he did on that occasion or what he did or is said to have done on other occasions not yet referred to it should be said – and I say it in all kindness but it needs to be said – that unfortunately Mr. Maloney on occasions drank to excess and that may explain some of the things he did or is said to have done.[25]

If James's name was not to be entirely cleared, it was not found that he had engaged in any criminal act. Roach's conclusions have to be seen in the context of the common, sloppy, occasionally dubious practises of the time, and the fact that James, as a lawyer, and as a politician, and as a human being, was a man of generous, sometimes feckless tendencies, given to use his power, whatever it was, expansively, and sometimes without much thought of the consequences. Some have spoken of him as simply naive, and easily influenced, although it should be remembered that he was a very tough, rough, and competent counsel. He was, as W.H. Auden once said of Yeats, "silly, like the rest of us."

The question of who prepared the Ramsay Club brief was never answered – nor who, claiming to be David Humphrey, had phoned the OPP Inspector to set the matter up. The criminals were prosecuted and convicted under the law, but Mr. Justice Roach could find no evidence of serious official impropriety, although he was not entirely comfortable with the way some of the lawyers had comported themselves, and there was a lot of odd comporting going on. He could not find "any improper relationship between senior officials of the legal staff of the Department of the Attorney General and any person or persons." That might well have been the case – but the lower orders had certainly been busy in a wild olio of criminality, corruption, and horseplay, which was often hilarious in its peregrinations, but also included the disappearance of one of the witnesses in a manner that suggested ultimate foul play.

Arthur was free and clear, but he could not entirely retrieve James, who is still remembered as the Minister of Mines who was involved in the sixties gambling scandal – and before that, the Northern Ontario Gas scandal of the late fifties. This latter public memory is the most damaging, and is not, in fact, true. He was not involved in the Gas case at all, save in a peripheral sense. It was Philip T. Kelly who was Minister of Mines when charges were made about manipulation of the gas stock, and Kelly resigned. He was succeeded by J.W. Spooner in 1957, and after the 1958 provincial election, James took that portfolio. But given the nature of public memory, the two scandals have been linked, and James has become the unfortunate beneficiary of both of them. Ever after, on appropriate occasions, Arthur, with ironic solemnity, would declare that "every Royal Commission needs a dead man."

It was not, then, a happy time for Arthur. The failure of his political career was assuaged, in part, by his relief in getting back home to his family and his practice, but the double blows of James's death, and the results of the Roach hearing, were disheartening. When Jimmy died, Arthur was deeply hurt, having lost, as he said, his best friend. They were an amusing pair, who enjoyed being together, like some odd, fraternal version of the two-sided pairing suggested by Aristophanes in Plato's *The Symposium*, complementing each other in their versions of the Maloney personality, at once the rough and the smooth. Their mother had once hoped that they might practice law together. They knew that would have been an impossible collision of personalities, but they dearly loved coming together in great clashes of familial celebration.

On top of that, in May of 1962, Lillian's father, Gilbert LaBine, had a serious stroke, which paralysed his right side and permanently affected his speech. He was to live for several years in that sad state, a fiercely frustrated man, locked inside his ravaged body. One of Lillian's fondest memories is the way in which the two men coped with the problem and the friendship that developed between them. Arthur spent a great deal of time with his father-in-law, and Lillian remembers how Arthur would often take over the bathing of LaBine, who would croon with incoherent pleasure while Arthur washed his hair. There was a great capacity for affection in Arthur that was naturally expressed in his relations with his wife and children, but the connection with James, and with LaBine was of a different kind, much more akin to the unspoken, inarticulate affection that he had for his students and colleagues, and which so many of them still hold, deeply imbedded in their memories as one of the most fulfilling relationships of their lives, although they would, given their natural tendency to eschew emotion, be hardly likely to express it, if, indeed, they could find the language to do so. It lies there, just under the surface of their anecdotage – an uneasy memory of an evanescent, idealized world of laughter and high excitement and endeavour – gone forever – as they move into old age.

8

Murder on the Run

In May 1963, Maloney defended Karafil Bleta on a charge of non-capital murder. The first eyewitness to the incident, Ordinary Seaman John McGuire, formerly of the Royal Canadian Navy, was on his way to the unemployment office on Dundas Street, Toronto on the 4 January 1963. He came down Keele Street and turned west on to Dundas:

McGuire: I was going down Dundas when I heard a bunch, I heard a woman yelling or screaming.
Crown: You heard a woman yelling or screaming?
McG: Yes, sir.
C: Where did the sound come from?
McG: The sidewalk just ahead of me there.
C: Ahead of you?
McG: Yes, sir. And then I walked over ...
C: And then what did you say you saw?
McG: I heard a woman yelling or screaming. I'm not sure right now.
C: Heard a woman screaming? Then what did you say?
McG: Then I seen these two men fighting.
C: Where were they?
McG: On the sidewalk on the north side of Dundas. North side of the sidewalk.
C: West of you?
McG: Yes, sir.
C: Did you know them?
McG: No, sir.
C: How were they fighting?
McG: At the time they were just fighting with their fists.
C: Their fists?
McG: Yes, sir.
C: Well, did either of them actually strike the other one?

McG: Well, I didn't see anybody, any punches thrown but I seen them bleeding around the eye and that ...
C: Could you give us any description of these two men in order that we might distinguish between them?
McG: Well, the victim –
C: Pardon?
McG: The victim, he was sort of tall, about six feet I guess.
C: A tall man, about six feet?
McG: Yes. Real heavy.
C: Real heavy?
McG: Pretty heavy, sir.
C: Pretty heavy?
McG: And the other one, he was pretty, well heavy built too but a little shorter ...
C: Do you see him here in court?
McG: Yes, sir. ...
C: You are indicating the prisoner in the dock?
McG: Yes, sir. ...
C: You say he was which one?
McG: He was the one that, he was the one that killed the other man, sir.
C: Well, do you mean the tall man or the shorter man?
McG: The shorter man. He was just getting off the ground.
C: Who was?
McG: The man over there ... Yes, sir. And then the other guy started to walk away. He started to chase him.
C: Why did you say they were fighting with their fists?
McG: One was bleeding.
C: Which one was bleeding?
McG: He was bleeding a bit around the neck.
C: You are nodding to the accused?
McG: Yes, sir.
C: Around the neck and you put your finger to the right side of your cheek or chin?
McG: I don't know what side it was on. I remember he was bleeding a bit.
C: Yes. Now, you see, you have said that they were using their fists. You are just drawing a conclusion, weren't you?
McG: Yes, sir.
C: Now, the rules of evidence are such that you shouldn't give your conclusions but just what you actually saw. Do you understand that?
McG: Yes, sir.
C: It is for the jury to draw conclusions. Well, you actually saw the accused on the ground and getting up?
McG: Yes, sir.

C: And a tall man near him or something like that?
McG: He was just walking away.
C: Just walking away from him?
McG: Yes, sir.
C: In which direction?
McG: He was coming towards me as I was walking down.
C: He was walking east?
McG: Yes.
C: What happened then?
McG: The man over there, he got up and reached in his pocket and pulled out a knife, and the other guy, he seen this, and he started to run ...
C: He started to run?
McG: Yes. He looked over his shoulder and happened to see it and he was running.
C: And the accused chased him?
McG: Yes, sir ...
C: Did you see where the accused pulled the knife out from?
McG: He just got up and then pulled it out.
C: Out of where?
McG: Inside his coat, heavy coat. A trench, heavy coat, winter coat.
C: An overcoat?
McG: Yes, sir.
C: And he pulled it out from where?
McG: I don't know. Either from the right hand – I think it was from the right-hand side, sir ...
C: Well, then, the other man, the tall man, looked over his shoulder and started to run?
McG: Yes, sir.
C: The accused started to run after him?
McG: Yes, sir.
C: They were then coming towards you?
McG: Well, they ran past me by this time.
C: Both ran past you? ... What happened then?
McG: Well, the other guy, the man he was chasing, he couldn't outrun him, I don't think. ... The other man couldn't outrun him. I thought he was turning around just to fight him, then it was too late. He got him before he turned around. He stabbed him in the back of the neck.
C: Could you tell us just in what fashion he stabbed him, how he held the knife or anything like that?
McG: Like this. (Indicating) Down.
C: Making a downwards motion?
McG: Yes, sir.

C: As if you had a dagger in your hand?
McG: Yes, sir ...
HIS LORDSHIP: Were they running pretty fast at first, sir?
McG: Pretty fast, yes sir.
H.L.: The one that was being chased, he was running at a good speed, you say?
McG: He was running pretty fast at first, sir.
Crown: What happened then?
McG: The man fell to the ground. When he fell to the ground ...
C: The tall man?
McG: Yes, he fell to the ground. When he fell the other guy kicked him.
C:Whereabouts?
H.L.: I'm sorry, I didn't hear that again.
McG: The tall man fell to the ground after he was stabbed and the man over there kicked him when he fell.
H.L.: Kicked him with his foot where?
McG: In the side.
Crown: The ribs?
McG: Yes.
C: The tall man, did he not do anything towards the accused before the accused stabbed him?
McG: No.
C: And after the tall man was on the ground, did the accused do anything to him besides kick him?
McG: No, sir.
C: What happened next?
McG: He just took off. Took off.
C: The accused?
McG: Yes, he took off west on Dundas again.[1]

There was no question of who did what to whom here, and no chance of suggesting that others might have done the same; Maloney's client was the only choice. It was the kind of bare-faced evidence that he often met, and to make things worse, the witness added another bit of damage when Arthur Klein, the Crown, asked him if he had heard any conversation between the two men. After admitting that he could not understand what they were saying to each other, he put his opinion of the matter nevertheless, as witnesses, when they become comfortable, are inclined to do – just trying to be helpful.

H.L.: Just a minute, now. I don't quite follow you there. Witness, you didn't, if I understand your evidence, you didn't actually see them fighting? By this time one was down but they were talking then?
McG: He was, the taller man was telling, I think was telling him to quit, he

wanted to forget about it. That is what I could get by the hand expression, he just wanted to leave him alone, just go, but he persisted.

Arthur Maloney managed to get this opinion slightly diminished in cross-examination:

Maloney: You said a little while ago something about the tall man saying to the accused, "forget about it." You don't know what he was saying at all?
McGuire: No, but it looked that way.
M: Well, whatever was being said was being said in Albanian? Isn't that right? Or some language foreign to you?
McG: Yes, sir.[2]

But the rest of that testimony stood up to Arthur's cross-examination, and the witness was of no use as to what had happened previously, since he had only seen two blows struck – the one to the neck of Hairedin Gafi, the victim, with a knife, and the other to his ribs, with a boot, immediately before Bleta disappeared down the street. The matter of this evidence was, in a sense, of little consequence anyway – Arthur was prepared to admit that his client had killed Gafi. The real problem was obvious. Whatever had happened previously between the two men, Gafi had broken it off, and had walked away, seemingly satisfied that the party was over. Bleta had got up, pulled a knife from his pocket, took after Gafi, who, seeing him coming, had tried to run away. Bleta caught up, and stabbed Gafi in the back of the neck, with such force and accuracy that "the first and second vertebrae of the cervical column and as part of that wound the upper spinal cord had been almost completely – sorry – had been completely cut across so that death in the case of Hairedin Gafi was due to a deep penetrating stab wound of the neck with complete transection of the spinal cord."[3]

It was not a case to fill a defence counsel with much enthusiasm. It was, however, to be one of Maloney's most satisfying cases, and was to break new ground in the defence use of psychiatric lore. Arthur had, from early on in his career, made extensive use of psychological defences, particularly in murder and manslaughter cases, but the Bleta defence was as far as he ever went in depending upon the doctors to get him out of a losing situation. Bleta was charged with murder, and the reason for that was simple. Whatever might be discovered about what McGuire had not seen, whatever punishment Gafi might have imposed on the man the seaman had seen on the ground, the matter seemed to have come to an end. Gafi had gone on his way, seemingly wanting to end it; indeed, he did end it, striding away, and more to the point, when he saw Bleta coming after him, he started to run away. In a legal sense, it could be argued that two separate incidents had occurred: the initial fight – whoever was to blame – and the attack on Gafi, some distance down the street when Bleta ran after the fleeing man, stabbed him in the neck, and after Gafi fell, kicked him in the ribs, and ran off. It looked like murder to the Crown.

It must have looked like murder to everyone in the courtroom by the time McGuire, disinterested and confident about what he had seen, and not seen, told his story. Maloney might have slightly diminished the evidence as to what was being said by the two men, but body language is a common way for humans to express themselves, and John McGuire had read Gafi's gestures as signs of having had enough, and his immediate departure seemed to corroborate that attitude.

The only thing that Bleta might have had in his favour was a rule of law that could have convinced the Crown to charge him with manslaughter, rather than murder. There is a defence that will reduce murder to manslaughter if the defence can prove that (1) the accused was provoked either by word or deed, or both, in a way that might lead a reasonable person to physically attack his or her tormentor – but it must be conduct of an egregious nature that can be accepted as likely to so upset a reasonable person that it would be understandable for him to strike out, not with the intention of killing, but to simply respond physically and uncontrollably to the enormity of what has been imposed on a sudden upon him. But (2) the attack must be spontaneous, and almost instantaneous. The offended party cannot stand about and think about it, since the defence is based upon the presumption that a reasonable person, so insulted, momentarily loses control, and, on the moment, blinded by excruciating rage or sorrow, strikes out. It will not obtain if one decides to think about it – it is basically an act of an unthinking, enraged person who, not unreasonably, given the circumstances, has good reason to be unreasonable.

It can, for instance, be a defence to an attack made on the revelation of infidelity on the part of a loved one, if it is so suddenly and so upsettingly presented that the betrayed party strikes out on the moment, and strangles the betrayer. But the insult has to be so extreme that a normal juror or judge could understand how one might lose control for an instant, *and* on the instant. That, perhaps, might be the case with Bleta if Gafi had said something to him while he was down and out. He certainly reacted immediately, running after Gafi and striking him in full flight. Obviously the Crown thought that the beating, if there was a beating, wasn't enough, and that no reasonable man would have lost that much control under the circumstances. That he had the presence of mind to arm himself before he reached Gafi suggested that Bleta was not acting blindly, but with some determination and preparation, however short the time between Gafi's withdrawal and the violent collision just a short way and a short time down the block.

There was, however, some evidence that might well have been considered sufficient by Arthur to try for a defence of the type discussed above, but there was one thing that could have convinced Arthur to take a more dangerous and difficult road. A defence of this kind, if it did work, did not allow the accused to go free – it only allowed for the murder charge to be reduced to manslaughter. It was obvious from early on, however, that Maloney was going for something else – something quite radical in Canadian law. He was going to prove that Bleta was, in fact, temporarily unable to control his actions, not because of some sudden attack by Gafi, but because he was, in a very particular sense, out of his mind temporarily. Not insane, as in the M'Naghten Rule, which requires the accused to have no idea of the nature and quality of the criminal act, but literally out of control mentally because of the beating he had taken. It was very risky.

The first witness to the fight had been little help, and the second, Rustem Kaziu, was even less helpful. The district in which the fight occurred was something of an immigrant haven for Albanians, and Kaziu had been in a local cafe, The Albanian Coffee House, just prior to coming upon the two men in combat. He knew both of them – Bleta to nod to – and Gafi as a friend. He had never seen them together, until he came upon them fighting. The first witness had claimed that Gafi had walked away while Bleta was still on the ground. Kaziu refuted that idea.

Kaziu: I got in the centre of them and took ahold of both of them with my hand by their shirts.
Crown: Go ahead.
K: I parted them and I yelled to Gafi to run and get away from here and I was hanging on to Bleta ...
C: Well, why did you do that?
K: Because they were Albanian and I knew them.
C: I know. Why did you hold on to Bleta and why did you tell Gafi to go away?
K: It appeared to me as if Bleta was more nervous.
C: What do you mean by "nervous"?
K: I don't know why I thought he was more nervous. He just looked more nervous to me and he took a knife out.
HIS LORDSHIP: Just a minute. Put it to him this way. When he used the word "nervous" does he mean nervous or angry?
K: Yes, My Lord, angry. As I was hanging on to him an old woman was yelling to me to let go and get away because Bleta had a knife and I was telling him to put the knife away.
H.L.: How did he know he had a knife?

K: He took the knife out as I was holding him by the shirt – And as I was hanging on to Bleta, Gafi left and I stopped Bleta. I let go of Bleta and started to walk east on Dundas myself. As I was walking along I noticed Bleta running along Dundas and got in front of me at a running speed. I couldn't reach him to catch hold of him. He caught up to Gafi and hit him with the knife.[4]

There was no joy in the cross-examination. Kaziu did not see Bleta being knocked down, nor did Bleta seemed dazed to him. He did agree that Bleta looked the worse for wear, and he saw Gafi strike Bleta in the face. But Kaziu left the jurors with an impression of Bleta standing toe-to-toe with Gafi, with a knife in his hand when Gafi walked away, and the look in his eye was not dazed, but angry.

If there is one thing, however, that is constant in trials it is the surprising way in which witnesses, who are disinterested and determined to tell the truth, see things differently, and sometimes damagingly so, without realizing it. Maloney did not kick against the pricks with Kaziu; he did not even suggest that Kaziu might be mistaken, or that his perception of the incident might be coloured by the fact that he was something of an acquaintance of the dead man, while only a nodding passer-by to Bleta. He simply let it lie, without giving any one, including the jury, any indication of where he was going, save for his attempts to suggest that Bleta was getting the worst of it (which Kaziu agreed to). And might be dazed at the time (which Kaziu did not notice).

The next witness was enormously helpful. Eleanor May Trimble was out shopping, and came out of a shop, next to Reitman's, the shop before which the two men were fighting. She knew neither man. She couldn't help Arthur on the matter of how much punishment Gafi's blows were doing to Bleta, or vice versa, since what she saw were two men flailing away, but not striking each other. She did see Bleta fall down, and most importantly, she saw him hit his head on the tile step of the Reitman's entrance.

Trimble: But it was a winter day and it was slushy and the taller man of the two went to hit the shorter man – and he didn't hit him – but the shorter man lost his footing on the slushy tile entrance to Reitman's and he fell backwards and he hit his head on the tile. And I never thought he would ever get up ...
Crown: Why did you think that he wouldn't get up?
T: Well, the back of his head hit that tile so hard, well, the only way I can explain it, you know – a coconut – and he hit it in a manner to open it up. Well, that is the sound it made when that man's head hit the tile.[5]

It is possible in looking at the trial record to determine what particularly interests Maloney, since he has a habit of drawing vertical lines on his copy, through the middle of the passages which he thinks are important. The preceding testimony, and the following were so marked:

HIS LORDSHIP: Witness, the one that was knocked down, did he stay down for long?
T: He stayed down for a few minutes and I just stood there.
H.L.: One moment. You mean a few minutes, not a few seconds?
T: No, I don't mean a few seconds, I mean ...
C: Moments?
T: A minute and a half, maybe two minutes.
C: By the watch?
T: By my timing, that is all.
C: Pardon?
T: By my timing it seemed a long time that he laid there.
C: Yes. Well, what did the other man do, the taller man, while the shorter man laid there?
T: Well, he just turned round and proceeded towards Keele and Dundas. I thought that was it.[6]

Gafi walked off, according to Mrs. Trimble, and then the smaller man got to his feet, and Maloney got another break:

T: I was still standing at the doorway at Reitman's and I stayed there until the shorter man got up and staggered and then he proceeded towards Keele and Dundas and I thought it was all over so I just walked behind him.
C: You just walked behind him?
T: Yes.
C: In what manner did he proceed?
T: He was staggering.
C: Staggering?
T: Yes.
C: Well, how far – or how slowly, did he walk or move?
T: He was very much slower than the other man and not steady either.[7]

So the running chase of the first witness had now become a staggering, slow pursuit, and the presence of Bleta on the ground had become a head-splitting fall, followed by a short stay on the tiles as Bleta sought to get himself straightened around. Kaziu's story of having held the two men apart seemed untrue. For the rest of her statement, Mrs. Trimble was less helpful. Somehow, despite his staggeringly slow walk, he caught up to Gafi. Although Mrs. Trimble said nothing of a running attack, she was so close to Bleta that he almost knocked her over as he pulled back after striking Gafi.

The shorter, stockier man, he seemed to hunch his shoulders up and all I saw was the arm raised. I just thought – by this time he had caught up to the taller man – I just thought he was going to hit him with his fist but I didn't know anything different until I saw the man slump on the sidewalk. Because when it happened he turned around and he knocked me flying. He turned around in a daze and I didn't – these things happened so quick that you just don't realize what had happened but he knocked me flying.[8]

There was no hope of avoiding Bleta's attack on Gafi, but again Mrs. Trimble had, unprompted, used the word "daze." There was another innocent observation to follow: "all I could see was this accused running zigzag like this up Dundas Street." Klein was interested in the way Bleta was running, probably to establish that he was trying to evade capture, but the answers didn't entirely help that theory:

C: Was there anything in his way that might have given him a reason to zig zag?
T: Oh. Unless it was terror.
C: Were there any people in his way?
T: There were a few but not as many as there usually is on a Friday in that section.

Arthur went immediately to the points he wanted to emphasize, beginning with the staggering. Mrs. Trimble agreed that had she not seen Bleta fall, she would have presumed that he might have been drunk when he walked off. But she could not help with the question of whether he looked dazed. She was very helpful on the fall.

Trimble: I was glad to see him get up because I didn't think he ever would.
Maloney: You mean you felt that the blow to his head that he received was so severe you were surprised he was even able to get up? [An example of Maloney leading a witness.]
T: Yes, because with the cracking sound, the terrible crack, I thought the man's skull, you know, that he had cracked the back of his head open.
M: That was on the back of the head?
T: Yes, sir.
M: Well, when he did finally get up were his movements uncertain?
T: His movements were uncertain and his balance wasn't right at all. He was backward. I mean he wasn't standing up like you.

Arthur was always happy to help a witness who was helping him, even if it meant a little deft posing.

T: He was out of balance, he was backward and the motion you went through a second ago, you sort of had your body reared backwards. That's right, exactly.
M: He was walking in a sort of a list?
T: That's right.

And then he got the other bit of evidence that he had tried for earlier; it came out in a way that he could hardly have hoped:

M: Just before he knocked you flying you said he turned around and in a daze he knocked you flying.
T: That's right.
M: Is that what you said?
T: He had the funniest look in his eyes. I mean, it was a shock to me.

In fact, Mrs. Trimble, who had earlier told Arthur that she didn't notice Bleta's eyes when he got up, had earlier told Klein that when he turned after the attack, he had turned "in a daze." The judge, for a moment, was unsure of whom Mrs. Trimble was speaking. He interrupted, but it didn't break the line of her thought.

HIS LORDSHIP: Who are you speaking of now, witness?
Trimble: The accused, sir.
H.L.: The accused?
T: He looked like a man that wasn't in this world.[9]

Arthur could not have done better himself. After establishing, as he had with other witnesses, that Bleta's head was bleeding at the back, he went on to the "zig zag" escape that Klein had made nothing of, and might, one would have thought, have left well alone since it might be presumed that Bleta had enough of his wits about him to dodge about to avoid capture. But Arthur often had a sixth sense about "fishing," which one of his students spoke about as being astonishing and unnerving, since the first thing a law student learns is not to ask questions if the answer is either not known or could be damaging. The "zig zag" might well have been that sort of trap, particularly if Maloney was going to argue that Bleta had no idea what he was doing. Nevertheless, he went right for it:

Maloney: Then after he knocked you flying, he, you said, walked over towards Keele, walked away from Keele Street, I'm sorry?
Trimble: Yes.
M: In a zigzagging fashion?
T: Yes, sir.
M: Was he still staggering?
T: To an extent, yes. He wasn't on the sidewalk all the time.
M: He was sometimes on the road?
T: On the road.
M: Sometimes on the sidewalk?
T: Yes, sir.[10]

Now came an example of how well Maloney listened, as he turned the Klein examination to his advantage:

M: And I got the impression from what you said to Mr. Klein that there didn't seem to be much reason why he would walk that way, why he would have to zigzag like that. The people weren't in his way?
T: It wasn't for the want of people on the sidewalk.
M: He could have, there was nothing preventing him from walking straight along the sidewalk, was there?
T: No, sir.
M: But instead of doing this he was walking in this unusual zigzag manner, sometimes on the sidewalk, sometimes on the road?
T: Yes, sir.[11]

On re-examination, Klein tried to discover if Mrs. Trimble had seen anyone attempting to part the men, but she could not help. Then the judge tried to get the matter cleared up, and ran right into a bit of hearsay that might explain Kaziu's story.

HIS LORDSHIP: Witness, just a minute before you leave the witness box. I heard some evidence that some man came along at one stage and separated these two men. Did you see that?
Trimble: I didn't see that in the part of the fight that I saw, sir. I understand that the fight previous to what I saw took place on the other side of Dundas.
H.L.: You don't know anything about that?
T: I don't know anything about that because I didn't see it.
H.L.: All right.[12]

It was a wry moment when the witness instructed the judge on the rules of evidence, but it was also a puzzling one. Kaziu had told a simple tale of holding the men apart, of Bleta drawing a knife, and Gafi leaving. It might have been an earlier encounter, as Mrs. Trimble's comments suggested, save for one further fact – Kaziu went on to describe how Bleta had followed and struck Gafi down with the knife. Surely it had not happened twice. No wonder the judge was puzzled, given the difference in the stories being told.

The next witness was also helpful to Maloney on the matter of Bleta's condition. Mrs. Mazie DeGeer was on the combat spot earlier than any previous witness – with a privileged view from inside the Reitman's store, where she worked. She saw the men appear outside the store, punching each other, and she saw Bleta knocked to the ground by Gafi. Not so much a blow, as a push. She saw men trying to part the two, but no specific man in control of both of them at any one time. She also saw something else:

Crown: You saw the taller man push the accused down?
DeGeer: Yes.
C: What happened after that?
DeG: Then he got up and he was knocked – you see, they were up closer to the door and he was knocked down and hit his head with a terrible blow.
HIS LORDSHIP: This was the second time?
DeG: This was the second time and I was amazed that he ever got up because his head hit the ground so hard.
C: The back of his head?
H.L: How could you tell he hit it so hard? Was there a sound, a noise?
DeG: Oh, it was a terrible thud. I mean, you could just ...
H.L.: A thud?
DeG: Yes, you could just hear it.[13]

Arthur must have wondered why he was needed with the Crown and the judge working so hard for him. The pair went on, sharing the witness in an attempt to discover whether Bleta had been knocked down or simply pushed, but without much success, and the testimony ended as Maloney would have wanted, if only in part.

DeG: He hit his head and I didn't expect him to get up again. He hit his head so hard.
C: All right. What happened then?
DeG: Well then he did get up and they both disappeared from the store and I didn't see anything after that.

The one disturbing aspect of this statement was the omission of the departure of Gafi before Bleta got up – had she seen that or was Bleta up, as Kaziu said, when Gafi left? Arthur, in cross-examination, was more successful in getting Mrs. DeGeer to say that it was a punch that had knocked Bleta down, although she did not, in fact, see the punch that did it. She would not admit that she saw any punches landing, and though she had Bleta down twice, and his head hitting the pavement both times, it was the second fall that she thought most damaging. She could be led by Arthur to stress her description of the second collision with the concrete: "Was it a sort of a sickening sound?" DeGeer: "It sure was." Mrs. DeGeer was also able to support Mrs. Trimble's description of Bleta's condition after the fall:

Maloney: Mrs. Trimble, who gave evidence just before you, said that after that terrible blow to the head of Bleta, when he got up he was staggering almost like a drunken man would stagger. Did you notice that?
DeGeer: Well, I noticed it took him – you know – when he got up he was dazed and in a dazed condition because, I mean, he had hit his head.

HIS LORDSHIP: Was he down for very long the second time, witness?
DeG: He was down longer the second time than he was the first time. Lying there longer the second time than he was the first time.[14]

The judge, who admitted being concerned about getting things right, persisted, and the witness was prepared to go as far as five minutes for Bleta's second downing. While she did not exactly agree with Mrs. Trimble's description of Bleta being out of this world, she answered in a way which was sufficient, and had the tang of common sense that makes some witnesses so effective.

M: She said [Mrs Trimble], if I remember her words rightly, "He didn't seem to be in this world." That is the way she put it. Is that the impression you got?
DeG: I imagine he wouldn't be after he had such a blow on his head, that he would be in a dazed condition.

She didn't see the knife, and she left the stand agreeing with Maloney that Bleta was "getting the worst of it."

By this point in the testimony, Arthur's interests were apparent. He had no intention of disputing the evidence of the fatal attack. What he wanted to discuss with the witnesses was almost exclusively confined to (1) who was doing badly in the fight, (2) how severely hurt was Bleta as a result of his falls, and (3) what was the physical and mental state of Bleta before, and after the stabbing? What he planned to do with this material was still unclear, since the fatal attack was separated from the prior battle between the two men, and however badly Bleta had been doing in the fight, he was certainly the aggressor in the final confrontation.

Maloney's attempt to picture Bleta as a stumbling, confused wretch was not aided by the testimony of Sidney Coles, who was driving by and saw the two men, as he put it, "burst from the crowd."

Coles: The man who was pursuing seized the man who was in the lead around the back over the shoulder and around the chest in this manner and raised his hand up on high (indicating) ... The right hand, raised his hand up on high and brought the hand down with a swift thrust into the back of the neck. There was something in the hand. I can't say that it was a knife. It was a flashing object that struck the man in the neck ... The man who was struck threw up his arms in a stiff manner like this and quivered a little bit and fell over backwards to the street with his head into the gutter, towards the gutter. The man who done the striking stomped him twice on the stomach and turned to his left and made off.
HIS LORDSHIP: He did what, witness?
C: He stomped him, sir.
H.L.: How do you mean?
C: With the right foot on the stomach.[15]

Coles was no help to the defence. He admitted having seen nothing prior to the pair chasing down the street, and he wasn't close enough to see Bleta, as Arthur coyly put it (getting it fixed in the jury's collective mind): "You wouldn't get an opportunity then, I suppose, to have noticed what one or two of the ladies noticed who had seen the fight earlier, the very dazed appearance of the accused man Bleta?" Arthur often got the answer he wanted into the minds of the jury, without actually getting anything at all from the witness.

A further witness had only seen Bleta pull the knife and strike Gafi. Maloney got part of what he wanted, despite the witness: "There were two ladies gave evidence earlier this morning, Mr. Randell. They told us about Bleta having been pushed to the concrete pavement and his head hitting the pavement very hard. This must have happened before you began to take notice of the fight?" On this occasion, Maloney is using a variation on the rule about not asking a question of which one does not know the answer. He knows, from what the witness has already said, that he does not have this information – he knows that the witness will say he does not know – what he wants to do is simply put the prior evidence in front of the jury again. Randell's answer, "Well, I didn't see any fight" is irrelevant – it is what Arthur says that is important. It was a trick of Arthur's that has faint echoes of the Irish habit of asking a negative question, well knowing that the answer will be "no."

The next witness was more helpful. Philip Rosenfarb, a store clerk, was watching the fight from the south side of the street and saw the two punching away at each other. Bleta went down "and the bigger chap went over to him and started to punch him quite a few times." He saw Gafi back away, and someone, possibly Kaziu, step between them. He saw Gafi leave and "the little chap broke away from the one he was with and ran after him and I saw him raise his hand to hit him, that is all."[16] So Kaziu's story might well have been true; it was just a matter of different witnesses judging time differently. Bleta was down and beaten by Gafi while still on the ground – Bleta started to get up and Kaziu came between them, sending Gafi off, and Bleta, breaking away, went after him. Perhaps that was how it happened – and it would be very fast, not at the pace of the witnesses' memory, which would slow down the incident. In fact, a police officer saw the fight in progress, but by the time he parked to get over to it, it was all over. Bleta had killed Gafi and was fleeing.

Maloney obviously saw the Rosenfarb testimony as a chance to deepen the evidence on the question of Bleta's lesser accomplishment in the battle – he was especially interested in Roserfarb's statement about what happened when Bleta was on the ground.

Maloney: How many times did Bleta get knocked down to the ground in the course of this fight between him and Gafi the deceased man, that you saw?

Rosenfarb: I believe twice.
M: And on one of those occasions that he was knocked to the ground did you say Gafi kept on punching him.
R: Yes.
M: What was he punching him with?
R: As far as I know his fists.
M: His fists? Could you see what Bleta was trying to do to protect himself from the blows that he was getting from Gafi as he lay on the ground?
R: No.
M: But here we have Bleta lying on the ground and you say Gafi, as far as you could see, was administering punches or blows to him with his fists?
R: That's right.
M: Could you see what part of his body, Bleta's body, he was striking?
R: The head. The accused was in a sitting position, and he went over, the deceased went over and grabbed him and was punching him on the head I believe.
M: At this stage was Bleta doing anything to attack Gafi or was he just sitting there or lying there on the sidewalk?
R: No, he wasn't fighting back. I think he was trying to get up.

Arthur had a deft way of getting words into the mouths of witnesses in cross-examination, and he was clearly colouring the evidence in the following exchange:

M: Did the blows that Gafi administered, did they seem to be pretty severe blows? Did they seem to have a lot of punch behind them?
R: Yes.
M: And they were all in the general area of the head of Mr. Bleta?
R: In the general area.

Rosenfarb went on to support Kaziu's claim that he – or someone had attempted to part the pair.

On the matter of how quickly this all happened, the testimony of Charles Bond, an off-duty policeman, is helpful. His description of what he was able to see may put the proper tempo into the various descriptions of the fight:

Well, I was driving with my wife and son westbound on Dundas Street in the vicinity of Keele Street in my own car and as I passed the intersection of Keele Street I observed what appeared to be a fight on the north sidewalk; two men at a stance, a crowd of people around these two men. I pulled into the curb a little bit west at this point when I got the opportunity ... and I got out of the car and started to proceed towards the scene of the fight. At this time I saw a man walking towards me on the north sidewalk. He was walking quickly, the accused man. I recognized him as being one of the persons involved in the fight. He had a bit of blood on his face. I took ahold of the accused and told him I was a Police Officer.[17]

A matter of moments, and the whole affair was over, and Bleta was in the hands of a passing officer – who saw part of the last moments of the encounter.

What Maloney had by this stage in the trial was some agreement that Bleta had got the worst of the fight, had fallen or had been pushed or had been struck down, at least twice, and had hit his head the second time with such force that two witnesses actually heard the impact, and were surprised that he was able, after a short rest, to get up again – in a dazed condition. It would seem that upon rising the second time, the battle had continued, although someone (possibly Kaziu) had tried to part them. Soon after Bleta rose for the second time, Gafi walked away and Bleta broke away from whomever was holding him, pursued Gafi and stabbed him. In Bleta's favour was the evidence that he was losing the fight, that he had fallen twice, and cracked his head badly, had been beaten about the head while on the ground, and got up, dazed and staggering – although there was some difference of opinion on whether he moved quickly or slowly. When Gafi saw him coming, it seemed, on balance, that both men started to run. Then Bleta stabbed his tormentor. What Maloney seemed most interested in was the beaten-and-banged-about state of Bleta.

Maloney was only rarely inclined to fiercely provocative attacks on witnesses. He was not temperamentally disposed to the sneering disbelief that some counsel presume is the requisite demeanour when cross-examining. He treated most witnesses with considerable courtesy. He was, however, doggedly stubborn, and he would attempt to get an answer, particularly out of expert witnesses, even if he had to put it into their mouths. He was also possessed of a determined way of trying to stretch good news into better news – which did not always work. Bond, the off-duty policeman, was prepared to go part of the way on the matter of Bleta's mental state. "I would say he appeared to be dazed when he approached me and when I took hold of him but he appeared to understand me when I spoke to him."

Maloney: But until you spoke to him and identified yourself, he seemed to be in a daze?
Bond: He would have a dazed look on his face as he came towards me.

The answer gave Maloney the opportunity, seemingly by chance, to re-use the earlier evidence of one of the women – with the hope that the officer would add to it: "As a matter of fact I think, to borrow one of the expressions of one of the ladies – I have forgotten which one – she said he looked as though he was not in this world, was the appearance he conveyed to her. I suppose we all have different ways of expressing the same things but does that add up to you now as you recall his appearance?" Police officers were generally inclined to co-operate with Maloney, but they also have a wary pride in not being led by the nose, and Arthur, for all his diversionary, informal, seemingly "by-the-way" style was trying to do just that – and Bond knew it. He turned laconically stubborn: "No, I wouldn't say he was that far."[18] Then Arthur tried to get Bond on to the injury to the back of Bleta's head, but Bond did not notice it, and remained un-cooperative, refusing to allow Maloney to lead him into saying that Bleta was holding his head at the time of his arrest. Well, at least, he admitted that Bleta was dazed before he caught on to what Maloney was trying to do.

Now that he had got Bleta down and out, he started to concentrate on the head injury; he tried it again on Detective Sergeant Norman Hobson, who had questioned Bleta at the police station. Bleta had not said much, aside from "I don't know what to say." He went on, "About that murder, I should say no about that. I didn't murder anyone." Arthur wanted to link his terseness to his mental state: "Well, now, you have heard the evidence of Mrs. Trimble and you have heard the evidence of Mrs. DeGeer. We now all know that he suffered a very, very severe blow to his head. You recall that evidence, don't you?" Hobson seems to be trying, in his answer, to comment upon the way in which Arthur was presuming that the head injury was generally accepted: "I heard that evidence, yes." Arthur then went to his Irishism: "And you, of course, would have had no knowledge of that head injury at the time you made, took this statement or of the extent of the head injury. You didn't know what Mrs. Trimble and Mrs. DeGeer had seen." Hobson kept himself to himself: "No, I didn't." That was all in aid of Arthur attempting to undermine the statement that Bleta had made, however slight it might be. "I suggest to you that with your experience as an officer in this field that had you known about what they had observed, and had you been informed, as subsequently you were, that he had had this extremely severe blow to the head, you would have taken greater cautions before questioning him to satisfy yourself you were dealing with a man who really understood what was going on, apart altogether from the language difficulty." Hobson knew what Maloney was trying to do, and he attempted to slip away: "The way you put the question, it is hard for me to answer, Mr. Maloney." He did, however, relate how the officers had taken Bleta to St. Michael's Hospital for examination – where Bleta was found to have a bruise on the back of his head, but not a particularly serious one. The officer was helped in his attempt to escape by the judge, who asked him what state Bleta was on the evening of his arrest. Hobson's answer reveals some gift for irony:

> Expecting that such a question might be asked either by the court or by counsel, Sergeant Noble and I made it a point to see the accused after this day as many times as possible and his demeanour on this night was the same as it has been every day we have seen him since. We made it a point to see him in the City Hall cells and speak with him and he seems just the same. If he was dazed then, he is dazed now.[19]

Many counsel would have backed away at this point, but Arthur did not. He came back again, suggesting that had Hobson *known* "you would have taken different precautions before trying to question a man who had been the victim of that kind of injury." Hobson, by now, had the same bit of stubbornness between his teeth, and was not going to concede anything. "May I say that if I suspected that there was the slightest possibility that he might have suffered a fractured skull, there would have been no question but he would have been taken to the nearest hospital." That might have been a sufficiently strong answer, but Maloney would not leave it alone, and he was determined to make it work for him.

> In other words, you would have taken, if you had known what Mrs. DeGeer said, what Mrs. Trimble said – if you had been aware of the large bruise on the back of his head, I suggest to you that if you followed the course you usually follow in cases of this sort, before interrogating the accused you would have brought him to the hospital, you would have had him x-rayed, you would have had him thoroughly examined. Is that a fair way to put the thing to you? Is that what you ordinarily would do in that case if you were aware of these facts?

Hobson was unsure how to deal with this game of presumptions, and was lamely, tentatively, exploring the options: "I can only say, Mr. Maloney, in answer to that question ..." Well, how was he to answer it? The judge stepped in to help him: "What you mean is that you must get a good many people that have had blows of one kind or another on the head but if they show no signs of being abnormal, you don't do anything special but if there is anything you see which indicates some abnormality then you take special precautions. Is that what you do?" Hobson: "That is correct, my Lord."

Arthur might well have wished that the judge had kept his help to himself, because Hobson could not have got away without him, but Arthur reacted immediately to the judge's statement, getting the officer to admit that it was possible that some people could, in fact, come into his ken who were, in fact, severely injured, but showed no signs of the same – but he could not remember that having happened in his experience as a police officer. It was grudging, but it was an admission that it could happen, and that was something of a victory for Arthur that he could not have got had he stopped when the officer had proclaimed that Bleta had shown no signs of being dazed or, indeed, badly bruised. The judge had let it go on but was restless: "We are getting close to giving medical evidence now." Arthur, with that mild chattiness that was an occasional fillip to his examinations, took the pressure off the moment – and off the officer – with his reply: "He is graduating from the medical faculty. I guess I am to blame, my Lord."[20]

It was all "ifs" and "buts," yet it served its purpose in establishing the possibility that whatever Bleta might have done was the result of mental impairment, even if the officers did not see it, and obviously did not believe it. After all, it mattered little; it was a matter of what the jury believed ultimately. If Hobson would not help much, another officer, Constable Kiekebelt, who was involved in Bleta's arrest, was prepared to confirm his mental state: "He seemed to be in a sort of dazed condition. For instance, when I spoke to him he just seemed to stare right by me as if he didn't hear what I was saying or when I asked him to take his hands from his pockets, it didn't seem to register with him at all."[21]

Dr. Alexander Golab, the St. Michael's intern, who examined Bleta sometime shortly before 10:00 p.m., admitted that there were cuts about the face and a blood bruise on the back of Bleta's head, but it was of minimal proportion. He admitted that it would take a fairly severe impact to cause such a bruise, but he was not concerned about it at the time of the examination. Arthur led him past the bruise, which seemed to be of little consequence, to the same line that he had used in dealing with Hobson's scepticism about Bleta's condition. "I am right, am I not, in stating that people can sustain quite severe blows to their head and as a result suffer very real damage to their brain and to their heads and often, to the inexperienced layman, not convey the impression anything is wrong with them at all." Golab: "True, very true."

There might go Hobson, but Golab was a doctor, and he had not found any such injury – Arthur had an answer for that: "And a somewhat more complete examination would be required of the individual in question to ascertain the extent of the injury that had been done to him, isn't that right, than the kind of examination you had an opportunity to conduct on January 4th on the accused?" Golab tried to explain the cursory examination on the grounds that the condition of the patient was the touchstone for closer care, and Bleta seemed not to merit it. Maloney moved in on that – the doctor had been told by the police that Bleta had been in a fist fight, and that was all the doctor had to guide him.

Maloney: Because I take it that the case history, the origin of the injury, the cause of the injury, would be something that would be fairly relevant as a medical man to know about in assessing the gravity of the case?
Golab: True. Most cases, yes.
M: For example, have you since found out how this blow to the head was caused to Bleta?
G: No, I haven't.
M: Because evidence has been given here this morning by two ladies who were standing in the vicinity of where this altercation took place and they both said that Bleta hit the concrete pavement, his head hit the concrete pavement.
G: True.
M: With such force that both of the ladies were amazed that he was able to get up.
G: Um, hum.
M: And that when he did get up he was staggering and he seemed not to have any proper balance and that he appeared to be dazed and to be confused.
G: Um, hum.
M: Now, if you had been given this history when you examined him on the night of January the 4th, I am suggesting that your examination of Bleta would have been a good deal more complete.[22]

It would seem that Maloney had him, but he didn't. The doctor quietly insisted that given Bleta's state, as he found it, he would have done no more than he did. Maloney got him to admit that he was not a specialist in head injuries, and got him to admit that Bleta had a headache, and had been given two aspirins, but otherwise, there was nothing he could do to make the young doctor budge. It started so well, and was a masterly shaping of presumptions but it had slipped to Bleta at ten in the evening, cut and bruised, with a minor headache, but otherwise sensible, courteous, and too healthy for his own good; "he looked to me as an oriented man and well behaved."

At 4:00 p.m. the court adjourned, and Arthur had the night to think over his defence. It might well have been presumed that he was on his way to getting the charge reduced to manslaughter, if the jury was prepared to put the best face on the evidence, and accept the attack as instantaneous – a blind act that a reasonable man might have done under the circumstances of being beaten half senseless by a bigger man. Particularly if there was some reason for Bleta to fear Gafi. No one had said a thing about why these men were fighting. That might well be the key to getting it down to manslaughter – if that was what Maloney had in mind.

What Arthur had in mind was not a reduction of the charge. Nor had he any intention of doing what he often did – make straight to the defence of insanity under the M'Naghten Rule. It was not to be egregious incitement to violence that would allow for a manslaughter conviction, nor was it to be mental illness. He was, in fact, not going to allow Bleta to be convicted of anything! He was determined to walk him out of court – a free man. That would have been a surprise to both the judge and the prosecution. As it turned out, the surprise came much sooner than either expected. It came out in Maloney's opening address to the jury.

Laymen are accustomed to the prosecution setting out the case at the opening of a trial, stating the facts to be proved and the manner in which the Crown intends to use witnesses to prove it. They are less accustomed to the idea that the defence has the same right, which is usually not used, since in most criminal cases, the less said by the defence the better. Arthur, however, chose to instruct this jury. That was his first surprise. The second was his statement that he intended to use a long list of character witnesses to support his defence. Usually character witnesses are used after a conviction to persuade the judge as to the sentence, but it is possible to use them for the simple purpose of persuading the court that the accused is unlikely to be the sort of person who would be likely to do the supposed criminal act, and to support the credibility of any testimony that the accused might care to offer. It is not often used, and as one criminal lawyer said, it is not worth much to a criminal lawyer with a dubious client – "It is usually a 'Catch-22' situation; they usually commit such terrible crimes that anyone who is willing to admit to be their friends are automatically morally dubious to a jury, since no respectable person would have the accused as friends." But it is a possible addition to a defence of an accused who is a person of good character – and Bleta was that. That, however, wasn't the last surprise, as Arthur began to develop his argument. It became apparent that Maloney was not looking for a reduction in the charge, nor going to prove Bleta was insane, under M'Naghten, at the time of the killing. He was attempting, as Klein saw it, to invent a new defence, obviously related to all that constant cross-examination about the bang on the head, and Bleta's subsequent dazed condition. Maloney seemed to be going to defend on the simple grounds that Bleta had been knocked into a mental state in which he acted without responsibility because he knew not what he was doing and acted as some sort of zombie. Klein was astonished!

In the *Esposito* trial, Arthur had managed to elicit sufficient detail of a helpful nature that he could construct his contrary version of the events without needing to put in any evidence at all. It was simply a matter of making a construct of persuasive credibility that the jury might contemplate as a reasonable alternative to that which was presented by the Crown. In the *Bleta* trial, however, no such accumulation was available – there was no doubt that Bleta had killed Gafi. All that could be said was, as Arthur repeated over and over in his cross-examination, that Bleta had been beaten up by a tougher man, and in the course of that beating, had suffered a fall on to the back of his head that two witnesses considered serious. But there was no evidence about why this killing took place, or who started the fight. The Crown did not need it; all it had to prove was that Bleta had killed Gafi, and it did that. It was for Maloney to take that brutal fact and build a story around it which would either, on the one hand, prove such extenuating circumstances that the jury could find that Bleta did not commit murder, or, in the alternative, that Bleta was insane when he did it. The point to be remembered is that no-one is guilty of anything, whatever they have done, until they are so proven to be to the satisfaction of the court. Bleta, for instance, could admit that he killed Gafi, but it was not for him to decide if he had murdered Gafi. No one could just deem him a murderer – policeman, judge, lawyer – that was for the court to decide.

It was Arthur's job to put the evidence presented to the court by the Crown and by the defence into a context that would belie such conclusion. It looked daunting, and Klein might well have presumed that he might be asked to agree to a manslaughter conviction, but he would have been unlikely to presume that the case would slip entirely out of his hands. However, as Maloney's students say, when Arthur took a case, he went all the way. He came immediately to the sticking point in his jury address: "The accused Bleta did in fact wield the knife which inflicted the blow which caused the death of Gafi so that there is no problem for you there. This is not an issue, really, in this case. That is a matter of fact about which there isn't any controversy or disagreement or dispute." Which must have bemused the jury, and the Crown, and the judge who presumed that it was why they were there. Maloney put the real problem, as he saw it, in the next sentence: "The only thing about which the controversy arises is the responsibility in the eyes of the criminal law for that." But surely that was clear – Bleta chased Gafi down the street and stabbed him to death. It was not so simple for Maloney:

> Now you will recall that evidence has been given about this very severe blow he got to his head, the behavior of the accused immediately after the blow; you will recall the evidence of Mrs. DeGeer and Mrs. Trimble about how severe that was and how amazed they were that he was even able to get up and how when he did get up he was staggering; how after the stabbing episode he walked in that zig zag fashion; you will recall their evidence about his appearance of being dazed and confused and you will recall the evidence of Officer Kiekebelt about how confused and dazed he appeared to be.

Then came another surprise. Arthur announced the presence of a witness who had sat through the trial to the moment, watching the proceedings. It was to have something to do with Bleta's condition. "This you will see, in the light of the evidence for the defence, becomes very significant because the accused Bleta has been examined by medical people highly trained in this field, highly skilled, whose qualifications I am sure you will accept without question, one of whom has been sitting in the courtroom throughout the greater part of the trial – Dr. Stokes from the Toronto Psychiatric Hospital, frequently a witness in cases called by the Crown or by the defense."[23] That was sensible if Arthur wanted to establish extenuating circumstances either to meet a conviction for murder or for a lesser charge. What he then said, however, might not have surprised the jury in their layman ignorance, but it astonished the Crown:

It will be his considered opinion that he was suffering what he describes as severe trauma, severe trauma to the brain. This brought on a state of clouding of the consciousness, and in consequence of which Bleta behaved in a manner that was devoid of rational control of his brain. It was accompanied, he will explain, by a patchy type of amnesia, by confusion, by other tendencies that he will himself describe. As a result of this he will express the psychiatric and medical opinion to you that Bleta was incapable at the time of that stabbing to form any rational judgment, his actions were not the voluntary actions of a rational man. In other words, he was an automatant [*sic*], he was in a condition that would be akin to that of a sleepwalker. He wasn't insane, that is not insane, but he was possessed of this state of mind that was brought about by the severe blow that he got to his head and is therefore not criminally responsible.[24]

Arthur went on to tell the jury that he would call character witnesses to prove the benign character and conduct of his client, and the relation with Gafi prior to the fight. Bleta would take the stand, although he was unable to remember the time of the killing. But the jury would be told how Gafi started the fight, and the history of the long relationship between the two men. On that point, Arthur called his first witness.

Or he tried to. Arthur Klein had listened to enough of this nonsense, and he jumped up, and asked the judge to retire the jury, as he did – then Klein had his say:

My Lord, my submission is that the defense has introduced a legal issue before the jury which is not known to our law ... Counsel has put it to the jury that the defense will be that because of severe trauma to the brain – that his actions were not voluntary, the voluntary actions of a rational man, that he was acting like a sleepwalker; although he was not insane, he was not responsible for his actions. Well, according to our law, I submit that just isn't so, my Lord, and that is something which should not have been brought before the jury. It is not properly a matter to be considered by the jury. It is clearly established on the authorities that blackout, for instance, is no defense in our law.[25]

Questioned by the judge, Klein admitted that it might be possible to compare such blackouts, if such existed, to that of an intoxicated man, but "a man in such a case would be still guilty of manslaughter, my Lord – but counsel for the accused has put it to the jury the accused is not responsible at all." If the idea was a new one to the Crown, and he complained later in the trial that he had no idea that such a defence would be offered, it was also something of a surprise for the judge – but he was already beginning to think about it as an interesting possibility. "I would have thought that if it could be shown that this blow had so affected the accused he didn't know what he was doing at all he would not be guilty of anything." Which was exactly what Arthur was aiming at. Klein was not convinced. "He would be guilty of manslaughter on the authorities." Neither the Crown nor the judge seemed certain, and Klein was ruefully reluctant to go rummaging around in the legal precedents. "That will take a little time, I suppose." Maloney waited patiently for the two men to get back to him, and finally the judge did, asking him for authority for his peculiar argument. He had a Saskatchewan Court of Appeal case, *Regina v. Minor*, 1955, Vol. 122, *CCC*, p. 29, in which it was argued successfully that in a motor manslaughter case, it was legitimate for the defence to argue that at the time of the accident the accused was unconscious and therefore he did not know what he was doing. The judge had ruled that it could not be used as a defence. In a sense, the argument put by the defence was that the accused was literally out of his mind, since he was unconscious. On appeal the judge was reversed.

The *Bleta* judge moved very cautiously. He put a version of the M'Naghten rule in juxtaposition with the idea that the accused would have to meet a stringent test: "It would have to go so far as to show that the accused not only didn't know what he was doing but didn't know what he was doing was wrong. If what he was doing was wrong, then, as Mr. Klein says, it would amount to manslaughter anyway." Maloney pulled him back from this improvisation.

Maloney: I think you get into a different realm altogether, my Lord. It is not insanity because it is not a disease of the mind. It is, on the other hand, a state of mind of a person who really has no mind at all by reason of the blow he got to his head.
HIS LORDSHIP: Say for the sake of argument he was a sleepwalker. Is it the same sort of thing?
M: That is the very sort of thing and he would be entitled to be found not guilty completely.

The Saskatchewan case, although a driving offence, was an advantage to Maloney since the accused had, in fact, "received quite a severe blow and suffered an injury to his brain as a result of the blow which injured his head as to render him unconscious for an unknown interval." That case had, in turn, referred back to an Ontario case, *Kasperek* in the Court of Appeal in which the following had been said: "The only conceivable defense to the presumption mentioned other than insanity or drunkenness, might be that at the time of the commission of the offence the prisoner was walking in his sleep or otherwise acting with his mind a total blank."[26]

Maloney followed with a small handful of cases where the accused were suffering in some way or another from physical impediments to the mind over which they had no control, and which, in the ordinary sense, did not constitute madness. He finally came around to a House of Lords case, *Bratty v. Attorney General for Northern Ireland*, 1962, 46 *Criminal Appeal Reports*, p. 1. Here he sprung the key word on the court.

M: In this case the accused had been convicted of murder. At the trial defense counsel had asked that the accused be acquitted on the ground that he was in a state of automatism ...
H.L.: He was in a state of?
M: Automatism.

The headnote for the case put the matter clearly, but it added obligations that the Crown and the judge were to fasten upon:

The defense of automatism may arise from circumstances such as a blow on the head received by the prisoner after which he acted without being conscious of what he was doing or a condition of sleepwalking. Before a judge can leave a defense of automatism to the jury, a proper foundation for the defense must be laid. Defending counsel may be able to point to some evidence either from his own or from the Crown's witnesses from which the jury could reasonably infer that the prisoner acted in a state of automatism, before the defense can be left to the jury.[27]

This seemed to put an end to it, since the judge put it bleakly:

Mr. Maloney, there is precious little evidence here that goes that far. It is true there is evidence – and medical evidence too – that he was in a sort of a shocked, dazed state – he had got a bad crack on the head – even at the time he was placed under arrest, but, on the other hand, he started out slowly, remember, after he got up. He broke away from the man that was holding him and trying to restrain him and he ran – he finally got going – and he ran quite a little distance and was able to grasp this man with his left hand and stab him with his right. There is very little evidence to indicate that, the reference you made, if there is any at all.[28]

It must have been the lowest point of all in the trial for Arthur. Everything he had done to the moment had been in aid of the defence of automatism. He had shown that such a defence existed in law, but he hadn't enough evidence to convince the judge that Bleta was in such a state. It looked as if a reduction to manslaughter was the best he could get. But almost instantly, after a moment's pause, the judge offered him another chance at the golden ring:

HIS LORDSHIP: Or is it a matter for me to decide?

Maloney was off and running, arguing on the basis of the *Bratty* case that all the judge was obliged to do was decide if there was any evidence that might support the defence, and leave it to the jury to decide if there was enough. Indeed, part of the *Bratty* decision could have been written by Maloney: "When the cause assigned is concussion or sleepwalking, there should be some evidence from which it can be reasonable inferred before it should be left to the jury. If it is said to be due to concussion, there should be evidence of a severe blow beforehand." Arthur argued that the evidence they already had "plus the evidence the doctor will give you, plus the evidence of the accused himself about his mental state from a certain point on during the course of the episode, would be ample evidence on which to leave this defense to the jury."

By this time, the judge was moving closer and closer to Arthur's point of view, working his way in tandem with Maloney through the English judgment.

H.L.: What we have so far is this severe blow on the head, severe enough that they heard the impact, that the two ladies didn't know whether he would be able to get up at all. We have that evidence plus the evidence of the Police, the arresting Police Officer, that he was affected in some way. Just a minute now: "Where there is evidence of a severe blow" and there is such evidence here, it would be pretty dangerous for me to refuse to leave it to the jury.
M: I would think so.[29]

The judge was not inclined to let Maloney have the running too easily. He intimated that he might have his own opinion of whether Bleta had been in such a state, and "from my point of view it is not particularly impressive but the jury might well feel differently." To nail the matter down, Maloney added one further case, *Regina v. Schonberger*, 1960, Vol. 33, CCC, p. 107, and the judge seemed satisfied.

While Arthur and Mr. Justice Aylen were having such a good time chatting and passing law reports back and forth, Arthur Klein, a solid, phlegmatic man, disinclined by temperament or skill to indulge in the ironic scepticism of many Crowns, had sat silently watching, seemingly bemused and slightly concussed by the legal traffic between defence counsel and Judge that was swiftly passing before his eyes, and seemed to have run his case over, and out. He could not have been sanguine about the increasing enthusiasm that Mr. Justice Aylen was showing for the *Bratty* judgment, especially as the judge kept quoting from it in a way that seemed to suggest that Arthur was going to be allowed to use this defence, which had come out of the blue.

H.L.: This is quite a case, it covers a great deal. It refers to the difficulty in some cases of deciding whether it is a matter of automatism or mental state but in one case referred to the learned judge put it to the jury this way: "If he did not know what he was doing, if his actions were purely automatic and his mind had no control over the movements of his limbs, that he was in the same position as a person in an epileptic fit, then no responsibility rests upon him at all."[30]

Shortly after, the judge seemed to become aware of the fact that only two of them were playing, and he attempted to get Klein in on the fun: "And there is much evidence here. Mr. Klein, can you help me further on this problem?" Klein, who had said nothing for some time, was obviously frozen in his tracks by the Maloney proposition, and feeling a bit betrayed and sorry for himself. "Well, my Lord, I had no idea this defence was going to be raised. I haven't had any opportunity to prepare my argument." Aylen, full of enthusiasm and willing to help, offered the *Bratty* case to Klein with the comment that "it seems to me to make it fairly clear I should admit the evidence and then be very careful how I put it to the jury. A lot will depend on that. If you would like a short recess to study this, it covers the thing pretty well."

It was starting to gain comic proportion with Klein laying low and Aylen, excited by this new defence, urging him to come out to play. Klein seemed not quite to know how to handle this evangelical fervour. He had not read, or indeed, heard of the *Bratty* case, and was not eager to change that state of ignorance, but he thought that a bit of stalling might just slow down the judge's avalanche of excitement. "Well, there is a vast lot involved on this point, my Lord, of a rather profound nature." But Aylen was not to be stayed – "Well, with respect, according to this judgment there isn't." Klein took a flyer at this, claiming that there was a Supreme Court of Canada case that spoke to the contrary, and being Canadian would surely take precedence over an English decision. The judge called the bluff:

If there is any judgment of the Supreme Court of Canada which is in conflict with the judgment of the House of Lords in England, or the Privy Council, we would have to follow our own judgments, especially if they were made since it became our final court of appeal. Would you like to give the matter some thought, Mr. Klein? We are going to have a recess.[31]

Well, what could Klein do? It was the civilized congress of the law at its best – first in the geniality of the dialogue between Arthur and the judge, sensible, coherent, energetic – what is probably meant by a "meeting of the minds," ending with the judge drawing the reluctant Klein into the discussion, giving him all the time he needed to undo what Arthur had wrought – willing to be convinced to the contrary – presuming that Klein knew what he was talking about. Klein seemed eager enough to have his chance: "Oh, yes, I would like an opportunity of turning up the relevant authorities, my Lord." Whether or not the judge knew Klein was whistling in the dark or not, he put his instructions to him ever so delicately, sending him off with *Bratty* in his ear: "You let me know when you are ready. I suggest you study this case carefully. It seems to be very helpful." Who was kidding whom?

Shortly after, Klein came back, admitting that he couldn't find the case he had in mind, but manfully confessing also, in his imploded embarrassment, that upon further reflection, he had misremembered not only the facts of the case, but the further detail of it being decided before the *Bratty* decision. In short, it was not on point, nor on time. Gracious in defeat, Klein gave up in a dying fall: "So I am quite content to let the matter stand as it is. I have no further authorities to submit, my Lord."

H.L.: Very well, gentlemen. I have decided that there is sufficient evidence to enable the defense to call evidence on the issue which has been raised on automatism.

When he had begun that morning, Arthur had nothing but a bloodied client with a knife in the neck of the murder victim. Now, without calling a single witness, he was halfway home. Bleta, who had originally been charged with capital murder, had come to trial on non-capital murder, and by this stage of the trial, given the evidence, Arthur Klein might well have expected that Arthur Maloney would be talking sweetly to him about reducing the charge to manslaughter, rather than having passed it by on his determined way to seek an acquittal. But, as the judge had darkly, if tersely suggested, there was not much evidence for automatism. Two women had commented upon the fall, and there was some evidence about Bleta being dizzy, but the latter state might well be explained as a normal consequence of the fall without it necessarily transmuting a normal human being into a lethal sleepwalker. Arthur had some work to do that could not be done simply by using a single psychiatrist – particularly one who had not examined Bleta until some weeks after the murder. Arthur's idea of the defence, therefore, was three-fold, and the medical evidence was only part of it. He was also determined to show two other things – that Bleta was not the kind of man who would attack another man so violently, and that he had reason to fear Gafi. That latter aspect of the defence is where the very odd story began.

It was a very odd story indeed; a part of that larger tale of European immigration after the Second World War that went on for years as distressed and abused groups of ethnic waifs with a bit of luck and determination worked their way to Canada. One of the groups, smaller than the others, but no less determined to get out of the internecine struggle of post-war political chaos, were the Albanians, and by the late fifties a number of them, mostly men in their early thirties, who had struggled through the ruins of Europe, arrived in Toronto, where they gradually put their lives together. Gafi and Bleta were two of these, from the same village, although they were not friends. Bleta was a farm boy; he had been in the Albanian army between 1944 and 1948, but he wanted out of the mess, and in 1949, he actually walked out of the country into a refugee camp in Greece, and from there, in 1950, he managed to get to Germany, where he worked for the American army for four years. In April 1954, he came to Toronto. "Maloney: Did you have anything when you got here? Had you saved any money or did you own any property or anything when you got to Toronto? Bleta: Nothing." He was unemployed for twenty days; then he got work at the Canada Packers slaughterhouse, and he was still working there at the time of his arrest. By that time, he was a husband, father, a small property owner, and he had some money out on mortgages. Nothing had come easily to him; he wasn't very intelligent. The Albanian men had difficulties settling down. Many of them were Muslims, an incongruous fact of Balkan atavistic turmoil, and they had trouble finding wives in Canada. That is where Bleta and Gafi got together. Gafi was a part-time marriage broker, bringing women in Albania into contact with the Toronto men for a fee. Gafi started such a deal with a woman for Bleta, but the woman soon refused to deal through Gafi, and she and Bleta made their own arrangement. Gafi never forgot it. He tried to block the marriage and when that failed, he harassed the couple and their in-laws. Through the years, he continued to threaten Gafi, sometimes to his face, sometimes to his friends. Bleta's wife was terrified of Gafi, and in order to settle her fears, he moved the family away from the Albanian district in Toronto. That was the story Maloney wanted the jury to hear; much of it bordered on hearsay, and most of it was third-party tale-telling, so its evidentiary worth was suspect. Arthur and the Bench met in a bruising head-on confrontation over it, particularly when it dwelt on Gafi's general conduct.

Gafi had once pulled a knife on a witness, and Maloney wanted to get that sort of conduct in to show why Bleta might fear him. The judge was determined to keep this kind of general, past evidence out:

HIS LORDSHIP: Supposing, for the sake of argument – I hope there won't be too much of this in the press because the jury is excluded – supposing you could show that Gafi had knifed half a dozen men in the past, it wouldn't be relevant in this trial except perhaps to show – and as far as evidence is concerned, that is the basis to supply a motive for what he did. [*i.e.* for what Bleta did]

Arthur replied with the information that he was going to present evidence that Gafi had pulled a knife on Bleta when the fight began, and that he was only attempting to show that such was characteristic behaviour on Gafi's part. The judge was adamant, even when Arthur added that the evidence of Gafi pulling a knife on the previous occasion had been witnessed by Bleta, and would therefore affect Bleta's attitude. The judge refused to budge. "We'll deal with that issue when we reach it. Independent evidence as to the character of Gafi or his actions, I'm not admitting." The judge was determined not to allow Arthur simply to blacken Gafi's character. He bridled against a further witness reporting a conversation he had with Gafi, which Arthur wanted in to prove that Gafi was hostile to Bleta on the day of the attack. Surprisingly, Arthur Klein had no objection to it, so the judge let it in, reluctantly.

After much battling back and forth, they agreed that Arthur could put in evidence of a continuing animus on Gafi's part, so long as it was not used to build up the accused at the expense of Gafi, who was not on trial. They also agreed that the judge would have to instruct the jury on how to treat such evidence. "His Lordship: It may be regarded, I suppose, in a general way as part of the *res gestae* if the jury look upon it in the proper light." Or as he put it to the jury:

You are not trying Gafi; he is not on trial before you, nor is he here to defend himself, but I have decided to admit the evidence partly because it is not seriously objected to but partly because it shows some of the surrounding circumstances and might have a bearing on the defense of provocation which no doubt will be argued, that this man had a good deal of provocation ... you must not take the evidence against Gafi and his actions as having any real direct bearing on the issue of the innocence or guilt of the accused person before you. It is admitted in that limited way.[32]

It was another example of Maloney stubbornly hanging on, circling the judge and the Crown, nudging them further towards his point of view. He was, of course, helped considerably by Arthur Klein's co-operation, and by the natural reluctance of the judge to stop him chipping away at the original blanket refusal to let him get this sort of evidence in. A lesser counsel might well have given in earlier, not wanting to take the banging about that the judge gave him, although it was considerably milder than he took from a lot of judges. It did make things so much easier if he was able to show that Gafi had a determined intention of doing Bleta harm in his marriage, and also a tendency, witnessed by Bleta, to pull a knife when he was angry. As a result, Maloney was able to get evidence of Gafi flashing a knife at a rowdy guest at a party – and he got it from an independent witness and Bleta.

But it was Bleta's story of the fatal encounter that best displayed his reason for avoiding Gafi. Walking along Dundas, after work, he was suddenly attacked, and knocked to the ground. He got up and was knocked down once more. Once more he got up and recognized his assailant as Gafi. He started to run away from him. Gafi caught him, knocked him down again, proclaiming that he was determined to kill him.

HIS LORDSHIP: What is that again, witness?
Bleta: I stand up the second time I say to him, "Why don't you say something before you hit me?" He says to me, "I have tried five years to kill you and I haven't so now is the last time for you."

Bleta tried to escape into the store, falling down over and over again: "During that time he was saying to me, he was showing me one knife, was saying, 'With this one I'm going to kill you; with this one I'm going to scalp you.'" Bleta claimed that he seized the knife, and realized that Gafi had, in fact, two knives that he was displaying, "and I tried to twist his arm but he tried with the other knife to scalp me like that. (*indicating*) So while he was doing that, was moving this one too. And from then I don't at all what happened [*sic*]." Bleta was familiar, in an odd way, with bloodshed and death – he worked at Canada Packers, and the Crown thought that something might be made of that:

Crown: But you were using a knife in your daily work all the time.
Bleta: Oh, yes. In the work I was using but not in fighting.
C: But your work at Canada Packers, you have been using a knife to kill animals all the time?
B: No, not kill animals.
C: What do you do with them?
B: I have used knife there to cut meat once in a while.
C: Wasn't your job to remove the tongues of the animals with a knife?
B: Yes, recently.
C: So you were quite skilled in the use of a knife?

B: Pardon me?
C: You were quite skilled in the use of a knife?
B: Yes, like work.[33]

Not quite the same as knife-fighting, however, and Klein sensed that he ought to get away from it. He took Bleta back to the fight, but he didn't get much more out of it than a reiteration of the testimony that Arthur had drawn from Bleta – of Gafi threatening him with both knives, and occasionally hitting him with the handle of one of the weapons. Klein, however, did have one bit of evidence that suggested that Bleta knew what he had done – the statement that he made to the police, which included this version of the encounter: "While I was walking. He jumped on me. I was coming from my work and going to the bank. He jumped on me and hitting with a knife, and I fell down. Then while I was down I took his knife and while I was taking his knife and he then left me and he stand up. When he stand off I ran away. While I was running away the Police catch me. That's all." Significantly, he said nothing about stabbing Gafi in the statement. He remembered getting the knife off Gafi, remembered Gafi moving away, and running away himself – but the significant gap was there – he said nothing about stabbing Gafi. And the statement supported his claim that the knife belonged to Gafi.

A handful of Albanian witnesses corroborated Bleta's claim that Gafi had pulled a knife and threatened another guest at a party, and that Bleta had helped to restrain him on that occasion. There was evidence that Gafi had spat at Bleta and made an aggressive gesture behind Bleta's back in a restaurant, and that Gafi had often shown a violent temper, and was known to carry a switch blade. It was also well known that Gafi believed that Bleta owed him money for his matchmaking, and that he continued his personal vendetta of abuse about Bleta for years. Maloney was also able to show, through a succession of witnesses, including Bleta's wife, that Bleta had no reputation as quarrelsome or bellicose, and that he was regarded as a mild, hard-working fellow. It was to turn out that if he wasn't very smart, he wasn't dumb about money.

Aside from the relatively generous conduct of Arthur Klein, whose expostulations over automatism and over hearsay evidence were short-lived, nothing came easy in the case. Once Maloney got the law straightened out, he had to fight very hard to get Gafi's previous, threatening conduct in, and he might have felt that all the hard fighting was done by the time he got all the Albanian tall tale tellers off the stand. But he still needed the psychiatrist to give the defence the touchstone credibility of science, and his problem there was a simple one. He had a psychiatrist with impressive credentials, who believed in the automatism theory. What he did not have was any psychiatric evidence concerning Bleta at the time and place of the murder, or in the immediate time before or after. Dr. Ronald Stokes, his man, had not examined Bleta until 30 April 1963, weeks after the fight, and by then, although Bleta was still complaining about headaches, he certainly was not under the spell of automatism. He was a perfectly sane murder suspect.

Dr. Ronald Edward Stokes, an assistant to the Director of the Forensic Clinic at the Toronto Psychiatric Hospital, had been specializing in this kind of practice since 1959, and had a record of appearances in court on behalf of both defence and prosecution. He had hardly established his credentials when Arthur revealed his next turn in the defence. "I think you have been present throughout practically all of this trial, have you not? Stokes: That is correct." This seemingly odd fact was to be a masterstroke – not only would Maloney be able to question the doctor on what he personally found in his examination of Bleta, but he was going to be able to question him on what the psychiatrist made of the evidence of the witnesses who had testified as to how Bleta had acted at the time of the murder. It looked like a good idea – it was, ultimately, to lead the case all the way to the Supreme Court of Canada. At the trial stage, however, it seemed to work well:

Maloney: And you were particularly interested in hearing the evidence of the witnesses who witnessed the episode that occurred on January the 4th in the vicinity of Keele and Dundas Streets.
Stokes: Yes."
M: You heard the evidence of Mrs. DeGeer and Mrs. Trimble concerning the blow the accused received to his head on the concrete?
S: Yes, I did.

Arthur led the doctor through the whole list of witnesses who had testified as to Bleta's condition. In short, what he did, without a peep out of the judge or, more surprisingly, the Crown, was to use the doctor, as the expert, to comment upon the evidence of previous witnesses, and to come to a conclusion, partly as a result of his own examination of the accused, but mainly, as a result of hearing what the other witnesses remembered. It was breath-takingly confident stuff:

As a result of my examination of the accused Karafil Bleta, it is my opinion that this man, as a result of a moderate to severe head injury, a closed head injury, sustained on the day of the offense, had a state of clouding of the consciousness ... And that during that period of time the accused man would be unable to rationally form intent.

The doctor was prepared to go farther, and suggest that there were still touches of the injury in Bleta's conduct during his examination at the trial. Asked if Bleta's performance on direct and cross-examination had revealed anything, the doctor was happy to oblige.

Well first of all, his hesitancy which I think is partially language difficulties and partially related to his intelligence level [which the doctor had characterized earlier as "dull to dull normal"] but also the sort of bewilderment and confusion particularly in discussing matters touching on the offense at that time. In other words, the area that I feel he was amnesic and the times just before and afterwards in the Police Station I sensed the confusion and bewilderment in his thinking about it. It seemed to me that he exhibited this on the stand.[34]

The doctor was so much in control of the situation that he was able to use a sport anecdote to undermine the worrying fact that Bleta had run after Gafi.

HIS LORDSHIP: Doctor, there is nothing strange in your mind about the fact that he chased the deceased down the street before he stabbed him?
Stokes: No, my Lord. There was an article that might perhaps explain the difficulty in trying to present this type of information, there is an article in one of the journals of a fight in which the former champion Gene Tunney was engaged and he fought more than two rounds of the fight and went out to a cocktail party afterwards and had absolutely no recollection of his behavior, the fight, the attacks on his opponent in the ring whatsoever. He was fighting in the ring as an automaton, an automatic individual.
H.L.: So he might have gone on fighting even to the extent of going some distance down the street? It would be all automation, there would be no knowledge of it at all?
S: That is correct, my Lord.[35]

To the doctor, Bleta's actions, as related by the witnesses, were all of a piece with the fact that he was suffering from a head injury, and his inability to remember parts of the incident was also part of the same illness.

Arthur Klein tried to get around the doctor by suggesting that Bleta, at least, should have been able to be more specific about what happened to him before his head hit the sidewalk, but that didn't work – that kind of injury "not only involved the individual following the injury to the brain but also will supersede or come before this injury for a given period of time, probably as much as one or two minutes." Nor was Klein any luckier in suggesting that Bleta was simply lying, since the doctor stuck to his opinion that Bleta's contradictions were consistent with the damage done to him, and that his performance in court was, in fact, confirmation that he had suffered the injury claimed.

Crown: Did you not think that might be due to the fact that he didn't want to admit he said those things?
Stokes: No, I do not.
C: Why?
S: Because I think that this is consistent with the apathy amnesia which one would expect. I don't see why he would avoid some questions and answer others. The questions he avoided were no more damaging to him than the questions ...
C: And you are assuming he did, in fact, receive a severe head injury?
S: Yes.

If he got anything out of the doctor, it was at the end of the questioning when Stokes admitted that Bleta, given such an injury, might well have attacked his assailant – it seemed to get into the realm of conscious action for a moment – until the doctor quickly qualified it:

C: Gafi was as far from you to that doorway over there to the jury room, that far away, when Bleta started after him and Bleta caught up to him and stabbed him. Wouldn't Bleta know whom he was going after when he did that?
S: Yes, he would have. He would have known because this was the last person to inflict injury, if you will, or stimulation, or irritation to this individual. This would have been the last person he saw before his head hit the pavement.
C: And on those facts wasn't he stimulated to go after Gafi?
S: He would be stimulated to go after him, yes. The same way an animal or a worm would be stimulated, if you trod on it, to wiggle away. This was the last irritating source.
C: Yes. And he would be stimulated to take a knife and stab him?
S: He could, yes.
C: Don't you think that is what happened in this case.
S: I am assuming it, I didn't see it, I have only listened to what the witnesses said.[36]

It was Arthur Klein's best moment at the trial – if, of course, the jury remembered that the doctor admitted that Bleta would be prompted to attack Gafi, and forgot that he also said that it would be quite beyond Bleta's control – the automatic behaviour of an animal or a worm.

Arthur put one further turn on the defence in his short re-examination of Stokes. It was evident that Klein was determined to go along the line that suggested that Bleta was lying, not only about not being able to remember, but on the matter of those things that he claimed to remember. One part of the evidence that had not been corroborated was Bleta's claim that Gafi was threatening him with two knives at the same time. Maloney went right to the heart of that:

Maloney: Let's assume for the purpose of argument that the accused was not telling the truth about that. Would that fact have the slightest bearing on what his state of mind was at the instant of the stabbings?
Stokes: No.
M: Or would it in any way affect the opinion you have given here as to what that state of mind was at that time?
S: No.
HIS LORDSHIP: Doctor, I think in answer you said it depends what you mean by the statement being true. Actually, in fact, it is probably not true according to the evidence of independent witnesses but from his point of view it is an attempt at reconstruction but it is actually not.
S: Not only that, my Lord, but he would be highly suggestible to any idea put into his head also.
H.L.: Supposing a proper conclusion is that his account of what happened insofar as it differs from the account of independent witnesses is not correct – the independent witnesses are right – that doesn't shake your opinion because you say it is not true in a way but it is the best he can do by way of reconstruction.[37]

According to Dr. Stokes, even if the jury disbelieved Bleta's version of what happened, it would not be a confirmation of an attempt on his part to lie, but simply another symptom of his condition. The judge went on to do the Crown another disservice. Klein had suggested that Bleta's claim that he could not remember anything just prior to the knife attack was an indication that he was lying. The psychiatrist had claimed that amnesia from such a blow usually pre-dates the time of the blow, and the judge wanted to talk about that.

HIS LORDSHIP: Does the fact that Bleta, with the low I.Q., in his account to you, gives you an account of amnesia that starts a little before that incident, is that significant?
Stokes: It is highly significant because the person who is trying to fake an amnesia will often – I would say the average lay person who is trying to fake an amnesia would say that the amnesia occurred at the precise instant their head hit the pavement, not for one or two minutes before, and I don't think that Mr. Bleta has enough medical sophistication to have known that previously.[38]

That was the end of the defence case. The matter was now for the jury to listen to three addresses. First to speak would be Maloney, then the Crown, and then the judge. But Arthur Klein turned obdurate and wanted to call another witness – it could be presumed that he wanted a psychiatrist to answer Dr. Stokes, and that would have been fine since the Crown had no warning that Arthur was going to bring on the automatism defence. But Klein wanted to call the detective sergeant who had taken Bleta's statement in reply to the automatism defence. The judge was puzzled, "If you called the Detective Sergeant in reply to evidence of automatism, I don't think he would be qualified to speak on it. You could call a psychiatrist."

What Arthur Klein was really up to had a two-fold intention. The lesser of the two was his concern for the credibility of the statement that Bleta had given in the police station, since Bleta on the stand had stated that he could not remember giving certain parts of it, and he specifically could not remember telling them of the fight and the aftermath of the same, although what he had said did not include any mention of the stabbing. Klein had not put the statement in as part of the prosecution, but had used it in his cross-examination of Bleta. He now claimed that since Bleta had denied part of the statement on the stand, the Crown was entitled by law to prove that he had, in fact, made *all* the statement, not just the bits he now remembered. This bemused both the judge and Maloney, who were of the opinion that Bleta had admitted making the statement, that it had been adjudged a voluntary statement at *voir dire*, and that all he had done, in fact, was say that he couldn't *remember* having made certain bits of it – which was not quite the same as denying that he had made them, but that he couldn't remember doing so.

The other, more important reason for bringing the police on once more went directly to the doctor's testimony. Bleta had claimed that he had been suffering from some sort of amnesia, and the doctor supported that. What Klein could have done, and was expected to do with this request for another witness, was offer his own psychiatrist to undermine the diagnosis. What he wanted to do, however, was to bring one or two police officers on to have them testify to the fact that Bleta made the statement, however disjunctive, only a few hours after the killing, and in so doing, they might be able to undermine the claim that he had amnesia *then*, because he did not complain to them of his head injury, and he did, at that time, certainly remember quite a lot of what happened. This, Klein claimed, was to be his reply to the automatism-amnesia defence.

Yet the statement had been read out to the jury, and it had been used in the cross-examination of Dr. Stokes, who gave his opinion on its disjunctive contents, calling them perfectly consistent with Bleta being in a concussed state after a period of automatism – and arguing that his confused reaction to the statement, when being cross-examined on the stand, was also consistent with the after-effects of such condition.

Maloney: If the Crown had wished I suppose that the Crown could have put this in as part of the Crown's case but in point of fact I wouldn't think that this statement proved anything as regards the assault. As a matter of fact, it is an exculpatory statement.

HIS LORDSHIP: We have argued all that out before, and, of course, at that time didn't know what other evidence would be put in. It is one of these borderline statements where it is in a sense exculpatory. On the other hand, he admits certain things ...
Crown: The accused, my Lord, did purport to give an account of it. And at no place in that account did he claim that he was suffering from any amnesia. He didn't make any claim he suffered from any injury to the head.
H.L.: I don't suppose he knew himself.[39]

Klein was still trying, and he put the matter to the judge once more. It was a question simply of whether or not Bleta really was suffering from amnesia on the evening after the killing.

And this statement is nevertheless relevant to that question of fact. Now, an important factor in Dr. Stokes's reasons for his opinion that the accused was suffering from a mental condition amounting to a statement of automatism is the alleged amnesia on the part of the accused. Alleged amnesia. Well, the evidence of amnesia eminates [*sic*] solely from the accused, my Lord. It is only the accused's statement that he didn't remember anything from a certain moment on until a certain moment that constitutes any evidence of amnesia and as against that we have this statement made to the police, and reduced to writing by the police and then signed by the accused, and that, I submit, is of the utmost importance. It couldn't be more important; it is the most important single bit of evidence in this whole trial at this stage.[40]

All this, despite the fact that the statement displayed no description of the fatal attack itself. The judge was not convinced that the police could come back in. Arthur tried to help by going over the way the statement had been used, and by affirming that the accused did not deny making a statement – he just couldn't remember making some parts of it.

The problem was that Klein had got himself into a bit of a mess by not putting the statement in as part of his case. He had used it in cross-examination, and at that time Bleta had simply said that he did not remember making some parts of it, particularly the following: "While I was walking he jumped on me. I was coming from my work and going to the bank. He jumped on me and hitting with a knife, and I fell down. Then while I was down I took his knife and while I was taking his knife and he then left me and he stand up. When he stand off I ran away. While I was running away the Police catch me. That's all." He couldn't remember having said that, although he did remember other parts of the statement. It was not any more damaging than other parts that he did remember. What Klein wanted was to confirm that such was in the statement, and in the process of so doing, show that Bleta was not entirely blank-minded after he was arrested. Mr. Justice Aylen was not convinced that he could do that, since it looked to him, and to Maloney that "what my friend is really asking for now is permission to re-open his case-in-chief." Aylen refused Klein such privilege, and the matter was closed. It was, finally, time for the jury addresses.

The Maloney address was considerably slimmer than usual, in part because Maloney had been addressing the jury from the very moment he began cross-examination. Every line he took went to the proposition that Bleta had been attacked, beaten to the ground, had fallen at least once, and probably twice, very badly, on the back of his head, and rose near the end of the fight, dazed, staggering, and unaware of what he was doing, but continuing to fight back without any idea of what was going on through the fatal blow and the zigzagging run down the street. The real legal tussle had already been won – first in drawing the evidence of Bleta's physical condition out of the prosecution witnesses; second, in the argument over the defence of automatism. Once that was in, it was a matter of getting support for it from the accused and the psychiatrist, who might have proved a liability, given the fact that he had not examined the accused until weeks after the incident.

In the course of the trial, however, the doctor had become something more than an expert on Bleta's condition. Stokes had proved to be the strongest part of the case, not simply in providing an informed lecture in how automatism worked, but also in using the condition to explain away whatever inconsistencies the Crown attempted to suggest in Bleta's conduct not only after the killing, but at the trial itself – even to the point of suggesting that if Bleta was sometimes not telling the truth, it was not intentional, but a symptom of the illness, lingering months after the attack had occurred. If he fabricated it didn't mean he was lying, but that he was still suffering from the trauma – in a kind of mad logic, lying was proof of the truth of his condition. It must have made Klein suspect his own sanity when proving an accused was lying proved that he could be believed.

Maloney's address to the jury is an example of how he tended to cut through irrelevancies and focus the minds of his jurors. After his general preamble as to the legal responsibilities of the jury, he went straight to the point: "Well, we know the charge against him, we know the issue that is involved, we know that he stabbed Gafi, we know about the burden of proof, we know about the presumption of innocence. Where do we go from there? What is the defense to this charge?"[41] It was a good example of how Arthur tended to skew the positions of the participants. It was not a question of the defence attempting to tease the jury into a point of view, but of the defence joining the jury in finding out the answer to their mutual problem. It was not Arthur and his client against the forces of the Crown, and judge and jury, but Arthur leading his gang of jurors, in something akin to a class project, to solve the mystery. Together they would get to the heart of this matter. Luckily, "I made some notes of the evidence of Dr. Stokes because it is really in the framework of his evidence that the conduct of Bleta becomes explained." He tends to avoid addressing the jury *de haut en bas* – it is much more a matter of a ruminative quest for the truth in which Arthur is first among equals. He tends, for instance, to ask rhetorical questions that turn the address from a straight-forward statement of fact – lawyer to jury – into a seemingly mutual discovery. On the doctor's testimony, for instance, he leads into the matter with a question: "What does he say in effect? He says that the accused was suffering from a severe trauma or blow to the head." Then he goes on to paraphrase, in simple terms, the doctor's evidence. He puts himself into the position of the juror: "What does that mean?" Which leads him to the proposition that the mind must follow the same course as the action – that a man is not guilty if he doesn't know what he is doing. Then he quite disappears – it is not Maloney who is defending Bleta, but someone else, someone far more able than anyone else to do so under the peculiar circumstances: "The theory of the defense, as stated by the doctor, is that Karafil Bleta was an automaton whose behavior was automatic, whose actions were not the voluntary actions of a rational man ... It all hinges really, doesn't it, on Dr. Stokes's evidence?"[42] The interjection of "doesn't it" draws the jury into the dialogue over what really is the central simple problem they must somehow work out between them. It is a question not of believing Bleta, but of believing Dr. Stokes. If Stokes is believed, the matter is solved. It is, in a sense, then, Stokes who is now on trial – not Bleta.

"You may say to yourself, 'Well, we have listened to Dr. Stokes. He may well be right. We don't know.'" What Arthur is doing, before their very eyes, is drawing the jury into a premature experience of the jury room discussion, presuming the pattern the discussion is likely to take (and in a sense imprinting that pattern on a group who, inexperienced in the main, are likely to be quite happy to be shown how to do it, especially by someone as experienced as Arthur Maloney.) Of course, had they thought of it for a moment, it might have crossed their minds that the jury room was the one place in which Arthur Maloney had no experience at all. He is giving them the questions to be asked, and eventually he will give them the answers. There is a seemingly unpressured flexibility in this imaginary dialogue. What if the jury or a jury member isn't so sure of Stokes? Arthur thinks that unlikely, but it might happen.

Well, you may say to yourself, "Well, we have listened to Dr. Stokes. He may well be right. We don't know." Well, then, you are in a state of reasonable

> doubt. Dr. Stokes may well, as I submit he should have, convinced every one of you of the correctness of his opinion, but he may not have. We are all inclined, or have a tendency to be our own lawyers and our own psychiatrist and our own doctors. It is a temptation we should perhaps avoid in this case particularly but even if you are so inclined, even if you do say to yourself, "Well, with all the respect we have for Dr. Stokes, we are still not sure that what he said by way of opinion was right." Don't you see, then, you still have a doubt – and the doubt of a reasonable person – and you must acquit him.[43]

Again, Arthur puts himself in the position of a juror, struggling with the problem of an expert, who ought to be believed, despite our inclination as human beings to fancy ourselves experts; he suggests that it is a human weakness – but not to worry, since even if Stokes has not entirely convinced, he has made the juror unsure – and certainty is the only position for a juror in convicting a man. Of course, it is a bit of a quick sleight-of-hand argument. Stokes is not on trial – Bleta is, but if the juror is not sure about Stokes, that means he is, in a sense, not sure whether or not Bleta was suffering the injury Stokes claimed for him, and if the juror is not sure, one way or the other, he must acquit. Arthur acts out the possible position of scepticism, while intruding on it informally, judging such a position mildly ("we should perhaps avoid ..."), putting it into the context of common human fallibility ("we are all inclined ...") and leaves the jury with the comforting idea that a man who doubts is a man not entirely convinced, and therefore a man who can acquit.

It is a variation on what in literary circles is sometimes called "technique as discovery" in which the very nature of the questioning process leads through the labyrinth of questions to the proper conclusion. It is, in fact, a form of "dramatic monologue" in the tradition that runs in English literature from the sonnets of Wyatt and Surrey through the soliloquies of Shakespeare, through the lyrics of John Donne, the dramatic monologues of Browning into the psychological maunderings of T.S. Eliot's *J. Alfred Prufrock*. The most important thing is to choose the "voice" carefully. Browning's voices, for instance, are not always inclined to engender sympathy, but disdain and disgust, although the speakers seem to have no sense of how distasteful they sound. Donne's are full of ardour and high, witty intelligence. Maloney seems to grasp instinctively the artistic nature of what he is doing, and the voice he uses in jury addresses to move into concert with the jury varies from case to case. Here he knows that the presence of Dr. Stokes makes it unnecessary for him to take a position of authority, which he often does in addressing a jury. He can, for instance, be quite peremptory with a jury. Dave Humphrey remembers that in the *Bencardino* case, he demanded an acquittal, and demanded it "quickly," so confident was he that the evidence was in his favour. In this case, a light, tender, tentative, nonprofessional voice is appropriate. The authority belongs to the doctor. It only lies with Arthur to lead the jury to contemplate medical opinion, to think about the authority figure, and our natural suspicion of such, and to suggest that it is all right to be not quite sure, since a doubt is as good as certainty in a criminal case – a kind of variation on the old saw: "A miss is as good as a mile," applied to the obligations of a jury in a criminal case.

Who is Dr. Stokes? He is obviously a professional man of very considerable background and experience. He has been at the work for quite a while – The Toronto Psychiatric Hospital – a witness, I presume right in that box, on a number of past occasions. He has certainly been a witness before, called not just as a witness for the defense but called as a witness for the Crown, whose integrity is vouched for in those circumstances by both the defense and the Crown.[44]

He always has a strong sense of those widely held suspicions of the common citizen. He knows that they look upon doctors, and especially doctors as witnesses as likely to say what their hirers want them to say. Most lawyers would prefer to leave such ideas alone, but Arthur likes to think about them, not only to get them out of the way, but to deepen his identification with the commoner in the jury box. "I know what your are thinking – why should you trust a paid expert? Well this one is so good that both sides use his services – that wouldn't happen if he was just a mouthpiece for defence counsel. This man is trusted by all of us." He does not say that, but that is what he and the jury know he means.

Of course, there is the possibility that one or two of the jurors are quite beyond doubt, and simply do not believe Stokes. How is that to be dealt with?

You would really have to say to yourselves, "We have considered his evidence and we have come to the conclusion that we are satisfied beyond a reasonable doubt, we are morally sure that that opinion isn't right." And, frankly, with the greatest respect and without usurping a single one of your functions, I submit to you just how could you possibly do it, really, in view of the weight that I submit must clearly be attached to that evidence?[45]

It looks as if he has reverted to the role of the authority figure at last, but he suddenly shifts it into a personal context. If that is the problem – if you don't trust the doctor – let's bring it closer to home. You've heard of his qualification, so "if you and I were to walk out of this City Hall tonight and suffer a severe blow to our head; the first thing we would hope to happen to us would be that somebody would get us into the care of somebody like Dr. Stokes."[46] So what is the problem? If that is the man or the kind of man we would want to help us, surely his opinion about Bleta ought to be taken seriously? Particularly when other witnesses who saw Bleta support Stokes's findings, and Bleta proves them in his conduct after the killing, and in his testimony in court.

It is a simple, person-to-person form of rough logic which can be picked apart easily enough after the fact, but on the ground, with Arthur using that seemingly unstructured informal style, full of syntactical flaws and improvisational back-fillings, it achieves a spontaneity and immediacy of intense sincerity. Much is said of Maloney as an eloquent counsel, but what is meant is not a polished, rhetorical style, but a very loose, sometimes quite ungrammatical, unbuttoned, conversational struggle to find what looks to be the truth that a juror can take into the jury room and depend upon to lead him to the correct verdict.

The jury addresses are not in any formal shape, but consist of a series of notes with the occasional full sentence prepared beforehand. There are, of course, common introductory statements on the function of the various elements in the court structure, with special emphasis placed on the role of the jury, and there is a tendency for the conclusions to have a somewhat more formal rhetorical shape, but the main body of his addresses are always flexible and inclined to common sense, expressed in an open, seemingly unplanned manner that is somewhat deceptive since he does move very strictly from one point to another, quite logically, but not with any air of superiority.

There is something vaguely Proustian about the way Maloney created this kind of first-person narrative for the jury's consideration, which is best described by the narrator Marcel in the last volume of *Remembrance of Things Past, The Past Recaptured.*

> The writer's work is merely a kind of optical instrument which he offers to the reader to enable him to discern what, without this book, he would perhaps never have perceived in himself. And the recognition by the reader in his own self of what the book says is the proof of its veracity, the contrary also being true, at least to a certain extent, for the difference between two texts may sometimes be imputed less to the author than to the reader. Beside, the book may be too learned, too obscure for a simple reader, and may therefore present to him a clouded glass which he cannot read. And other peculiarities can have the same effect as inversion. In order to read with understanding many readers require to read in their own particular fashion, and the author must not be indignant of this; on the contrary, he must leave the reader all possible liberty, saying to him, "Look for yourself, and try whether you see best with this lens or that one or this other one."[47]

In Maloney's mind, what it all amounted to was, quite simple:

His Lordship in due course will charge you. You will be instructed that you may bring in a verdict of "guilty as charged." Probably open to you to bring in a verdict of guilty of manslaughter or not guilty at all. Manslaughter. If Dr. Stokes' evidence is right Karafil Bleta is guilty of nothing, not a thing in the eyes of the criminal law. Don't compromise and say, "Well, we don't really think he is guilty of anything at all – we agree with the opinion of Dr. Stokes – but he stabbed a man." That is not judicial behavior, that would not really be in conformity with the pledge you took when you became jurors, compromise of that sort has no place in your deliberations, because go back to what I said a moment ago. If Dr. Stokes' opinion is right, he is guilty of nothing all, not a thing. His Lordship will tell you the law of self defense, the law of provocation and that sort of thing, your rights in regard to manslaughter. These are matters that he must leave with you but remember what I said; the opinion of Dr. Stokes, if valid, says that the conduct of Bleta was not a crime at all and that he is entitled – if that is so – he is entitled after the four or five months he spent out at the local bastile, to walk out of this courtroom with you and me and all of us tonight and back to his home and to his properties and to his children. And so I submit that is what your verdict should be. Thank you.

All very simple, to the point, avoiding any touch of sentimentality until the penultimate sentence, using the language of the common man, particularly in that dismissive suggestion, that whatever the judge said – "that sort of thing" – it was just a question of trusting the good Dr. Stokes.

The jury retired at 12:40 p.m. and returned at 2:47. The accused was found not guilty. Not surprisingly, the case went to appeal, and was not finally resolved until the Supreme Court of Canada. But it was not the "automatism" defence directly, or the judge's refusal to allow the Crown the re-examination that precipitated the appeal by the Crown. It was on a matter of legal procedure that seems not to have bothered any of the legal participants during the trial. At the Ontario Court of Appeal, in November 1963, before Chief Justice Porter, and Judges MacKay and Kelly, the Crown won, and a new trial was ordered. Bill Bowman appeared for the Crown and Arthur Maloney defended. The appeal record reveals the reason for the Crown complaint:

The defence advanced on behalf of the accused man was automation. To establish this defence counsel for the accused called Dr. Ronald Edward Stokes, a psychiatrist. This witness expressed the opinion that the accused, as the result of brain damage caused by the impact of his head with the pavement, acted in a state of automation so that he could not form the necessary intent to commit murder. In the course of his evidence Dr. Stokes admitted that he had not made any examination of the alleged brain injury, and relied chiefly on information given him by the accused prior to trial. He also commented upon the evidence of a number of the witnesses and expressed his views as to their credibility.[48]

Arthur argued that if there was anything wrong with the way he had used the witness, the Crown, or failing that, the judge, should have objected, and neither had done so. Nevertheless the court was adamant – Maloney had used the witness incorrectly – the proper way to elicit a professional opinion was to put the question to the expert in a hypothetical form. The reason for this caution is best expressed in the second hearing of the appeal, which Maloney took to the Supreme Court of Canada in June 1964. Whether Bleta was or was not in a state of automatism was a question of fact, and that was a matter for the jury to decide without being unduly influenced by expert opinion. In the case at hand, it was the most important question of all:

... it is because the opinion of an expert witness on such a question can serve only to confuse the issue unless the proven facts upon which it is based have been clearly indicated to the jury that the practice has grown up of requiring counsel, when seeking such an opinion, to state those facts in the form of a hypothetical question. In cases where the expert has been present throughout the trial and there is conflict between the witnesses, it is obviously unsatisfactory to ask him to express an opinion based upon the evidence which he has heard because the answer to such a question involves the expert in having to resolve the conflict in accordance with his own view of the credibility of the witnesses and the jury has no way of knowing upon what evidence he based his opinion.[49]

Chief Justice Porter at the Ontario appeal, had no doubt that it had been all wrong, even if the judge and the Crown seemed not to know it: "Counsel ... asked the expert questions concerning his view of evidence given by witnesses. Dr. Stokes, in fact, was improperly permitted to express an opinion based on his own assessment of the evidence ... Indeed the evidence of Dr. Stokes was the only evidence that in any way touched upon the subject of automation."[50] As such, in Porter's opinion, the evidence was inadmissible, and the lack of objection by someone or anyone was irrelevant, since, as the judge explained, the verdict might well have been different had the objection been made and had been accepted. Maloney argued that there ought to be some discretion practised by the appeal court, given the fact that the error in not objecting was made by the Crown, and in effect, a reversal put the accused in double jeopardy. The Ontario court was unmoved.

At the Supreme Court of Canada, however, the matter was seen in a wider context. Although it was acknowledged that the best and usual way of using an expert witness was as stated by the Ontario court, it was possible for the trial judge, in his discretion, to permit the opinion of an expert in "so long as the nature and foundation of his opinion and the evidence upon which he is asked to base his conclusions, have been clearly indicated by other means." It was the opinion of the court that there was, indeed, sufficient evidence, clearly apparent to the jury, upon which the doctor had come to his conclusions. "Provided that the questions are so phrased as to make clear what the evidence is on which an expert is being asked to found his conclusion, the failure of a counsel to put such questions in hypothetical form does not of itself make the answers inadmissible." On examining the trial judge's instructions to the jury on the question of Stokes's evidence the court was "of the opinion that the learned trial Judge was justified in proceeding on the assumption that the hypothesis on which Dr. Stokes based his opinion has been made clear to the jury and that he was accordingly also justified in admitting the evidence of that opinion and commenting on it as he did."[51]

The jury verdict was restored, and Bleta, according to the newspapers, was finally able to take things easy. "Twice cleared on murder charge he plans to relax, go fishing" was the unusually long headline. For Arthur, it was a bit of the same old story that bedevilled his bank manager: "Mr. Bleta, who owned a $20,000 equity in four houses when the trial opened, said his lawyer, Arthur Maloney, is only charging him a fraction of the usual fee for his defence."[52] Which may have been something of a self-chastisement for putting the question to the psychiatrist in a way that precipitated the appeal in the first place.

9

Coming to the Rescue

Arthur Maloney's return to private practice, after the 1962 defeat, burdened with old political debts, and failed hopes, was also marred by the fact that he had been unable to fulfil his ambition to do something lasting. Aside from personal ambition, there had always been that deeply held determination to do something about capital punishment – and he never quite got the chance, save for his speech, which stirred his audience on the moment, but did not change anything. When he came out of politics, however, he was not so disillusioned by the failure that he turned his back on social action.

As early as the summer of 1962, he was back in the thick of social comment in the "Robert Roberts" case, along with many of his fellow criminal lawyers, many of whom were his former students. "Roberts" was the self-imposed name that a Toronto man, with a previously clean record, took to protect his pregnant wife and six children from public harassment, after he confessed to a string of fires in 1960, '61, and '62, which caused some $65,000 damage, but no loss of life. Born in 1930 to an east-end, working class family who had struggled through the thirties, poorly educated, and prone to depression, he married in 1950, had several children very quickly, and was in and out of ill-paid jobs through the decade, drinking too much, often falling out with his wife as they struggled to keep the family together. On 7 April 1962, he presented himself at a police station, gave the false name, confessed to setting nine fires, and begged the police to get him some psychiatric help since he was convinced that he was would be unable to stop this destructive conduct otherwise.

He pleaded guilty before Magistrate Tupper Bigelow in the old City Hall on 30 June. Bigelow, one of the older, tougher magistrates, quickly settled his problem by giving him a twenty-four-year sentence. Everyone was astonished, although Bigelow seemed satisfied. Roberts attempted to make him think again:

May I say something, your worship? I gave myself up on the grounds that I receive psychiatrist's help, and I have a wife and six children. My wife is expecting again. I never meant to hurt anybody in my life, and I knew within myself that I needed medical help and that was the reason I gave myself up. I couldn't face myself or face my wife or my family.

Twenty-four years, your honor – I'm only 31 years old and I never expected nothing like this. I could've not said nothing and done nothing. I couldn't face myself and my family and I figured I needed psychiatric help. That's why I gave myself up.

There was medical evidence that this simple, bewildered soul was quite right – he was, in fact, mentally ill and could be helped out by psychiatry. Tupper Bigelow, true to his reputation as a hard man, brushed aside the plea with a quick rejoinder: "They've got the psychiatric help, if that's what you need, in the penitentiary."[1]

The Bigelow decision was met with such public indignation that the lawyer for Roberts soon discovered that there was a grass-roots movement in the city to do something about the situation, and a meeting was called in a church (which Roberts had, in fact, attempted to burn down) to see what might be done. One of the first citizens called to help was Maloney, and he and several other lawyers formed the legal backbone of the group that fought to get Roberts out from under the egregious sentence that Bigelow had handed out with such thoughtlessness.

Arthur was not alone in this particular case, but it represents the kind of thing that moved him, so often, to extend himself beyond the role of leading defence counsel. There were many trial counsel as good as Arthur, and there were some who were better than him, particularly in the matter of arguing the mandarin subtleties of the law, but there were few who were so constantly inclined to go out of their way to help the unfortunates; who for one reason or another, often of their own making, were down and out and at the mercy of the courts – which, quite often, as in this case, showed no mercy at all. Many lawyers came forward, and Roberts, as a result, received a much-reduced sentence, but it is significant that the lawyer to whom they first turned to stand at the centre of the fight was Arthur Maloney, whose statement to the newspapers gives some idea of how his mind worked, and why he was fast becoming the social conscience of the city:

I was approached by Mr. James Babson, who informed me of his concern about the disposition of the case that was made against Mr. Roberts. He told me this concern was shared by what appeared to be a large number of fellow citizens in the Metro area.

> I replied that I would only be too glad to associate myself with Roberts' lawyer, Mr. Kott, in meeting with him and with other interested citizens to discuss with them the legal procedures involved in the case and to advise them of any future action that is possible to take on behalf of Roberts with a view to assisting his rehabilitation and his release.
>
> I look forward to meeting with the group who propose to assemble in the church hall next Wednesday night to discuss these matters with them, and to assist to clarify their understanding of how the law functions in cases such as this.
>
> One aspect of the matter that impressed me was the fact that in the Metro area there should be such a large number of people who demonstrate this kind of interest in the administration of justice. This is a heartening thing, because the administration of justice would be in danger if the public were to be apathetic about it or indifferent as to the manner in which it operates.[2]

The response among the younger criminal lawyers was so strong that Arthur did little of the work, and allowed them to carry through the negotiations and legal procedures that eventually lifted some of the frightful burden that Bigelow had dropped upon this sad creature, but it may well have been the sudden uprising of public indignation, and the accompanying interest of so many members of the legal profession that convinced Arthur that he could do something about capital punishment despite his lack of success in Ottawa. He clearly had a natural constituency among criminal lawyers, and to a lesser extent among lawyers in general, and he had enough sense of his capacity to attract the general public to lead him to the conclusion that he might still do something about building public pressure that might eventually lead the legislators to the idea that killing people was wrong, not only for the murderers, but also, and perhaps more so, for society.

Lawyers often bear the brunt of public dislike, and there are good reasons for this, although it should be remembered that in the main, without a society constantly at war with itself, trial lawyers would hardly exist. Since they depend upon problems that no-one wants in the first place, and charge for services that are generally played out in stress and worry, their accounts can hardly be viewed with much enthusiasm, especially if the clients do not get quite what they want – however well they deserve it. Few clients ever get quite what they want, and rarely anything to take home in a smart shopping bag, however brilliant and expensive the counsel may be. There isn't a criminal lawyer about who hasn't spent his entire professional life defending what he does to self-congratulatory moralists at dinner parties who feast on the old, boring question of how one could defend a party who is obviously guilty. No deft argument or Jesuitical suavity can defeat the smugness of the lay moralist determined to take advantage of the good manners of a criminal lawyer trying to avoid an argument and get on with his soup. Yet, prior to the legal aid system, which only came into play in the late sixties, there was constant free work being done by trial lawyers, some as prominent as Maloney, and many of lesser gift or experience, who did what they could to alleviate the misery of those in society who often had the single talent for getting into trouble, but little skill in accumulating any funds to pay for legal counsel.

No-one seemed to understand this better than Maloney, who was his own best example of how a lawyer could help out by doing what he did best, practising what he preached, while arguing for change. In 1964, he and a group of criminal lawyers, many of them his former students, founded The Canadian Society for the Abolition of the Death Penalty, and not only became its first members, but went out into the public on their own time to educate, debate, cajole, and plead for a change in public opinion on this dreadful subject. Arthur Maloney became the founding national president of the society, and like so many of the other busy counsel, he held himself out as a speaker, willing to travel throughout the province and occasionally the country in an attempt to civilize the Canadian public to a new way of thinking about the most despised member of society – the murderer. It is now difficult to remember how strong the feelings were on that matter, although the occasionally vicious exercise of that vile habit of man in killing his own kind still brings out the cry for the return of the hangman. Roy McMurtry, who had helped Arthur in his work on the Coffin inquiry, had been persuaded of the validity of the anti-death penalty position by Arthur, and he became the president of the Toronto chapter of the movement; this, in a sense, was McMurtry's first entry into public affairs. "Our financial angel was Senator Wally McCutcheon; he didn't want to go public, but he was it."[3] Arthur's old Parkdale constituency came in; Jerry Wilk became chairman of the National Ethnic Group Research Committee. In the sixties, there was still very strong support for capital punishment, which was only gradually eroded over the years by enlightened social reformers, among which the Society members can take an honourable place. How much they influenced the general populace is difficult to assess, but they were there, organized, articulate, impassioned, and informed, and they gave much of their time, through the period, long into the nights, arguing for a different way of dealing with the problem.

When the Parliament of Canada finally rid the country of the death penalty in the late seventies, Arthur's speech in the 1960 Commons debate on capital punishment was remembered as the clarion cry of the movement. Charles Lynch, in his *Ottawa Citizen* column of 21 September 1984, at the time of Arthur's death, spoke of its importance: "it has been quoted ever since as a model of argument against the noose." He went on to quote several passages from the speech:

> This I say with all humility, is the only subject on which I feel I am qualified to give at least some measure of guidance to my colleagues in this house ... To me, the sole question to be determined and the only question we are called upon to decide is this: Is the penalty of death the only effective deterrent available to stamp out the crime of murder, or is there another alternative penalty that is equally effective and less drastic? The evidence demonstrates to the point of moral sureness and certainty that the penalty of death is not the only effective deterrent to the crime of murder and that a sentence of imprisonment for life has proven to be equally effective.

Maloney went on to speak of the anguish of waiting convicts "dying a thousand deaths, suffering more torment and torture" than was commensurate with their crimes, the possibilities of miscarriages of justice, and the awful fact that so many murderers, as well as so many convicts in general, came from "slums, broken homes, poverty, drunkenness, divorce, lack of opportunity, lack of education." One of his last sentences touched on his general concern with the way the criminal law operated. "I detest any law or system that discriminates unfairly between the rich and the poor." It is a speech better remembered than re-read. It is not a great piece of oratory. But it is organized, sensible, and informative, and it succinctly illustrates the vagarious, chancy nature of the legal system with its dependence upon counsel of various skills, judges with arbitrary power, witnesses with dodgy memories – all of which is bad enough when it puts an accused in jail for the wrong reasons, but devastating when the hanged man allows for no second thoughts.

Joe Sedgwick in introducing Arthur at the Royal Canadian Military Institute on 8 June 1977, after the federal government had gotten rid of the punishment, thought he knew how much Arthur and his determined, happy band had done: "For many years he campaigned for the abolition of capital punishment. In season and out, he raised his voice in the cause, before public audiences, on radio, on television, and in print; and when finally the barbaric punishment of hanging was abolished in Canada, I think we may attribute that step as much to the advocacy and zeal of Arthur Maloney as to any other person."

Maloney had been informally campaigning against capital punishment for several years. Arthur Martin remembers him working at it in the fifties:

> Arthur used to organize discussions on capital punishment. I remember one occasion when at the mid-winter meeting of the Canadian Bar Association, he

arranged for me to speak against the penalty and Mr. Justice Kieller McKay spoke in favour of retention. He organized groups to travel around the province. Father Kelly would be there, and Joe Sedgwick, and myself. We used to refer to it among ourselves as "the travelling road show." Joe Sedgwick would speak in favour of retention. He had no strong feelings about it, but he thought somebody should put the case for the other side. I recall one time being invited by Arthur to speak in the House of Commons dining room when he was a Member. I remember one of the people there was an American who had proved statistically that it did not act as a deterrent. I made speeches at Arthur's request before the Society, when it was formed. He played a very important role, in organizing it, and expressing his own views.[4]

It was never simply an intellectual matter, or a matter of morals; he cared passionately about it, and any execution would set him off, haranguing his friends. He was good-natured about it, but he could be frankly bemused by those who did not agree with him. Frank McGee found himself a source of long-lasting mystery:

I had this curious experience in about 1953. I was called for jury duty and the first case was a man who had murdered his wife, and Austin Cooper was defending. Henry Bull was prosecuting, and Jim McRuer was on the Bench. The defence was on the M'Naghten Rule – also the curious fact that the defendant fell asleep in the courtroom, and Austin argued that it proved how insane he was. We convicted him – and I got home that night and I cried – I was terribly upset. The phone rings and it's Arthur, and I told Arthur why I was upset. And Arthur, for whatever reason, concluded that if I were ever on another murder jury, I would not convict. The panel was still held and I was still on it. Four of us were selected for another murder trial, defended by Austin Cooper again, and Cooper put us on, and we convicted again! And Arthur till the day he died used to shake his head, and say, "McGee, I'll never understand it! How in the name of God, on the basis of how you felt, you could convict! I'll never understand you, McGee!"[5]

Bob Johnstone, whose father was a policeman, had been brought up to know what was good for murderers, and he spent many hours arguing the toss with Arthur, whom he realized was often personally troubled by executions:

Arthur would be shaken by a hanging in a case he had nothing to do with. He still would be shaken. He'd talk about it for hours. I remember the case of Louis Baldwin Fisher, a mental defective who killed a lady he had picked up. All the evidence showed that he was mentally substandard, but they hanged him. I guess I remember his name because Arthur talked about it after, for months and months and months. You'd be sitting shooting the breeze about football or the weather, or something else, and suddenly he'd introduce it again. It was an awful shock to him, but I don't think he had anything to do with the case. It hit him hard.[6]

Johnstone was finally converted, after a long time under Arthur's tutelage, to the uselessness and cruelty of the death penalty, but Arthur couldn't convert everyone, although it seemed not to harm his friendships. George Karmanin had gone through too much bloodshed in his homeland to be kind to his enemies, and he was frank in his reluctance to follow Arthur without certain exceptions being made. "I explained to him that in the situation such as an opponent, as the Axis regime or the Communist, is different. We have to deal with an opponent who doesn't have any ethical restrictions. In other words, it is almost an impersonation of the Satanic force. And in the defence of our religion, of our convictions, everybody has the right to fight this enemy, and we don't see any other situation where it applies. We said that High Treason should be excepted. He said that God's law is one law for everybody. In the perspective of time, this attitude makes Arthur Maloney ever greater in my eyes."[7]

Arthur spread his net very wide in the attempt to get the word out on the question, and he was often prepared to go at a moment's notice to speak to any who would listen, however small the group might be. There were, of course, given his taste for spreading out in his expansive way, moments of wider endeavour. Doug Crane, who had stood on the corners of Parkdale with him during the last election campaign, was still presumed to be at his call after he came to the Bar.

He got me involved as one of the people in the Society. I think I eventually became secretary, and then president, and organized ethnic rallies to promote the idea. Then Arthur got a rally going in Ottawa with Bishop Carter, who later became Cardinal Carter – with two or three experts on the death penalty. He wanted the political parties represented, so I got Stanley Knowles, and a Conservative, Jed Baldwin from Alberta, and the Liberal was from the York Mills area – I've forgotten his name. As soon as Arthur got into a hotel room, it was off with the jacket, and he'd want a drink. The first time I met Bishop Carter was in a hotel room and he said, coming in the door, 'Maloney, where's the Scotch?' He was rolling up his sleeves, obviously a good friend of Arthur, and certainly enjoying himself.[8]

It must have given Maloney some satisfaction to see so many of his colleagues, so many of his former students, taking up the cause that he and Robinette had felt so deeply, years previously, at the double hanging of those feckless rogues, Suchan and Jackson. But it was not simply that which brought Arthur to the fight – it was part of what he was – a man who candidly admitted his deep hatred of the act of murder – but a deeper hatred of the idea that a man should lose his life as a result of killing another. It was simply impossible for Arthur to accept such public revenge, just as it had always been impossible for him to ignore the cry for help of the lame, distressed humans, who came to him in his early career, with big trouble and empty wallets. John O'Driscoll's sense that he was not simply a fine lawyer, but a man prone to not only listen to the troubled who searched him out, but to go looking for them, was simply part of his character, and by the mid-sixties, part of his public reputation. As Michael Starr said, when he was in the House, despite the fact that he was a newcomer, others came to him for advice when they were in difficulty. A human being in need could always count on Arthur.

His career as a Bencher of the Upper Canada Law Society was marked by the same concern for the despised outsider. He was not a particularly serious member of this group, which is the governing body of the legal profession in Ontario, although he was, among the profession, often its most popular member. Benchers are elected to the post, and it is considered a great honour, since the entire Bar is involved in a free vote. Arthur not only came early to the group in 1956, only thirteen years after graduation, but he often topped the list, with more votes than any other lawyer. His attendance record at the regular meetings, and at committee meetings was often spotty, particularly during his Ottawa years. Some Benchers found his constant popularity with the general population of the Bar upsetting, given his lack of attention to the post. He did have one abiding, and sometimes irritating weakness – he was most likely to be flexible on matters of bar discipline, and his position on the matter of dealing with wayward lawyers was always, and sometimes comically, determined by a desire to see their faults in the kindest light possible. As one former Bencher said, "if Arthur was in attendance at a discipline hearing, you could presume that he would take the role of defending the lawyer with the same tenacity that he would use in court." Eric Murray saw him rarely before the Ombudsman business, but he knew of his reputation as a Bencher:

> I used to do both prosecutions and defences for the Law Society, and I was prosecuting a lawyer on a case that was cut and dried; normally prosecution counsel keep quiet; I had my say and the fellow was disbarred. Arthur didn't appear, but he was indignant that he missed that one – he'd have voted for the lawyer –

that's the way he was. I was once assured that Arthur would have been made the Treasurer of the Law Society [its highest office] if he had ever shown up once at Convocation.[9]

Stephen Traviss, trained as a lawyer, has long served in the offices of the Law Society, advising lawyers on professional ethics. He has seen Benchers come and go through the years, and remembers Arthur as elusive in person, but always available to help on difficult problems of legal conduct.

He was always attentive when he attended. He was chairman in 1973 of the Professional Conduct Committee. He was always extremely concerned about the fairness of the proceedings; one might say he was a little biased in favour of the member who was being hauled on the carpet – if I can quote colleagues from the audit department who gave testimony before the committee – they always said that after Arthur cross-examined them, although he was a member of the panel, they felt that they had taken the money, and not the lawyer who was being examined. I know that when they heard that Arthur was sitting on the panel, they would roll their eyes, anticipating what was going to happen to them. Arthur was very much the defence counsel.

On matters of criminal conduct, he was always available, would explain the problem, and the solution, and he would also tell me, "if the lawyer has any doubt at all about what I mean, he can phone me at home, and here are my phone numbers, and I'd be happy to discuss it with him." A lot of our difficult ethical problems would arise from criminal cases, and he would always help. He didn't run in '75; he had won four successive elections, so he had the right to become a Life Bencher – which he chose. In debate, he was always very fair, and he was always interested in how things could be improved.[10]

He simply hated to see a human being punished without some attempt to see the miscreant in the best light possible, however obvious it was that the party was the sole author of his or her own trouble. It wasn't, therefore, a requirement for Arthur that the troubled suppliant be necessarily down and out, although most of his charges were such. He would help anybody, even those who were perhaps least worthy of succour. As he would often say, the most despised members of society had a right to be protected from society taking more vengeance than was deserved. One did not have to be worthy of help to get it from Arthur, nor did one have to be innocent of his own undoing.

Probably the best example of Arthur's tolerance can be seen in his jury address at the trial of Gary McCorkell, a teenage stock boy in a

Mimico furniture warehouse, who in the act of molesting two very young boys, panicked, and in order to keep them quiet, stopped their mouths with his hands. What he didn't, couldn't know, is that children that young could be easily smothered, and that is what happened. Seeing what he had done, he tried to revive them and when that failed, he ran to a nearby hospital, got help, and displayed the babies, lying side by side, past any hope of being revived. McCorkell, taken into custody, was an easy suspect for the police to coax into a statement, and he was charged with murder. A working-class boy with no money, and little intelligence, he came into the hands, in the first instance, of Monte Harris, the young lawyer who had helped out in Arthur's last campaign, and Harris was able to convince Arthur to come in and lead the defence. There wasn't much of that to be had, although Arthur was critical of the way the police had kept the young boy sequestered without any refreshment for several hours, until they were satisfied that they had obtained sufficient information from him. In his address to the jury, he turned that indignation into a general comment upon the arrogant manner in which the police took on their authority. He often used the jury address as a forum for education on the duties of the citizen to be constantly vigilant to the dangers of official power:

> His lordship will instruct you as to the matters of evidence that you will have to take into consideration in determining whether or not to act on the confessions, but bear in mind that there was no evidence at all to speak of against this accused until Inspector NcNeely, Detective Alexander and Detective Crawford went into that little room in No. 13 Division. There was no evidence against him of any consequence ... but when he comes out of that room there is plenty.
>
> Then you have the verbal statement and you have the whole history of the evening: several hours practically of silence, nobody to talk to him, nobody to say anything to him, and the mother discouraged, really, from coming down to see him. ... are these confessions valid? That is up to you to decide, and you alone.

Arthur did not deal in misrepresentation, or in taking advantage of a situation unfairly. He did not like the *mise en scene* of the statements. He did not attempt to blacken the officers, but to put the statements before the jury with some sense of the terrible pressure imposed upon an eighteen-year-old boy. It was the system he wanted to talk about, in a way that went beyond the particulars of the specific case:

> But as I listened to their accounts of how they conduct these interrogations, I wonder how fair that system really is. No one wants to hamper the police in their efforts to investigate a crime, especially this kind of crime, but when it is

proposed, in the course of that investigation, to elicit answers from a young boy that they are later on going to repeat in that witness-box, I very much question the fairness of that ... Are we getting to the point where we are being tried by police, and is all this ritual that we follow in this room, with his lordship on the Bench, with counsel and court reporters? Is this all a farce ... Surely all this procedure that has taken centuries of effort to build up means something more than that. This is not just a ritual we go through here, surely. I would hate to think that Gary McCorkell was tried by reason of answers he gave out in No. 13 Division in that little room on the second floor to which the public did not have access. It would make quite a farce out of our system of justice. ... do you feel that they have fairly presented what was in this boy's mind at the time? Or do you feel that we are dangerously close to where this boy might have been tried by the police?[11]

Maloney knew that the statements were likely to be accepted, and he got down to the really serious business of the charge of murder. It is not an easy set of facts to deal with. McCorkell evidently found the children playing outside the warehouse, and brought them inside, took them into the basement, and played with their private parts. His employer called him, and in a panic, he clamped his hands over their mouths to stop their crying out. He did not intend to kill them, and there was some evidence that, given his limited intelligence, and his conduct, that he did not know that they were dead. There was no semen found on his person or on them, no bruising, and save for a small tear in the crotch of one of the children's trousers, no damage to clothing. However, he did not have to intend to kill them if their deaths occurred during the commission of this sort of criminal offence. If the muzzling occurred while he was molesting them, he was then on the way to a murder charge. It was Arthur's task to convince the jury that such was not the case – that what had happened was in two parts – that he was playing with them improperly – heard the call of his employer, and stopped touching them, but in order not to be caught out by his boss, he had attempted to stifle their cries – then you might, just, have manslaughter.

That was quite enough for any jury to handle, but Arthur wanted more from them than that, and wanted them to consider the sensitive idea that, in a way, McCorkell was not really being judged by a jury of his peers at all – that he was different, and in two ways.

It is a crime which, when a person is charged with it, must be tried by a jury of his peers. But you are not really a jury of his peers at all, are you? You are infinitely his superior – in age, in wisdom, in experience, in vocation, in walk of life, and above all, you are not afflicted with an abnormal appetite that he never sought nor wanted.[12]

It was Arthur going, once more, where other counsel might fear to tred. In the Bleta case, he had spoken directly to the common inclination of society to look upon expert witnesses with some suspicion; here he had a much more sensitive problem – the general personal and social disgust for child molesters. It wasn't sufficient to point out that McCorkell was just a boy – but that he was a boy who had been cursed. He didn't set out to become a molester of children, nor was it something he desired – he too was a victim. Maloney essayed the idea and then left it with them, moving on to consider the connection between the indecent acts and the stopping of the breath. He would, sometimes, do this in his jury speeches. If he had an idea that was difficult to understand, or, as in this case, emotionally dangerous, he would show it to the jury, almost as an aside, and leave it with them. Here he went on to the necessary connection between the criminal act and the stopping of the mouths.

> You have got to satisfy yourself that you are satisfied beyond a reasonable doubt that the stoppage of the breath was for one of two very definite purposes; that is, that the stoppage of the breath was for the purpose of facilitating the commission of the offence of indecent assault or for the purpose of facilitating his flight after committing or attempting to commit the offence of indecent assault.
>
> Was it for the purpose of facilitating the commission of the offence? All the evidence is to the contrary. Every line of it, every word of it, every syllable of it, in my respectful submission to you. He put his hand over their mouths when they started to cry – "when they started to scream," the officer said ... Whatever he may have done on April 18th, one thing he did was not to run away. He got a first-aid kit; he wet cloths at a hose to revive them; he carried them up to bed; he went to a man at the hospital; he waited until the police came. If that is flight, it is news to me.[13]

Then he went into one of those intimate patterns of one-sided dialogues in which he anticipated what was going to happen in the jury room. The defence and the jury were rummaging about in the evidence together – it was "let us," not "let me" that is the secret of this rhetorical method. "Let us take these elements apart again in the light of that evidence and within the framework of that presumption of innocence, bearing in mind that all these things must be proved beyond a reasonable doubt to the satisfaction of every single one of you."

The questions come in quick, simple succession: did he put the hands over their mouths to facilitate the offence he had been engaged in? No. Was there an indecent assault? There was no physical evidence of such. What about the tear in the pants? "There was no evidence as to how that tear got there, and there is no evidence as to when it got there. Good Heavens, we cannot assume in a capital case that the accused put it there, not unless we are going to act on supposition. We wouldn't even do that in a civil case, let alone one concerning a serious matter such as this. And there is no evidence of semen and no evidence of bruising around the privates."

That all sounds fine, but Arthur had the statement to contend with, and in that statement the accused had admitted putting his hands over their mouths. But in order to convict, it has to be a wilful act, a willed attempt to stop their breath. "Did he wilfully stop by any means the breath of Ronald MacLeod? Wilfully, gentlemen. He didn't sound very wilful in what he said to the police. No sir. This is what he said:

> Someone came downstairs, I think it was Mr. Roberts, but I am not sure. I put my hand over the boys [*sic*] mouth that had his hands tied behind his back as he was crying. He really started to cry so I put more pressure on his mouth to cover the sound up. The other one started to cry then, so I did the same thing with him ... I didn't realize that I was going to kill them, it was an accident, and I just put my hand over their mouths to prevent me from being discovered.

It is not the best evidence in the world, but Maloney made something of it, linking it with his earlier complaint about the way in which the police got the statement from such a young suspect. "And nobody has the right to poo-poo that or water it down. This is a statement made by a boy, after three hours of silence, to a policeman who was typing down what he said in circumstances which Dr. Kaston said were highly unsatisfactory."[14]

Maloney had another difficulty to meet. Even if the jury came to the conclusion that they could not convict of capital murder, they might consider it non-capital, if the boy did something that he ought to have known would cause death. Maloney's response to this hypothetical question was to return to the evidence of the boy's conduct, immediately after he realized that the children were unconscious. By now, he seemed aware that he was fighting up hill, and he took to instructing the jury on their duty – they must do the dirty work:

> You will bear in mind the statement and its contents and what he said in the warehouse. You will bear in mind that he said it was unintentional; you will bear in mind that he said it was an accident; you will bear in mind that he stated he thought they had only passed out. You will bear in mind that all his subsequent conduct indicated that he believed that they were still alive – the first-aid kit, the white cloths, the visit to Sheehan [at the hospital], when he said they were hurt.

It was a case in which the return to the starkness of the evidence was the best thing Arthur had to work with, and where it was necessary to go to the most unpleasant aspects of the scene to make his points. "You will remember that Sheehan said, 'It was obvious to me that the boy thought they were still alive.' He might be wrong, but that is what he said. Eden [a police officer], when he went up to see them, said he thought they were asleep at first."

Then the speech became intimate once again. Having given the jury their head to work their way through the matter of the accused's intent and actions – in a sense, stepping back in order not to crowd them – he moved back into their space, and suggested what is the reasonable conclusion. It has an oddly, man-to-man simplicity and directness that ends in a vulgar, tough fillip of seeming indifference.

> All right, if that is the case, if you agree with my submission there, then he should be found not guilty of non-capital murder, which leaves, then only one other verdict – manslaughter. Now, in the light of all the facts, isn't it that? In the light of the statements, within the framework of the doctrine of reasonable doubt, in view of the fact that you are the ones who decide, isn't that the proper verdict here? In my respectful submission it is. Because once you overcome that first hurdle of whether or not he did the act and you come to the statements, and once you are prepared to act on the statements, isn't that the only proper verdict? If the statements are right, if he did what they say, then he is a pedophile and his attraction is to little boys, and where he would go then he would find no little boys.[15]

Maloney was not quite finished yet. He knew the inclination of juries to oversimplify, to react with a coarse cruelty to one of their own who had failed, and he was still worried about it, about the atavistic cruelty of tribal anger at an act forbidden and feared. He went right to the point:

> I know it is not easy, and I know how I would feel if it were my two little children, and I know how you would feel, and there is very little in the way of consolation which can be held out to their parents and their relatives other than the fact that in their sweet innocence they were taken away by Providence, whose ways have always been inexplicable to mankind, to a place which, if everything we are taught is right, as I firmly believe it is, they feel no pain.

This of itself had a kind of credibility in Arthur's mouth that might not lie so well in that of other counsel; his deep religious faith and his ability to express it unselfconsciously allow it to have a tonal credibility that might be missing with other lawyers, particularly so since his religious and social beliefs were well-known. However, he was not through, and he took that idea of Providence, quite astonishingly, to another matter that he knew was the real danger in this case:

And bear in mind, too, as you try to disabuse your minds of the natural prejudice which must be lodged there, that the appetite that afflicted this young boy was one he never sought or wanted and the same Providence that took the lives of these two little children planted that appetite in him. You have a duty to society, it is true, and that duty to society includes your duty to him. You will approach the facts of this case, no matter how much they fill you with horror, with all the decency and humanity of which you are capable.[16]

Any number of counsel could have worked the jury through the alternatives of capital, and non-capital murder into a consideration of manslaughter for this dim, bewildered child, but very few of them would dare to intrude on Providence. The last step into asking the jury to consider the hapless nature of Gary McCorkell's personal hell as yet another aspect of the universal Creation which we, as human beings, cannot quite understand, was a particular example of how Maloney brought his deep, forgiving Catholicism into his work, without apology, and with intense sincerity.

He did not win that case. McCorkell was sentenced to hang, but the sentence was later commuted. That was not to be the end of the association. As McMurtry said, "he passionately believed that everyone was entitled to a defence, however disgusting the crime or the criminal." McCorkell had more misery to come. In that peculiarly disgusting attempt to prove themselves worthy of social and moral credibility that convicts indulge in when let loose to attack helpless sexual offenders, particularly those found guilty of molesting children, McCorkell was beaten almost to death in the Kingston Penitentiary riots of 1971, in which good old-fashioned enthusiasm for hurting other human beings was masked by supposedly righteous indignation. Only a few of the prisoners indulged themselves therein, but they had a good time. Maloney defended one of the men who went wild. When McCorkell recovered, he was sent to Penetanguishene, where, through the years, he kept applying for parole. In the early eighties, he got in touch with Maloney, asking him to help, but by this time, Arthur was unwell; Monte Harris took the hearing, and managed to get McCorkell released. It was not a happy conclusion to his miserable life. He re-offended, and fled to the United States, where he was arrested for the same thing, and was again in jail when last heard of by Harris.

I think criminal work requires a special kind of personality. The thing about Arthur – he honestly believed in giving the best defence, and sometimes in obtaining the acquittal of a person who may have been guilty of the act, he was doing something that was for the benefit and greater freedom of all. That's a hard ideal and conviction to maintain, because sometimes some of these cases are very difficult.[17]

His sense of obligation to anyone in trouble was not confined to those with criminal difficulties, which made for some chance for one man whose friends came to Arthur for succour in late 1966. John Diefenbaker was troubled, down and almost out, but hardly worthy of Arthur's help, since he had never done anything for Arthur (some felt he had done him an injury), and he was certainly the main culprit in his own downfall.

Lillian remembers the moment that it started. They were at home one evening, and the phone rang: "I can remember the time, too, when Mike Starr phoned that night. It was only about six weeks before this thing in Ottawa, and Mike asked him to run for the presidency of the party. And him saying, after, when someone else phoned, 'My God, Camp's been campaigning for a year, crossing the country!' But he finally said, 'I don't owe Diefenbaker anything, but I'm going to do it because I think it's a terrible thing to do to your leader!'" Mike Starr might have saved himself a trip to Toronto, since Arthur had made up his mind, shortly after that phone call, to do the decent thing as he saw it. Nevertheless, Starr came down as the bearer of what could hardly be called good news – a small group of members in the parliamentary caucus wanted Arthur to run for the presidency of the party against Dalton Camp, who had been at war with Diefenbaker for several months, and whose election to the post was seen as the beginning of the end for the Chief. Diefenbaker and his small band of loyal followers were in such disarray that it was not until a few weeks before the election that they thought to put up an alternative candidate. Starr remembers himself as the initiator of the idea: "I was instrumental in getting him against Camp. We had a little caucus, Gordon Churchill, etc., and we said, 'We've got to get rid of Camp. He's working against Dief.' They said, 'who should it be?' And I said, 'Well, if we can get Arthur Maloney that would be great – if we can.' 'Well, all right,' they said, 'you're the guy to see him.' I phoned Arthur and made an appointment with him at the Royal York. Just the two of us."[18] Peter Newman has a more detailed description of the event, which puts a slightly different slant on the enlistment of Maloney into that unhappy band of brothers, attempting to hold the breach:

At this point, Gordon Churchill was trying to recruit a member of the parliamentary caucus (either Erik Nielsen or J. Waldo Monteith) to oppose Camp for the presidency. Finally, Senators David Walker and Harry Willis and M.P.'s [*sic*] Hugh Horner, Terry Nugent, Russell Keays, and Michael Starr were able to persuade Arthur Maloney to contest the office and on October 27 he made his announcement. He would run against Camp on two planks – unqualified support for John Diefenbaker and opposition to any review of the party leadership.

Maloney, a highly capable Toronto lawyer, had supported Donald Fleming against Diefenbaker at the 1956 leadership convention, but he later was elected as a Tory back bencher and came to believe in the Prince Albert politician with the fierce emotional loyalty of which the wild Irish are capable ... it was never clear why Maloney's fervent devotion and distinguished legal record didn't win him a Cabinet position in the Diefenbaker government.[19]

This idea of fervent devotion to Diefenbaker was not quite true. He was often highly critical of how Diefenbaker had frittered away the popular mandate that he had been given in the late fifties. Ralph McCreath recalls an incident in the 1962 election that reveals some of his frustration at the time of Diefenbaker's appearance in Toronto for the big ethnic rally.

To me [on the matter of Maloney coming to the rescue against Camp] that was a change of heart because he wasn't too happy with Diefenbaker after '62. For some reason or other – I guess he felt some indebtedness. Can you imagine two people more different than Diefenbaker and Arthur Maloney? During the '62 election, we were having lunch at the Royal York and the head waiter came over and said that Mr. and Mrs. Diefenbaker were out in the lobby waiting – Arthur was to take them to some meeting in Parkdale – and I said, "Come on, Arthur. I'll go and get the car." And he said, "Oh, fuck them, I haven't finished my coffee." He left them out there for half an hour! I went out there three times before he came out with me![20]

However disillusioned he was with Diefenbaker, he was ready to do his best for him, despite the lateness of the call. Roy McMurtry remembers two things which preceded the meeting – he, Norm Atkins and Camp had been discussing the matter of a possible late opponent just days before Starr came to town – Arthur came up as the only candidate who might possibly cause them trouble. McMurtry was at the centre of Camp's Toronto support among the younger members of the Party, and Camp suggested that McMurtry sound Arthur out, since they were, at the time, involved in a defence of two police officers charged with assault. He didn't quite find the right moment to ask – but then he didn't have to:

We had been visiting some police witnesses at the station where the alleged assault had taken place, and in the cab on the way back, Arthur suddenly told the cabby, "I want to be let off at the Royal York." Then he turned to me, "I've got to meet Michael Starr. And I'm sorry on this occasion (he knew I was sympathetic to what Dalton Camp was doing), I'm afraid I can't invite you in for a drink, Roy, because I'm not sure you can be privy to our discussion, given your relationship with Dalton Camp."

Dalton had said to me previously that "of all the people who are going to come out against me, you know, there is only one I'd be concerned about." "Who's that?" I said. "Arthur Maloney." I said, "I can't believe that Arthur would get involved in this. In conversations we've had, Arthur was never a great admirer of John Diefenbaker." So to me, it was a remarkable sort of insight on Dalton Camp's part.[21]

The Starr meeting went quickly to the point, and Arthur was not difficult to persuade, despite the late start. "He said, 'All right. How much support have I got in the caucus?' I said that I'd find out. I said, 'Arthur, I'll see what I can muster, and I'll phone you.' So I went back to Ottawa, and talked to Gordon Churchill, and he said we had about twenty-five to thirty guys, and we had a meeting with Arthur and so he ran."

Jack Horner recalls his involvement in the slow movement towards stopping Camp:

Three or four weeks before the annual meeting in November, Gordon Churchill phoned me to come over. Mike Starr was there. So was Donnie MacInnes [Cape Breton South]. Gordon said, "We've got to put up somebody against Dalton Camp. Mike's going to see Arthur Maloney. He's the one man we can rally the troops behind." I agreed. Mike explained he'd seen Arthur the previous week: "Arthur said he might consider it, but he wanted to know where the Horner boys and Donnie MacInnis stood."

Doc [Horner's brother] wasn't in town, but I pledged us both; "You've got the Horner boys. Get Arthur." When Doc hit town at the first of the week, he asked, "What are we doing? Dief should retire." "Sure," I said, "everybody says Dief should retire, but you and I know he's not going to, particularly when he's got a fight on his hands. Here's the story. We're trying to get Arthur Maloney to run against Camp, and I've assured him that the two Horners will be right behind him." "You did the right thing," was Hugh's reaction. "No question. We can go with Arthur."[22]

In Toronto, nothing had been announced, but Roy McMurtry was waiting for the other shoe to fall.

A few day's later, I phoned Arthur and Lillian said, "He's down in Ottawa." And I said, "Lillian, for God's sake, surely to God he's not going to get himself in the middle of this." And she said, "I sure hope not. I'm very upset, but I'm worried about what they're talking him into."

Then I can still remember getting a phone call from Arthur early next morning, and he said, "Brother McMurtry, have you got the Maloney signs on your lawn yet?" And I said, "Arthur, you're not!" "Yes, yes. I'm running for the presidency against your friend Camp. A leader's a leader ... blah, blah, blah." So we had a great debate about John Diefenbaker's leadership, and I said to Arthur, "With all due respect, the sincerity of the views – Arthur, you seem to be confusing the leadership of the Conservative party with the papacy. It's not a job that is given to somebody for life, and Diefenbaker's not the pope of the Conservative party." So I was faced with a very serious personal dilemma. – I thought I was just going to drop out of this thing. I remember pacing around the kitchen one evening. I sat down and wrote a letter to Arthur explaining myself – Arthur told me, a few days later, he got an almost identical letter from Mulroney.[23]

Arthur set out to get himself organized as quickly as possible. He turned in the first instance to his former students, and legal buddies. Dennis O'Connor, the son of Tom O'Connor of the old O'Connor, Coutts, and Rogers firm, a big man of genial temperament, who was to be a close intimate of Arthur's during his time as his student, recalls that they were driving to or from court in Willowdale, when Arthur told him that he was thinking of running, and O'Connor agreed to go to Ottawa. It was fecklessly hit-and-miss from the beginning. Things began to fall apart almost from the start. Pat LeSage had breakfast with Arthur the morning he was going down to Ottawa to run for the presidency. If LeSage had any politics, they were Liberal, and Arthur liked to talk to him in order to get some idea of how the other side saw things. LeSage found Arthur to be mildly optimistic, given the short time he had to prepare for the election.

Then I remember speaking to him, probably a couple of weeks after the event, and he said, "When I was getting off the plane in Ottawa, I met Wallace McCutcheon, who was getting on (he was a Senator at the time), and McCutcheon called me aside, and said, 'Arthur, I know I promised you my support, but things have changed. I can't support you any more.'" Arthur was somewhat taken aback, since McCutcheon seemed to intimate others had also changed, and he said, "You know, I can't understand what caused McCutcheon to change; something had happened." He was quite intrigued by it.[24]

Aside from defections, there was the matter of the loose, informal way in which Arthur put the campaign together. After the fact, some of his supporters wondered what was going on. He was joined in Ottawa by O'Connor, Doug Crane, Bob Barr, all members of his Toronto legal clan. Tom Edmondstone had a delegate's role initially, but he was reluctant to get involved, and gave his vote to Tom Conway. "I was amazed how little organization there really was; Tom Conway was a very gifted, local politician (a cousin of Sean Conway), and a nephew of John Conway, the biggest Tory lumberman in the area – he was a bright man, but he had no standing across the province, and suddenly he's at the centre of Arthur's organization."[25]

Michael Starr thought Arthur had everything in hand, but he became uneasy as he watched the battle unfold. Arthur did not ask him to get involved in the campaign, and he presumed someone else was doing it. He had arranged for Arthur to run, and his job was done. But he noticed that something was missing.

A lot of individual guys were with him, but that wasn't enough. Dalton Camp had an organization. To be honest with you, I don't think anybody thought there was a need for an organizer or else somebody would have started something. There were some get-togethers, but nothing in a specific way. We thought Arthur was going to win. No one asked for funds. Arthur didn't organize it. He had to do that – he had to ask, but he didn't. Perhaps he thought that he was so well-known that he didn't need to.[26]

Neither Crane or O'Connor can remember it being much of an organization. There was some intrusion by supposedly professional communications people, but Dennis O'Connor thought they were a bit of a joke.

The night before the speeches, in his suite, he was in the bedroom working on his speech. I remember someone from an advertising agency talking about the content. I remember thinking how odd it was to have these guys telling Arthur how to make a speech; they didn't look like they had the experience – and then, next day, Arthur came out with that great speech! Arthur had asked me to come and help out, and there wasn't much organization there. The people around Arthur weren't from our milieu in Toronto – the Toronto group were with Camp.

Crane was equally bemused by who was with Arthur and who wasn't, and by the ramshackle nature of the organization.

Arthur didn't have half a dozen people working with him. But he almost turned it around, singlehandedly. We had a parade around the hotel lobby, and I think I had a sign, and if I could have played the drum, I'd have been playing it. We were on a shoe-string. People came to us, like Jack Horner, but we didn't have any real organization – if you took the Maloney family and the law students out, it wasn't much. I didn't see a hell of a lot of money – I don't think it cost much. We had Maloney buttons, a few placards, a couple of hotel rooms. It isn't like he had an expensive phone campaign across Canada. The reason we lost was the delegates-at-large. Arthur won the ladies from the small towns, but he lost the Premiers' appointed delegates-at-large, but only by a few votes. There was a lot of hostility – the first time I was annoyed by Conservatives – guys threatening to rip down the Maloney banner – rah, rah, vicious in-house campaigning – I remember being in that hall when Camp's boys occupied all the seats.

The famous line of Arthur's speech: "When John Diefenbaker enters the room, Arthur Maloney stands up!" is not to be found in the files held by Maloney, although a draft of the speech is otherwise on hand. It seems to have been an extemporaneous addition in response to the way in which the Camp supporters had refused to rise when Diefenbaker entered the meeting. It made little difference finally, although the results were very close – certainly much closer than might have been the case, given the long-time preparation that the Camp people had put into the operation, and the short time and loose organization of the Maloney group. Camp received 53 percent and 43 percent supported Maloney. *The Canadian Forum* of December 1966 broke the votes down:

The most significant observation was the relationship between age and voting preference. The results substantiated the general impression that Camp derived his support mainly from the youth of the Party, for 54% of his supporters were under 35. In contrast, only 23% of Maloney's supporters came from the under 35 group. A division of the delegates on a male-female basis showed that 63% of the men polled supported Camp, whereas 37% favored Maloney. The women illustrated a near-reversal of opinion, for they gave 60% of their support to Maloney. Consideration of the urban-rural distribution presented a similar reversal. 60% of urban delegates supported Camp, while rural delegates preferred Maloney to the same degree.

Had Maloney begun earlier, had his organization been larger, more organized, spent more money, had the Parliamentary caucus spent more time on the battle, he might have won. Certainly he did himself no harm. His effort was seen by all sides as an exercise in old-fashioned party loyalty – which is what he said in his speech. O'Connor saw how genially Arthur took the defeat:

The only thing he said to me, and he said it several times, was how important it was to have loyalty to one's leader. Arthur had respect for people in the position of Diefenbaker. He always treasured later praise about how he had acted, especially from Diefenbaker. Arthur felt honoured in being honoured by certain people. I remember Jack Horner being quite upset, but in Arthur there was no outward show of anger or hostility.

Michael Starr, who genuinely believed they could win, was very disturbed. "Arthur was such an easy-going fellow. His attitude was 'Here I am; take me or leave me.' I cried after he lost, right in front of other people. He'd have got help if he had asked for it, but he didn't."

Once he was back in the safety of his enclave of associates and friends in Toronto, it became something of a joke. Bob Johnstone remembers how they helped to take the sting out of the defeat, "A bunch of us kidded him about it – he always kidded too. In fact, he told me it wasn't a very serious attempt. And I said, 'Jeez, Arthur, not very many of us came away with that impression!' 'Well,' he said, 'you didn't think I had a chance. I didn't think I had a chance.' I said, 'Aside from that, Arthur, what were you going to do if you got it?' I can't remember what he said exactly, but it was a long list of things, and I said, 'Jeez, Arthur, you gave it a lot of thought for a guy who didn't think he had a chance! All you needed was another week, to turn it around!'"

He and McMurtry made up almost immediately, and continued to agree to disagree – at least on some things. They never settled the difference on Diefenbaker, but McMurtry wanted to go on to the future, and forget what was quickly becoming the past for the Conservative party. He was so impressed by Arthur's performance, and the general reaction to it in the party that he suggested that Arthur think about the leadership, and offered to take part in the attempt.

> Arthur said to me, unequivocally, that he was not interested in the leadership, and then he sort of – a little light-heartedly – I still remember we were sitting in a bar – I think we were sitting in a bar – the Prince George or the Metropole or someplace. I think we were sitting behind the bar – we had taken it over. It was closed down. He said, "No." "But why Arthur, why?" And he said, slowly, "For the simple reason that if I was leader of the Conservative party, you and I could not be sitting at two o'clock in the morning having a drink like we are." He was not prepared to put up with the sort of life that a leader – he didn't want to live in a fish bowl. Of course, people were talking about him – he'd developed a hell of a following as a result of his candidacy for the presidency. I mean, he would have had a very good shot at the leadership in '67. He would have had great support. His political star had certainly risen as a result of the Camp incident. It helped his reputation. From then on, he enjoyed the role as Diefenbaker's sort of warrior, and he made an effort to maintain a relationship with Diefenbaker for the rest of the old man's life. Diefenbaker came and stayed at the farm, and they kept in touch.

Maloney's file on the matter is certainly full of letters of praise for his attempt to stop Camp, and suggestions that he think about running for the leadership, but Michael Starr, who tried for the leadership in the '67 battle, with Arthur's blessing, never considered him a viable candidate, not simply because he had no really solid base across the country, but because he simply didn't have the stomach for the long-run dreariness of political wooing and genuflection – he didn't want it that badly.

Lillian, who was enormously relieved by the Camp defeat, has the last word on the matter: "He was willing to do it, but he was just as glad he didn't win; it would have been a year just crossing the country."

"The Wary Eye," Arthur as a child.

Photo from the Maloney-French family

Maloney home, Eganville.
Doctor's office entrance on the side (left), 1993.
Photo from author's collection

The Maloney family, late 1930s. Back row, left to right: Pat, Nell, Mary, Henry, Catherine, Anna, James. Front row, left to right: Arthur, Mrs. Maloney, Margaret, Dr. Maloney, Frances.
Photo by Karsh (Comstock/Y. Karsh 0129747-F300-434)

The boys with their father, late 1930s. From the left, standing: James, Pat, Dr. Maloney, Henry; Arthur seated.

Photo from the Maloney-French family

"The eyes have it." September 1948.
Photo from Lillian Maloney

Dressed for the Privy Council, London, 1950.

Photo from Lillian Maloney

ONTARIO

ONTARIO PROVINCIAL POLICE

$26,000 Reward

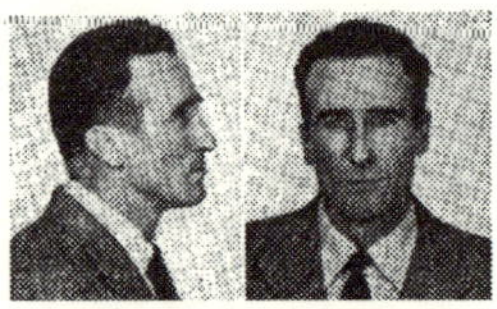

EDWIN ALONZO BOYD, Alias Chas. B. HUNTER; alias Charles HUNTER; alias Jack THOMPSON; alias John HAWKINS, Age 37. 5'7⅜". Slim build. Black hair (grey). Blue eyes. Fresh comp.

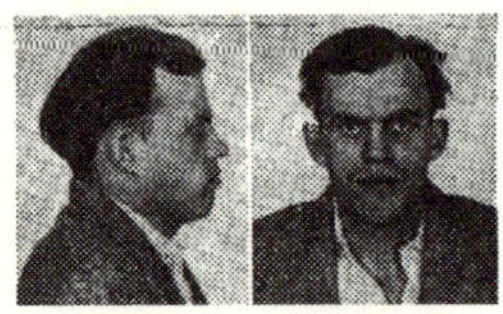

WILLIAM RUSSELL JACKSON, alias A. GIBSON, Age 25. 5'7½". Medium build. Dk. br. hair. Blue eyes. Medium comp. "Eleanor" Tatooed right forearm.

LEONARD JACKSON, alias Robert KENT, Age 29, 5'9½". Medium build. Dk. br. Hair. Brown eyes. Dark Comp. Left foot artificial (limps).

VALENT LESSO alias Steve SUCHAN; alias Victor J. LENNOFF, Age 24. 5'10". Medium build. Brown hair. Brown eyes. Medium comp. Face pimply and pock-marked.

The GOVERNMENT OF THE PROVINCE OF ONTARIO will pay a reward of TWO THOUSAND DOLLARS for information resulting in the arrest of EACH of the above named persons who escaped from the Toronto Jail on the night of September 7th, 1952.

The BOARD OF COMMISSIONERS OF POLICE FOR THE CITY OF TORONTO will pay a reward of TWO THOUSAND DOLLARS for information resulting in the arrest of EACH of the above named persons. THIS REWARD IS IN ADDITION TO AND APART FROM the similar reward offered by the Province of Ontario.

In the event of more than one person claiming either, or both, of the above mentioned rewards or to be entitled to a share therein, the rewards will be apportioned as the ATTORNEY-GENERAL FOR ONTARIO deems just.

The CANADIAN BANKERS' ASSOCIATION, in addition to and apart from the rewards mentioned above, offers to pay a total reward of TEN THOUSAND DOLLARS for information resulting in the arrest of the persons named above.

The CANADIAN BANKERS' ASSOCIATION retains the unrestricted right to fix the amount to be paid in respect of each claim where more than one claim is made and to apply any part of the total reward in respect of each of the said persons arrested and the unrestricted right to reject any claim for reward. No claim for the BANKERS' ASSOCIATION REWARD will be considered unless made in writing to the Secretary of the Canadian Bankers' Association within thirty days after the date of the arrest in respect of which the reward is sought.

The CHIEF CONSTABLE OF TORONTO holds warrants for the arrest of VALENT LESSO alias STEVE SUCHAN and LEONARD JACKSON on charges of MURDER, ATTEMPTED MURDER and ROBBERY ARMED; and holds warrants for the arrest of WILLIAM RUSSELL JACKSON and EDWIN ALONZO BOYD on charges of ROBBERY ARMED.

ALL OF THESE MEN WILL NOW BE ARMED. THEY ARE EXTREMELY DANGEROUS AND THE UTMOST CARE SHOULD BE TAKEN IN EFFECTING THEIR ARREST.

Extradition proceedings will be instituted immediately in the event of these men being arrested in the United States or any foreign country. The identity of the person giving information will be kept strictly confidential.

Any person in possession of information regarding the whereabouts of these persons, or any one of them, should immediately communicate with the nearest police authority, the TORONTO CITY POLICE authorities or the undersigned.

Parliament Buildings,
Toronto, Ontario.
September 10th, 1952.

WILLIAM H. STRINGER
Commissioner of Police for Ontario.

(SEE FINGERPRINTS ON REVERSE SIDE)

The beginnings of celebrity, 1952.

Photo courtesy of the Metropolitan Toronto Police Museum

A bit of the Jimmy Cagney swagger – Boyd on his way to face the music.

Photo courtesy of Toronto *Telegram* – York University Archives

Still smiling – Boyd second from left and Willie "The Clown" second from right. On a short ride to the Don Jail.

Photo courtesy of Toronto *Telegram* – York University Archives

Martha Maloney and parents, 1958.

Photo from Lillian Maloney – Ashley & Crippen

Visiting Daddy at work, 1961. House of Commons, Ottawa.

Photo from Lillian Maloney

Early 1960s: "Then there were two." Left to right: Matthew, Lillian, Arthur, Martha.

Photo from Lillian Maloney

Politics and the family, 1962. Left to right: Sen. Yuzyk, Father Henry Maloney, Arthur, Mrs. Odelle Wilk, Lillian, The Hon. John Diefenbaker, Dr. Pat Maloney.

Photo from Jerry Wilk

Before the storm, early 1960s. Left to right: Dalton Camp, Arthur, The Hon. John Diefenbaker.

Photo from Maloney-French collection

Arthur and Roy McMurtry, the best of friends, working together just before Diefenbaker-Camp battle, mid-1960s.

Photo from *The Toronto Star*/R. Innell

"Ottawa, Nov. 15 – MALONEY IN ELECTION BID – Toronto lawyer Arthur Maloney acknowledges applause of supporters as he is nominated for the presidency of the Progressive Conservative Association at Ottawa Tuesday. He is opposing incumbent Dalton Camp."

Photo from Canapress Photo Service/Lyn Ball

Arthur's favourite publicity photo.

Photo from Ashley & Crippen

Three Wise Men: David Humphrey, Arthur, G. Arthur Martin, early 1970s.

Photo from David Humphrey collection

Local masters meeting an itinerant colleague. Left to right: Robert Carter, Edward Greenspan, F. Lee Bailey, Arthur, David Humphrey.

Photo from David Humphrey collection

The Ombudsman and the home of the adversary looming at his shoulder, 1975.

Photo from *The Toronto Star*/B. Spremo

The Coronation: Arthur Maloney shakes hands with Speaker Russell Rowe after being sworn in as Ontario's Ombudsman. Premier Davis at right.

Photo from *The Globe & Mail*/Barrie Davis

"So that's how ombudsmen make their decisions! Arthur Maloney, Ontario ombudsman, gazes into a crystal ball yesterday at a steering committee meeting in Toronto of Canadian ombudsmen. With him are, from left: Dr. Harry Smith, Nova Scotia ombudsman, George Malty of Manitoba, Ernest Boychuck, retired ombudsman of Saskatchewan, and Dr. Randall Ivany of Alberta."

Photo from *The Toronto Sun*/David Cooper

King Arthur's Court.

Photo from *The Toronto Sun*/Barry Gray

On the run – little does he know!

Photo from *The Toronto Star*/K. Beaty

The Political Piety Quartet. Left to right: Arthur, Roy McMurtry, Judy LaMarsh, Premier Bill Davis.

Reprinted with permission – The Toronto Star Syndicate

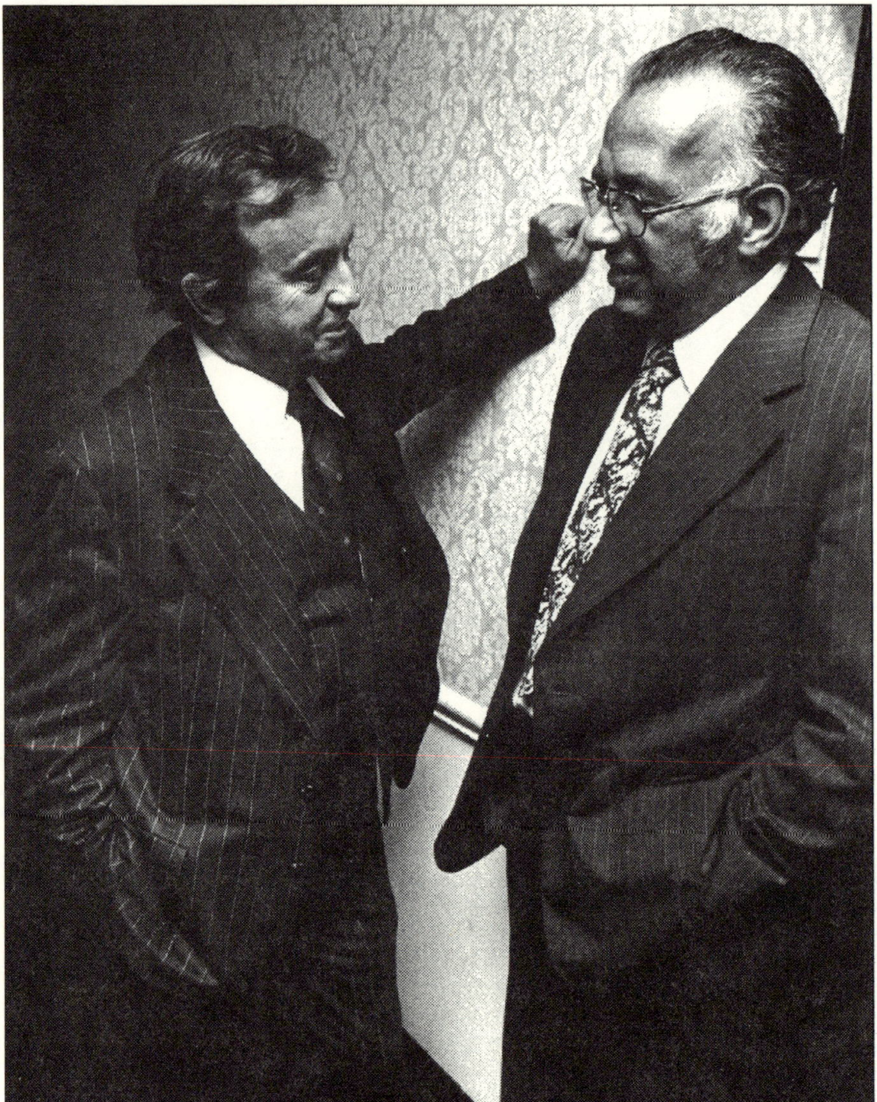

"Can't we talk it over?" Arthur and Housing Minister John Rhodes in pin-striped confrontation.

Photo from *The Toronto Sun*/Hugh Wesley

King Arthur. Not as easy as he thought.

Reprinted with permission – The Toronto Star Syndicate

Thinking it over – during last year of ombudsman confrontations, 1978.

Photo from *The Globe & Mail*/John McNeill

Reprinted with permission – The Toronto Star Syndicate

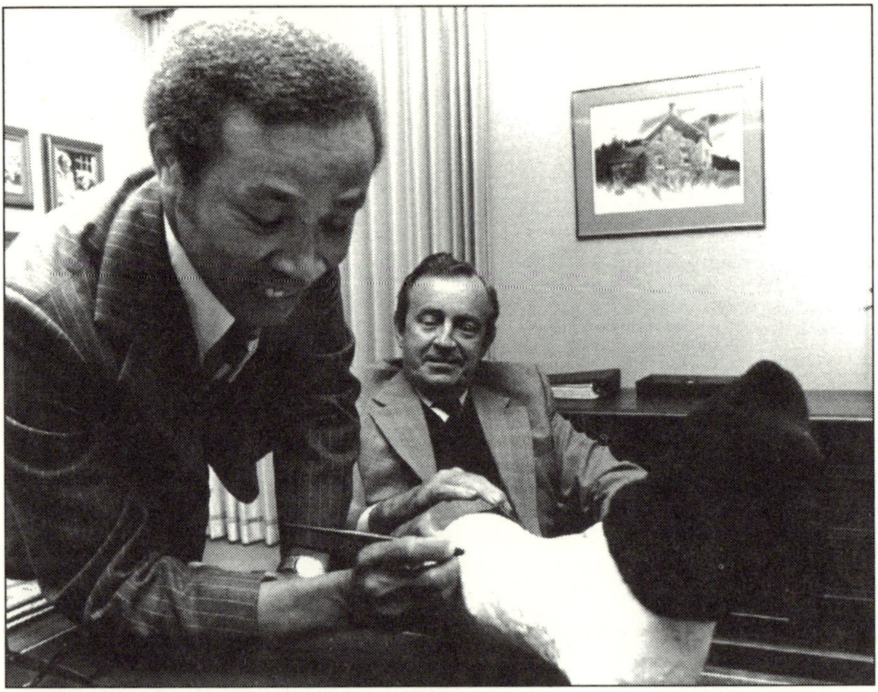

"The New and the Old – Keith Hoilett, newly-designated temporary ombudsman of Ontario, signs a cast on Arthur Maloney's ankle in Toronto Friday. Maloney, who had been ombudsman, resigned to return to private law practice."

Photo from Canapress Photo Service/Bill Becker

Late 1970s, Arthur and Lillian "smiling through."

Photo from *The Globe & Mail*/James Lewcun

Arthur with Roy McMurtry's painting of "Malafield," the Maloney Guelph line home.

Photo from *The Toronto Star*

The Diefenbaker visit – on the way to the Highland Games, 1978.
Sporan slightly out-of-place.
Photo from Maloney-French collection

At home, 1978, Cortleigh Blvd., Toronto. Left to right:
Lillian, Matthew, Martha, Arthur.

Photo from Lillian Maloney collection

A late meeting with some of his 1970s and '80s students. Left to right:
Philip Patterson, Arthur, Glenn Hainey, Rory Cornale.

Photo from Phil Patterson

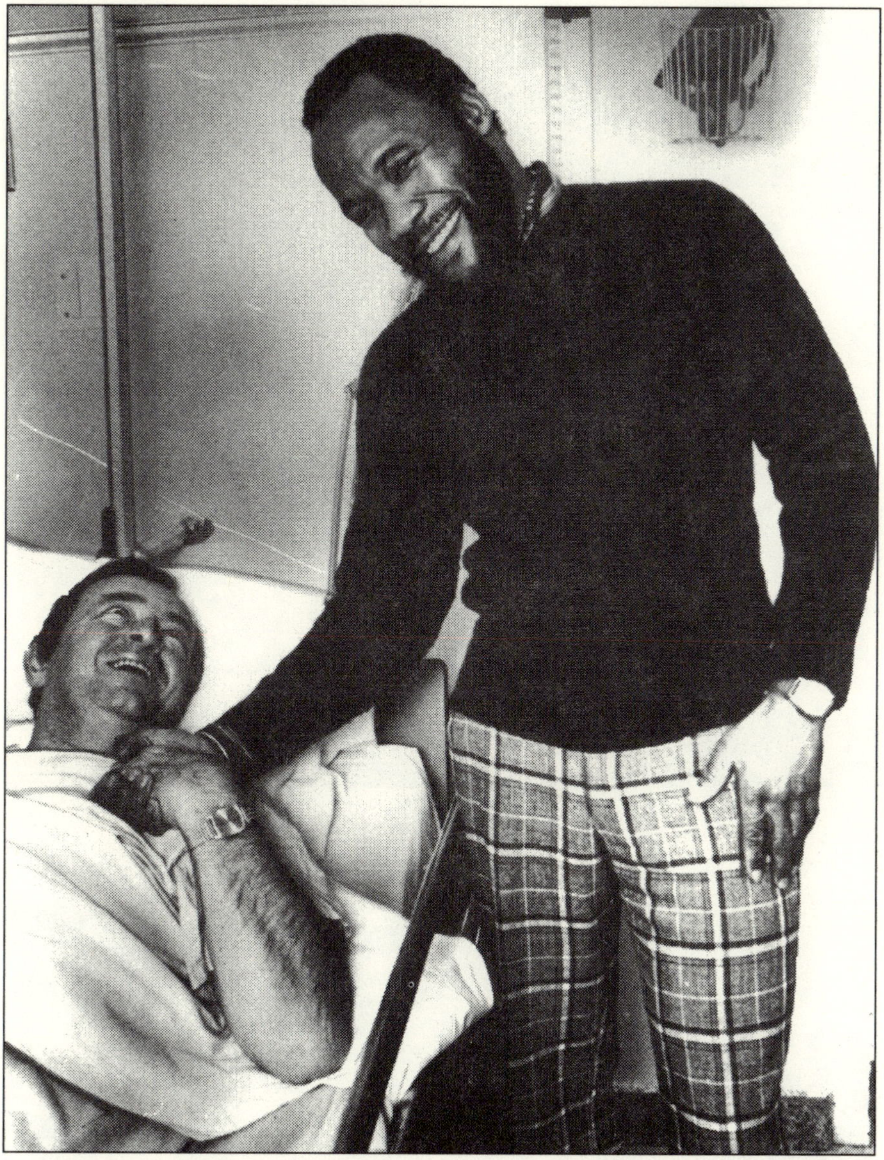

After the strokes began. Arthur receives congratulations from Al Peabody in 1979 for winning the poll as Toronto's most respected and trusted white.

Photo from *The Toronto Star*/E. Combs

The last summer, 1984.
Photo from Phil Patterson

"The Last Visit."
Reprinted with permission – The Globe & Mail/Ed Franklin

10

Murder, a Woman Scorned, and the New Criticism

The early seventies were an exceptionally busy time for Arthur not only in the courts, but in his public service commitments. He was at the top of his form as a defence counsel, and took many of the major cases, not only in Toronto, but throughout the province. He was particularly proud of the Gary Staples trial, with which he was involved in January 1971. Arthur was not the first lawyer to defend Staples, but as was often the case, he came into the matter on an appeal from the original conviction. He won the appeal, and then led Staples's original attorney in the second defence of the charge.

On 5 December 1969, a Hamilton taxi driver had been robbed and murdered in his cab in a lane just off the CNR tracks, close to the Hamilton Place shopping centre. The man had been shot twice in the head at close range. There were no clues in the cab, and it looked to be a case that would be unsolved. Four-and-a-half months later, police were searching the home of a woman called Mary Conklin, who lived on a farm just outside of Dunville, Ontario, a small town some thirty miles from Hamilton. During the conversation between the police and Conklin, some snatches of complaint emerged about why they were picking on her. They were looking for evidence pertaining to a robbery that had occurred in a nearby town, Selkirk, and ought to be questioning Gary Staples, not her. The police allowed that they had, in fact, searched Staples's home, but had found nothing. Conklin, upset by the news that Staples was seemingly free and clear of the Selkirk robbery, gave the police an earful – not just the same old complaint about police insensitivity – but something in the way of a gift. She told them that Staples, on the night of that murder in Hamilton some months before, had visited her after the fact, displayed the gun used in the robbery, admitted shooting the cabby, and complained about only getting forty dollars for his trouble. The police were impressed. Why would Conklin lie about such a serious thing, especially when it was well known that she and Staples were partners, sometimes in crime, and sometimes in love? More to the point, how did she know that forty dollars had been stolen, since that information had not been made public. On the basis of her story, Staples was arrested, despite his claim that he had not been in Hamilton, and could not be in Hamilton, since he was in a local garage, fixing his car, when the murder took place. He was, nevertheless, convicted.

At appeal, however, Maloney was able to make the case for a new trial on the grounds of new evidence that had not been available at the time of the first hearing. Whether that new evidence would have been sufficient of itself to bring about an acquittal in the first trial cannot be known, but it was obvious from the manner in which Arthur went about the matter that he was not content to depend upon it, and that he was determined, as he often was, to get some real value out of the Crown's witnesses.

Most young counsel have little idea how to get their case out of witnesses on the other side, but Arthur often depended on little else. He had a way of skidding along the boundaries of the most confident evidence presented by a Crown witness, picking up details that had been missed, or re-modelling the story they told to suit a defence theory, which was not immediately apparent either to the witness or to a wary Crown. Even more irritating to the prosecution was the way in which he would make use of witnesses who either didn't know anything, or were determined not to know.

In this particular case there was no question that Staples and Conklin were lovers at the time of the murder, and that they had something of an on-going career as thieves working together. If Staples was going to tell any dirty secrets it would seem reasonable that he would tell them to Conklin.

There have been two previous articles on the Staple case, one, unpublished, by Chris Kates, a lawyer and legal writer, who was lucky enough to begin an oral history file on Maloney for the Osgoode Society – but was not lucky enough to finish it before his last illness. A second article was written by Neils Ortved in the *Advocacy in Court* tribute to Arthur.[1] Ortved confines himself to the Mary Conklin cross-examination, since it was the centre of the case against Staples. It was Conklin, and only Conklin, who claimed that Staples had admitted killing the cabby, and she stated that a relative, Ken Shellard, was close at hand for part of the conversation. It was she who stated that Staples gave her the details of the murder, as he sat before her in her living room, wrapping the gun in a package to hide it away, just a short time after the killing.

The big problem for the defence was Conklin's detailed knowledge of the killing, and her intimate relationship with Staples, and she wasn't shy or inarticulate about either. At the first trial, the defence had tried unsuccessfully to get conversations between her and Staples into the record which would suggest that she, too, had a gun in her possession, long before the robbery occurred. He also tried to simply besmirch her reputation, showing that she was a woman of generous sexual exploit with several men. The judge ruled out the conversations about the gun, and in his address to the jury, rounded on the defence for moralizing over, and mocking Conklin's sexual conduct, and dubious physical attractions. After all, as the judge said, Staples seemed to find her attractive, and Staples was possessed of a longer criminal record than Conklin had accumulated.

Arthur's attitude to Conklin was much more constructive. While he was determined to destroy the character and credibility of the woman, he was also determined not to allow his questions about her sexuality to become so judgmental that sympathy would build up in the jury or the judge – and he was determined to build something on revelations about her promiscuity. It might be best expressed thusly: "Given the necessity of destroying the value of the opponent's evidence, is there anything that can be positively drawn out of that destruction that would go beyond the exclusion of the material itself and would become of value for the defence?" The first counsel had been right to bring her sexual busyness into the open to diminish her character, and therefore her credibility – but he had to avoid gratuitous cruelty. It might have worked – usually it would work, but in this case, the judge took offence. Not only did he find it irrelevant, but he used it in his remarks to the jury to attack the counsel and his client.

Arthur, on the other hand, saw her lively career as a lover of many men in an entirely different way. He let social distaste take care of itself. In his jury address, he declared himself thoroughly uninterested in the sexual exploits of both Conklin and Staples, thus attempting to take some of the sourness out of the fact that Staples had been cheating on his wife, who had, since the arrest, left him and was contemplating divorce. What he was interested in was not what Conklin did with so many men – but the men themselves. Who were they?

Conklin knew the details of the murder. Either she did it or was part of it. Or someone had told her about it. She claimed Staples. He denied it on the stand, but what she knew was still true. So Maloney did what he was very good at – he turned the courtroom into an investigation centre. If Staples did not tell her, who else could have done so? Was Staples the only one who could, without a reasonable doubt, have told her the tale?

When Maloney questioned her about her social life, it was not simply a matter of winkling out her sexual secrets. It was a question of with what sort of fellows she associated. If Staples, a petty thief and an adulterer, was not much to boast about, her other male companions were of similar stripe – questionable, shifty, erratic, content to come and go without any serious commitment, and occasionally threatening. They ought to have been seen to.

Luckily they were not. Once Conklin had named Staples, the case was closed as far as the police were concerned. This is where Maloney's creative mind worked best. As in *Esposito*, he had a strong inclination to look around the farm, beyond what had been done by the police. His whole defence shifted from the simple question of Conklin's credibility to what the police did not do. They, like Staples's first counsel, saw them as simply a matter of her character. Maloney saw them as potential killers. What made that leap of the imagination more viable was the fact that no-one else had ever done so. Staples was out in front, like the rest sans trousers, but with the gun in his hand. All the others had been allowed to slip out the back window of the case with their pants in their hands as they legged it across the scrubby fields of the Conklin farm. They were an *embarrass de choix* that a simple country constable would have found a nuisance – Staples was the man.

Certainly he deserved to be the man. He was a part-time, break-and-enter thief with a bit of a record. He owed money (but what working man doesn't?), and he had brandished a little revolver on one occasion at his place of employment, and was so dense that he had to be ordered not to do it again. But he never admitted the murder, and no gun was found. Conklin admitted, grudgingly, that when she named him, she was more than a bit miffed by the fact that he seemed to be slipping out of the Selkirk robbery, and was avoiding her in her troubles. More to the point, they had fallen out recently. She had expected him to join her in a lease on another farm, where they would live together. He had refused to sign the lease, and gave no indication that he planned to abandon his family and join her. She was not an easy witness; she didn't lose control, but Arthur eventually worked her down to a whimper of complaint:

Conklin: I was more hurt than anything, really.
Maloney: That's why you told this story on Gary, isn't it?
C: No, not really.
M: Not really?
C: No.
M: A little bit?
C: I wasn't really that mad. I could never get mad at him.
M: A little bit?
C: No, I was hurt.
M: Not mad?

C: Well, I might have been a little bit but not mad enough that I really wanted to tell on him you know.
M: Not angry?
C: I'm not a person that would get mad, not really angry.
M: You were not blowing steam or anything like that?
C: You might say that.
M: You might say you were or you weren't?
C: I was maybe, yes.

It is a lovely example of Maloney becoming intimate with a hostile witness – not so much pressing her as exploring the problem of what were her intimate feelings at the time of her revelation to the police. In a sense he lets the questions find their own level where Conklin is comfortable and where she is prepared to accept the characterization of her feelings as reasonable, particularly in the face of the alternatives.

What Maloney possessed was patience, and the ability to gain time without arousing the suspicion of the judge that he might be on a fishing expedition. The repetition of "a little bit" and the terseness of the questions – "Not really? – "Not mad?" – "Not angry?" – allow for a development of something closer to conversation than confrontation. It could have been small talk between two friends, one consoling the other in a moment of lament. If he didn't get the woman to admit that she told the story to the police because she was mad at Staples, she certainly left the jury with the impression that she was disappointed with him at the time and – just maybe – she was "blowing off steam" in snitching on him. "I was maybe, yes." That last word, like Molly Bloom's at the end of Joyce's *Ulysses*, seemed to sum up all her hopes and fears. Maloney had led her from outright denial to reluctantly hurt awareness, which they had found together, that, perhaps, her information was not uncoloured by disappointment with a man who had such hold on her that she "could never get mad at him."

Of course, it might still be true. Some of the details certainly were – but it did explain why it was Staples that she had named. Because, as Maloney was to show, she had plenty of candidates for the role of murderer. That is where he really went to work. Not only with Conklin, but with the investigating officers, who were well aware of her popularity with the itinerant males of the Dunville suburbs. It was here that Arthur did something of the same thing that he had done in *Esposito*. Arthur loved to ask questions that he knew the witness would have to answer with the admission that he or she didn't know the answer. He was counting on the fact that the police had paid no attention to Conklin's other male associates in their enthusiasm for Staples.

Neils Ortved, who worked on several trials with Maloney, knew exactly what he was doing: "The purpose, of course, was to alert the jury's attention at an early stage to the fact that there were many men other than Gary Staples around Mary Conklin's farm ... the questions are more important than the answers. And Arthur Maloney was careful to protect himself at the outset of his questions regarding each man so that he would not be surprised by an answer."[2] It was only in part a matter of quantity – how many men were hanging about Mary – but also, and as importantly, a matter of quality – what kind of men were hanging about Mary? Arthur asked the officers not only who, but what they knew about the men, and those things he wanted to know, if they knew, were of a particular kind. He didn't ask if the officers knew if they were good dancers, or sang in the local choir. Everything he asked had a sinister aura about it; he asked if the officers knew about criminal records, of possible guns in the possession of these men, of any associations with criminal conduct, of court appearances, of any mention of the names in the Staples's preliminaries, of any kind of suspicious conduct.

Most of the time he got exactly what he wanted – blank stares. The officers knew nothing. On once occasion, he got a bonus that he could have hardly expected. In the matter of Shellard, the man who may have supposedly heard part of Staples's incriminating conversation with Mary, the officer put words right into Maloney's jury address:

Maloney: What about him? Did you check him out to find out if he has got a record?
Answer: Yes.
M: A long one or a short one?
A: It is long and growing longer.

It was money for jam. The one male friend of Mary, whom the officer had checked, had a criminal connection – perhaps the others did as well. Which is why Ortved is not quite correct in suggesting that the answers were less important than the questions. The answers, which in the main were negative, were slowly piled up by steady questioning of a seemingly uninspired kind:

M: What about a chap named Wilfred Davenport? Did you ever check him out?
A: No, sir.
M: You don't know anything about him at all?
A: No, sir.
M: Or how close he was to Mary?
A: No, sir.
M: Or what kind of relationship she had with him?
A: No, sir.

M: Or whether he had a record or anything of that sort? You don't know anything about him at all?
A: No, sir.
M: A chap named Gino – I just know his first name – do you remember his name being mentioned in earlier proceedings? If it was, you don't recall it?
A: That's correct, sir.
M: You certainly made no check on him?
A: No, sir.
M: To see who he was?
A: No, sir.
M: To see whether he had a truck?
A: No, sir.
M: To see whether he had a gun in it?
A: No, sir.[3]

They were enormously helpful in suggesting that the police had not quite done the job – that they ignored the fact that Conklin's associates, *déracine* males of unknown age, habits, records, accoutrement were hanging around at the same time as Staples and were just as capable of doing murder. Not only had Shellard been shown to have a criminal record, but when Arthur got Conklin on to talking about her male friends, further suspicions were aroused. One Roland Savard had assaulted her, and she had thrown him out because he was on drugs. Again Arthur went to the specific question that would hurt, whatever the answer – did she know if Savard had a criminal record – she did not. Did she know, as Arthur did, that he had three convictions. She did not. Did she ever discuss guns with another friend, a truck driver, Guy Hall? She did not. Was he ever in trouble with the law? She did not know. One Ray Stirling was dealing in horses – and he had a red car. (A car, a mix of red and white, had been seen near the murder site.) "It could have been red or white. I know the bottom was red. I don't know what the top was." Then there was Wilfred Davenport, the roofer, who tried to move in and was rebuffed by Mary – he left for Vancouver just after the murder occurred.

This unsavoury gang of males, none of whom had sufficient connection with the murder to be of interest to the police, came together in an accumulation of suspicion that was much more than Arthur on an aimless trawl for some kind of break in the case. What he was building was a small community of drifters, labourers, drivers, horse men – each of whom fitted a bit of the jig-saw, but not all of it. Gino might have kept a gun on her property – she didn't know anything about it. One Hans Willamanka, whom she admitted had been a lover, worked at the dump, and had been involved with her before she left her husband. She had lied about him when questioned about entries in her diary – but it was just a little white lie – and not the only one that Maloney got her to admit about her personal life. Even under oath, she admitted that she was prepared to lie, but only if she thought it was "my personal business." But Maloney, earlier on, had been assured by her that she would not lie under oath. She qualified that – well, only if she deemed the question personal and of no importance to the trial.

By the time he got through with the police and with Mary Conklin, the matter was getting murky. Conklin stuck to her story that Staples had told her of the murder. But she had also admitted that she had a gang of men coming and going at the time, and had no idea who had criminal records and who did not, although some of them were very rough customers. This rum gang, whom no-one seemed to know much about, loomed threateningly in the background. What was, in the first instance, a rag bag of bits and pieces, ambiguous, uncertain, unknown seemed to be of little help to Staples, who was named and numbered. But what Maloney had done was establish this gang of shifters and slippery characters – not to solve the mystery, but to unsolve it. It was a perfect example of what was later, in literary criticism, to be called "deconstruction," which is best defined as allowing for the idea that one person's opinion is as good as another's, however uninformed it may be. Because if anything was clear by the time he got through with the Crown witnesses, it was that the tale could have any number of prime suspects. There were an awful lot of rogues to choose from, and it was anyone's guess who was the best candidate for the role of murderer. There wasn't much difference between Staples and the rest of them – save for the fact that Mary Conklin had named him. There was no physical evidence and there was no gun. Just Mary Conklin telling a tale about a disappointing lover. What if someone else had told her that story? If Staples looked ripe for the job, it was equally true that almost every one of her associate males could have been in the prisoner's box – if Mary had so deemed it appropriate. Reading the transcript of these cross-examinations is a cross between boredom and hilarity as the "No, sirs" and the "I don't knows" pile up, and what was the certainty of a one-to-one confession between two little thieves together becomes a milling mob of Dickensian thugs in check flannel shirts standing in line to service sweet Mary.

As Ortved put it in his article: "Judgment is all-important when deciding how a case is to be presented, and will in the end govern one's argument or address. It is crucial in determining how one handles a witness; an accurate perception of ordinary human reactions and therefore the springs of human behaviour can provide the key to the motives and probabilities of a witness acting in the manner alleged and thus, whether the witness is to be challenged, and, if so, in what fashion."[4] Attacking Mary Conklin would not do it – what Maloney did was try to find a reason why she did what she did, and once that was found, it could be turned to the advantage of the defence. By the time Arthur got through with her, it was obvious why Mary did it – Staples had hurt her. But just as obvious was the fact that Mary was leading a life in which many men might have hurt her – and also might have confided in her in the deep of the night after doing murder. She had the inclination – and she had the opportunity to learn of the criminal act – and not necessarily from Staples.

> Members of the jury, any one of these weird collection of males could have been the source of Mary Conklin's information. If she had chosen to turn against any one of them, he could find himself in the same dilemma this man now faces, Gary Staples. She knew too much to get it from the press, no doubt about that. The four items not contained in the news media must have come from him or those who were in the know. [The four things Conklin knew were the time of death, the calibre of the gun, the fact that the slugs had been filed down to prevent identification, and the amount of money stolen.] If she didn't get her knowledge from personal involvement in the murder, who told her all the details? I repeat, we know it was not Gary Staples ... Who was it, then? I haven't the slightest idea. I don't know. The failure to investigate all these other men as possible sources of her information must, I submit to you, leave you in a state of very great uncertainty, indeed distress. Let me hasten to say that I, in questioning Mary Conklin with respect to this strange assortment of men, have no concern whatsoever about her moral habits, none whatever. I couldn't care less. That is none of my affair. Her male acquaintances had to be explored by me for the purpose of finding out the possible sources of information she might have had.[5]

Much has been said about Arthur's vanity, but he loved to admit ignorance in a criminal case about who did the act, particularly after he had assiduously pursued a line of questioning with the Crown's witnesses that stealthily made the Crown's case disappear up his arm. "I don't know – my friend doesn't know – the judge doesn't know – the accused doesn't know – and you, the jury don't know" was his idea of the ultimate perfect state of defence heaven. He often got it, in part, out of the police not quite doing the job, not anticipating that Arthur was going to come along with his habit of sweeping the horizon for strangers who might be swimming in the vicinity of the crime. It was not necessary for Maloney to get his client out of the way entirely – he simply would manage somehow to get someone, or if lucky, several someones, in the boat with the accused, and then he would happily row them about in circles.

In this case, he was helped by the fact that Shellard, who was supposed to have been present when Staples came courting with the smoking gun, was not put on the stand to corroborate Mary's story – it seemed a simple enough thing to do, but he was used in neither trial. Unused witnesses were often ripe pickings for Maloney, and in his jury address he went after that strange omission. After naming and exploring the qualifications for suspicion of Mary's lovers and acquaintances, one by one, he came to the last man:

But the prime suspect I have left to the last because his name, in my submission to you, casts a shadow that is really quite sinister over this case, and I refer to Ken Shellard, cousin of Mary Conklin, Crown witness. Crown witness. There is the back of the indictment. There is a list of witnesses. There is his name. Of all the witnesses in creation, he is the one to confirm the truth of Mary Conklin's evidence. Ken Shellard is surely the prime star, and incredibly, unbelievably, the case for the prosecution closes and he was not called. What did Mary Conklin say that he would have overheard? Let us just refresh our memories with respect to that. "I seen Gary December 5th at night between 10 and 11. He drove car in, came in house, took off shoes, walked straight into living room where TV was. I was on chesterfield. He sat in the middle of the floor. He took a little gun out of his pocket, a plastic bag out of the other pocket, put the pistol in the bag, took black electric tape, wrapped it all around the plastic, and he put it in his pocket. I said: 'What are you doing that for?' He said: 'I got to get rid of it for a while.' 'What for?' 'Just used it on someone.' I said: 'For heaven's sake, who?' He said: 'A taxi driver in Hamilton' 'What detachment?' – He said: 'Kenilworth.'" Listen to this, listen to this, members of the jury: "My cousin Ken lying on other chesterfield. Accused motioned as though he didn't want him to hear any more. He wanted coffee. We went into the kitchen. I made him coffee." That is what Ken Shellard was supposed to have seen; that is what Ken Shellard is supposed to have heard. Just think of what he could have added to the case. He either would have said: "That's true," or "That's false." The Crown left him outside and left you and me wondering, and deprived me of the opportunity of asking him about his white fur collared jacket, the size of his boots [there was some evidence of what the assailant was wearing], an account of his movements on December 5th, and deprived Sergeant Williams, I suppose, of the opportunity to arrange for taking of his fingerprints so that they might be tested.[6]

Maloney was always sensitive about another problem that arose out of the rules of the game in criminal cases. If the defence does not choose to call any witnesses, it is allowed to speak to the jury after the Crown. If, however, it calls witnesses, it has to go first. Which means, of course, that the last man speaking has a chance to rebut anything that might be said by the other side. He was a great one for anticipating problems that might arise, and in this case, he seemed to sense that he might have gone too far in complaining about the absence of Shellard. He had put in a defence, so the Crown was lying in wait. After all, he had gone on to say "No jury can rest easy who has been deprived of all the evidence by the Crown." Arthur had another gift essential to a trial lawyer – he listened to himself carefully, and he knew immediately that he might well have provided a chance for the Crown to have back at him. He responded to his excess with alacrity, not only to cover himself, but to deepen the argument.

> I have no way of compelling the Crown to call any witness. The failure to call Ken Shellard as a witness is the decision of the Crown and the Crown alone. [Now he begins to cover his weakness.] Would my friend dare suggest: "Oh, you could have called him?" Imagine, I, counsel for the accused, call this cousin of Mary Conklin, this young man with a record, presently long, growing longer [An example of how he holds things in his head for later use, if the chance comes along.], this young man at whom I was prepared to virtually point a possible finger of guilt. Some way of administering criminal justice. I don't think we would feel happy about it if we thought that that was the way things were done. And the decision of the Crown not to call Shellard will ever remain a mystery, and a jury which is not allowed to convict any man of any crime unless satisfied beyond a reasonable doubt of his guilt must surely be left with an abiding feeling of doubt in a case where the Crown chooses to hold back the one witness that could confirm the evidence of Mary Conklin.[7]

Chris Kates, in her article, discusses this inclination to tidy up, and to be unafraid of admitting limitations in general. Many counsel avoid any suggestion of vulnerability, but Arthur, given his tendency to identify with the problems of the jury, to trying to get them to see that they were all trying to get things straight, usually included an *apologia* near the end of his address to cover any possibility of having missed something, or having gone too far in his arguments.

> If I have taken too long today, indeed, if at any time during the trial I have pressed a point too hard or taken any action with which you disagree, it is only because, I can assure you, of my anxiety to make certain that no stone is left unturned to establish the innocence of this accused. You could imagine what a sense of torment I would feel if tomorrow he were found guilty and five or ten years hence his innocence was to be established, and if I thought that that mistake had somehow or other been brought about by any oversight or omission on my part.[8]

Kates is sceptical about this. "Indeed, it is questionable whether a statement of this sort would go over with the jury particularly when the defence is Arthur Maloney."[9] What Kates seems to suggest is that

Maloney's reputation as a master of the trade would lead a jury to suspect the sincerity of such comment, and thus, undermine their confidence in Maloney. In isolation, that might well be the case, but it is important to put that statement in the context of the entire jury address – indeed, in the context of Maloney's conduct during the trial. Arthur did not work out of arrogant display of his talents – he did not browbeat, he did not score points with any display of superiority, he did not crow, or preen himself. He tended to use a plain style, and to assume the role of an intelligent, but simple man looking for the truth. Indeed, this was not the first time, in the jury address, that he had admitted some concern about how his comments might be taken in the jury room. Very early on, discussing the problem of going to the jury first, he took the same modest tack:

> You may wonder why it is that I speak first to you and not last. The rules that govern the conduct of the trial of criminal cases in Canada prescribe that, if in a criminal trial the accused person exercises his basic fundamental right to give evidence in his own defence and to call witnesses to testify in support of that defence, as he has done, then his counsel or his lawyer forfeits what otherwise would be his right to speak last to you. Gary Staples chose to exercise that right ... I have no right to reply. I have no right to get up after my friend finishes and take issue before you with this comment he made or that. So I want you to understand, if remarks are made in the speech that follows mine that you feel call for a reply, I am not permitted to make such a reply. If need be, I ask in those circumstances that one of you make that reply on my behalf.[10]

Of course, it is a rhetorical ploy, but made with that same consistent strategic stance of being at one with the jurors – "I am trying to help you, and I hope that you will try to help me." Arthur always interpreted the idea of a jury of peers as a matter of the jury being there not to simply do justice on behalf of society, but on behalf of the accused – "peer" meant, as he always put it to the jury, one of us – not one against us. One of his students, after his first jury trial, was approached by one of the old court bailiffs, and told that he must be one of Maloney's students. The young lawyer, bemused by how the fellow knew, asked him what gave him away, and the bailiff said, simply, that it was the way in which he addressed the jury as friends. Arthur, for all his celebrity and skill, always assumed the position of being at one with the jury – trained in the law, perhaps, but just trying to do the job sensibly. Which is one of the reasons why so many of his cases wound up so genially, and why his after-trial parties often included not only his clients, but Crowns, police officers, and occasionally the judge. There was a general air of good will, and tender concern that this kind of comment to the jury made tenable at the worst of times.

Kates, in her article, makes a very full analysis of the jury address, and in doing so, noted the rather unusual order in which Maloney deals with the evidence. Instead of ending with the defence case, he put it first, and then closed on the Crown's case. She is of the opinion that he might have done that because the defence case was somewhat complicated, and he wanted the jury to be fresh as he spoke of it. That may have been so. It was certainly an odd collection of facts that Maloney had to present, and which may, in themselves, have made all the difference in the first trial. Staples had claimed he was neither in Hamilton, nor with Conklin on the night of the murder, but working on his car in a local garage. But there was some question in the first trial of just *when* he was in the garage with the car, and there was sufficient doubt to suggest that he might have been able to get down to Hamilton and back and still be at the garage for part of the evening. The first jury believed that he was able to pop down to Hamilton, and get back quickly.

What was missing was a witness who could specifically remember seeing him at the garage at exactly the right time to exclude any possibility of him also being in Hamilton at the time of the killing. There was evidence that he was at the garage, supported by the garage owner, Peter Stollar, who helped Staples put a universal joint in his automobile. Another customer, Roy Graham was washing his car at the garage; he got to the garage at 9:30 p.m., and Staples was there. But in order to do the murder, he had to have been in Hamilton just a half hour previous, and that might be too narrow for Staples to have got back to the garage in time for Graham, who hardly knew him, to see Staples at work on his vehicle. A few minutes one way or another might just give him time, and the Graham evidence of itself would not quite do the job.

The best evidence came from a young boy, Ronald Stire. He knew Staples. When Staples was arrested, Stire remembered that he had seen him sometime around the time of the murder. Here is how Arthur put that experience into play for the jury:

Further we come now to the evidence of Ronald Stire. He was born on the 6th June, 1955, will not be 17 until later this year. He was fourteen and a half in December, 1969. He knew Staples, not personally, just from seeing him in Dunnville. He said he was not what you would call a friend of the family, although he knew his older brother. He said he learned of Staples' arrest. That arrest took place on April 26th, 1970. He heard about it shortly after, and his first thought was: "When did I see that fellow last?", and he recalled clearly that the last time he had seen Gary Staples was at Stollar's garage, and it was the night, it was the same night he had been at the hockey game at the arena, and it was the night before the Santa Claus Parade, an event that he planned to attend but didn't because he slept in, and, further, it was the night of the school dance. Can't you picture the enquiring mind of that young boy who doubtless, like so many of his age, watched these plays on TV? Can't you picture him as he recalls to mind after learning of the arrest of Gary Staples when it was he last saw him? Can't you picture him piecing all these bits and pieces together like any boy his age would be expected to do? And it all fits into a pattern. "I remember when I saw him last – at Stollar's garage after being at the hockey game. I remember another thing. It was the night of the dance at the school. There were more kids going to the dance than at the hockey games. That's why I remember that. I remember for another reason. It was the day before the Santa Claus Parade and I slept in for that parade." Now, what date or dates did all those events occur on? And he checks and finds it is December 5th. The check out showed the Santa Claus Parade was December 6th; the minor league hockey games were Friday, December 5th; there was a school dance Friday, December 5th. Therefore, the last time he saw Gary Staples was Friday night, December 5th.

Bald speaking was the needed touchstone here. This is the kind of thing he often does – speaking with homely simplicity, often without much concern for sentence structure, spontaneously moving from idea to idea, taking things as they come, but ultimately accumulating a structure that makes perfect sense. In this case, however, he needed more. Stire added another voice to Staples's presence during the evening at the garage, but what was needed was a specific time. Maloney might well have announced at the start of the Stire narrative that he possessed such, but he wanted the jury to go through the process with him – he rarely liked to simply "say" the facts – he wanted to put them into a context of reasonable consideration.

He said that he left home around 5:45, went to the arena to the minor sport all star hockey games. He remembers the Humberstone team playing a game against Dunville. He remembers leaving at 8.30, going to the gas station ... He went to Pete Stollar's station at 8:30 to see if his brother was there and to have a cigarette. He had to be home, or wanted to be home, at nine o'clock because his mother said that he had to be and she worked and held down two jobs and she would phone home to check up on him and to make sure he was there. He got to Stollar's about twenty to nine, 8:40. He walked over there from the arena, six or seven blocks. It took him ten or fifteen minutes to do that walk, and he stayed at Stollar's about 35 minutes. He got there at 8:40, members of the jury: he stayed for thirty-five minutes. That would bring him to 9:15. His home is two blocks away. When he got to Pete Stollar's service station, Pete was there and Gary Staples was there. Any doubt about it? No. Pete was in the office. Gary was working on the car. Pete helped later. The car was on the hoist. Gary was working under the car. Talked with Gary and Peter. Saw the green car in the other bay but couldn't tell the type. It was new, and it was still there when he left. So Graham [who moved the green car to wash his] hadn't come in yet ... he puts Gary Staples in the garage from twenty to nine to a quarter after nine on the night of Friday, December 5th, 1969, and the execution of Gerald Burke happens about nine o'clock at a place thirty-three, thirty-four miles away. While that execution was happening, this accused, Roy Graham, Pete Stollar and Ron Stire, at different times, were together in Stollar's garage ... My friend wouldn't dare suggest either of these men were liars. They have no motive to lie ... The Crown concedes they are telling the truth.[11]

But the Crown had not given in without a fight, and might well have done considerable damage, if he hadn't made a mistake that Arthur was able to make use of when he needed a hand. Stire, the schoolboy, under cross-examination, had to admit that although he had said he was at school on the Friday, he, in fact, had not attended. He had also told the police in an early interview that his brother's car was at Stollar's garage; that proved to be untrue. Then the Crown probably went too far, in alleging that the boy had been subject to nervous problems. "'Oh, this boy had a nervous breakdown.' It must have been some breakdown," said Maloney, "cured by a few pills, and it seemed to have escaped the notice of his mother."

But he had lied about being in school, and about his brother's car. And if he was so honest, why did he claim that he was watching the Humberstone team playing against Dunville when he left the arena at 8:30? The Crown threw him badly off stride, when he asked him: "Would it surprise you to know Humberstone didn't play a game until nine o'clock?" Despite this revelation, the boy held up reasonably well under cross-examination, but there were the little white lies, and the big one about watching Humberstone. Maloney, however, was nothing if not thorough, and he did not let that pass. The boy "is stating the facts correctly, and is suddenly led to believe that he has made a terrible blunder and that he couldn't have seen the Humberstone game because it didn't even start till nine o'clock, and, unfortunately, this error wasn't discovered until after he had left the box and we called Mr Schram, who was able to show you and show my friend that he was wrong and that the Humberstone team did play at six o'clock as the boy said." Point taken, but not without Arthur making something more out of it, and he does it with a slight flash of his celebrated eloquence, using his indignation to rise to a higher level of oratory for a moment.

You can imagine how this would shatter the confidence of any witness, to be confronted by a lawyer in cross-examination with a statement of fact that subsequently was proven to be based on a bit of misinformation, but imagine how it would shatter and devastate a fourteen-and-a-half year old boy. The fact that it

> happened so early in the cross- examination makes it particularly unfortunate. But, notwithstanding that, this young lad stands up there and unequivocally establishes the whereabouts of Gary Staples at the crucial time on December 5th. The whereabouts of Gary Staples at the crucial time are not established by his mother, by his sister, by his father, by his wife. They are established by people to whom he means nothing. He means nothing to these people. Not even his friends. They are the witnesses who establish his whereabouts at 9 o'clock.[12]

That evidence had not been available at the first trial. It was not that the boy did not realize what he had seen, nor that he was not aware of its significance. His mother, however, told him to keep it to himself, and however many times he asked her to release him, she would not do so. But Staples's mother had heard what the boy knew, and finally Stire's mother gave in. Oddly enough, that was not the only piece of evidence that had been withheld from the first trial. One Marily Burdiak, a young girl who knew Mary Conklin, had heard Conklin and Staples arguing on the Saturday, 6 December because Staples had not come over to the farm, as he had promised, on the Friday night – and she also had seen a small hand gun in one of Mary Conklin's dresser drawers earlier that year, although Conklin had denied ever possessing a firearm. That evidence was also withheld, and again it was by a mother's command, who had told Marilyn not to get involved.

Kates is probably correct in presuming that Arthur wanted the jury to be fresh when he put together the jigsaw of that Friday night, bringing the garage proprietor, the customer, and the high school boy into conjunction between the car wash and the grease pit at a time between 8:45 and 9:30, which would make it impossible for Staples to do the killing. It was done with great care, and with sufficient repetition to get it fixed in the jury's mind so that the recital of the facts in the jury address made perfect sense to them.

There is also considerable sense in putting the Crown's case before the jury in the latter position. The alibi evidence might stand on its own, and might save Staples, but there was no gainsaying his intimacy with Mary Conklin, and no way around the fact that she knew too much about that murder. It was, therefore, essential, that the work that had been done in cross-examination on her credibility, on her motivation, be well-remembered by that jury. If there was the slightest chance that the panel might reject the alibi evidence, given the fact that the timing was given to them by a teenager who had revealed some disturbing memory lapses as to the whereabouts of his brother's car, and his school attendance on the very day of the murder, the second line of defence was obvious. If the jury chose not to believe that he wasn't able to be in Hamilton, it was essential to suggest that given Mary Conklin's penchant for male companionship, he wasn't the only one who could have been there – even if he was the only one, at that later time, whom Mary Conklin had any cogent reason for putting in the soup. Maloney was using two lines of defence – the first, a complicated conjunction of several incidents remembered long after by more than one person, was pure alibi – Gary Staples could not have done it simply because he did not have the ability to be at the crime scene when the murder occurred.

The second line was pure criminal law. No-one is to be convicted unless the jury is convinced beyond any reasonable doubt that the accused did the act. Mary Conklin claimed that Staples told her he did just that. She had details that only the murderer would know. It came down to two points – was she to be believed, and could anyone else have done it? She was mad at Staples when she told the police – and she had lots of other male friends of questionable reputation, some with criminal pasts. And as Arthur said, revealing, as Ortved notes, his deep knowledge of human nature:

> Of course, you should realise the hopelessness, in a sense, of her position. From the time of her original sworn statement she cannot turn back. She could have been charged with making a false declaration under the Criminal Code and sentenced to prison, if she had ever changed the original story. Worse still, having been committed to the story under oath at the preliminary hearing and these proceedings, she could have been charged with perjury and sent to prison. There is no way Mary Conklin could get before you and say: "What I have said is untrue." She has got herself into a position where she can do nothing but stick to the lie, in my submission, she originally told. Even if she were overcome with the deepest feelings of remorse, there is nothing she can do about it now.[13]

Ortved, who spent so much time watching Arthur do it over and over again, deserves the last words: "What it is hoped may be seen in these passages is a glimpse of Arthur Maloney's insight into the human psyche – what prompts one's actions, what causes one to pause and reflect, what is right and just, what is wrong and unfair."

Staples was found not guilty. Both Neils Ortved and Chris Kates know why, and their articles, if prepared for legal readers, are quite accessible to lay readers, and display subtle aspects of his trial skills. This discussion of the trial is a complement to their excellent studies.

11

Sixty Thousand a Year, a Car, and a Driver

On Thursday, 30 October 1975, Maloney was sworn in as Ontario's first Ombudsman. It was no hole-in-the-corner affair. Arthur had convinced the Premier that a full-dress celebration should mark the event. Everybody who was vaguely anybody was there, and Arthur made it apparent in his remarks on the occasion that it was appropriate that they should be in attendance.

> I want to express my gratitude to Her Honour the Lieutenant-Governor for what she has said and on behalf of all assembled to express our gratitude to her for her kindness in inviting us to her reception which is to follow.
>
> I wish also to thank you, Mr. Speaker, and through you, Mr. Roderick Lewis, Q.C., and Mr. John Holtby, for the excellence of today's arrangements.
>
> As I view the Members of the Judiciary present today representative of all of the courts in the Province in all of which it has been my privilege for the last thirty years to have appeared I am filled with nostalgia at the prospect of not being able to appear before you again as counsel; certainly for ten years the prospect of never addressing a jury again in that period of time is not an easy one to contemplate.
>
> I am consoled, however, by the fact that it has now become my privilege to serve a much wider constituency of people which I look forward to doing with all my heart.

Arthur was not being entirely honest in this awkward piece of sentimental afflatus. It was his weariness with the grind of trial work that had led him to seek government employ. More to the point, however, was the yet-unknown fact that whether he was filled with nostalgia or not, he was going to be back in the courts much sooner than anyone expected. By the early months of 1978, he was working on his letter of resignation.

Some citizens were exultant at the news of his early resignation – Claire Hoy, the *Toronto Sun* columnist, who had been sniping at Maloney from the start, headed his Wednesday, 16 August 1978 column triumphantly: *King quits! Long live the taxpayers*. What had gone wrong? Just about everything. Several years later, the affair is remembered by members of the public with no particular prejudice or personal knowledge of the matter as entirely Maloney's fault. Claire Hoy may not be a journalist of much distinction, but his influence on Maloney is proof of the power of the press, particularly in a society that hasn't much time to find out the facts – or any real interest in doing so. Which is not to say that Maloney was not, in several ways, responsible for providing the kind of conduct that yellow-press journalists feed upon. But the Ontario government, in several of its hydra-headed forms, must bear some responsibility for the failure of what started out as the perfect match of an enlightened government finding the best man to do a civilized job. It might, however, have been seen, from the start, to be ripe with the chance of failure – a sad example of a government trying to pat itself on the back for providing a badly needed service to the public, which it wanted to be seen as supplying, but which it really could not face in its full consequence.

Maloney was well-known to many of the members of the Conservative Cabinet, and generally to the party as a whole. He had been, if inactive for several years, an independent member of the Progressive Conservative party elite from the mid-fifties. As late as 1971, he had contemplated, momentarily, but sufficiently long for the newspapers to get on to it, a run for the leadership of the provincial party at the time that Davis won the nomination. He had been on the long list of possible aspirants to the federal leadership in the late sixties. He had often headed government commissions that were praised for thoroughness and social sensitivity. He was not simply a prominent name in the law, or a former politician – he was, in fact, something of an intimate, if at second-hand, since the politician (if yet to be confirmed as such by the electorate) who put his name forward for the office was his friend Roy McMurtry, who spent much of his time in those days at the ear of Premier Bill Davis.

The critics of Maloney as Ombudsman may have thought it began inappropriately as a coronation – Arthur may have thought it began with the dignity and panoply appropriate to the great task – but it actually began more modestly, in a second-hand car struggling through the early morning traffic on Avenue Road in Toronto. Arthur liked being driven about by others, usually his students. It was not that he did not have a car, nor that he didn't drive regularly, but he would cadge a ride if he could. His happiest arrangements for transportation would come from students living close enough to pick him up on their way to the office. He had no vanity about the cars – he would ride in any old wreck.

In early 1955, he had the luck of employing a student called Glenn Hainey, who lived slightly to the north of him, and who drove him to work regularly.

He had been at the Bar for just over thirty years, was still at the centre of the fight for the abolishment of capital punishment, and was affectionately remembered for his *bel gesto* in fighting the good fight for Diefenbaker vs. Camp. What was left for him was more of the same in the courts, since politics no longer interested him. He could have become a judge – many of his friends had already gone that way, and many more were to follow. In 1973, G. Arthur Martin and Charlie Dubin had both joined the Court of Appeal. Years previously, Mr. Justice Pat LeSage remembers discussing their respective futures while LeSage was still a very young Crown, and he was pleasantly flattered when Arthur presumed that LeSage would hope to become a Supreme Court judge. LeSage felt, modestly, that a County Court appointment (which is eventually how he started) would suit him quite nicely. Lawyers don't like to talk too openly, save among themselves, about the hierarchical nature of their profession, but there is a pecking order, not only in practice at the Bar, but in appointments to the Bench that is based on merit, but is also, of course, influenced by political connections. This structure has been seriously compromised by the "levelling up" of the Ontario judiciary by the Liberal and NDP governments of the nineties, but there is still a rigorous awareness that some lawyers, and some judges are patently better than others. LeSage had his own measure, and he thought he had Arthur's, but Arthur had other ideas.

> I know there were those trying to get him into the Senate. John Turner, when he was Minister of Justice, had offered Arthur the Court of Appeal. I'm sure Arthur told me that under Turner, he was offered that. But Arthur did not want to go to the Court of Appeal. If he was to be a judge, he wanted to be a trial judge. What he said was that the position that interested him – and I don't know whether he was serious – was the position of the Senior Judge of the County Court in Toronto, which was the position that Walter Martin had. And on more than one occasion, he said that was the only job that interested him. He used to say that at the Court of Appeal, you were not dealing with people, but reams of paper, and that would get him into more trouble than it did in his own practice.[1]

He told LeSage that it was the senior judge job or nothing, since in that position, he could pick and choose among the cases – but it is unlikely that he was really serious. He knew that sitting still on the Bench, listening to counsel hour after hour would not do, and he had, on one occasion, suggested, jokingly, that his own experiences before the Court of Appeal made it impossible for him to have much affection for the fellows who sat there. Yet, he was restless. Paul French saw his shuffling unease in the early seventies. French was in an unusual position since he was Arthur's nephew, and he saw Arthur in postures of disaffection with the law that he might not have revealed to anyone else: "He often felt that his practice was too narrow, and he would advise young lawyers who often came to him for advice to get some civil trial experience. I think he, unfairly, judged himself as limited. I say unfairly because he had the ability to do whatever he wanted. But he felt that he was branded as a criminal counsel, and that was about all that was available to him." This reluctance, bordering on insecurity, was unusual for Arthur, and he never got over it, nor did he ever make any real effort to move his practice in the direction of increasing his civil work. The Ombudsman offer, however, was a chance to do something new, and an opportunity to get away from the nagging sense that there was a sameness about criminal work that was boring him in his late middle age. French remembers him complaining, "There was no legal activity that he hadn't experienced. At the time I was involved with some matters in the Tory party, and one of my friends was in the Premier's office. I indicated to him that Arthur would like to do something different, and it was shortly after that Arthur's name went on the list for the Ombudsman's office. Whether my conversation with my friend had anything to do with it, I never knew."[2]

In the early seventies, Arthur had proven his skills in dealing with social problems in his investigation of the Toronto police force, and had offered the conclusion that an independent board should be set up to hear complaints against the police. It was praised by all concerned, but not implemented, and was to redound to Arthur's reputation several years later. It may have been this work, more than any other, that made his appointment as Ombudsman so acceptable to all. Neils Ortved, who had worked with him on that assignment, remembers that Arthur saw the Ombudsman proposal as a similar kind of job. "He felt very proud of his report on the police complaint procedure. He came to me, and said, 'Now, Neils, in accepting the Ombudsman's job, I've done it on the condition that I undertake precisely the same kind of investigation of the institution of the Ombudsman as we did for the Metropolitan Council in relation to the police complaint procedures."[3]

In the eyes of Glenn Hainey, however, the whole thing came about almost by accident.

I was probably the first to hear of the proposal that Arthur should become Ombudsman. The way it came about – I used to – quite often in the morning – when I was an articling student – pick Arthur up. I was living at home, not too far from where the Maloneys lived. Quite often we would pick up Roy

McMurtry, and Arthur and Roy were great friends. Of course, at the time, Roy had not been elected to anything, but he was a very close confidant of Davis. In any event, I had this rusty old Chevy Vega, which is a pretty small car. Arthur would sit in the passenger seat, and Roy, who's not a small man, would sort of pour himself into this teeny back seat. It was fascinating for me, as a student, to hear them talk, and they'd talk about politics. They rarely talked about their cases; it was just current affairs, and what was going on behind the scenes in the provincial Cabinet, because Roy, of course, had access to a lot of that information, and Arthur was interested in hearing it. It was great fun anyway.

One of these mornings, when we were driving down, I remember that Arthur was complaining; he was a little fed-up with practice, I think. We had a couple of cases where he had a rough time with the judges, and he felt he was getting pushed around a little bit and he didn't like it, and I think he was just a little disillusioned with the practice. And I remember the discussion started. Arthur said to Roy, "You know, Roy, if I ..." There must have been a vacancy of the chairman of the Liquor Board or Control Board. I forget which one. I guess it was the Liquor Licence Board. It must have been vacant or something – whoever was the incumbent was about to retire. I remember Arthur saying, "You know, Roy, if the Premier would – for sixty thousand dollars a year, and a car and a driver, I'd be pretty interested in that post."

I don't think the post mattered. I think it was the sixty thousand dollars a year and a car and driver. Especially the driver – that was very important. And I remember Roy saying, "Arthur, you're kidding. You wouldn't really be interested?" And Arthur said, "Yah, I'd be interested. I'd be interested in that." And I, as a young student, thought it was all sort of a joke. I couldn't imagine he would really be interested. So anyway, not long after that, we were driving down and they were on the same topic, and Arthur was saying how he, you know, for sixty thousand dollars and a car and a driver, would get out of this rat race. And Roy saying, "Well, you know, Arthur, we're going to be creating this new position of Ombudsman; would you be interested?"

And Arthur – I didn't know what an Ombudsman was. It meant very little to me. It meant something to Arthur. And he said, "You know, Roy, that's something I might be interested in. But it would have to be sixty thousand dollars a year and a car and a driver." So that's where it started, and it moved very, very quickly. That would have been in the spring, and if I'm not mistaken, it was announced in May or June.

Arthur confirmed that the idea began in Hainey's old car, and Roy McMurtry's recollection is similar in its casual, off-chance maundering about the job that was going to be so important to Arthur and his reputation, something less so in the long run for the province, and a sensation for the press over the three years of his holding of the office.

My memory is that Arthur Maloney expressed some interest to me in the Ombudsman's job during one of our drives together downtown in early 1975. There was no discussion about salary and emoluments initially but I recall being a little surprised that Arthur was interested in the job, given his continuing success as a trial lawyer. At that time I was in Bill Davis's "kitchen cabinet," not having been elected to the Legislature. At my next meeting with Bill Davis I raised the matter of Arthur's interest and he was so immediately interested that he asked me to pursue the matter further with Arthur. I also advised the Premier that the matter of a salary package might require some careful negotiations, but I was confident that Arthur would be reasonable. They were just beside themselves at the weekly breakfast! Eddie Goodman was there and he couldn't believe it! They all kept saying, "Do you think we could really get him!'"It was met with great enthusiasm. There were no nay sayers.[4]

McMurtry had no illusions about Arthur; it was not simply a matter of "jobs for the boys." Arthur wasn't looking for that; this was to be, in his mind, a real job with real things to do. McMurtry anticipated what might happen if Arthur had power, and he also knew that Arthur would only take it if power was involved. He remembers discussing the fact that Arthur might be a formidable opponent with the Premier, but Davis was unconcerned. "I only remember him having one concern, and that was a joke. 'Don't let him get Al Eagleson as his salary negotiator!' So I was put in charge of negotiating the deal, and we finally settled on a salary commensurate to what a judge would be paid. And we made it clear that we wouldn't give him any trouble with his budget."

The salary was to be a stick used constantly by the media to beat Maloney, although it was fair. Maloney was finally making what he was worth, and it was a good deal more than $60,000. He was also bringing reputation, energy, and enthusiasm to the job. Aside from the salary, the newspapers were happy with the choice. However unprofessionally loose the negotiations might seem, given the importance of the appointment, the power to be wielded and the money to be spent, Davis was right to leave it to McMurtry to negotiate with Arthur. They had been friends from early on in McMurtry's legal career. McMurtry may not remember the demand for sixty thousand dollars, a car, and a driver, but Lillian thinks that Hainey is probably correct. "I can see Arthur saying that to Roy. They teased each other a lot, and Arthur was pleased with Roy's success in politics."

Some men come to politics naturally, given their natural gifts and instincts (and sometimes social connections) that are often apparent while they are still barely children; some *will* themselves to office, sticking to their ambition through failure and derision, and sometimes they succeed; some are lucky to be in the right place at the right time; and some, like McMurtry, seem to wander in with an aimless casualness that ought to be an impediment. McMurtry's success must have surprised him quite as much as it did those who knew him, genially rolling along, seemingly unmindful of ambition or direction, well-liked and unthreatening to others of balder, more obvious ambition. He graduated from Osgoode in 1958, and started into trial practice almost immediately. His father was a trial lawyer in downtown Toronto, so Roy knew how to get around in the labyrinths of the Bar. In early 1959, Maloney congratulated him on his handling of a difficult rape case. It was a common sort of kindness on Arthur's part. He started to refer cases to McMurtry, particularly if they had civil implications, since McMurtry had, from the beginning, built his practice on both civil and criminal files. McMurtry was soon a member of Arthur's gang of Metropole drinkers. They became close friends, and McMurtry was involved with Arthur first in the Coffin inquiry and then in the abolishment movement.

Their first falling-out, which was quickly forgotten, was over the Camp-Diefenbaker battle in '66. It was, in fact, Camp who got McMurtry interested in politics, although he had no intention, initially, of running for office. When Allen Lawrence decided to go federal and left the St. George riding vacant in 1973, McMurtry was persuaded to run, and he lost. He presumed that would be the end of that. But Davis wanted McMurtry in the government, and in 1975, Len Riley, the sitting member for Eglinton, advised him that he would not run again, and McMurtry had a nomination.

It is often been suggested that the McMurtry-Davis connection was close from their university days in the early fifties, when they were both football players at the University of Toronto. It was not quite true. They had met while members of the Varsity intermediate team, but McMurtry had gone on to become a member of the senior team, the Varsity Blues. They knew each other in a cursory fashion, but were not friends, nor did they see much of each other in their early years at the Bar. McMurtry supported Davis for the provincial leadership in 1971; most of his close friends supported Al Lawrence. His first bit of political luck came from having back trouble, which put him in the hospital for several weeks prior to the convention. Given his enforced idleness, he did nothing to aid in the Davis victory, but he was the perfect go-between after the battle to bring about a reconciliation between Davis and the Eglinton group, who had supported Lawrence. He urged Davis to placate the young, ambitious men, most of them lawyers, and he arranged a dinner for them to meet. McMurtry sees this as the beginning of the "Big Blue Machine," and several members of the group went on to important positions with Davis. The Tuesday morning breakfast club developed out of that meeting, and Roy McMurtry's position as a confidant of the Premier was established. He was, therefore, the man to deal with Maloney, since he was, by chance, possessed of the ears of both men.

Not everyone was enthusiastic. J.J. Robinette could not understand why Arthur would bother, but Robinette went through his entire career gracefully turning down political temptations, although for a short time, in the mid-fifties, he thought of becoming a Supreme Court judge – and then thought better of it. Monte Harris thought it wasn't much of a job for Arthur, but Monte, one of life's great enthusiasts, adored Arthur, and would have considered anything less than Prime Minister below Arthur's merit. Doug Crane was sceptical:

> I was sharing space at Carrick, O'Connor when he came to me with the idea, and I said, "Well, Arthur, it's none of my business, but since you've asked me, I'd say you shouldn't do it. You've already run a clinic like that when you were at Parkdale, and I think you are better than that." To this day, I think it was a mistake. I think he wanted something different, but that was not up to his worth. He was a political animal but he sold himself short. I thought he should have tried earlier for the leadership of the national Conservative party. I think him becoming the Ombudsman was like a professor becoming the college janitor. He was way above the job.[5]

But most of the general public, who knew him from the newspapers, thought of him as absolutely right. Stephen Traviss recalls that "one friend of mine said that if Premier Davis hadn't appointed him as Ombudsman, he could have called a press conference and appointed himself."[6]

On 22 May 1975, the word was official, and the *Globe and Mail* used the language that was to be consistent throughout the province, and, indeed, throughout the country.

> *The people's new man*
>
> Arthur Maloney's appointment by the Ontario Government as provincial Ombudsman is news to be well received. Certainly, there can be nothing but admiration and respect for his credentials.
>
> There are his ample skills as a criminal lawyer and his readiness to make those skills available to the poorest and most miserable accused offender. There have been his many services to his community – to name some: member of Parliament, mediator who resolved Toronto's 1972 garbage strike, commissioner to inquire into citizen complaint procedures in the Toronto police department, member of the Ontario parole board ... There are, in addition, the many causes he has full-heartedly championed – prison reform, parole reform, court reform, reform for more human welfare and, of course, his more than 20-year advocacy of abolition of capital punishment.

Innocently, however, the *Globe* article had *en passant* indicated the area in which trouble was to lie: "Exactly what his job as Ombudsman will be, we suppose will depend to a considerable degree on what shape Mr. Maloney gives to it. The Ontario Government has not been particularly precise in defining it."

Time, in its Canadian edition of 9 June 1975, was equally complimentary, but again there were passages in the article that were to have ironic implication. Aside from the obvious misreading of Canadian politics and Arthur's position in them in 1975 ("Maloney, who was a Toronto M.P. in the Diefenbaker era, would effectively remove himself from the Tory leadership race"), the piece was reasonably accurate, but not completely so ("Maloney also is not about to pursue his office like a trasher. He does not have to. His reputation is such, observed Ontario Liberal Leader Robert Nixon, 'that if he were even to suggest any government was holding back on him, it would be enough to destroy that agency.'") Arthur was to quickly discover that when a government agency or department wanted to resist him, his destructive powers were going to be less lethal than *Time* and Robert Nixon presumed. Most ironically prophetic of all was a quote from Maloney: "The Ombudsman shouldn't go around stirring up conflict. He will have to operate on a big scale, without getting big himself."

The job quickly caught Arthur's imagination; it was suddenly before him in all its glory – the chance to lead a crusade! Who could blame him for such *hubris*? Everyone, including the government, admitted that things were out of hand – that big government had to be watched and restrained and, perhaps, chastised – so why not do it properly and with some style? It was the style that caused the first uneasiness. Arthur's inclination to expansiveness, was a well-known aspect of his personality, which, to the moment, had been expressed mainly in his social life. Usually it had a sophomoric innocence that went no farther than amusing anecdote. Clive Bynoe tells of the time a group of lawyers and wives were going to London for a meeting of The Advocates Society (Arthur was the President of the Ontario Chapter in 1973):

> Before we left he called me into his office, and said, "Doug Crane and his wife are coming, so are the Humphreys, and you're going – four couples. What do you say we go to Paris for the weekend? But you have to know right now – don't ask the price for this, because if you do, it will spoil it. But this will be the best weekend you'll ever have in your life!" So I agreed. "It's all right with me, Arthur." So he gets on the phone right then and there and he phones the hotel in Paris, and he asks to speak to the general manager at the Crillon. Then he called La Tour d'Argent, the great restaurant, and then he makes a few more calls to Paris numbers. So we take off for Paris. We walk into the hotel, and the general

manager's there to meet us, and we are taken into the Maloney suite and it's all flowers and wine and chocolates and champagne – and we all have adjoining suites. It was unbelievable![7]

It could be much humbler. His happiness in simply sitting back in his students' second-hand cars, being driven to work or to his trials in the county towns, is a common memory for many. His lordly demeanour was not unremarked by his relatives. Doug Crane tells of one occasion when family and student regard for Arthur's majesty came together:

We had a defence of an armed robber in Bancroft, and Father Henry was there, visiting with us. I had a pea-green, ugly Volkswagen – the cheapest you could buy. You had to get down on your hands and knees to move the seat. We had driven up there in it, and Arthur was kind of grumpy. He had a bad cold. We went to a local lawyer's house, and Arthur was grumping around. We had lunch, and a few drinks. When we were on our way out, and he was saying goodbye to everyone, he said to me, rather abruptly, "Is the seat back far enough?" Meaning, of course, had I moved the wing nuts back so he could get in. Father Henry, quick as a flash said, "I don't know, my Lord, but we'll go out and measure it." And everyone burst out laughing! Arthur didn't mean anything by it, and he would sit in the back seat of that little Volkswagen when I was driving, looking, as he was, the great king of the courts![8]

Now was his chance to indulge in the real thing. He was to set his own budget, hire his own staff, decide on his own method of working, even choose his place of employment. It is unlikely that the Ontario government had ever written such a blank cheque before, and it is surely unlikely that they will ever do it again.

More knowledge may be gained of a man's real character by a short conversation with one of his servants, than from a formal and studied narrative, begun with his pedigree and ended with his funeral.

– Samuel Johnson, *Rambler*, No. 60

The Ombudsman appointment was a great temptation to play at majesty, and Arthur did exactly that – and he did it on purpose. It was, perhaps, the most damaging and most lasting error that he made, but he always insisted that it was a conscious decision, made in good faith.

Years after he left the office, he was to argue for the manner in which he burst into the civil service like the king from over the water. His goal was to make the Ontario Ombudsman's office the best in the world. It was not the first to be established in Canada; four provinces already had offices. It would not be enough, however, for the Ontario office to simply be the best – it had to be seen to be the best – and he meant exactly that. He wanted it to look good, not simply to confirm the commitment of the government, but to symbolize its power. Bob Johnstone, watching the newspapers turn on Arthur, confronted him: "I ran into Arthur one Saturday in Simpson's. He was really bitter about how the press jumped all over him about the grandiose life style, and he told me, 'You know I'm not that kind of guy!' And he wasn't; he was a very simple, unpretentious guy. 'But,' he said, 'I've got to do it! Because when people come into the Ombudsman's office, they've got to see we've got some clout. We cannot have old, chipped formica desks over in some corner. We have to let them see that we are every bit as big and as important as the attorney general."[9] He had previously told Bynoe that, "We have to have the appearance of being able to combat the Crown, and you see the vast resources of the Crown, so now we've got something like that."[10]

The "appearance" came in two stages, neither of which passed without some public unease, although in the first instance, the criticism was good-hearted and, generally, amused. Arthur, quite simply, stage-managed his official investiture in a manner that smacked more of an ascent than an entrance into high office. It took place on 30 October 1975, in the House, and was immediately characterized by the wits, and the witless, as a coronation. Dave Humphrey, always intent on keeping Arthur earthbound, had a good seat. "I was at his coronation. The people got the best criminal lawyer in Canada. I told him that I took a tape with me to the ceremony, and when I played it later, I kept hearing this voice, 'When you were being sworn in. It said: this is my son in whom I am well pleased.'"

The press saw it as an occasion to be viewed as only just appropriate, and the sense that it had gone over the top and was risible began to build. It was his finest hour, but it was loaded with opportunities for mockery. John Diefenbaker, as well he might, proved gracious and generous – stating that he had always though that Arthur would be a future Prime Minister of Canada. Sally Barnes, the Premier's press secretary, must have been relieved to see the ceremony pass, since in the days previous, Arthur kept adding, like a bride who cares little about father's pocket book, names to the guest list. Bob Johnstone tells of her confiding in him. "Arthur really went crazy. He told me later, 'Listen, I had to impress on people that the Ombudsman is as grand as any other government office.' Sally complained to me once that 'Arthur's guest list just grew by 120 in the last 48 hours! He thinks it's a coronation! It's crazy; I don't know how to stop it. If Billy sees the list!' 'Well,' I said, 'you can always hide the list.' 'Yes, but when he gets there! The last time he went to London to see the Queen, the room wasn't this crowded!'"

It wasn't all window dressing. As soon as the appointment had been announced in the late spring, Arthur had set to work. He knew nothing of how to be an Ombudsman. Neils Ortved joined him to find out how to do it: "He engaged me to do exactly what we had done with the police matter. I was retained to undertake and supervise the investigation of the institution of Ombudsman – to look at a number of them, and distil the best from their work ... We met with all and sundry. We held public meetings, and we travelled all over the world, found out what worked, and produced a report."[11]

While Ortved did the book work, Arthur was everywhere. Nothing was done without his consideration, and nothing was too small. The choosing of a symbol, and a logo were as important as the choosing of office space, and the proliferation of expensive detail was to be used against him. A man of lesser imagination and energy would have been satisfied with the grand gesture of the investiture, and get down to quiet business, but Arthur saw the appointment as something beyond doing his job. His visits abroad convinced him that the Ontario office could be used to energize the Ombudsman movement throughout the world. It wasn't simply a matter of picking and choosing the best bits of what others had done – it became a matter of providing an example for the whole world!

Yet the one ineradicable stain on his reputation is the Ombudsman job. The most obvious reason lies in the way in which he did things, which were easily turned by the sceptical and the malicious into public derision. Even those who admired him sometimes used language that was to accrete sinister implication in the long run. Douglas Fisher, a political fan of Arthur from his parliamentary days, started his 13 October 1975 column in *The Toronto Sun* with an emotive touch: "The consecration of Arthur Maloney as first Ombudsman of Ontario took place yesterday in the Legislature." Fisher did not think it excessive, but "consecration" was an unfortunate word to use, particularly in the vicinity of his following sentence: "Sceptics could see the ceremony – one columnist labelled it a 'coronation' – a 'jumped-up' ritual which exaggerated the role that the Ombudsman may play or should play." Later in the same article, Fisher innocently did it again: "It is already clear from Maloney's staffing of his office and the fields he intends to operate in, that he is going to throw a very wide loop. Further the consecration with its august ceremonies was certainly staged to give the office a majesty and an authority that would make it immediately recognizable as important and very distinct from the government, the Legislature as a partisan place, and from the courts." Fisher touched upon the problem that was going to become the final aggravation in the affair:

> No one bothered to spell out the unique relationship which must be developed between the Ombudsman, the Legislature and the individual MPPs, particularly to make the point that the Ombudsman is not a super-MPP but an agent of the Legislature who has been given a unique writ to intervene through the mantle of ministerial responsibility and the traditional anonymity of the public servant to find out whether a decision or action or an evasion or a failure to act has been done fairly, thoroughly and in line with the powers and rights given by law and regulations to the bureaucracy and to the citizen.

The Legislature had time enough to get it right. The idea had been contemplated around Queen's Park since 1962; in 1965, Vernon Singer, the Liberal member from Downsview, brought in his first Private Member's Bill calling for a "Parliamentary Commissioner." He took the successful New Zealand system as his model, and he refused to give up on it, bringing it back into the House ten times in all, before the Conservatives decided to still him by taking over the idea in 1975. It was not that Singer was considered foolish; it was that many legislators and some legal advisers saw ombudsmen as intruders. In 1964, retired Chief Justice of the Ontario Supreme Court, J.C. McRuer, led the Royal Commission Inquiry into Civil Rights to the conclusion (1969) that it was not a good idea, just in time to sink Singer for the sixth time. In 1971, the Conservatives were on Singer's side, and Attorney-General Arthur Wishart announced a bill for the next session, but the government did nothing. There was always sufficient queasiness about the idea of someone looking over their shoulders, about an ambiguous, further level of power to deal with, that caused MPPs to push the idea away, suspicious of giving up part of that which was clearly theirs to do – albeit sometimes badly or not at all – the duty to represent their constituents' interests in government, and, sometimes, to protect them from it. By 1975, they had become accustomed to the idea. In the 11 March speech from the Throne, the promise was made, and the negotiations began in Glenn Hainey's old car.

It was an astonishing exception to the rule that governments act in mysterious ways – all of them slow. The government announced it – Arthur mused – McMurtry passed the message – Davis said "certainly" – and on 22 May, he announced to the House that Arthur would be nominated. Five days later, the Fifth Session of the 29th Legislature of Ontario started its first reading of a slim Bill 86: "An Act to provide for an Ombudsman to investigate Administrative Decisions and Acts of

Officials of the Government of Ontario and its Agencies." It was out of McMurtry's hands now – he might be inside the Davis machine, but he was outside the Legislature, and the Hon. John T. Clement, the witty, charming member from Niagara Falls, who was to lose his seat in the autumn election, presented the bill as the Attorney-General.

It was a simple piece of work. Perhaps too simple, too easily manipulated, and the Legislature, for once all on the same side, had a good time, tuning it up, providing Arthur with opportunities for creative improvisations that they could not have expected. From 10 June to 19 June, the debate on second reading went on, and Arthur and his rapidly expanding group of young, eager acolytes took notes on what the politicians were saying. The MPPs, with a largesse universal like the sun, were full of magnanimous suggestions. The ethnic multiplicity of Ontario had to be considered – which translated into Arthur building a staff large enough to cover most major language groups. The fact that the Act required all complaints in writing seemed a bit harsh, so it was suggested that the Ombudsman's staff should be flexible about that requirement. They were so flexible about it that on one occasion, as Michael Zacks tells it, when the office was full of beans, and flexibility gave place to comic invention, they got into air traffic control. Arthur was at the centre of the adventure.

> He insisted that somebody man the phones at night, until ten. We got a call one night from some guy who had to force land his plane on a highway in northern Ontario. He fixed the problem with his motor, and he wanted to take off again, but the OPP wouldn't let him. So he managed to get to a phone, and he called the Ombudsman's office. Why he called the Ombudsman – of all people! I can't remember who was on the phone that night; it was very democratic. Everyone manned the phones, including the senior officers. Arthur didn't do it, but everyone else did. Whoever was manning the phone didn't know what to do, so he called Arthur at home. Arthur got quite upset and called the Commissioner of the OPP, whom he knew personally and the commissioner called the detachment and let them know that it was appropriate to let this guy take off in his plane. They closed the highway down and he took off! That really happened!

The legislators could hardly have anticipated such importunities from on high, and it might be argued that a downed aircraft was hardly within an Ombudsman's authority, but sometimes the desire to help took strange, harmless turns. The MPPs had wanted to show what good fellows they were, and Arthur and his crew were good-hearted and imaginative. The MPPs knew that the public would not be aware of the finer points of the Act, especially in the matter of the limits to Arthur's authority. Some things were not to be done – obviously federal matters were forbidden. He was to deal exclusively with complaints against Ontario government offices, administrative units, commissions, boards, agencies, and the ministries. He had no authority over the courts or court officials, nor in municipal matters. The MPPs knew all the exclusions would be confusing, and they instructed Arthur to treat the distressed, if errant complainants tenderly, and to direct such lost souls to the right place for their grievance. That problem of directing people to someplace else was going to be a busy part in the work of the office, not only because so many of the early complaints were shotgun blasts of indiscriminate lament from aggrieved citizens who hardly bothered to think about whether they had come to the right place, but because most citizens seemed unable to tell the difference anyway. They heard that Maloney was publicly calling for customers, and making it easy (as the MPPs had urged) for them to get a hearing, long into the night, and often on weekends. As if the debaters didn't give Arthur quite enough flexibility already, the representatives from ridings far from Toronto urged him to get out into their areas, a suggestion that Arthur seized, since he knew, as a child of the back country, how far Toronto was from the lives of many people, particularly those in the north of the province.

It was a love feast, and the MPPs, knowing that the press was watching, attempted to outdo each other in generous exception to the narrowness of the Act. They did no harm – or so they thought. All the added services they urged upon Arthur were, or could have been, just hot air, in the best tradition of politicians taking advantage of a situation that cost them nothing. After all, the act was not amended – Arthur's ambit of authority was clearly defined: "Section 15 (1) The function of the Ombudsman is to investigate any decision or recommendation made or any act done or omitted in the course of the administration of a governmental organization and affecting any person or body of persons in his or its personal capacity." Nor did the debate lead to any change in the Act on the matter of all complaints being in writing, nor did it allow for any leeway in treating problems outside its ambit of authority. The suggestions to be kind and flexible were simply oral – but coming from the MPPs, they had authority enough for Arthur to use them, often with excessive *brio*.

The Act had Royal assent by the 3rd of July. It was in force on 10 July. Although he was not to officially take office until October, he was in the thick of things immediately, and he made no attempt to hold back complaints until the office was fully established. In a 1980 speech, Arthur recalled the result of the announcement:

> Simultaneously to the announcement of my appointment as Ombudsman by the press on May 22nd, I began receiving daily a great number of complaints from all parts of Ontario. At this point I was faced with a choice: I could either defer

or refrain from responding to the complaints received until I had been sworn in by the Speaker of the Assembly and my operation was staffed, equipped and fully operational, or I could attempt to deal with the complaints received on an *ad hoc* basis in the best manner that I could.

He chose the latter, and that inclination to *ad hoc* response was to be one of the problems he was to meet, though at the time no-one objected to Arthur starting before his time.

He began hiring immediately. One of the objections that was to be made, off and on, was his practice of bringing his own people into the new organization, rather than following standard civil service procedure of advertisement and interview. That was too slow for Arthur, particularly if he was to get on with the job immediately. What he did was what might have been expected of him – he turned to young lawyers and law students whom he had trained himself, or whom he knew through his practice. Some of them were very young, indeed, and very inexperienced, and hardly any had civil service experience. He presumed, ingenuously, that any person associated with him could work on a level of serious endeavour. As a result, the Ombudsman adventure, almost overnight, catapulted several very young men into jobs of major moment.

Glenn Hainey, who had been his student in the very year of the proposal, was not to be called to the Bar until 1976, but Arthur offered him the job as his executive assistant – he was only twenty-four years old. He was to be responsible for preparing the annual reports to the Legislature, among other important things. He was not officially in the office until after his call to the Bar in the spring of 1976, but he was there on a part-time basis from the start.

Phil Patterson was scheduled to join Arthur as his articled student in the spring of 1975. After his exams, he came into the office to be instructed on his duties:

I'd just finished my last exams at Osgoode, and it was the first or second week in May, and Arthur said, "I've been asked by the Premier to accept a position outside the law; I've been asked to be the Ombudsman. I've thought long and hard about it. I want you to stay with me; I'm going to need students. I undertake to you that if you're not satisfied in the Ombudsman's office, I'll get you the best articles I can."

I was in a tizzy, but I said, "I'd really like to work with you, and I respect you, but I've set my heart on doing criminal articles." He said, "Okay, I'll get you someone to article with." And two days later, he introduced me to Dave Humphrey. But I wasn't to join Dave until the fall, so through May, June, and the rest of the summer, I worked with Arthur as his executive assistant in the Ombudsman's office.

> I went to Dave in September; all the time I was moonlighting with Arthur. I wrote speeches for him, travelled with him. Then, when I finished articling and went to BarEd, I worked for Arthur, and after BarEd, I worked full time for him until he left. I was in charge of the correctional and psychiatric facilities in Ontario, taking care of all investigations and complaints.[12]

Hainey and Patterson, now successful trial counsel, were just boys – educated, but inexperienced, and with no civil service background. They were not exceptionable. Neils Ortved had articled with Arthur in 1971–72, and had gone on to civil work, as Arthur had urged, before returning to join the group of young lawyers who shared office space with Arthur at 330 University Avenue. Some few appointments were made outside the law, but in every case, the new employee was hand-picked for peculiar skill that Arthur thought might be useful. Sometimes they had been social workers or policemen or had special language skills. Milan Then, one of the few appointments without legal experience, remembers how young they all were, and how handsome they looked *en masse*. He recalls the hush that would fall in government offices among the secretaries, when Arthur would arrive with his entourage of young males.

There were a few appointments made with experience in mind. Keith Hoilett, born in Jamaica, had been a Crown Attorney for over nine years – in him Arthur got solid legal experience and his first ethnic appointment. In Tom O'Connor, he got a lawyer of maturity and stability. Tom, a large, florid, handsome, good-natured Bay Street lawyer whose specialty had been mining law, was winding down his practice at the time, and Arthur, who had shared office space with Tom at Carrick, O'Connor for years, saw the chance to get himself an in-house *eminence grise*, and at the same time, help O'Connor ease himself into retirement from the law. He became the associate general counsel in the office, and as it turned out, was to stay on long after Arthur left. He was absolutely right for the job – an older man who could provide some calming balance to Arthur's mercurial personality in an office staffed with very young, sometimes over-enthusiastic men and women, many of them in their first important job – and some of them in the first job they ever had as professionals. On occasion, when Arthur, upset by someone, went too far, Tom could talk to him and settle the matter.

"Team" is an appropriate way to describe the organization. It wasn't like any other civil service department. Maloney deliberately defined the office as, necessarily, given the job it was to do, *other* than the civil service. It was a kind of cuckoo in the nest, quite out of harmony with the rest of the civil service. Had he spoken to the Legislature about how he saw the office, as he did to his employees, they might well have been disturbed. Michael Zacks articulates the situation as well as anyone involved. He was not quite a Maloney acolyte, but was close enough to be drawn in. He had articled with Mike Wadsworth, who shared him with Tom O'Connor, and had done some minor jobs for Maloney. He suspects that Arthur had quite forgotten him, and that it was probably Glenn Hainey, on the lookout for young lawyers with connections to the old satellite Maloney world, who came up with his name. It was Hainey who asked him to come in for an interview. "I got a call from Glenn, and he asked if I might be interested in joining. It was in the fall, and I went down to see Arthur, who was delighted to see me, although I suspect he didn't really know who I was. He had a way of making you feel you were his long-lost friend, and he was able to make you feel that he was totally interested in what you were doing, and he made me want to come and join him."[13]

Zacks saw immediately that it wasn't just a matter of convenience that had caused Maloney to call, in the main, on young lawyers and law students. It was planned, not only because lawyers were trained to wrestle with the vagarious ambiguities of the law, but because they were used to the idea of being outside a question of conflict, able to weigh both sides of a question of confrontation, and assess, without prejudice, the nature of the problem, and the possibility not only of solution, but of compromise. In a sense, he put the Ombudsman's office together as he would have established a law office, partly because he knew no other way to do it, and did not want to follow any advice from the civil service that would lead to just another government department, and more importantly, because that pattern was consistent with the fact that he wanted a kind of anti-civil-service institution. Law students and junior lawyers are trained to depend upon senior counsel, and particularly, upon their "principal." Arthur had been through it with Colonel Greer, and he had carried on the tradition in his own office. His students belonged to him, and he took care of them – that is what he wanted to bring into the Ombudsman's office. As Zacks saw it, "Arthur single-handedly and by force of his personality made the office what it was."

"Arthur always had pet peeves, and it always bothered him," says Hainey, "that you could never get a government office after 4:30; so from day one, he said that was not going to be the case in this office. 'We're going to have someone at the phone.' And we always did until ten o'clock at night. It provided some great work for students in the BarEd course; we'd come over when the regular staff couldn't do it and man the phones." Lillian remembers calls coming in from the office during the evenings. "He insisted on somebody being there until ten. 'You know, Lillian,' he said, 'people can have problems at night, and if you can't reach anybody, it can be worrying.' Of course, as soon as he left, that was the first thing they stopped."

12

Culture and the Civil Service

Michael Zacks, a fastidious, wary man, who remained in the civil service after leaving the Ombudsman's office in the early nineties, looks back at the experience of working with Arthur with considerable warmth, despite the determination of Arthur to make Zacks over in his own image.

I didn't know him well when I started; he had excellent political "street smarts," unlike other people who had been involved in Ombudsman work in other jurisdictions. He really understood the process and beyond that he was a truly compassionate person. He always criticized me for being "too red-necked!" Constantly! It was, "Zacks, Zacks, you're thinking like a bureaucrat!" He took extraordinary pain and effort to create a separate culture in that office, separate from the civil service. He did everything he could to distance himself, and run it as a self-governing agency. He tried to create a culture in the office by bringing in people who weren't in government. In some areas he had to bring in a few with civil service experience because they had the special knowledge he needed, but he tried to avoid them if possible. He brought Keith Hoilett in, a former Crown Attorney, musicians, engineers, nurses – people who had no particular skills but lots of energy. He was sensitive about a good racial mix, and ahead of his time in that. We developed our own procedures, classification systems. It was his intention to use the government for *nothing*! They would simply transfer funds to us, and that got him into trouble. One of the reasons the office became as large as it did was the decision to do all this administrative work in-house.[1]

The dim public memory of Maloney's rise and fall rests mainly upon his supposed extravagance, which manifested itself initially in the theatrical sweep of his taking office, and was confirmed by other public gestures that were part of Arthur's plan to give the office instant *gravitas*. Thus the coat of arms – the gryphon – an innocent bit of dignity, but one that not only showed up on letterheads, but on everything from ashtrays to cutlery. The publicity release revealed an office determined to take itself seriously.

The Gryphon

Symbolic of the law, The Ombudsman's GRYPHON comes to us from ancient mythology, and is alluded to in the Scriptures.

The Biblical counterpart of the Gryphon – THE CHERUBIM – guarded the entrance to Eden.

In Hellenic mythology, the Gryphon was a sacred beast of the Goddess "Nemesis" as an offspring of a lion and an eagle and, with its resultant capacity for swiftness and strength, it sped forth to avenge arbitrary acts upon man.

With the Gryphon drawing the chariot of the Golden Sun God "Apollo," this came to represent justice and moderation.

All these qualities, as well as the modern symbolism which depicts the Gryphon as the Guardian of the Rights of Man, are embodied in the marque as chosen by the Ombudsman for the Province of Ontario.

It suspends over four representations of the floral emblem of Ontario ... "The Trillium."

One Trillium represents our Native people
One Trillium represents our people of French origin
One Trillium represents our people of Anglo-Saxon origin
One Trillium represents our people of other Ethnic origin

and thus 'THE OMBUDSMAN' represents protection for the Social Rights and Cultural Integrity of all.

Arthur made much of getting in touch not only with the public by such publicity puffs, but with other ombudsmen, who would fly in to see the wonder of Arthur's magnificent plaything. He was also careful to include Queen's Park in the celebration, drawing members of the Legislature, and senior civil servants down to the new Queen Street offices to explain what he wanted to do. He entertained them at lunch in his new dining room, and those lunches, catered by local restaurants, were to cause him trouble in the long run. His own office, which one would presume ought to have some dignity, added to the snickering and the backbiting. Most of the furnishings were brought over from his law office, but the newspapers choose to put it otherwise. Lillian was not altogether convinced that he made the right move, especially as things started to go wrong.

I don't know why he took it, because he didn't make half as much money as he did as a criminal lawyer, but he said, "If I'm going to be Ombudsman, Lillian, Ontario is going to have the best Ombudsman there is!" And he laughed with excitement. But he got an awful lot of criticism, especially about the money he was spending on the office. I'll never forget one article about him sitting behind this large desk in this "immaculately-tailored" suit – well, Arthur didn't give a hoot about how he dressed. I would have to say to him, "Arthur, you need to get something new." As long as he had something pressed and clean, he was satisfied. He had an old jacket on, and a pair of slacks which he had bought sometime earlier in Hamilton when he had split his pants during a trial – that was what he was wearing when this woman interviewed him. And his desk! Well, when he moved to the Bay Street office years before [1957], I gave him that desk and chair for Christmas! The breakfront was his, and the lamps, and the pictures. The government paid for the sofa, and the coffee table. They talked about these things all the time! He would laugh about it, but he never got it straight in the press.[2]

Zacks saw it as a determined effort not to get it straight. The press was corrected regularly, but they paid no attention. "He saw himself as giving himself to public service, and it's nonsense about the gold-plated faucets and the sandwiches from Winston's. Certainly he entertained, and he did it with some style, but food would be ordered from Simpson's or a good caterer. They weren't ordered from Winston's. That's nonsense! And the furniture in his office – it was all his! The art work was his! He spent his own money!" It was just a minor misrepresentation, but it became a truth through press repetition, and a supposed confirmation of arrogance when the real battle began.

Glenn Hainey knew what Maloney had in mind, beyond the decorations. "I think Arthur's view of the office, rightly or wrongly, was that it shouldn't really be answerable to anybody – other than the Legislature – and even the Legislature should tread lightly. He wanted it to be distinguished from the rest of the civil service."[3] One of the obvious indications of that difference was the fact that the office got off to a very fast start.

The *First Annual Report*, which covered the period of operation between the 22 May 1975 and 10 July 1976, came out in January 1977. Its 647 pages, which among other things covered the history of the organization, staff biographies, public and private hearings, statistics, case summaries, and conclusions, revealed that over 10,000 complaints came in the first year, and by October 1976, just a year after Maloney had officially come to office, 14,000 had been received. However, the office had to admit that many of its petitioners were outside the jurisdiction. The report made much of quantity, and it might have been better had it confined itself to that which was its own business – which it did very well. There was an obvious intention to show how limited the Ombudsman's powers were in the face of so much need. As early as page four, Maloney was on about it: "I have said from time to time that the Legislature should be urged to give the Ombudsman jurisdiction to deal with such cases." In fact, only 954 cases were on target, and hundreds of complaints against municipalities, universities, and other bodies financed by the government, but outside the Ombudsman ambit, were piling in, and reluctantly rejected. But not without some help from the office. "About 90 per cent of the complainants with problems outside my jurisdiction as of October 31, 1976, were given information or advice, or referred to an agency which could help them." It was in the matter of "advice" that the office was to get in trouble; it was willing to go farther than simply pointing the suppliant in the right direction.

Judged by civil service practice, Maloney never ran the office properly. He was, for instance, involved in too many of the cases personally, despite his responsibilities as the senior administrator, and he never sequestered himself from his staff. The normal practice of only getting to the top man through a chain of command was ignored, and it was common practice for him to leave his door open, and for his staff to simply walk in, if they wanted to talk to him. "There was a very flat hierarchy. It was Arthur and then there was everybody else. He was unique in government bureaucrats at the top level in that he permitted access to himself that you don't ordinarily see since you have to go through a chain to get to the senior person."[4]

Even more peculiar was his involvement in cases that somehow caught his fancy. A case that he often spoke about concerned an old *bête noire*, the unfeeling conduct of a police magistrate. In December 1975, a troubled father phoned the office, complaining about the fact that his seventeen-year-old daughter, who had no previous trouble with the law, had been jailed for three weeks while the judge considered her sentence for possession of a small amount of hashish. The girl had a lawyer and had pleaded guilty to the charge. She was involved with a young man, with whom she had been living, and that person had sold a very small amount of hashish on the day previous to the arrest. Arthur's long experience gave him an immediate solution to the problem: "The Ombudsman contacted the girl's lawyer and told him that a perfectly proper device to use in order to secure the girl's release would be to launch an appeal from conviction and sentence and obtain bail." Arthur speeded up the process by instructing not the complainant, but the lawyer.

Given the intimate nature of the lower courts, the judge was informed that an appeal was to be launched. He was surprised by two things – the odd idea, as he saw it, that someone would plead guilty and then appeal against conviction, and more disturbingly, that the Ombudsman was involved; he protested to Arthur, muttering about "very significant issues as to the administration of justice and the division of function between this Court and the Office of the Ombudsman."[5] Anyone, other than Arthur, might have backed off at this point, having successfully got the girl out of jail by a bit of a trick.

Arthur, however, wasn't finished with the judge. He was not much abashed by having intruded in a matter outside his jurisdiction, nor by the obvious displeasure of a minor judicial figure. Arthur wrote back in a way that is reminiscent of his battle, years before, with the Law Society. It began as acridly dry as those letters of 1943 had been: "Thank you for your letter of December 10th. I was interested in your comments." Arthur went on to state what was, as Ombudsman, none of his business. "The precise complaint about your Honour's conduct that was brought to my attention in my capacity as Ombudsman was that you had directed that a seventeen year old girl, not previously in difficulty with the law, should be detained in custody for a period of three weeks while you took under consideration the sentence to impose in her case."

In the next two paragraphs, Arthur expounded his theory on how his office worked in such a situation: "It is basic to the successful functioning of the Office of the Ombudsman that citizens who approach it be advised as to their rights and as to how they go about asserting them." This seems reasonable, but in the next paragraph, he put his duties to extra-jurisdictional petitioners on a much stronger basis than either the legislation or the legislators had suggested: "If the matter raised is outside his jurisdiction the Ombudsman *must never* [italics mine] send the complainant away in ignorance of where he goes to have his rights determined." Which, of course, was not quite what Maloney had done at all. He went further, underlining his supposed obligation: "A young girl in the position of the accused, once convicted, has a right in law to appeal her conviction. *It is the duty of the Office of the Ombudsman to so advise her.*" [italics mine] No, it was not. If he had a duty it was to advise her father, who was the complainant, that the Ombudsman could not interfere, and to suggest that he go to a lawyer who could advise him. The complaint against the judge was none of Arthur's business, and the judge had done nothing wrong, save exercise his authority harshly. It was Arthur's duty to send the father in the right direction, nothing more. But what did happen shows how Arthur and the office sometimes extended themselves into actually doing the job if it could be done quickly. In this case, he jumped past the complainant to the lawyer, who obviously did not know what to do.

He acknowledged that applying for bail after conviction and prior to sentence was unusual, but then he turned on the judge: "It is not common to apply for bail after conviction and prior to sentence, but it is uncommon also for a trial judge – especially in cases involving a charge of possession of marijuana – to put over passing of sentence for so long a time as was the case here." Again, none of Arthur's business. He went on to produce legal precedents on the matter of sentencing. He was still not finished. The judge, in his letter to Arthur had advised him that the girl and her lawyer had, by reason of a filing error made by the lawyer in the court offices, changed their minds after the child was released, and the girl had returned to custody. This seemed to prove the point to the judge: "As I dictate this letter, I have been informed by my Court Administrator that the accused girl has also apparently come to the conclusion that her release from custody was unlawful and she has been surrendered into custody again." Arthur wasn't having a lay person's timidity before the law used against him when he knew he was right, particularly since the return to custody had been caused by the fact that the lawyer had evidently filed the appeal incorrectly. "You say in your letter to me that the accused had come to the conclusion her release from custody was unlawful. If she and her counsel thought this, they laboured under a misapprehension. Even if the actions of the justice in releasing her were a nullity because the appeal had been launched in the wrong forum they remain in full force and effect until set aside by a proper superior tribunal."[6] Arthur loved to teach the Bench the law, particularly when he suspected peevish hair-splitting and bloody-mindedness. He finished this letter with unveiled swagger: "I trust this will serve to clarify your understanding of the role the Ombudsman in this Province is required to play and will continue to play so long as I am the incumbent."

He was particularly proud of this bit of extra-mural work. He spoke of it in detail in the speech he made in 1980 at the Second International Ombudsman Conference in Israel. The point that he seemed to be pursuing – that the Ombudsman owed a duty to those who strayed into the wrong office to send them to the right one – was only part of what he was doing. He suggests that not only is the Ombudsman there to tell those he cannot help where to go to pursue a complaint, but he goes one step further. "I pointed out that it is basic to the successful function of the Ombudsman's office that citizens who approach it be advised as to their rights and as to how they go about exerting them if they choose to."[7] Not just where to go, but *how to go* about exerting their rights.

This urge to take the office into areas that were obviously outside the jurisdiction could sometimes be spontaneous. John Loftis, a former RCMP officer, who joined as an investigator, tells of the time when he was suddenly called into Arthur's office and sent off on a trip that couldn't wait for a written complaint – and probably was outside the authority, but which had two elements of concern that Arthur could not resist: a mother in distress – and in Renfrew.

Arthur called me down to his office. I know he didn't go through the senior investigators at all. All of a sudden, he just asked for me, and I'm down there. He said, "I want you to go to Renfrew." I said, "Pardon me?" "I want you to go to Renfrew. There's some woman up there with five kids that they're kicking out of her place, and I want you to investigate this, and tell me what's going on." Well! A case like that with Arthur! A woman with five kids! He didn't give me the option of going or not. And just the way he said it, I knew he was in a no-nonsense mood for being jerked around, so I went back upstairs, and then went to get a car, and there wasn't one. I asked my superiors and they suggested I either take my own, or fly up there, but I didn't like flying so I drove all day and into the night. The next day I got the lady, and then the housing people, and next day I came back, made my report recommending that she be allowed to stay where she was while they straightened out the problem. Of course, as soon as they found out that Arthur was interested, they started to bend over backwards. You see, Arthur was that way – a big case, or a woman getting thrown out or anyone else in trouble, big or little – and it was often not done in the official way.

This kind of flying-squad conduct was not common, but sufficiently so for many of the group to have their own favourite story of Arthur using his power with questionable latitude, if always, as he saw it, in a good cause. He was easily roused by a sudden emergency, and a lot of complaints came in on the fly that could not wait for the formalities – they needed immediate response – which was one of the reasons for the evening telephone line. It was more than a matter of indifference to the rules; Arthur had been long enough at the law to know that rules were important, and had to be met most of the time. He also presumed, however, that he had some room for flexibility.

Most of the cases were complicated and often took months of work, and Arthur's insistence that the staff were not ordinary civil servants meant that they worked much longer hours than Queen's Park employees – and thought themselves privileged to do so. Hoilett still remembers the early days with pleasure. "Those were heady days in a new office with Arthur showing incredible energy, and not so much zeal as commitment. The amount of leg work that Arthur had done before I joined on the lst of July 1975 – before the office got off the ground – was remarkable, and the research that was being done to establish the best office possible, and the way he sought to have an office that could respond to, and represent the community, was marvellous."[9]

Michael Zacks agrees with Hoilett, and had the experience of spending several years under later directors.

He was different from other ombudsmen. As a lawyer he would look at people, as opposed to looking at the law. Issues might be technical, and he might not understand them, but it was our job to sort the technical problems out for him. It was always, "You're thinking like a bureaucrat! Let's look at the issues here. You are not really serious when you're telling me that this is fair! This is right?" My approach was, "Well, legally, yes. This is what happened." He would say, "Well, we have to look at it a different way. We are not a court of law."

The touchstone is an aspect of the law often lost in the rigour of government regulation. Maloney was a born equity thinker, prepared to give the benefit of the doubt to anyone, to ignore the time limit or the exclusion in the footnote. As Zacks puts it, "Oh, yes, it was an equity approach. It was fairness that mattered; we were not going to deny remedies because the rules were there. It was always, 'Let's find some solution, some compensation – some way!'" It was the way he would address a jury, trying to convince them that there was another, fairer way to look at the facts – to give the person in trouble the benefit of the doubt – to be fair rather than rigorously right.

It was not, however, unstructured. A very detailed, systematic way of investigating most complaints was in place from early on. The Pickering case, which was to be the centre-piece of his withdrawal was supposed to have been badly done, but it was done in exactly the same way most of the files were handled. Much of the time, the patterns of investigation that led to eventual recommendations were carefully followed. Phil Patterson, in his penal and mental institution work, where there was constant complaint, was very careful about how he dealt with his cases:

We'd start an investigation. We'd send a field investigator out. He would have certain guidelines he was expected to explore, certain things he was to find out. Then he would bring everything back to our office. He would bring back medical reports, reports of who was on duty, time sheets from the guards' office, statements of witnesses. If necessary we would retain our own experts to say how an injury might have been occasioned.

You then would take all this data and distil from it what you thought, as a lawyer (and I oversaw every correctional investigation), it led you to. Then I would have a case conference with my own people, and if after that I thought it should go on, we had a case conference with all the lawyers in the office, including Mr. Maloney, plus the investigators ... On the matter of using the oath, it was a matter of discretion. We would often use them at Penatang, because psychopaths are often extremely manipulative. The vast number of complaints, as a matter of fact, were not upheld. Maloney never got any credit for that – only a very, very few were found against the government.[10]

The investigators were expected to move carefully, and they looked with some apprehension on the days on which they had to appear in Arthur's office to make their presentation of case findings. Loftis, who had years of experience as an investigator in both the RCMP and the Immigration service, found these meetings as daunting as anything he had ever faced. "You were not only expected to investigate the problem, but you had to come up with an appropriate way to solve it. At King Arthur's court, it was looked at, and you knew that you had to have it all together. Arthur literally held court; he would listen with the rest, and then ask for opinions from his group of young lawyers."[11]

While the office was being built up around cases already begun, Arthur was also on to another idea that was to cause some uneasiness because of the expense, but was to redound internationally to the reputation of the office. In his early wanderings, Arthur had made a lot of friends in the business who admired and envied his young office, and he rapidly became something of a model for them; he, in turn, realized the value of their experience, and he believed that constant meetings between Ombudsman officials would be mutually beneficial. Hainey was deeply involved with the development of international connections, and he saw that "Arthur was regarded as a real phenomenon. Most of them had these shoe-string operations, and Arthur loved to invite them to Ontario. They would go away with stars in their eyes, hardly believing what they saw. He'd preach to them his idea of what an Ombudsman's office should be."

By 1977, however rosy the situation might seem to the visiting Ombudsman officials, the battle had long been joined. There was no doubt that Arthur was in trouble with his masters and with the press. The government had not given up on the office – yet. There were some observers who believed that what Arthur was doing was what the government wanted – establishing a large, solid department able to withstand opposition, and ready for the long-run.

There is a myth that something went wrong. There is a notion in the Ombudsman community that Arthur did something – that there was something inherently wrong, flawed, but it's not true ... Arthur Maloney was selected by the Premier and Roy McMurtry, later the Attorney-General, clearly knowing what Arthur Maloney was, and the kind of person he was. They knew exactly what they were getting. They wanted somebody of his stature, somebody of his intellect, drive and sense of purpose. They were going to get somebody to establish an office as *he wanted it*, and he was somebody who was not going to take a back seat to anybody, and not going to "kowtow" to the Legislature. When he read in the *Ombudsman's Act* that he was independent, he took it seriously. That meant something, and he thought that it meant that he made the decisions, and not the MPPs, and he wasn't going to permit any political interference. So the only thing that went wrong was doing what everyone ought to have known was going to happen.[12]

McMurtry has always insisted that he knew Arthur would be independent and stylish and fearless. What he and Davis did not know was how difficult and public the quarrels would be, or that Arthur would finally give up since he would not, could not, give in. McMurtry denies that they thought of Arthur simply as the hard man who would put the department on its feet and then go away, taking the wounds of organization on to himself. They hoped it would go on as it began – in mutual compliment and co-operation. But if Arthur and his fellow ombudsmen thought that he, gryphon-like, had flown free of the trammels of political power and the civil service, they were wrong – politics and bureaucracy, phoenix-like, go on forever.

13

The Children's Crusade Meets Reality in North Pickering

Maloney's career as Ombudsman might well have been different had North Pickering not been lying in wait. It seemed a simple problem: had a group of assessors hired by the Ontario government to deal with the purchase of land around North Pickering, a few miles north-east of Toronto, conducted themselves properly when they convinced residents to sell their land to the government for a new airport – and thus avoid inevitable expropriation? If they did not do so, how much money was involved in setting things right? Perhaps of less moment – who was responsible for any unfair conduct? In a way, it possessed all the danger of Ombudsman intrusion – it could confront a government department with suggestions, at least, of incompetence, if not the intent to cheat, and perhaps, more to the point, it would cost a lot of money to solve.

It was a matter of simply listening to the complaints, confronting those assessors who would be willing to talk, and if the Ombudsman was convinced that people had been treated unfairly, he would recommend compensation. The government would pay it – no doubt. As F. Marzo and A. Miles, the two Ombudsman investigators, put it, in an interim report to Maloney in January 1976: "the complaints can be boiled down to two: a) that the methods used by the acquisition agents in trying to induce property owners to sell their lands were highly questionable and suspect b) the actual appraisals done in evaluating the various properties were inadequate, incorrect and not representative of the true value of the property." By the time all the property owners had been interviewed, as well as the appraisers and the project director, the documents examined, the law of expropriation researched, and the properties valued again by independent professionals, the Ombudsman crew were of the opinion that they had done a good job.

There was a sense of irrelevance about the whole thing, since in late summer 1975, the federal and provincial governments had given up on Pickering, and closed down the project. It had cost millions of dollars, and it was going to cost more if the Ombudsman clients won their case. A large number of properties were in the hands of the provincial government, and the federal government had also been buying busily (as late as autumn 1993 the federal government was still holding thousands of acres). The complaints to the Ombudsman had roused others to wonder if they, too, had a chance of compensation.

The Ombudsman found that the owners had been treated unfairly – that some of the assessors had acted unprofessionally, either directly or indirectly, in a way that suggested that they had been instructed to make a hard, rather than a fair deal. There should be compensation for the same. The Minister of Housing rejected the report, claiming that the investigation was inadequate and unfair. What has been left in public memory is the idea that for once in his life, Maloney was caught with an ill-prepared case. Those Ombudsman employees who were involved in the investigation deny this; those in the office who were not involved are not quite sure. The fact is that the report was prepared in exactly the same manner as most others had been prepared by the office. It had been always presumed that a government organization found wanting by the Ombudsman might be unhappy with solutions suggested, but would, if reluctantly, accept the inevitable. What distinguished the Pickering case was the fact that the ministry in question would not accept the findings. One of the points of rejection came as something of a surprise, since it was on a matter of procedure. The Act, under Section 20 (2) (a) gave the Ombudsman the right to treat a complainant with legal rigour: "The Ombudsman may summon before him and examine on oath (a) any complainant." It also allowed him to use the same power with a government employee or, indeed, any other person testifying on any complaint. This power was rarely used by the office. It seems not to have even been thought about much, save in the case of Patterson's convicts and mental patients. It was presumed that parties involved in a complaint would tell their story, and that the investigators would, once they had both sides of the tale, be able to sort the information out, and come to a sensible conclusion. Complainants might be mistaken, or misunderstand, but they would not lie, and if they did, the investigators would, somehow, be able to detect the fib. The Ombudsman staff presumed that since they were in good faith, so was everyone else.

This informal procedure was, of course, open to abuse. But the use of the oath was discretionary, and the office usually felt that informality was the best policy. The children's crusade, led by Arthur Maloney, could muddle through simply, allowing the aggrieved to say it simply. Glenn Hainey knew where the trouble was: "It wasn't Davis; he was supportive, but I think he had a lot of pressure on him. We ran head on into John Rhodes, a powerful man, who was not about to back down, and Arthur was not going to back down."[1]

The other supposed flaw was also a matter of procedure, and again, it was not considered in preparing the recommendations, probably because it was presumed, if it was thought about at all, to be irrelevant. It fell under Section 19 (3) of the Act: "... if at any time during the course of an investigation, it appears to the Ombudsman that there may be sufficient grounds for his making any report or recommendation that may adversely affect any governmental organization or person, he shall give to that organization or person an opportunity to make representations respecting the adverse report or recommendation, either personally or by counsel." Given that the assessors had been questioned, it might be presumed that they had been given their opportunity to respond on their own behalf, but that was not quite the same thing as the Act provided. Kathryn Cooper, one of the lawyers involved, when asked why they simply did not take the report back and do it over in the manner that would meet the objections, stated that the investigation, save for the lack of oaths, and lack of formal notice to the parties criticized, was sound; if they had done it over again, they would have reached the same conclusions. Glenn Hainey saw the matter possessing implications that made a re-run difficult:

> I think he felt that he had to defend the report. First of all, he never questioned that the result was correct. There was never any doubt in our minds that what we recommended was fair. It wasn't a case where we could take it back and come up with any different recommendations. It would only have been a matter of listening to the assessors' point of view – I don't think it would have changed it. It would have appeared to be fairer to have taken it back, and re-do it, but why he stuck to his guns so vehemently is that we all thought we had got it right. We may have had a better process, but we got it right. And I think he also felt that this was the first real test of the independence of this office; if he backed off, he would have been undermining the whole concept of independence. It was a real battle of the Titans.[2]

Keith Hoilett was on the outside looking in at Pickering, although he was eventually to be a main figure in unravelling the mess, since he was to chair the Ombudsman committee that took four years of hearings, two years full time and two years part time, to re-hear the complaints, and to deal with latecomers. He saw the valuable lessons of the investigation. He found that most of the original findings were accurate, but that the language used in the report had moral connotation, and tended to inflame. But he also saw that the public wanted expropriation to be done fairly, not as it might be done in the open market, with the vendors and purchasers taking care of themselves. "One of the things that came out of Pickering was that the expectations of the public were seen. If the government takes land, as they have a right to do by expropriation, the rules of the game were to be seen. There had to be a sense of fairness."[3] But that insight and the final solution were years away. Rhodes stood his ground, as he had a right to do. The Act did not make it obligatory to do what the Ombudsman recommended. Often the parties did, and often they were inclined to do so very early in the investigation – on some occasions, the very threat of Maloney's gang descending was sufficient to get a minor injustice remedied. The Pickering matter was different: errors had been found that would cost a lot of money – and in being remedied, a major ministry would be brought into disrepute.

This, of course, was always the weak spot in the Act, which Arthur had not thought to anticipate when he was making his original deal. As Rhodes put it in a later statement to the Select Committee:

> His office is not a court nor are his findings binding judgments or determinations of the issues before him. He is an officer of the Legislature who is authorized to investigate certain complaints or matters and to form an opinion of them. Where he is of the opinion that corrective action is justified, he is required to report his opinion and his reason therefore to the appropriate governmental organization and he may make such recommendations as he thinks fit ... I am called upon by reason of my responsibilities not only to the Legislature but to the public at large and to persons affected by the report, to review such recommendations and the supporting material and to reach a decision on whether I can accept them in whole, in part or for that matter at all.[4]

The Act, however powerful, did not allow the Ombudsman to order anyone to do anything. The Ombudsman is to come to an "opinion."

> Section 22 (3) (g) the Ombudsman shall report his opinion, and his reasons therefor, to the appropriate governmental organization, and *may make such recommendations as he thinks fit* [italics mine] and he may request the governmental organization to notify him, within a specified time, of the steps, *if any* [italics mine], that it proposed to take to give effect to his recommendations, and the Ombudsman shall also send a copy of his report and recommendations to the minister concerned.

That, in effect, was where the Pickering matter stopped. Rhodes received the report, and found it wanting. He also felt that if the missing steps had been taken, the Ombudsman had another duty – to inform him in the case of conflicting stories why he accepted one person's word over that of another. Rhodes did not deny that there was a case to be made for the landowners. "Having carefully considered the extensive report and your recommendations, I am convinced that there may be cases in which the actions of negotiators misled property owners and that further government action is required."[5] He simply wanted the whole thing done over again, under oath, with the agents allowed a formal chance to reply, and reasons given for final recommendations. A more flexible, wilier man than Maloney might have seen this as a bluff to be called – if that was what it was – taken the report back, gone through the steps demanded to satisfy the Act at its most pedantically rigorous, and come up with the same conclusions. It would have been an interesting way to discover if Rhodes was in good faith, or simply determined not to accept the report however it was put to him.

It was particularly irritating since much of the criticism of the manner in which the agents conducted themselves came from the agents themselves – the Ombudsman was not coming to any conclusions on that – the project employees who had been interviewed complained about the method, and the fairness of the way in which they were instructed to deal with the landowners. On the matter of the oath, Maloney insisted on its discretionary nature. "It is easy to appreciate the difficulties, delays and expense which would have been involved in examining 150 witnesses on oath. In brief, although I value the oath as much or more as any person, I repeat there is no inherent magic in its application." On the matter of not warning the agents in writing that their conduct was being seen as possibly damaging to their careers, the answer was obvious, if somewhat ingenuous. "The Minister is concerned that I have not dealt equitably with the officials whose actions were being investigated. In reply, I point out that I found no evidence that any agent was not acting in good faith or that the conduct of any agent may have amounted to fraudulent misrepresentation. I have not suggested in any way that they be punished for their part in the events." Rhodes was unmoved. He wanted an independent body to deal with the matter. Maloney argued that it would be a waste of time and money for either the proposed committee or the Ombudsman's office to try again. He had not yet learned that wasting time and money was no deterrent to the internal workings of the government (although ironically it was on the subject of how he spent money that he was to find enemies). The haggling and bad temper increased.

It was not a matter of the report surprising the Minister. The possible conclusions had been conveyed to him as early as January 1976, and consultations were going on between the two offices by early May. The ramifications of the report were worrying, since the forty-four cases, if accepted as valid, would cost the government three million dollars plus.

That, however, was unlikely to be the end of it, if the remedy was to be extended to include other owners who might come forward; the cost might rise to over thirty million dollars. When the report came out on 22 June 1976, the Ombudsman stood his ground, and had not made any accommodation to the ministry's concern over oaths, or notice to the agents. The ministry responded by suggesting an independent tribunal. Maloney, in return, seemed to be making an admission of insufficiency in proposing that all further complainants would be examined under oath.

He, however, did not have to put up with the ministry's intransigence. He could send the report on to the Premier and "may thereafter make such report to the assembly on the matter as he thinks fit." He still had to wait on the Premier and the Legislature, who might not support his findings. *Rhodes, however, made it clear that if the Legislature accepted the report, he would do as bid by Maloney.* That would have seemed the best way for Maloney to go. But to get there was not easy. The report went to the Premier on 8 July, and seven meetings took place with Davis. Then Maloney made a big mistake, as his group soon saw. Bill Davis suggested that a Select Committee of the Legislature, representing all parties in proportion to their representation in the Legislature, should be established to consider the report. It might well have been the best way into the Legislature, but the wording of the motion that established the committee had Pandora's box written all over it: "to review *from time to time the reports of the Ombudsman* [italics mine] as they become available, to report thereon to the Legislature, and to make such recommendations as the Committee deem appropriate." Maloney had been in politics long enough to have known the "dead hand" of committees, and their inclination to grow like killer weeds in a Gothic novel. Most threatening was the fact that this committee was not to disband with the resolution of Pickering. Zacks was aware that Maloney should have known better, and that he had been warned.

> The Pickering incident was really the precipitator of the Select Committee; they were originally to look into that, and they became the standing committee. He was actually cautioned about accepting that committee, because once you set up the process, the Legislature will use it; that really was the source of a lot of conflict. He would provide the information, his reports, but he would not accept them questioning his decisions, which he saw as political interference, and, of course, they saw it as performing their public duty of looking into and reporting back to the Legislature. They were just not *ad idem* at all on their respective roles and that is where the conflict developed.[6]

The simple task was being drawn into the morass of the bureaucracy, quickly and surely. It was no longer a matter of an enlightened government providing unhappy citizens with a remedy for government bungling – that was only to be the beginning – one part of the government was now happily inventing obstacles to the solution of problems.

While the Select Committee was still getting organized, Maloney and Rhodes continued to attempt some compromise. It was supposedly only a matter of Maloney satisfying Rhodes that the findings were accurate, and if not, amending the same. They had several meetings, and while they were at it, another element was added. Five of the land acquisition agents who had been accused of misleading the owners decided to hire their own lawyer, unhappy with the protection given them by the minister. They chose John Sopinka, a formidable, younger Toronto counsel, who was later to go on to the Supreme Court of Canada. He brought a Notice of Application for Judicial Review in the Divisional Court on the Ombudsman's report – a move that would certainly delay any quick disposition of the matter. Maloney and Rhodes kept meeting, but now they had Sopinka shadowing them. The plot was thickening, and it had its moments of farce. Glenn Hainey was deeply involved in the negotiations that Maloney and Rhodes were trying to keep quiet.

We tried to settle it, and Bob Armstrong was acting for Rhodes, and John Sopinka for the land negotiators, and I remember that no one would move publicly. Somebody called somebody – I think it was the minister's office. Somebody called me as I recall, and said, "We think that we should have a private meeting." Arthur thought this was a great idea. Typical Maloney style – [Hainey laughs] he organized a suite. I think it was the Westbury; he got a great big goddamed suite at the Westbury and ordered in a bar and a big dinner. There was Arthur, myself, and one other from the office, and Rhodes, his deputy Crosbie, Bob Armstrong, and another lawyer. Arthur ordered dinner, and in a gentlemanly manner, we were going to sit around and he and Rhodes were going to sort it out. It was very hush-hush and secret because we didn't want the media to know about it. So we all arrived.

Well, of course, Sopinka finds out and wants to be there; he doesn't want a deal worked out without his clients being represented. I'll never forget it – it's all the more amusing now when I think of him in the Supreme Court of Canada. Arthur had a great deal of respect for Sopinka, but that didn't mean he was going to let him come to dinner with us. He didn't want Sopinka there because he thought he would gum up the works, keep raising the procedural questions, and Arthur wanted to do a political solution. So we are all in this suite, having a drink, and Rhodes and Arthur were trying to bury the hatchet, and there's a bang, bang, bang on the door, and we open it, and it's John Sopinka, and he says, "I want to come in." And Arthur says, "You get downstairs. You wait for us downstairs! We'll call you when we need you."

Arthur didn't want him in on the negotiations because then it would have been two on one, you know. So poor John Sopinka is left in the bar downstairs

> with Arthur's driver, a young guy, and Sopinka would come up every hour or so, and bang on the door, and Arthur would say, "Get down there! We're not ready for you yet." I don't think that Sopinka ever got into the room. By the end of the night there was a lot of scotch consumed, and lots of negotiation, and Arthur and the minister worked out a deal, and we were left to work it out – and the Hoilett Committee came out of that.[7]

They finally agreed on two committees. These had nothing to do with the Select Committee, which was another matter. It was an arrangement that made perfect sense to lawyers. G.K. Chesterton, Arthur's favourite writer, in a 1912 essay, discussed the nature of government bureaucracy and its inclination to compound its activities, with the "mad officials" in full constructive flight in "one vast vision of imbecility." The Pickering problem was fast accumulating such trappings. The new committees, however, made sense to the combatants. One was to be struck under *The Public Inquiries Act, 1971*, and this was something of a victory for Rhodes, who always wanted the complaints to be reviewed by an independent board. It was to deal with claims that the ministry disputed, and it was also to handle any cases that had been processed by any of the land agents whom Sopinka represented.

The rest of the cases in the report, and any new cases that had come into the office since the report (and many were accumulating) were to be heard by a commission set up in the Ombudsman's office. The oath was to be administered to the witnesses in both forums. Rhodes was able to rub that in when he addressed the Select Committee. "The fact that the Ombudsman proposed a hearing process for future complainants at which time they would be called upon to establish under oath that they were likewise victims of unfairness, clearly acknowledges that a test of this issue is necessary."[8] Maloney had some reason to be satisfied, however, since the minister undertook "to give effect to whatever recommendation the Ombudsman made" in connection with the cases to be adjudicated in the Ombudsman office. Somewhat ominously, given all the concern about expense that was flying about the Ombudsman's head, was the proviso that in both hearings, the parties could take counsel, and the Minister of Housing would pay the legal bill. It was a recipe for lovely, complicated procedural battles.

If Maloney put the best face on the compromise that he could, the newspapers were aware of his defeat. As early as August 1976, when Arthur got himself landed with the Select Committee, it was obvious that Davis had rejected the report and would not overrule Rhodes. Harold Greer, the syndicated columnist, saw what had happened: "To oppose the Ombudsman is one thing, but to oppose him without seeming to and without being criticized for opposing him, is a political thing at which Mr. Davis excels. The trouble is that Mr. Maloney, despite a term in Parliament, is still a political babe in the woods when it comes to dealing with the likes of Premier Davis. If his independence is not only to be real but seen to be real, he will have to learn, quickly."[9] Greer was no less sceptical about the deal made with Rhodes. Greer, who seemed to articulate better than anyone else what everyone was up to, knew that Maloney was, in part, caught out by his decision (if not thinking about it can be so called) not to inform the land agents that they might be in jeopardy. Maloney argued that he expected no harm to come to them, but he wasn't necessarily in control of that, particularly since most of them were not government employees, but agents hired in for the job, who could claim that their professional reputations were in danger. They might well have a cause of action in the courts. So something had to be done to get them to stop their legal challenge. In agreeing to the commissions, Maloney was, in a sense, giving way to Rhodes on two points, as Greer was to note: "In effect he was admitting his North Pickering inquiry and report were grossly inadequate and in need of redoing. This is what Rhodes had claimed all along." On top of that, Rhodes had got his independent board. He didn't get all the complainants into it, and he had to promise to pay the legal bills, and accept without question the findings of the Ombudsman committee, but on balance Maloney was clearly the loser. Greer also saw it as something more serious: "It is a fairly substantial defeat and discredit for Maloney which is already being used by his right-wing detractors, such as Claire Hoy in *The Toronto Sun,* to call for his resignation."[10]

If there was some consolation in Maloney having won the battle for one of the committees to be his own, with the appointment of Keith Hoilett to run that group, there was serious trouble with the commission set up by Public Inquiries. It showed how the sweet simplicity of the Ombudsman's activities was to be smothered in intricate legal and political grappling, in the pushing and shoving at close quarters of the parties thereto, like mediaeval foot soldiers caught in a cul-de-sac, unable to strike a lethal blow, and satisfied to rudely bump each other for the sake of doing something for their daily crust. It was a mess from day one. Initially, the Premier appointed three commissioners: the Honourable J.F. Donnelly, a retired Supreme Court Judge, as chairman, and Mr. R.M. Grant, Q.C. and Mr. Peter Marriott. Maloney had not been consulted. However, there was immediate, widespread suspicion that someone had consulted someone – and not to do Maloney any favours. It was well-known – indeed something of a notorious joke in legal circles – that Maloney and Donnelly despised each other. They had quarrelled on every occasion they had met in court, and Maloney had always made strenuous attempts to avoid Donnelly in trial situations.

I'll never forget when we heard that Donnelly had been appointed. Arthur was furious. He figured Roy knew his views of Donnelly, and it's hard for me to believe that the attorney- general would not have been consulted, and Roy certainly knew Arthur's views on Donnelly. One thing is clear – Arthur and Roy continued to be the best of friends – there wasn't a breakdown, but having said that, I guess Roy had to do what the government wanted to do.[11]

Maloney put up with a lot of good-natured abuse from associates in and out of the Ombudsman's office who saw the Donnelly appointment as either a joke or an insult; some were of the opinion that it was both. Eric Murray recalls Arthur saying, "'Oh, well, Roy wouldn't do that to me.' I said, 'Well, who else would ever pull Frank Donnelly out of the hat!' Frank Donnelly was to the right of Attila the Hun! He was retired at the time, and if that wasn't sending Arthur a message, I don't know what would! But Arthur refused to recognize it. Because it was his dear friend, Roy. Rarely would he say anything untoward about any of his acquaintances."[12]

McMurtry sticks to his denial of having anything to do with the appointment, but understands why Maloney and others might have suspected otherwise. However loyal Arthur was in defending McMurtry, there was a coolness for a time between the two old friends.

That's the only time that Arthur and I did have a bit of a falling out. [Forgetting the Camp-Diefenbaker occasion] Quite a few months went by when I didn't hear from Arthur. He felt I had been most unhelpful in respect of the Pickering Land Act. I told Arthur that it was an unprofessional and biased report, and I was not prepared to recommend that the government act on it. I remember Arthur was clearly annoyed with me, but it didn't last long – only a few months. Some people gave him a bad time; we never did as a government. We agreed to disagree, and then this damn thing went to another inquiry, and it went on forever.[13]

Roy McMurtry has always denied any involvement in the choice of Donnelly, nor does he remember the appointment as a tacit attempt by the government to send Maloney a message. He has always insisted that the choice would have been made in the offices of the judiciary, and that he, as Attorney-General, would have no right to intrude. He suggests that those who think otherwise are indulging in the fashionable nineties inclination to revisionist history. The fact is, however, that the opinion that Donnelly was chosen to thwart Arthur is not a new idea – it was the general opinion of all of Arthur's associates at the time, and McMurtry could hardly have been unaware of how it would look. As one of Maloney's close associates says, "He might not have been involved in the appointment, but he must have known what would happen, and he might have delicately suggested that another man should be chosen if the committee was to have any chance of doing any work." It was, after all, not a strictly judicial appointment, but at best extra-judicial, and it was certainly the case that Maloney had no sense of it being sacrosanct, since he insisted loudly throughout the months of ensuing quarrel that Donnelly should be replaced. There was no doubt in the minds of his associates that the government had sent Donnelly as a message that the party was over. And it was – from that moment on.

On the matter of whether McMurtry was involved in the appointment of Donnelly, it looks as if Maloney, in fact, presumed that he was. In his letter to the Premier commenting on the commission, he certainly seems to think that McMurtry is part of the process. "It is no doubt unnecessary to draw your attention or the attention of the Attorney General that not all of the Government appointments to the Commission are acceptable to me."[14] If there was one bright spot in the matter, it was that Maloney's objections to the make-up of the commission under Donnelly was partly amended; Marriott was taken off and Arthur was allowed his own man – the wily, fearless Dave Humphrey – that should have made a difference, but it didn't.

The Hoilett group commenced its hearings almost immediately, but the Donnelly group fell to squabbling. On the second day of its meetings, Ian G. Scott, hired by Maloney to represent the complainants, attempted to put some documents into evidence; the lawyers for the ministry objected, and the commission split, two with the ministry, and Humphrey against. This was to become the basic pattern, with very few exceptions. The first witness, Heather Dinsmore, one of the complaining landowners, hardly began her testimony when the ministry lawyer objected. Again the commission split, with Humphrey supporting the witness, and the other two refusing to hear her evidence. Ian Scott asked for an adjournment in order to bring a stated case into the Divisional Court to test the procedural decisions being made. The meetings began in late January 1977, but fell into stalemate almost immediately, and the only action was being taken first in the Divisional Court, which ruled in favour of the landowners, and then in the Appeal Court, where Scott won again, but where it was decreed that a single member of the commission could not dissent from the majority view on a question of procedure. That was in late March, and by then not a single case had been heard. Humphrey wanted off, in part because the fee Maloney promised him was not forthcoming, and in part because he could only see a constant battle with the other commissioners.

> With deference to my fellow Commissioners, we are incompatible and one might conclude that I am a voice crying in the wilderness ... it is clearly on a col-

> lision course with proceedings at present being conducted by the Ombudsman under *The Ombudsman Act* in which exactly the same issues are being tried but without the participants being subjected to "an adversarial" proceeding, and with full powers of investigation. ... this Hearing has in effect been turned into a court case and an incredibly expensive one at that.[15]

Certainly the landowners, who had been pushed into the Donnelly forum rather than the one being run in the Ombudsman's office, were getting nowhere. They were not, in fact, being handled at all as the lawyers and the commissioners battled with each other in the courts. Humphrey's resignation letter suggested that the commission be re-constituted as a one-man proceeding, but that was rebuffed.

The quarrel continued. The commission wanted to go on with only two commissioners. Maloney objected. The Cabinet was asked to solve the problem. Davis proposed to put Peter Marriott back on in Humphrey's place. Maloney objected. In early May, he was offered the chance to name a replacement for Humphrey, but he refused to nominate, on the grounds that the commission simply could not work as long as Donnelly and Grant were lurking there. The government went ahead and confirmed Marriott as the third commissioner. This time Ian Scott moved, complaining about the way in which the two commissions differed: "the two tribunals may have been necessary for technical reasons but was never, as I understand the matter, intended to bespeak different treatment of the claimants or a different standard of re-investigation."[16] In Scott's opinion, those in the Donnelly group were being treated as if they were in a civil trial, put in direct conflict with the ministry, and, unlike the Hoilett group within the Ombudsman's office, treated in an adversarial manner. He refused, on their behalf, to have anything more to do with Donnelly. Donnelly was left without a complaining party, but attempted to carry on nevertheless with the real estate agents voicing their concerns about their reputations, but that, too, quickly wound down, and nothing more was done for the landowners on Donnelly's list. They would not appear before him. As a result,they were stuck in a bureaucratic no-man's-land.

It was not the last time that the Maloney dream of quick justice was to be caught up in the labyrinth of law, politics, and personality, charged with its own dynamic of bureaucratic futility and disregard for those who had come innocently into the Ombudsman's office to avoid exactly that which was now happening to their supposed champion. And as Maloney, Humphrey, and Scott said, in their numerous letters asking for a dismissal of the Donnelly Commission – this thing was costing a lot of money – it wasn't being spent on sandwiches from Winston's.

While all this was not going on, some lucky creatures had managed to get into the Hoilett hearings. Their first meeting was on 6 December

1976, and by June 1977, Hoilett was hearing evidence on the thirty-fourth complaint, with forty-one more to go. As of 30 June 1977, 122 witnesses had been heard. No wonder Ian Scott wanted to get his group back into the Ombudsman's hands! That was not to be easy. On 30 June the Ombudsman received notice that the Donnelly Commission was back in business, and that on 3 August they were meeting – the commission was turning itself into a perpetual motion machine despite the fact that its original passengers had left the vehicle. It was made clear that the Ombudsman could come along if he wanted, but they were going ahead "without further notice to you." By November, the commission, still without testimony from the landowners, wound up their sittings, having solved nothing.

Hoilett had the bulk of the complaints, and moved through them slowly but surely, although Sopinka, who was representing the real estate agents at both the Donnelly and the Hoilett hearings, withdrew from the latter on the grounds of prejudice against his clients. Thus Ian Scott had withdrawn his clients from the Donnelly hearings, Sopinka had withdrawn his real estate agents from the Hoilett hearings, and Maloney was still trying to rescue the poor innocents from Donnelly's jurisdiction. The matter wore on into 1978. Rhodes left the Ministry of Housing, and the new minister, Claude Bennett decided to show his mettle. He would not agree to the removal of Donnelly, and whatever Ian Scott might claim, he accused him of really staying away because of Donnelly, which was certainly true in part. He also supported Sopinka's withdrawal from Hoilett. Now came the chastisement. In the light of what was going on, Bennett claimed that he was not bound by Rhodes's promise to accept the Hoilett findings – he would look at them, and make his own judgment. It was just another turn of the tit-for-tat screw.

On 23 August 1978, more than two years after the original report, and more than three years after the first letters came into Arthur's office, Heather Dinsmore, the owner who had almost got her complaint out before the Donnelly Commission in one of the first meetings in 1976, let out a *cri de coeur* in a letter to the Select Committee. She had no quarrel with the Ombudsman or his staff, but, as she put it, why should the "Johnny-come-latelys" [*sic*] be getting a hearing? "WE WERE THE ORIGINAL COMPLAINANTS." [Her capitals] If the government had injured her in taking her land improperly, it was now compounding it by obstructing her right to have the case heard. The civil service was, to her mind, running the Cabinet and the government, and was all too easily able to thwart the Ombudsman. "Justice delayed is justice denied and even the Ombudsman would seem powerless to prevail."

Maloney would be gone before the matter was settled. It did finally end with some sort of justice in the early eighties for most of the complainants, but hardly within the time that could have been hoped for when the report came in, just over a year after the complaints arrived at Maloney's office. Hoilett sat for 360 days over three years, and dealt with 83 complaints. In October 1979, just a year after Maloney had resigned, the Ombudsman managed to rescue the imprisoned group of complainants from the moribund Donnelly Commission, which had never settled a single case. Despite government opposition, Chief Justice Gregory Evans ruled that the Ombudsman's office still had authority over those poor creatures. At least no individual had to pay legal fees – the ministry was to take care of that. In July 1980, one part of the legal cost was revealed. Three young lawyers had represented the complainants before Hoilett, Mike Wadsworth, John Rook, and John Collins. By the time they were through, Wadsworth was owed $513,268 plus $10,453 for disbursements. Rook wanted and got $183,348 and $10,453 for expenses, while Collins, who came in sometime later than the other two, put in a bill for $76,475 and only $1,023 in expenses. That was just one group of lawyers. Trying to get the government to do the right thing was an expensive matter. It added some sobering proof to the argument that the whole idea of justice speedily and reasonably done by the Ombudsman was no match for one single government office – when it decided not to co-operate. Pickering, albeit finally resulting in remedy for the parties long after Arthur had left, was his greatest failure, and has always been the blackest mark on his record in that office.

The *folie a deux* of two strong-willed men, determined to protect their personal and public reputations, one with an office in comparative infancy, believing he must not flinch, and the other, with a ministry of accomplishment and reputation, was not helped by the naturally deadly drawing power of the black hole of committees, legalisms, and bureaucracy sucking at the life's blood of common sense solution. The lawyers could not be blamed – it was their brief to fight their clients' corners. Anything less would be unprofessional. Yet one suspects an increasing rigidity in their conduct. Lawyers, in fact, are not only present to fight for their clients, right or wrong – they also have a duty to advise them on when it is sensible to stop the nonsense.

Sadly, what is remembered of the case has become, in the minds of those who remember it at all, simply a matter of Maloney allowing a sloppy job to be done. What it really was, however, was an example of how the Ombudsman's office met the facts of life in the world where politics and bureaucracy, supposedly prepared to co-operate in their own chastisement said "no," and got away with it, although in the end, years and thousands of dollars later, the government had to pay up after all. But that didn't do much to save Maloney's reputation.

14

Circling the Wagons

Much is made by apologists for Maloney of the continual attacks of Claire Hoy, the *Sun* columnist. In fact, Hoy only occasionally turned his splenetic attentions to Maloney. Some friends think that Hoy had some specific reason for attacking him, but the truth may be much simpler. Hoy treated most of his subjects with a sour puritanical dismissiveness – he rarely wrote a column of praise or approval. He struck a popular note, and a popular intellectual level in confirming the suspicions of the beverage room that one of their betters was having a good time at their expense. He had a preternaturally sensitive nose for the odd smells of public life that often were emanations of political hypocrisy, and he was aware that politics often travelled beyond true concern to plummy oratory on its way to hot air and finally to political flatulence, which Edward Pearce, the British *Guardian's* columnist once characterized as the noise and inert reflexes that remind us that a corpse breaks wind. Hoy suspected the same in Arthur's busy vanity. He detected something of the same in Roy McMurtry's tendency to trumpet social changes in his work as the Attorney-General. Hoy preferred his politicians to be less publicly pleased with themselves – certainly a bit less self-regarding than either Maloney or McMurtry, who had the air and swagger of populist triumphalism in the way they grasped the inequities of society, and announced their intentions of putting them right immediately.

The fact that McMurtry had brought Maloney to the Ombudsman's office was not simply a matter of friendship, but of like-mindedness. They had idealistic ideas about public service. McMurtry's ambitions for the Attorney-General's office, which he was given, as of right, upon his entry into the House in the autumn of 1975, were similar to those that Arthur espoused for the ombudsman job. They attracted the same kinds of criticism, and Hoy was just the most obviously simplistic example of an uneasy reaction to the grand insouciance and declamatory style with which Arthur took his place at the centre of the public forum, albeit with nods *pro forma* to the idea that it was a great honour, but clearly overshadowed by the pervading sense that it was a position which he, naturally, was destined to occupy. Hoy had a beady eye for that kind of political *entrechat* and was determined, from the beginning, to bring Arthur back to earth.

Bob Johnstone, who was a familiar of both Hoy and Arthur, was aware of how Arthur was putting himself into positions susceptible of derision, and he excuses Hoy's reaction, in part, not as a matter simply of yellow press mischief so much as an expression of Hoy's innate conservatism. "When you see Claire Hoy jumping on people, there's less to this than meets the eye. Meet Claire and you realize in a couple of minutes what I'm talking about. He's a nice guy."[1] Johnstone understands that Hoy would see Arthur as a rabble-rouser, appealing to the baser instincts of the social mix. It is an interesting idea, not unconnected to the comment of a member of the senior judiciary, Mr. Justice Archie Campbell, who, in discussing Arthur's political career, suggested that Arthur's natural gift as an orator, and his instinctive desire and capacity for arousing public affection, might well have been dangerous had he ever attained high office. Coming from Hoy, however, who himself practised outright yahooing, it is a bit suspicious.

It was not a matter of Maloney snubbing or insulting Hoy. He seemed initially bemused by the rancour with which Hoy attacked him, but he put the best face on it. Lillian remembers him regularly bringing home the *Sun* to show her the latest insult. In July 1977, he attempted to take some edge off the sniping by sending Hoy a clipping from the *Eganville & District Old Home Week* booklet of 1 August 1948, which described his maternal grandfather as the "King of the Bonnechere."

Dear Claire:

When you refer to me in your column I am usually designated as "King Arthur." It may be that I come by this title honestly as you will see when you read the enclosed extract taken from the booklet published in 1948 in my home town of Eganville in conjunction with the Eganville & District Old Home Week – With all good wishes, I remain,

Yours faithfully, Arthur Maloney.

Hoy continued to batter Maloney until and beyond the end, and as late as the public installation of Donald Morand in Maloney's place in January 1979, call his time in office one of the great boon-doggles of Ontario politics. It was never much better than that at any time during the Maloney tenure. It was always "King Arthur" or variations thereof, with accusations of elitism and snobbery, and constant demands for resignation. It was not, however, Hoy alone who went after the

Ombudsman. There was a considerable amount of superficial comment as the press stripped the office of its seriousness and density of purpose and re-shaped it in print as an expensive palace of thoughtless arrogance. What Arthur thought was good press – the display of no-expense-spared to surround the aggrieved public with the trappings of power – was seen by the press as posturings of celebrity. In the beginning, he seemed to have presented himself as the defender of the distressed citizens, bringing a swift, lively efficiency to the office, and therefore, it was presumed, to the government as it rubbed against the Ombudsman. His self-portrait was widely accepted – but quickly, it was turned into the derisive perception of vanity and waste.

Expense was part of the problem – and the expense was not confined to the trappings of office. The budget Maloney requested was to be fought over year after year, at a time when the government was beginning to react to the general slow-down in the economy. It went further than that. As the first year's work developed, there was an increasing concern not only about expense, but about what Maloney was doing. Nothing seemed to be too much trouble for the busy, young investigators, and it was an unusual spectacle to see a government department working fast, determined to get things done, and demanding the right to do more. The First Annual Report may have looked self-serving in its multiple listings, but it indicated an eagerness to go anywhere to help. This desire to search out new fields of complaint added to the uneasiness of some of the legislators as they saw the Ombudsman doing what they were elected to do – doing it faster, and taking all the credit for solving their constituents' problems. Allied to this was the legislators' growing suspicion of Maloney's practice of getting out to meet the people, and sending his attractive staff to the farthest parts of the province – it looked too political to many of them, who were not Conservative members. It was an office too eager to please, and too eager to praise itself for doing so.

The unease of his friends about the fulsomeness of the report was consistent with their concern about how he was comporting himself in general in his attempts to publicize the office. He particularly annoyed his critics with the amount of time that was spent on people who had no business coming to the Ombudsman in the first place, since their complaints were outside his authority. He may have presumed that he had the Legislature's blessing for his service to those not qualified to receive it, but it was to be one of his activities that was viewed suspiciously.

His intrusion into the court to rescue the young girl from an unfeeling judge may have seemed to him to be a good example of how he could help, but it did leave him open to the charge of too-energetic meddling, and the judge had the last laugh. Judges have ways of taking care of themselves, and in this case, the girl wound up with a $1000 fine – her boy friend, who had been charged with possession for the purpose of trafficking, and who had a previous record, got off with a suspended sentence. Maloney knew he had been mocked, and urged the father of the girl to appeal the sentence (another intrusion that was none of his business), but by that time, the father had enough of people helping his daughter and preferred to pay up. Harold Greer had two points to make – one on that matter – Maloney may have done more damage than good. On top of that, he could not really do anything about the judge, given the fact that the Ombudsman's Act forbade revealing, publicly, specific information obtained during an investigation: "That such a judge, identity unknown, should be sitting on the bench is intolerable, but what can be done? – Maloney cannot report the case to the Judicial Council, which is the formal agency for reviewing the fitness of judges – he can't even identify the judge to the government because the Act enjoins him to confidentiality." Greer was also worried about another aspect of the Ombudsman's activities. Given the high number of complaints made in the prisons and mental institutions, Maloney had decided upon two major investigations: one in the adult penal system, and one in the juvenile training schools. The Ministry of Correctional Institutions had an open mind about these intrusions, and saw Maloney as taking some pressure off the constantly bad-tempered stew of prison confinement. Greer felt, however, that Maloney should confine himself to dealing with the individual complaints, and avoid making up his own troubles, although, legally, Maloney had the power.

> Unless the Ombudsman's Act or the common law tell him he can't do something, he does it – Maloney, for example, is currently completing a major inquiry into the province's correctional system, the kind of inquiry that is normally done by a commissioner appointed, if the government chooses to do so, under the *Public Inquiries Act*. The Ombudsman's Act clearly doesn't envisage such a function and is geared to individual cases and complaints rather than "class actions." But it doesn't say Maloney can't either, so when he found he was getting literally hundreds of complaints from inmates, he decided to lump them all together into a general inquiry into the correctional system.[2]

Greer was not an enemy of the office, and had some admiration for the imaginative manner in which Maloney used his power, but he could see that Maloney might be going too far: "the Legislature may never have intended it, but there's a cat in the henhouse of government and the barnyard will never be the same again."

Despite the concern about expense, and extra-jurisdictional intrusion, Maloney was determined to go his own way, in his own manner, and he may still have felt able to do so as late as the autumn of 1977. There was a rumour around at that time that he might not have to put up with such criticism for much longer. At the September conference of legislative ombudsmen, the question of a federal ombudsman was considered – the rumours naturally included the possibility of Maloney moving to a higher place. Arthur, if not deeming himself the man for the job, had suggested that the Dominion government should have such a position, and two senior federal civil servants were sent abroad to look at ombudsmen in foreign lands. *The Bancroft Times* knew where this might lead.

> Will the next step from the Hill be to lure our ombudsman to a federal post? There is a good and sufficient reason for such alarm. Two and one half years ago when Arthur Maloney, one of Canada's top defence attorneys, accepted the mandate from the province to become its first ombudsman, in no way could the tremendous impact of his humanitarian investigations into government bureaucracy on behalf of the "little man" be envisioned. Now, this compassionate forum has achieved growing respect, not only from all parts of the jurisdiction over which he has control, but across the nation ... the people know, now, they have a champion at Queen's Park. But they are beginning to wonder, in the light of the Prime Minister's interest in the office, for how long this man of understanding will remain in the provincial jurisdiction.[3]

It was one of the few unqualified compliments that Maloney was to receive in the next few months, and it came from a newspaper in his home area, so it has to be taken with some scepticism. Nothing, incidentally, came of the federal investigation, although some suspect that Maloney's increasingly bitter battles may have caused Ottawa to back away. The inclination to inflate the numbers and the expense led to the damaging conclusion that if Maloney wanted to prove his effectiveness by quantity, he ought to produce more results specifically within the ambit of his authority. After all, the office was costing a lot of money. The numbers started to fly in the press – it was noted that Quebec ran an ombudsman on $743,000 a year with a staff of only thirty-one. Maloney had a staff of 122, and his budget for 1976–77 was $2,809,000, and he asked for a further $633,000 in the autumn.

It was suggested that Maloney and his staff were holding too many public meetings, and running up travelling expenses which were contrary to the way the rest of the government was economizing. The fact that the supplementary request of the autumn, 1977, asked for four more full-time workers, and a further $67,000 for additional office space did not help. Nor did the $169,000 that he wanted for supplementary professional services, which included extra-mural legal advice, medical experts, psychiatric consultants, and miscellaneous experts. The Board of Internal Economy was not happy, although it allowed a substantial addition to his budget as a result of his autumn request. It was noticed, however, that some expenses might be cut – the Swedish ombudsman made do with an annual report of four to five pages. Maloney had 647 in his first report, and went to 804 in the second. An already-sceptical press was aware that all was not well by the late months of 1977.

The Toronto Daily Star, in a 2 December 1977 editorial, made the matter apparent in its headline: "Maloney is losing his friends." In part, they saw it as a problem of how Arthur responded to adverse comment. "Maloney dismisses criticism of his expensively furnished office, specially made china and embossed stationary with an airy, 'The office of the ombudsman belongs to all the people of Ontario. The people would not like their ombudsman to have to do without, or operate in bargain-basement fashion.'" If that was exactly how Maloney put it, it was badly done. He might have taken the chance to say, once again, that his office was, in the main, furnished with his own possessions. The idea of the people – some adoring mob – being upset if their ombudsman was housed frugally was inept, smacking of populist arrogance that has echoes of some tin-pot dictator. The *Star*, however, was not looking for a fight. "Maloney is doing an important job. He and his staff are sympathetic and polite to the people who flock to his office. His investigations are thorough and his recommendations usually sound." But the paper worried about his testiness. They admitted that other ombudsmen had been defeated by too much deference to the governments that had invented them, but there was a difference between rigorous independence and self-destruction. The government had made the office – they might well choose to unmake it. "Maloney in parading his trappings is enraging members of all parties and tempting them to shoot him down. The result would be tragic – not to Maloney who could always return to his law practice – but to the hundreds of people who suffer some wrong at the hands of the provincial officials and have nowhere to turn except the ombudsman." It was the best advice that he ever received from the press. By the time of the Second Annual Report (25 November 1977), covering the work between July 1976 and March 1977, the office was fighting on all fronts. Public demand had not decreased, Pickering was still going on, some legislators were upset, and some government organizations were refusing to recognize the Ombudsman's right to investigate complaints. The Select Committee was up and running, and was intent on becoming his master. Despite this, the Second Report displayed an office still eagerly pursuing the public interest, with numbers high in all areas of complaint, including those in which the office had no jurisdiction. Maloney again called for power over municipal police forces, hospitals, universities, children's aid societies, and boards of education. In response to the somewhat hectoring tone of the report, the mildest criticism consisted of pleas to Maloney to take it easy, to quit asking for more money and power. At the other end there were howls of indignation at his extravagance, arrogance, and administrative inabilities.

The office furnishing scandal was always small potatoes (although it is the one best remembered years later), particularly when Arthur's own contributions were taken into consideration (which usually was not the case). There were also complaints about automobiles and chauffeurs. There were certainly cars, but they were not expensive models, and there was considerable need for them in an office that was sending investigators out in dozens to view evidence firsthand throughout the province. On the matter of the "chauffeur-driven" vehicles (a common way in which the cars were described in the newspapers), there never was a chauffeur in the proper sense of the word. Maloney rarely drove himself anywhere – in large part because he generally travelled with at least one member of his senior staff, and they would do the driving. Only Arthur ever had a driver, so designated, and that was not always the case. When he did, it was usually a law student, paid a basic wage, who also acted as an aide and researcher when he wasn't driving. It was not a matter of someone in livery, idly dusting the hood ornament while Arthur was performing. In December 1977, the *Sunday Star* did a piece on the office, and found that there were eleven cars owned outright by the office. The average price of the cars was $7000, and what seemed alarming was the fact that "two are air-conditioned and luxury-equipped with radios, digital clocks, fancy trim – all things that strict rules in all government offices forbid." Six other cars were being leased at the time. "Six cars are used by senior staff for unlimited personal use. The gas is charged to the office."[4] The intent was obvious: the cars were lavish objects, being misused, although the paper presented no evidence that such was the case. Nor did it acknowledge the fact that most of the staff, and especially the senior group, were always on call, and did not expect to keep regular hours or to know from minute to minute where they might be sent. Stephen Lewis, the former NDP politician, was the only sensible voice on a page of blatant exaggeration. "And yes, he asks for a lot of money. But the public purse could hardly make a better investment. Here's a man, with a staff of 125, potentially facing the entire bureaucracy of the government of Ontario. He does it with a budget less than we spent last year on municipal road subsidies for the counties of Middlesex and Wellington!"

Maloney did not entirely ignore the attacks. Somehow the office ashtrays got into the public domain, and he wanted to know how serious the matter was, so Alice Murray went on the hunt. "I obtained the following information and passed it on to John Dysart of *CBC – 24 Hours*: We had 24 ashtrays made by Ryerson Avenue Pottery of Toronto – arranged by Harry Gower of Government Services, interior Design [*sic*] at a unit cost of approximately $8.00 each. John Dysart agreed that this was a very reasonable price for such a good-looking ashtray."[5]

It was the press manipulation of this kind of irrelevant chattel that helped to ruin any chance for Maloney to be remembered fairly. Arthur's simple idea of instant credibility based upon the restrained richness of Bay Street legal decor, could be easily reduced to silliness. It may have been a mistake on Arthur's part to think that such money-is-no-object conduct would show that his office was different – a confirmation of the Ombudsman's distance from the restraint and cheese-paring of ordinary civil service practice. But it was not Arthur at the trough. What he had not anticipated was a handful of newspaper reporters of "small and envious mind" (as Evelyn Waugh would have put it) who would fasten on, in conjunction with a few MPPs who were equally inclined to envy. Patrick Reid, a Liberal MPP, who carried on a long-running fight with the office since he suspected that its visits to his constituency were being used to support a Progressive Conservative candidate, put it candidly in a *Star* interview on 11 December:

"Certainly I am jealous," says MPP Patrick Reid, discussing the flow of frills and luxury through the ombudsman's office. He sits behind his cluttered institutional desk, in his regulation drab office. [As always the furniture comes up.] Not only don't most MPPs have sofas, they also don't have enough store space. So files and papers are crammed into cardboard cartons or stacked on chairs. Icy breezes blow across desks from ill-fitting windows.

"As an MPP, when I travel I get off the plane and hope that maybe a friend will pick me up. I put an ad in the paper telling people I'll be there. I have no advance man," says Reid. "And if I have a wine and lobster dinner, it comes right out of my own pocket."

Maloney is still remembered as the big spender. "$16,000 a day to solve 7 Cases" was a *Star* headline on 11 December 1977. This kind of creative accounting was first essayed by the Conservative MPP, Larry Grossman when the battle was joined with the Select Committee in earnest in March of '77. On David Shatsky's radio show *Metro Morning*, on CBC, 15 March 1977, Grossman coarsely juggled the figures.

Well, Mr Maloney keeps telling everyone that in his first year of operation, his office opened 3,700 files. What he doesn't tell everyone is that only 900 of them were within his jurisdiction. And those 900 cases cost the taxpayers $2.8 million dollars. That's $3,000 a case – that's nine cases for every employee he has. He has 125 employees. That isn't money working well. And of those 900 that were within his jurisdiction I can tell you a lot of them were complaints by inmates that their eggs weren't cooked well at breakfast. I just don't think those are the – let me put it another way. There's maybe a dozen or two that are of true Ombudsman variety – What is the value of it? And is it actually happening? Deal with it on the merits of what is in fact happening in the office. Don't just keep piling bureaucracy on bureaucracy – cars and drivers and fancy stationary – the whole works – and pretend that you're doing – you know – 4,000 cases a year.

It was true that there were silly complaints, many of them coming from the penal institutions, but silly or not, the office was obliged to investigate them with care, and as soon as it was clear that the complaint was frivolous, it was abandoned. With the extra-jurisdictional cases, the matter was less easy of despatch – care had to be taken to send the complainants on their way to the proper remedy. It wasn't a matter of simplistic long-division as was claimed, but there was no chance for sensible rebuttal on the morning talk show.

The Ombudsman knew that they were heading for a public relations defeat, and internal memos indicate that concern, but little idea of how to solve the problem. Maloney continued to insists that his expenses were legitimate, and the "show" of the office an external proof of its power. His intimate group of young (and sometimes irritatingly self-righteous) lawyers, knowing that they were working night and day, were outraged by what they saw as political intrusion by the Select Committee, delay by the civil servants, and misrepresentation by the press.

When the Board of Internal Economy suggested that Maloney cut down on the constant travelling, he refused their advice, and the newspapers, who had learned from Grossman how to play the numbers game, made mincemeat out of the travellers:

In order to publicize hearings around Ontario, front man Cavanagh spends more money travelling than does Premier Davis ... Four interviewers then moved on to Arnprior where they heard 22 complaints, 13 of which were within their auspices to investigate. The other four went to Hawkesbury to hear 13 complaints, five of which they could take on under the Ombudsman's Act. Similarly, the ombudsman sent 12 people to Windsor by plane where they rented four cars to go to the same places together. They heard 75 problems in Windsor (6 and a half per person), 18 in Wallaceburg, and 44 in Sarnia.[6]

All of this tricky long-division might have been explained by the Ombudsman, who, after all, had a trained media man in Ken Cavanagh.

Yet the office seemed unable to get into the public consciousness the fact that they had no control over how many complainants turned up, and when they did, even if jurisdictionally illiterate, they still had to be dealt with. Nor were these visits simply an attempt to find people in immediate trouble – they were to instruct the public on what the office had to offer, not simply on the moment, but in the long run. However, as J. Earl McEwen, the maverick Kingston MPP put it, if the public didn't know about the Ombudsman already, they would never know. McEwen carried on a private war with the Ombudsman from early on as a result of a misunderstanding about who should get credit for straightening out a Workman's Compensation problem for one of his constituents, which McEwen had started and which the Ombudsman was asked to expedite. McEwen chose to believe that the Ombudsman was trying to steal his laurels, but it is well to remember that McEwen had a reputation for flogging dead horses if there was an ounce of publicity in it for him. He was one of the oddest characters in the House, beginning as a Grit MPP, and ending up, in the early eighties, as a Tory.

On the travel matter, Maloney finally blinked, and cancelled a December 1977 trip to Sault Ste. Marie. Glenn Hainey, Phil Patterson, James Stewart, Gilles Morin, Bruce Churchill-Smith (the infamous Maloney driver), and Gary Speranzini paid their own way (about $300 each) to fulfil the visit: "'We're doing it because we really believe in the work of the Ombudsman's office and because we promised the people in the North we would be here.' Hainey said, 'We couldn't let them down.'"[7] But this sentimental siege mentality was part of the problem, aggravating the feeling that everyone was against them, and it was this sense of being unappreciated and hounded that was to lead, in part, in the early months of 1978, to Maloney beginning to work on his resignation, years before his contract expired. The arrival of Eric Murray, the vagabond sceptic, was helpful, but by then, in mid-1978, it was too late – Arthur was already packing.

Aside from the fact that Hoy kept coming back to it, other columnists worried about it continually. It even came into the hands of Gary Lautens, the humour writer for the *Star*. Lautens rarely got involved in politics, tending to be a genial, benign commentator on the follies of Ontario society, but he had a very long life as a columnist, in part because he had an instinctive sense of what interested provincial readers. His column of 14 December 1977 mocked the problem, but also spoke part of the truth of the matter as some saw it: "We need an ombudsman's ombudsman's ombudsman. The only flaw in my plan, as I see it, might come from complaints by politicians, taxpayers and the media on how the second ombudsman is conducting his office. In that event, it might be necessary to appoint a third ombudsman to watch the second ombudsman, who is overseeing the first ombudsman." Lautens may have been only trying to make the taxpayers laugh at another example of the fatuity of human beings, but there was some truth in what he said. He might, however, have thought of doing a second column, investigating the idea of an ombudsman's ombudsman, not for the purpose of watching the ombudsman, but for the ombudsman to complain to about the way the bureaucracy was thwarting him.

The running fight with the newspapers, however, was only an occasional irritant. Hoy might be persistent, but he tended to be repetitive and had nothing very new to say as time went on. Given the reputation of the *Sun* as excessively inclined to the intellectual subtlety of a shot gun at long range, and Hoy's own history of always taking the low road in his nagging, the attack from that direction could be rationalized as amusing to read on the rocking subway in rush hour, but not to be taken seriously.

The real skirmishes, which by the spring of 1977 went on continually, were not so easy to put aside, and increasingly occupied the staff. Even that imbalance might have been borne for a short time had not the matter become serious – the tail started to wag the dog as the Select Committee insisted not only on barking, but on being in charge of which way the animal went.

15

The Monster in the Committee Room and Kitty Bar the Door

The Select Committee is presumed to have been the last straw in the battle that prompted Maloney's withdrawal from office in 1978, and is often seen as a stroke of bad luck occasioned by Pickering. The truth is somewhat different. The idea of a permanent committee had been mooted as early as late autumn 1975. Section 16 of the Act allowed for the possibility that the Legislature might give the Ombudsman further instructions on how he was to conduct his office:

(1) The Assembly may make general rules for the guidance of the Ombudsman in the exercise of his functions under this Act.

On 29 October 1975, McMurtry proposed the setting up of a Committee of the Legislature to consider the Ombudsman's powers. Vernon Singer was to be its chairman, and Patrick Reid (Liberal), Patrick Lawlor (NDP), and four Conservatives, William Hodgson, Keith Norton, Larry Grossman, and James Renwick were its members. They were limited to setting out "general rules and guidelines for the guidance of the Ombudsman and to provide formal recommendations to the Legislature thereon." They were to make their recommendations to the Legislature before 1 December 1975. It did not seem a problem if the legislators were handled with care, and care was obviously to be taken, since some of the group immediately launched into complaints about the Ombudsman. Patrick Lawlor felt that it was too soon to be making specific recommendations, and William Hodgson thought that the Committee had too little time to spend any of it on detail. Larry Grossman, however, felt that something should be offered as advice – some rules cobbled together on the spot: "he thought that if any recommendations were to be made they should be made now rather than after some abuse had manifested itself."[1] The Committee met three times, and on 13 November, Arthur attended, to convince them that the least said the better.

Our office is still in an evolving stage and while we are trying to cope with these problems as they arise we do not yet even have a clear picture as to what all the problems will be. For these reasons, it is my position that this Committee ought not to act prematurely and make regulations which, although appearing appropriate at this point in time, might unduly hinder a subsequent Ombudsman, and wait until the areas requiring a regulatory framework are clearly apparent.

He made an error, however, in suggesting that a permanent committee might not be a problem for him. True, in his travels he had only come across one such group – in England, and he could be forgiven for not being unduly concerned, since it confined itself to examining "the Reports of the Parliamentary Commission for Administration [the English version of the ombudsman] which are laid before the House and matters in connection therewith ... who will highlight the recommendations and criticisms contained in his Reports and then call before them representatives of the various ministries, whether senior civil servants or ministers themselves, to ascertain the action taken as a result of the Parliamentary Commissioner's recommendations ... This is a concept to which I am giving very serious consideration of drawing up in my blueprint."[2] He seemed to think that he was going to be responsible for fashioning the Committee. After all, Maloney and his staff were the experts. They had done the research, taken the trips to the various jurisdictions. Maloney might have been wise to stress the fact that only one country felt the need for standing committee presence.

On 11 December 1975, the Committee reported back to the Legislature. The more sympathetic voices had their way, agreeing that it was too early to "define or recommend general rules for the guidance of the Ombudsman in the exercise of his function," but they clearly wanted a committee. Someone had to deal with the reports, and facilitate the recommendations of the office – it would probably be all right.

When the real thing did come along on 15 July 1976, it was supposed to be just that – a help, not a hindrance, born out of the Pickering stalemate. Maloney was determined to get the report into the Legislature, to pick up support in his dealings with Davis and Rhodes.

The discussions with the Premier were at that time proceeding well. However, the Ombudsman did not want to forfeit the opportunity of reporting to the Assembly while it was briefly in session and thus necessitating a delay of some months before his Report could be brought to the Legislature in the event the talks between himself and the Premier broke down.

> Accordingly, the Ombudsman agreed with the Premier that a Select Committee of the Legislature representing all political parties in the proportions they are represented in the Legislature should be appointed to consider the Report and recommendation if they did not reach agreement in the matter.[3]

It would not be the last time that Davis worked his ways of political sleight-of-hand on Maloney. Both Davis and Maloney were lawyers; Davis may well have played on Maloney's natural presumption that pound for pound, the Premier was a journeyman at the law in comparison with his celebrated Ombudsman, and therefore Maloney would assume that he had nothing to fear from Davis's amateur attempts to get the better of him. He seemed to think that he could use the Legislature to make Davis do his bidding in North Pickering, and that this new committee was his instrument of choice for putting Davis in his place. Both men ought to have known better – one of them did.

Whenever Maloney had occasion to speak of the Select Committee's history, he always put its appointment into the context of North Pickering. But the natural dynamics of committees have always shown the inclination to expand and absorb power, and one of the first things that the Ombudsman's supposed group of tame legislators did was to get themselves a good lawyer, John Bell of the Shibley, McCutcheon firm, and Bell set about putting the committee in shape, providing it with a methodology to deal with the flow of material that it was to feed on from the Ombudsman's office. Bell did a splendid job, according to his and their lights, in making the committee more than simply a way station in getting the recommendations of the Ombudsman implemented by the Legislature.

If the early days were spent in seemingly innocent attempts to help Maloney and Rhodes get out of the half-Nelson that they had got themselves entangled in (with Sopinka's help), the committee and Bell were busily at five-finger exercises in turning themselves into combatants in their own right. On 16 December 1976, the terms of reference were extended from time-to-time review of Ombudsman reports to a much headier power: "To formulate general rules for the guidance of the Ombudsman in the exercise of his functions under the Act." Relations by this time had become mildly testy, and relations were not helped when James Renwick, the new Chairman, sent a letter out to members of the Legislature, on the 22 December, asking them for opinions on the Ombudsman's work. "It is our hope that you will be frank in your comments, whether favourable or unfavourable."

Most of the legislators couldn't give a toss, and failed to answer the letter. Somewhat surprisingly, given the old Valley loyalties, Paul J.

Yakabuski, the Renfrew South Member, delivered a turgid, aimless lament: "I have thrown the above together very quickly and I must confess that I have not spent the kind of time on this matter that it warrants, but I did want to make the above observations known to you and your Committee." In the hapless style of the common legislator he tried to express his disquiet. The office was too large, some of the staff went too far and too fast (although no specific problems were listed, and only one staff member, Ellen Adams, was named – without stating what she had done wrong, although her former zealous connection with the NDP had made her suspect from the outset), and some of the work could have been done by lawyers or MPPs themselves. Yakabuski seemed unable to remember that the office was instituted by the government because no one – Member or not – was doing anything. The cogency of his thought may be best illustrated by his lame conclusion: "The Pickering affair would make one wonder whether the Ombudsman or the Government should be the one to make certain and final decisions." Whatever that meant, it was consistent with the rest of a letter that revealed a mind not entirely at home with clear argument. Arthur might have been wise to ignore it, but the Committee seized upon it, since they only had two further complaints. One from J. Earl McEwen who had decided that the Ombudsman would be his limpet-eel target for the session (but no one took J. Earl seriously), and another, which, in fact, did not come out of the Chairman's trawl of the House at all, but was being pursued independently by Pat Reid about the Ombudsman politicking in his riding. Neither of these complaints was particularly serious, and all three were flawed in one way or another.

Just how determined the Chairman was to have a run at Maloney was revealed immediately. Reid's complaint had never been formally made to the Committee. It had already been investigated, and Maloney was involved in apologizing to Reid and the Premier for any misunderstanding that might have occurred as a result of a staffer appearing, innocently, on two TV programmes with a Progressive Conservative candidate in Reid's riding. It, in fact, had nothing to do with the Chairman's request for comment, and Arthur was not going to discuss it with the Committee. Reid, who was tenaciously trying to make as much noise as he could, was not unhappy to be included in the Commission's investigation. It was not a matter of Maloney trying to keep things quiet. He had informed Renwick about Reid's complaint, and that he was dealing with it personally. His memorandum of 2 March 1977, sets out his thinking on the matter:

I had a conversation with Jim Renwick about this about 6 o'clock tonight concerning the suggestion that Ken Cavanagh, Gary Speranzini and I should appear before the Select Committee to deal with the complaint by Pat Reid, M.P.P. about Gary Speranzini's TV appearance in northern Ontario on a programme that was apparently hosted by the conservative candidate, his political opponent.

I told Jim that the terms of reference of the Select Committee empowered it to deal with my reports and also to draw up rules and guide-lines for my guidance as Ombudsman. This was the limit of his authority. I explained to him that I was of the view that where a complaint was made by an M.P.P. against the Ombudsman or someone on the Ombudsman's staff, the Select Committee was not the proper forum to deal with it; that it had no jurisdiction to deal with it. Such a complaint should be referred to the Committee of Privileges and Elections (I subsequently learned that this was called the Committee of Procedures). I told him I had the matter under investigation and that my investigation would not be completed before March 14th. When it was completed I would send a report to Mr. Speaker. With the permission of Mr. Speaker I would send a copy to the Committee as well. Jim was of the view that the matter was not to be dealt with this formally and he intended to go ahead on the 14th to deal with the Reid complaint. I then explained to Jim that it was not my intention to participate in any discussion with the Select Committee nor would I permit any of my staff to do so. While I would attend on the 14th of March to discuss the complaints of Mr. Yakabuski and McEwen I would withdraw when the discussion of the Reid complaint commenced.

I said the reason I would agree to participate in the discussion of Yakabuski and McEwen was because they wrote in response to the original letter of invitation sent out by Mr. Renwick to all members of the Legislature in December. I reminded him that I was not consulted about the letter and I would have suggested certain changes in the format. I told him that the Reid letter was in a completely different category.

The Reid matter did come up, and Maloney did walk out. The battle that preceded it made the television news on the evening of 14 March 1977. It was not a fortunate moment for the Ombudsman, not because he was in the wrong, but because it was manipulated to be seen as a show of arrogance, and it is one of the incidents that is well remembered by those who denigrate his work as Ombudsman. It ought to be taken in the context of the Renwick memo, since the Chairman knew that Maloney intended to withdraw if the matter was pursued. It was interpreted as a spur-of-the-moment insult; in fact, it wasn't an act of spontaneous *hauteur*, but a planned response – Maloney's staff knew it might happen – and so did the Committee.

Unfortunately, the grand exit was also read in conjunction with a preceding confrontation between Maloney and Paul Yakabuski. The legislator was no match for Arthur, and the latter was able to brush aside Yakabuski's wooly maunderings. What he ought not to have done, however, was use all his oratorical skills on the poor fellow. It was considered particularly unfair of him to break a butterfly upon the wheel by proclaiming that while Renfrew South had a population of only 7.9 percent of the Ontario citizens, the number of complaints received by the Ombudsman's office was 16.3 percent of the total. "Granted the bare figures do not indicate whether any of the seventy-two individuals had tried to resolve their problems by seeking legal counsel or the assistance of their elected Member, but whatever their own reasons were, they thought it necessary to approach the Ombudsman for assistance." It was the kind of aside that might have been appropriate in the flyting of an acrimonious trial, and there was good reason for Arthur to be incensed by these feckless trivialities, but it was unworthy of him as the champion of the little man to beat Yakabuski into the ground like a tent peg. It is possible, however to understand, in part, why Maloney went at Yakubuski so strongly; they were both Ottawa Valley Conservatives. Arthur may not have ever run back home, but he always considered himself part of that gang, and had often taken part in the politics of the region through the years. What Yakabuski had done was, in Arthur's mind, more than a simple political act – it was a family betrayal. Yakabuski would have known that, but the public did not, and the subsequent sweep of Arthur and his associates from the Committee room, did him no good. He had won the argument, but it fed the claims that he was becoming a bully.

Grossman, who had been circling Arthur ominously, weighed in with complaint about how Arthur had used statistics unfairly to rebuff Yakabuski – which was pretty rich, given the way in which Grossman went into arithmetic contortions over the Ombudsman financial figures in his CBC attack. He went further, claiming that there was a general feeling that Maloney was not to be criticized, and that there was a pervadingly peevish air about him that made it difficult for the individual MPP to chastise him, since he might take offence and resign. There was never any real evidence that such was the case, and it must be remembered that Grossman was preparing for his run to a higher place. Certainly his attempts to prove that Maloney was not doing the job were very cute, but hardly possessed any serious particularity. However, Maloney may have won the day intellectually, and an internal memo, written after the television film had been viewed by several staff members, suggested that Arthur had done well, but it was the kind of half-truth that campaign workers use to buck up a candidate who has made a mistake. What Arthur saw, quite legitimately, as an attempt by the Committee to grab power had been skewed about to look like a battle between a weak, muddled legislator, just trying to do his job, and the grandeur of political *noli me tangere*. And he had done most of the damage by himself. It was an odd thing to happen to him, given his intuitive talent for reading public response, which was a part of his reputation in the court room. But he could be imperious if angered, particularly if he felt that he was in the right, and fighting for principle. It was, perhaps a matter of inexperience of a peculiar kind – in his courtroom work, much of the hard, tough talk would take place with the jury out of the room – just the judge, and opposing counsel to deal with – in this case, he seems to have forgotten that the public was watching – in the unblinking presence of the television eye. He should have been aware of the fact that he wasn't simply putting his opponents in their proper place, but that the unsophisticated, uninformed public was also watching – and that he had to take that into consideration – that was a new thing for Arthur, and he had to learn the hard way. An old St. Mike's man ought to have known Marshall McLuhan's warnings about some forms of oratory being too hot for the new medium, and Arthur was hot! What was most damaging was the fact that it was such a *bravura* performance that it could hardly be resisted as good copy for the hungry eye of television programming.

By the time of this confrontation, neither the Committee nor the Ombudsman had much illusion about their relationship. Maloney saw the Committee's attempt to discuss the Reid affair not only as an invalid intrusion, but an attempt to take an active role in the process of decision making, which was solely the right of his office under the provisions that existed at the time. A further bit of bad luck for the Ombudsman was the appointment of John Bell, who possessed the legal knowledge and the determination to give the Committee the power they wanted, and who was, as often as not, more than simply counsel. As one of the Ombudsman staff put it, "The committee was easily led. Some were more committed to getting their way than others. They relied a great deal on John Bell ... It became fairly routine to battle with the committee." Phil Patterson, who often had the dirty job of dealing with the Committee, saw the relation going wrong from the beginning:

> We would have absolute dog fights. Arthur, after things went bad, would very rarely attend personally ... Some of us thought the members of the Select Committee were using the Committee to show off their political powers. Every time I went up to the Committee, they would criticize what I investigated and how I did it. In a way, we were on the wrong foot from the beginning. The Select Committee saw their business to oversee not only his expenditures, but what he investigated and how he investigated it.[4]

It was Arthur's contention that the powers given them to formulate general rules did not give them the right to review the affairs of the Ombudsman's office. Their review powers were still confined to the

Ombudsman's reports. As one of his internal memos stated: "Other than problems of procedure, which affect the performance of the function of the Office, the Committee has no jurisdiction to make rules pertaining to the day to day operations of the Office." The Reid affair was exactly the kind of thing they were not to do. "I know of no other legislative Ombudsman where the political arm of the Legislature has attempted to assert a right to exercise the kind of control over the operation of the Ombudsman's office that your involvement in the Reid complaint would entail."[5]

The battle settled down eventually to five subjects: (1) the Committee continued to ask for more specific powers from the Legislature, (2) they continued to attempt to intrude into areas of investigation, such as the Reid affair, (3) the Ombudsman officers were treated in an bellicose and suspicious manner when appearing before the Committee, (4) the annual reports were treated with increasing rigour, and (5) the recommendations of the Ombudsman for improvement, as he saw it, in the service, were sharply criticized. "It is submitted that counsel's line of questioning develops an 'adversarial atmosphere' and is somewhat intimidating to the staff who appear on behalf of the Ombudsman ... One is left with the distinct impression that Counsel to the Committee controls the proceedings and that the Ombudsman's office is on trial. It is as if there is an onus of proof that the Ombudsman's Office must satisfy before the Committee will support a recommendation of the Ombudsman."[6]

Rejections of the Ombudsman's recommendations were rare – in the first three years of operation, less than thirty recommendations sent to the government were rejected, but there was no question that the Select Committee made the Ombudsman work to satisfy them. (Interestingly enough, given the length of time passed, the Select Committee and the Ombudsman are still battling in the early nineties, and the quarrel is still over contending powers.) How much personal ambition had to do with the breakdown of the relation is difficult to assess. Certainly the Committee went the way of most committees in attempting to draw more power to itself, and into attempting to give itself a dignity and authority which it did not, originally, possess. Minutes of its meetings show a determination to find some way to get beyond the Ombudsman into the public domain, where it could speak directly to the public on the matter of Ombudsman failings. On occasion, the committee was confused, and confusing, and in the long run, it got years behind in its reports. Its chairmen often complained in Hansard, when it brought its reports to the Legislature, that no-one was in attendance, since the natural inclination of the legislators was to display considerable lack of interest in the battle between Maloney and the Committee. On 5 June

1978, M.N. Davidson, speaking for the Committee on the matter of their fourth report, asserted that, "It's unfortunate that the government House Leader is not in the chamber to respond to this recommendation, as it is a very important recommendation, and I would hope that someone on the benches opposite would be in a position to make some comment today on it." (Ontario *Hansard*, No. 78, p. 3152) On 27 November 1978, Mr. Lawlor peevishly tried to rouse some curiosity among the legislators.

> The consuming lack of interest in the report of the Select Committee on the Ombudsman consumes me ... considering the amount of both plaudits and resentment that this particular office has aroused over the last period of time, I would have thought that particularly the snipers would have shown up in abundance simply to unload their shotguns and what do we have? We have a peaceful little gathering, basically composed of members of the Select Committee ... As far as the Cabinet is concerned, either they are indifferent or their refusal to appear here tonight casts some aspersions and a dim light upon the work of this Committee and upon the Ombudsman's office as such. That is a renegade gesture on the part of the Cabinet Ministers who might have appeared.

Why the legislators' lack of interest should be read as casting aspersion on the Ombudsman's office is an example of the way the Committee thrashed about, attempting to draw the Ombudsman into what was, in fact, the Committee's problem. What Lawlor means by the last sentence is confusing, unless he is suggesting that the Cabinet is attempting to tell the committee by their absence that they simply do not want to know, and have had quite enough of the Committee. At this time, Maloney had just left office, but the ambitions of the Committee had not ceased, and they found the lack of interest in the House insulting. There never was, in fact, any serious, organized dissatisfaction with Maloney in the Legislature, although individuals such as Grossman and McEwen claimed otherwise. Renwick's failure to collect more than two letters in his December 1976 trawl was significant, particularly given the fact that Yakabuski had no specific point to make, and McEwen's complaint was trivial and consistent with his reputation as an eccentric troublemaker. But the Committee was determined to catch someone's eye; one of its reports was surrounded by a black border, as an expression of dissatisfaction with the powers it had to curb Maloney.

Maloney was determined to protect the office and its rights and he was not flexible, even on matters of little importance, if there was the slightest chance that in being so the sacrosanct powers of the office would be impinged. A more cunning politician (a Davis, for instance) might have disarmed them with modest praise, and the Maloney of old, the Maloney of politics long past, could have done it without effort. The older, assailed man, trying to complete his dream of the perfect public office dedicated to the protection of the common citizen, surrounded by problems, numbers, budgets, critics, constant importunings, legitimate and otherwise, had less coating on his nerves, less space to think the matter through, and constant combative advice from his young, idealistic staff, urging him to fight back. He took to disdain – when a bit of his old Valley charm might have been a better weapon.

The Committee never let up in its determination to get the Ombudsman under control. In its third Report, there was a slyly worded paragraph that suggested more dependence on the Committee than the Ombudsman would acknowledge, or in fact, ever allowed: "Because of the newness of the Office and the policies adopted by the incumbent Ombudsman with respect to his functions, it has been the source of confusion and misunderstanding. The Ombudsman has himself sought the advice and assistance of the Committee in matters wherein he and his staff have had no previous insight and experience." One internal memo from Brian Goodman, one of the liveliest and most confident of Arthur's aides, put that quotation in its place:

> These remarks are presumptuous. After all, the Select Committee only came into existence as a result of the impasse in the Pickering matter. Only two members of the original Committee (the past and present Chairmen) continue to serve, the counsel still being John Bell. However, the second sentence quoted implies that the Committee *does* have insight and experience which we lack and further that we have sought the advice and assistance of the Committee in respect to these matters. I can not recall a single instance of us having done this.[7]

The Committee went so far as to emulate Maloney's trip abroad to visit other ombudsman offices, and they came back convinced that they now knew better than the Ombudsman, and that a little more respect from him would solve their problems. P.D. Lawlor (NDP) claimed that the *Globe*, which had recently suggested that the battling was a healthy sign of the Ombudsman doing his job, and Maloney had got it all wrong. "I say to them they wholly misunderstand the function. That is not the way the Ombudsman operates in Sweden ... The greatest care and delicacy are exercised on both sides ... The Ombudsman on his side – and in Denmark and in every other jurisdiction – goes about his job with tact, diplomacy and a sense of the rather thin-skinned, if you will, position of people in elected office."[8] But there was considerable dubiety and some hilarity in and out of the Ombudsman's office on the question of whether the Committee members had learned anything at all. The press considered the cost of the trip – $63,000 – inordinate. It was one of the few occasions when Maloney and Claire Hoy were on the same side, although Maloney and his office made no public comment on the matter:

> These same honorable members who quite rightly reacted bitterly against the ombudsman's outrageous demands for a 64 per cent budget hike – and still gave him 49 per cent – now have the nerve to announce they plan to slip off to Europe and Israel between Jan. 6 and 28 to study other ombudsman's operations. I'm sure the 10 or so MPP's going on this jaunt to Denmark, will have a marvellous time but, since the ombudsman and many of his staffers have already been on a similar jaunt – and were properly criticized for the expense – one wonders where they get the gall?[9]

The *Star* was also critical, but made their point visually in a cartoon on the editorial page in which a handful of middle-age gents with smug smiles informed a fellow wearing a *pince-nez* (presumably an indication of being a European) that "We're the Ontario Legislature's Select Committee to Study European Ombudsmen. As a European Ombudsman, what can you tell us?" The next frame found the gang glum, in the face of a laconic rebuff: "Go Home. You're wasting the Taxpayers' Money."[10]

The final gesture of frustration was made by Maloney after it was no longer important to him, since he had handed in his resignation. On 29 August 1978, he appeared before the Committee and let fly. Again, it made the newscasts.

> In a brief to the Select Committee, Ontario's Ombudsman claims the Legislative Committee has been an adversary in getting his Office to run smoothly. Arthur Maloney has just over a month to go before his resignation takes effect and he found it hard this morning to keep from sounding bitter as he spoke to the Committee. He says the group formed three years ago to study his Office and ways it might run has been an adversary and has kept the relationship with his office at arms-length. Instead of the many discussions he hoped for with the group, Maloney says there's only been one informal meeting. He also criticized Committee Counsel, John Bell for what he calls "aggressive, impertinent and dictatorial questioning of his staff." He thinks the Committee has moved away from its original purpose and says that if changes are not made, he'll go to the Premier to see what can be done. (Chris Gaynor, CBC, Queen's Park)[11]

There was a further element in Maloney's disillusion which is hardly known of at all, and it, also, contributed to his final withdrawal. In order to combat it, he had to resort to the work of an outside counsel, who was associated with him until the end, and stayed on after Arthur left, to continue to defend the Ombudsman's power. Arthur loved to have his cadre of young students and lawyers provide him with "opinions" on all the aspects of the ombudsman battles. North Pickering and the Select Committee were the subjects of dozens of long essays by his in-house lawyers. However, he sometimes went out to get help from more experienced members of the legal community. One lawyer whom he used was Eric R. Murray, Q.C., a member of the Cassels, Brock firm in the mid-seventies. Murray is still in practice in the nineties, as a senior member of Genest, Murray, Desbrisay, Lamek. He has vivid memories of his work for Arthur in the last months of his time as Ombudsman. Murray, a solid block of a man, glowers with energetic spleen about what was happening to Arthur in 1978. He has a reputation as a mordant wit – a master of the pessimistic aside on the vagaries of humanity with some special interest in its eccentric conduct when it comes into contact with the law. He is the author of a long string of *bon mots* which float around the profession, possessed as he is by a talent for choosing his words carefully without mincing them. He is known to look with undisguised jaundice on the administration of justice, and the re-organization of the judiciary in the early nineties has left him with a perpetual case of legal apoplexy, which he has not been reluctant to express to politicians and legal associates. He is, for all his gloom, a funny man, and his association with Maloney must have been a great knock-about farce, given Maloney's taste for optimism and Murray's sweet tooth for disaster. He looks and acts like a character out of a Smollett novel – a great raconteur of the law, capable of puffing his cigar and talking at the same time, and with an odd kind of lugubrious cheerfulness (since he never expects anything of the rogues anyway), he recalls Maloney's troubles with doomsday relish.

You know, one thing is clear. They appointed Maloney as the first ombudsman, and I suppose they knew they would have their hands full, but not to the extent that he would make life difficult for them. He wasn't quarrelsome, but when he got the bit in his teeth – and that's the point – if he felt that something or someone was being abused – I have a theory that the Conservative party has the most regard for the individual and the individual's rights. And I would think that is what made it attractive to Arthur. He was the best kind of Conservative. He would see somebody being shabbily treated and he wanted the government to step in. And he wouldn't back down. I thought he was the best choice of man to be the Ombudsman, and clearly the best Ombudsman we ever had. Now the public doesn't know who they are. It is now a matter of politics. I once asked Ian Scott why he had made a certain appointment – nothing to do with the

Ombudsman's office – and he said, "Somnolence." That's what they wanted – and didn't get with Maloney.[12]

Murray first shows up on the occasional payroll in early 1978, when he was asked for an opinion on one of the Select Committee problems, but his more intimate relation develops on the drafting of Maloney's resignation, and on the developing problem of government agencies claiming that the Ombudsman's writ did not run to them. This latter problem was to continue for some time after Arthur left, and Murray was to serve as counsel in some of the major cases. During his time, he appeared for the Ombudsman in the trial courts, the Court of Appeal, and the Supreme Court of Canada.

At least, the Minister of Housing co-operated in the investigation of the Pickering case, if proving stubborn over the results. Later, a new kind of game began to be played in which government groups, informed that a complaint had been made against them, refused to allow the Ombudsman access – attempting, in a sense, to nip any meddling in the bud. There was more than one of these cases, which, from a non-professional point of view, may seem to have a disturbing sameness about them. The first and most influential case arose out of an attempt by the Ombudsman to address a complaint against the Health Disciplines Board of Ontario. It started as did some of the others of this stripe while Arthur was still in office, but given the natural delays of the law, it did not come to court until just shortly after he had withdrawn. It was a new wrinkle on how to deter Maloney.

The case resulted from a simple complaint brought by a woman about her treatment in a provincial psychiatric facility. The College of Physicians and Surgeons had rejected her claim. She appealed to the Health Disciplines Board, which confirmed the early decision. Then she turned to the Ombudsman, alleging that relevant evidence had not been considered, and certain other evidence had been acted upon which had not been tested by cross-examination. The Ombudsman moved to examine the complaint, and was informed by the Board that he had no power over them.

On 13 December 1978, Eric Murray appeared before Mr. Justice Labrosse asking for a declaratory order on the matter. The judge had no difficulty in rejecting the Board's claim – it was a government organization, however distanced it was from the government, and was clearly covered by the Act. Despite the bare-faced certainty of the judgment (23 *O.R.* (2d), pp. 485–92), the Board and the Attorney-General (Roy McMurtry's ministry) took it to appeal, where the judgment was upheld, and where the Labrosse statement was accepted without reservation (26 *O.R.* (2d), pp. 105–25).

This new defence of attempting to stop the Ombudsman before he got started was to continue into the eighties. In 1978, and again in 1980, Murray defended the Ombudsman's right to re-open the cases of the landowners of North Pickering who had been marooned in the Donnelly Commission, after the Minister of Housing, and the land agents (represented by John Sopinka) tried to stop the retrieval of these poor lost souls on jurisdictional grounds. The decision was in the Ombudsman's favour at both the High Court (26 *O.R.* (2d), p. 434), and in the Court of Appeal (30 *O.R.* (2d), p. 768). At both levels Murray relied on the *Health Disciplines* case, and Chief Justice Evans made the position obvious: "I consider that the Courts should not approach the powers of the Ombudsman in the same manner as it approaches the powers exercised by the executive branch of Government ... I have been driven to this conclusion by the nature of his function, and the broad discretionary powers to investigate and to report and the freedom granted to the Ombudsman to act on his own motion." (p. 456)

Murray is very proud of the *Health Disciplines* case, and the way it proved so flexible in knocking back the various improvisatory arguments that were cooked up every time the matter came to court. In 1984, the case was to receive recognition at the Supreme Court of Canada in a hearing in which Murray "intervened" on behalf of the Ontario Ombudsman. The judgment was quite explicit:

> Read as a whole, the *Ombudsman Act* of British Columbia provides an efficient procedure through which complaints may be investigated ... It should therefore receive a broad, purposive interpretation consistent with the unique role the Ombudsman is intended to fulfil. There is an abundance of authority to this effect; see particularly, *Re Alberta Ombudsman Act*, supra; *Re Ombudsman of Ontario and Health Disciplines Board of Ontario, et al* ... also see *Re Ombudsman of Ontario and Ministry of Housing of Ontario* (1979).[13]

Despite this kind of decision, the game went on. As late as 1985, the Ontario Labour Relations Board tried to deny the Ombudsman's authority, and on this occasion, given the swings and roundabouts of the law, John Sopinka represented the Ombudsman, and cited Murray's case. Mr. Justice Steele tried to finally settle the matter: "In my opinion, the wording of the Ontario Act is more strongly in favour of the Ontario Ombudsman than the wording of the British Columbia Act with respect to the British Columbia Ombudsman. Far from overruling the decision in the Health Disciplines case, I believe the Supreme Court of Canada reaffirmed it."

Why then did government offices keep doing it over and over again? A question, perhaps, that only the non-legal mind would entertain. Like a mountain, it was there, and they did it because it was there. Or more to the point, they did it because that is what government offices did – thwart any intrusion into their claustral independence. Which brings one full circle to the reason why the Ombudsman was appointed in the first place – to intrude – because the bureaucracy had always done exactly that! It is, if one puts the very best face on it, an example of the peculiar dynamics that develops when politics, government bureaucracy and the law mix, particularly in an atmosphere of frustration and ill-will. From inside the government bastions, it would seem normal that an office should refuse to co-operate, and should make Maloney do everything the hard way, despite the time wasted, the petitioners waiting for a remedy, and the expense of first-class lawyers, judges, and court time. It puts a new light on the complaint that Maloney was extravagant when these acutely expensive legal battles were forced on the office by sundry government agencies, seemingly without concern, despite the fact that the same defeats occurred over and over again in cases that were blinding losers from the start. As Murray remembers it:

> I had a handful of cases where the jurisdiction was objected to, and those people were fit to be tied, and determined that he was not to be able to investigate them. This was a very important test for them. I remember two members of the Health Disciplines Board coming into court. They reminded me of the two old men in the box in the balcony on the "Muppets." They were there to listen to this outrage that anyone would check into the workings of their board! Which was, in fact, the very reason for the creation of the Ombudsman's office – so that if someone was badly treated, they could go to someone for help. That case wound up in the Court of Appeal and eventually we were successful at both levels. But the government agencies attacked again, time and time again, in attempts to erode his jurisdiction.

Asked if he might characterize these efforts as attempts to obstruct the Ombudsman, Murray, warily determined not to go too far, put it this way: "Well, their policy was constantly to try to narrow the Ombudsman's jurisdiction. I never thought of it as a conspiracy; I just thought that whenever someone complained, they would want to run to court and say that Arthur had no jurisdiction to investigate their organization. Those were pretty strong statements made in the judgments in the Court of Appeal, and at the trial level by Mr. Justice Labrosse." Pressed again on the possibility that there was some policy, stated or unstated, to stop Arthur, Murray said,

> I have no evidence of that. What I say is they created this office with great fanfare. They gave him wide powers in the Act. He was empowered to try to fight

wrongs that the ordinary citizen would have a dreadful time getting anywhere on, and as soon as he trod on somebody's toes – Bango! – we have a jurisdictional dispute. You may say on reading the Act that it was perfectly obvious that he had jurisdiction, and I say it was perfectly obvious, but even in the face of the judgments, they still came on again! And they continued to do so after he left. He set the standard for his successors. Just because the government says "no" – that doesn't put an end to the matter. I took some to court, and I was consulted on several others, and often we would get some compromise, but they often kept trying. Frankly, when you had the decision in the *Health Disciplines Board*, where Labrosse, and then Justice Morden at appeal, didn't mince words, they certainly knew they had their work cut out for them, but they would always throw in another twist of the argument. They didn't win one of them that I was involved in, so I don't know if they ever won any of them, but all of these were attempts to save their own little bailiwick from investigation.

Murray never saw Maloney in despair over what was going on, but he had his suspicions: "You know if you can delay and harass, and frustrate – you get to a point of saying, 'How much of this can I take?'"[14]

Roy McMurtry says that there was no antipathy to Maloney in Cabinet during the troubled months; he thinks that the real problem for Arthur lay in the Select Committee. He admits that there was sometimes a bit of world-weary eye rolling when the Ombudsman confrontations came up in conversation among Cabinet Ministers, but he does not remember anyone chiding him for bringing Arthur into the government. Nor is there any evidence of substantial discontent with Maloney in the Legislature; certainly the Select Committee had little luck in their attempts to inflame the Members. On the matter of the piling on of the jurisdictional cases, McMurtry is sceptical of Murray's conclusions, since Murray is well known to have always had a strong anti-governmental attitude. Yet Murray cannot be easily dismissed as some kind of malcontent clown, even if he is a man inclined to say things wittily; he was there at the end, fighting the battle, and he certainly put the government lawyers out of court every time they met, including those who were representing McMurtry's department.

McMurtry certainly does not believe that there was any organized instruction given to anyone to block the Ombudsman at every turn. Yet the accumulation of difficulty, particularly in these jurisdictional fights, in which the outcome was obvious, does have an air of obstruction about it. It was not that there is any evidence that Davis ever told anyone to do anything. McMurtry is probably correct in saying that Davis just put Arthur into office, and presumed he would get on with it. But given the hopes, the expense, and the obvious gifts that Maloney possessed – and the fact that everyone knew there was a problem of governmental cack-handedness at best and downright obstruction at worst that had to be solved – it might be suggested that Davis ought to have done something positive. Those who defend Davis on this point make the perfectly valid argument that it would have been difficult for him to tell Rhodes or any other senior minister what to do, although a general word to the lesser powers that the Ombudsman was to be accommodated when he came knocking on their doors, might have been possible. Yet even the argument that senior Cabinet Ministers would be hard to handle has to be considered in the light of the fact that it was just this kind of conduct that the Act required of the Premier, since if those found wanting would not do as suggested, it was up to the Premier and the Legislature to order them to do so. Rhodes, significantly, knew this, when he stated that if the Premier and the House told him to reimburse the complainants, he would do so. It is of little use to suggest that the Ombudsman's office was intruding in areas that ought to have been dealt with by the Members of the Legislature, and therefore was acting above itself; it was not acting above itself. That was what it was supposed to do. It was not an office invented by Maloney, but by the government, agreed to by all the Members of the House, who recognized that the citizens of Ontario were not being sufficiently well-served when it came to confrontation with the bureaucracy. The mandate that they gave Maloney, and had cooed over with inordinate pleasure as they adopted it, made it clear that the Ombudsman was expected to intrude. It may be the sad truth, but it is not an excuse, to suggest that such is human nature, particularly among politicians, to take back with one hand what they had so publicly and willingly given with the other, particularly when Maloney's reputation has been permanently diminished in the process.

McMurtry is right in suggesting that the fine hand of Davis was nowhere to be seen in the death of a thousand cuts applied to Maloney. Some of these cuts were certainly self-inflicted, but Davis, if he had so chosen, might well have made it known, subtly, that a lot of money and prestige and government reputation for fairness was riding on the Ombudsman doing his job, and that government departments were supposed to co-operate, not obstruct. His refusal, or reluctance, or lack of interest in doing so – in a sense to govern by example rather than by silence (with its implication of not being concerned) – may have been his greatest fault and an early sign of the feckless, loose-ended way in which his government unravelled in the early eighties as he lost concentration. Eric Murray was around the battle long enough to sense the way the atmosphere had thickened into sullen conflict: "They sure would have liked to see him quit; there is no doubt about that. They had a tiger by the tail – somebody who was taking the office really seriously."

Ultimately, however, it was Arthur who brought himself down. He could have stayed on, battling the Select Committee, facing the occasional thin-skinned legislator who felt undone by the Ombudsman services, taking the jurisdictional fights one by one, and winning them, given the power in the Ombudsman Act. Hoy's wailing was losing its point in stale repetition, and there was considerable support in the press from respected journalists who gave an even-handed picture of what he was trying to do. There was no serious movement to be rid of him. He just decided that he did not like it anymore. It was, again, an example of that peculiar aspect of his personality that never allowed the dignity of office to get in the way of his refusal to suffer fools gladly, or hang around for very long in their presence.

16

Running on Empty

Maloney, who resigned officially in the autumn of 1978, began to work on his official resignation statement in March. The first draft shows that he thought of leaving as early as 22 May, but the date was struck, and October was chosen, with the official resignation to go to Davis in early August. As early as January, there were rumours in the hands of the *Sunday Sun* reporter, Gary Dunford. He, unlike Hoy, was sympathetic.

Arthur Maloney, Ontario's much-maligned ombudsman, is on holiday in the sunny south. When he returns, watch for a bombshell: he may be resigning – in style. Nipped for months by the rabid media jackal-pack who've brought you exciting bulletins on his office wallpaper, Maloney's said to feel that, at his age, he doesn't need to stay centre stage, the target of sarcastic sniping. (Much of Maloney's fabled lifestyle – tut-tutted over by his enemies – comes out of his own pocket. Most of those office furnishings – which so impress the reporter corps – were picked out and paid for by Mrs. Maloney.) He'll be returning to private law practice.

Maloney's expected to hang in as two major reports from the ombudsman's office are submitted to the legislature, but resign before his report on the office of the ombudsman is released.

That way, the recommendations he makes may finally escape the usual screams of "Empire building" and the tedious King Arthur epithet.

It's ironic that Maloney apparently feels the air is so poisoned that he can do the office more good out of it than in it.

It's also ironic you should read of his decision to resign here, in the newspaper that dubbed him King Arthur.

There is one final footnote that I have saved for last, because I like it best. Maybe it says something about the style, grace and good humor of the guy that the newspapers haven't told you.

He's musing about announcing his resignation on St. Patrick's Day.

And a tough one to follow.[1]

Claire Hoy was quick to the scent, determined to sour the story, claiming that if the government would give him a job, Maloney would be off. "Word has it that if the government offered him say, a judgeship, Maloney would be out of his crown and into his judges' [*sic*] robes in a flash," Hoy reported in the *Sun* of 26 January 1978. Not satisfied with one cuff if he could get in a flurry of blows, Hoy informed his readers that Maloney was still making $60,000 a year and was "off sunning himself on a tropical isle." Hoy salted it with another idea: "News of this may cause some people to grieve although I can tell you that outside his cadre of loyal staffers – which, myth to the contrary, doesn't include all his staffers – it would cause some more general rejoicing than sadness."

Things went somewhat better for Maloney in February 1978, when the report on the Correctional Services came out, and was accepted by Frank Drea, the Minister, as a fair and helpful comment. The *Globe* was pleased, and saw the report in the larger context of the criminal justice system: "The first textbook for all these bodies should be Mr. Maloney's report." (10 February 1978) The report not only measured the physical limitations of the justice system in a society with a rapidly expanding criminal problem, but it also repeated one of Maloney's long-standing commitments to justice tempered with understanding and mercy. "But the real solution is not to impose so many prison sentences." He calls for a change of emphasis "to decrease the public's reliance on the highly symbolic but discouragingly failure-ridden and costly resort to incarceration either before or after the trial of an accused."[2] It was typical of Maloney to see prison as an empty symbol, hiding the real nature of the problem.

In late February, he asked for $3.3 million, some $89,000 less than he had in the previous year, explaining that the reduction was part of the return to normal expenses as the battle over Pickering settled down. To that moment, $395,000 had be spent on trying to get Pickering straight. He presented his Third Report to the Legislature, and again asked for expanded powers, although he was, at the same time, working on his resignation.

The resignation statement was tinkered with through the spring and early summer. Eric Murray was asked to comment, and he was not impressed. "I do however caution you against too much sop because if you praise everybody in sight, the leaders of the parties, the members of the Legislative Assembly, your staff, the news media, the children of this land, etc., it will become readily apparent that you and Frank Donnelly are the only swine left." Murray knew that he was supposed to add sardonic backbone to this toothless speech, which would present Arthur as a magnanimous man, leaving more in sorrow than anger, but not without some indication that he felt betrayed, without whining about it.

"You must also understand that my proposal is what I consider the extreme position that you can take." To give Arthur a bit of a lesson in how to turn civility upside-down, he ended his letter of 19 July 1978: "With a singular lack of love and affection. Eric Rutherford Murray." Just a little bit of Jonathan Swift at no extra charge. Murray wanted the following comment on the Bennett matter: "The final blow is a letter I have received from the Honourable Claude Bennett, Minister of Housing, date June 13/78, which in effect accuses me of breaking our agreement and advises that the Minister is therefore no longer bound by its terms and can accept or reject the findings of the Hoilett hearings as he sees fit." John Beaufoy, one of the staff, was against it: "Pickering will be seen as the major reason and the Minister's most recent letter will be viewed as the straw which drove you to throw up your hand and quit."[3] As a result, that part of the final resignation letter read less consequentially: "It follows I was much surprised to read early in July on my return from Russia a letter dated June 23rd sent to me by the Minister of Housing – the Honourable Claude Bennett – in which he puts forward the totally unwarranted suggestion that I had breached the agreement entered into by you, me, and his predecessor the Honourable John Rhodes on October 1, 1976."

The whole idea was to get the tone right, and to make points about having been let down without suggesting that Maloney was leaving because of it. "I would be loathe to go as far as Mr. Murray suggests, and suggest that you ensure that in no way do you allow your resignation to appear to be triggered by the Minister's position. You are *not* leaving the Office because of his position – in fact I gather you are leaving in spite of it – and your statement should reflect your confidence that the Government would not renege on its agreement."[4] That was how the final letter read: "I can't think he seriously feels this to be the case nor can I bring myself to believe that your government, when the time comes, will not honour its agreement and keep its word solemnly entered into with the Ombudsman. To do otherwise would be very grave indeed."

On 3 August, he met with the Premier, and the matter was settled. The letter of resignation was simply posturing *pro forma*, which gave him, he thought, the last word. By the evening, the story, on the radio, was fleshed out and was getting some of the comment that Maloney wanted:

Maloney says he wants to return to his law practice but Opposition Leader Stuart Smith feels that the real reasons for his resigning centers on a broken promise and the government's handling of the North Pickering land dealings. *Stuart Smith* – "He discussed it with the Premier at the beginning of August as far as I can make out and in mid-August Mr. Maloney resigns. The man who had intended to serve for 10 years as Ombudsman resigns after less than 3 years. Personally I am very upset by this and I would like an explanation from the Premier and from Mr. Maloney as to why this has happened."[5]

Jonathan Manthorpe, the *Star's* Queen's Park columnist, who had been a cautious and perceptive recorder of Maloney's three-year battle, was not convinced that Maloney was leaving to get back to the law, nor because he suddenly wanted to make some money. He had information from "friends and associates that he is unhappy with the way he has been treated by the select committee on the ombudsman ... One confidant of Maloney's said yesterday he thought the ombudsman would have stayed yet a while were it not for these frustrations." If Manthorpe was cautiously sceptical about why Maloney was leaving, he knew what Maloney had accomplished – sometimes despite and sometimes as a result of his way of doing things. "The qualities for which Maloney has been criticized – the pomposity, the lavish spending, the arrogance, the keen temper – were the qualities that established and gave form to the ombudsman's office. If you couldn't ignore Maloney, you couldn't ignore the ombudsman. Every day that, by some outlandish act, Maloney demanded attention was another day when the office became more deeply rooted in the government process." He was not convinced that it had always been foolish: "People laughed at the adoption of the Gryphon – that mythological righter of wrongs. Just another sign of Maloney's grandiose dreams, they said. Perhaps, but these little touches of instant tradition leave their mark. They are the embroidery at the hem that makes a blanket into a cloak."

The *Star* was certain that he would not be easily replaced, and Frank Drea, the one Cabinet Minister who had consistently praised him despite the fact that Arthur had deeply infiltrated his area of responsibility, stepped forward once again, "We've had the most successful ombudsman's office in the country and it was due entirely to the personality of Arthur Maloney." Stuart Smith even found a way to defend his expansive, expensive practices: "It doesn't surprise me that people try to build up their own areas – that's what you get when you get an energetic person who believes in himself."

Some papers were suspicious, seeing it as a squalid example of how Queen's Park managed always to get away with clean hands. The *Cambridge Reporter* of 25 August, thought it knew what had happened: "Arthur Maloney got wise and finally realized that fighting the provincial government in its own ball park is futile." That attitude was closer to the truth than it knew; some time later in the autumn, Arthur let down his guard for a moment, and Phil Patterson saw a different man:

We were in Thunder Bay where he was giving a speech, and I remember that we had just got back from a long day; it was the fall, some time after the resignation publicity had died down. It was a slushy, rotten day. It was blowing and icy. He had recently broken his ankle, and he was in a cast and on crutches. We got back to the hotel and he was very tired, and I turned on the radio and the announcement was made of the appointment of Donald Morand, and he was thrilled. He thought it was a great appointment. He was lying on the bed, and I looked at him, and he said, "I'm so happy to have this yoke off my back. I'm so happy to be leaving it. I'm so tired of fighting it." And I looked at him, and he just lay there, exhausted – and I had a tear in my eye for him.[6]

Lillian had seen the distaste building up for months before the final decision to leave. "Arthur often did things on the spur of the moment. He decided he was going to quit and that was it – it was common for him to do things without much planning. One night he just came home and said, 'I've had it!' He wasn't bitter or unhappy."[7]

In the end, disillusioned, and disliking what he was doing, he tried to get out gracefully. Murray, who knew that trying to please everybody would not be believed, wanted him to show something of the old panache.

I wanted to have more teeth in it than he did. He certainly didn't want it to be sweet, but it was part of his grandiose nature to put everything in it. He wanted it both ways, and we fought to a compromise. He was somebody, who, generally speaking, could bury the hatchet quickly. I don't think he carried many grudges. Frank Donnelly was an exception ... He wasn't trying to cause trouble. We have many people today determined to destroy the Establishment, and Arthur was perceived by some, at the time, as trying to destroy parts of that Establishment. But in actual fact he was a stalwart upholder of it, and his rage was directed at the abuse of the Establishment. He wanted it to be perfect, and therefore, since it was an imperfect world, at the least, his attacks, as he saw them, were not planned to knock down the structure, but to make it better. That I think is the real key to Arthur. I've said it many times. He would be seen on the warpath, banging at the doors of the ministries, but he was only trying to make them better and more responsible. He was not interested in destroying any ministry. It would have been sad for him to act against the Minister of Housing in a way that would cause the Minister to resign. That would be the last thing he wanted.

I don't respect many people, but I liked him very much. A warm, genuine human being.[8]

There was considerable personal support, some of it amusing in its suggestions of how to stick it in the government's eye. Tony O'Donohue, the Toronto alderman from Ward 2, suggested that he run for mayor. "It would be a most suitable position for you. Naturally, I would be most pleased to support you if you should choose to lean towards this office!"[9] More than one supporter suggested that he return to federal politics, and head for the Prime Minister's office. A prisoner in the Toronto West Detention Centre sent him a poem which included the rather depressing line "Only God could take Arthur Maloney's place." Mr. Bill Johnson of Rockwood suggested that Arthur might run as the NDP candidate for the federal seat in Halton. "We in Halton have a formidable organization, the opposition Dr. Frank Philbrook and Otto Jelinek can be beaten and you are the man to beat them."[10]

Zacks, who stayed on in the Ombudsman office longer than any of Arthur's appointees, saw the changes made by Morand, who came to the office from the Bench, and provided the calming effect of judicial solemnity, which was appropriate after the raw activism of the Maloney period. Morand also came into conflict with the Select Committee, but there was less sustained rancour. It wasn't simply a matter of method; it was also a matter of intention. It was not surprising, for instance, that Maloney defended the right of the Ombudsman to initiate investigations. He saw the office as the watchdog for the citizens, even before they might be aware that they were being abused by a government so huge and so intrusive that the citizens lived in ignorance of what it was up to. Morand, and later Dan Hill took a more clinical approach, and were not inclined to personal outrage or to look for trouble. Morand, ever the judge, would sit back and weigh things, and Hill, a mediator, would try to get people together. Arthur had grand ideas for the office; his successors were content to keep it operating.

For all his talent and enthusiasm, Arthur had a large part in his fall from grace. Despite his natural charm, reputation, skill, energy, and idealistic ambitions, he never seemed to understand that it was not simply a question of having ideas, however admirable they might be. He had to express them adequately, and he was never able to do that, despite his surround of advisers. For all his reputed eloquence, and for all the time and money spent on sending his handsome, young spokesmen through the province, his message was simply not a sufficiently persuasive mixture of principle and pragmatism that could withstand the onslaught of the press, hungry for sensational conduct by a man whom they had deemed more celebrity than doer of real deeds – a perception aided by the way in which the government blunted his attempts to get things done. The Legislature was no help, since it, too, wanted to be noticed, and was inhabited by men who wielded little power, and saw a chance to grab some off the overloaded table of the Ombudsman.

Early in his public career, when he spurned the Parole Board in the mid-fifties, he displayed a flaw in his political character that was to keep him from high office – he was unable to "trim," to compromise, and that inability to wheel and deal over principles, was, in the new Jerusalem of the Ombudsman's office, fostered and urged on by his band of children at the evening switchboard, was to drive him further and further into the corner of intransigence and despair. In a public world in which celebrity is more important than skill, Maloney thought that the former, which he had in full, would allow him to practise the latter, which he also possessed in abundance. But the press turned his celebrity into notoriety, and the politicians and civil servants knew how to use that perception of Maloney to do their job as they saw it, while the public were preoccupied with the appearance, and sometimes, the reality of his extravagance. It was a classic case of appearance demolishing reality. Maloney never knew what hit him until it was too late – it was proof of the sad proposition that it is perfectly possible to keep a good man down, if he is vain enough to think that his natural gifts, seemingly admired by all, are of such talismanic power that no-one would attempt to thwart him. He believed, as Thomas Carlyle stated, that all power was moral; his opponents knew that it was only a matter of political expediency.

Arthur often talked about it. Gordon Meiklejohn, who came to him as a student after the Ombudsman years, learned that he had ambitions for the office that went beyond simply serving the public. "He spoke of his idea of running young people through the Ombudsman's office – perhaps cleaning them out every three years or so. But giving them the experience of helping people."[11]

In the last weeks of his appointment, there were opportunities for the uneasy relation between Maloney and the Davis government to break into public quarrel, but Davis kept quiet, and Arthur, though urged privately and publicly to do otherwise, was equally politic. Having chastised the Select Committee in the late summer, he was satisfied to go no further. On 30 September, *Tab International,* a sensationalist tabloid, hoping for trouble, gave him the chance: "Ontario's Ombudsman Arthur Maloney, the top-flight criminal lawyer was virtually driven from office because, in the parlance of the street, 'he knew where too many bodies were buried.'" The reporter seemed not to know the meaning of the phrase about buried bodies, which, if it was true, should have guaranteed Maloney's position rather than put it in jeopardy. Maloney said nothing, and there was some disappointment that the man whom the newspapers had sometimes chided for being arrogant, went – without at least a last riposte. The *Star* felt betrayed: "Nobody expected Arthur Maloney to quit this way. The fire-breathing dragon, who at every turn took on the Tory government that made him Ontario's first ombudsman, might at least have come out with one final blast at the legislators who dared try to interfere in his affairs." For the press, looking for something, some bit of trivial fluff, Maloney provided a visual metaphor when, just before leaving, he broke his ankle, stepping out of a cab. "Instead ... he hobbled down from his self-created throne today with a broken ankle – from a recent fall – and hardly a whimper. 'The battles are over and I'm not a person who battles just for the fun of battling,' Maloney said, resigning after three years of helping the little guys tackle the government's bureaucratic maze."

It was, therefore, surprising but understandable that immediately upon his resignation, seemingly unaware that Arthur had left their employ under a cloud, the government thought of inviting him back. Not to the Ombudsman's office, but to investigate the problem of religious cults in Ontario. Maloney let them know that he wanted $1000 a day. The government bridled at this, but as the newspapers said, Maloney was expected to make something in the range of $200,000 a year in private practice. There was not, given the short memory of the public, any comment upon the fact that shortly before there was much complaint because the man was costing the province $60,000 a year. "What Davis and McMurtry want is someone who has a reputation for being a civil libertarian so the public see that rights will be protected, and there won't be a witch-hunt. Maloney, with his history as a defence lawyer and his recent tumultuous career as the Ombudsman, everybody's champion against the government, obviously has the right credentials."[12]

Maloney did not get the job (Daniel Hill, the former Chairman of the Ontario Human Rights Commission did), but the fact that he was considered, and the reasons why, leads inevitably to the question of why didn't Davis and McMurtry do something to keep him at the Ombudsman's office if they thought so highly of him? The looking-glass world of political and bureaucratic hypocrisy was revealing its lunacy in these second thoughts on Arthur Maloney. In late October, his name came up again as a possible head for an investigation into the City of Toronto purchasing and inspection department. Again he asked too much. He suggested that $60,000 would be needed to fund a two-month study, and the council would not pay it. But Maloney was their first choice. John Sewell urged the appointment of Maloney as a way to restore public confidence in the honesty of the project.

This collective amnesia about Maloney, the mad, bad, arrogant, incompetent failure, may have been in part prompted by his dignified retreat from office. It might also have been, at Queen's Park, a matter of the Conservatives trying to hold on to the bits and pieces of an organization which was starting to unravel. In August, not only had Maloney handed in his resignation, but Darcy McKeough, who was as tough inside the Cabinet as Maloney was supposed to be outside it, resigned, a serious blow to the strength of the Big Blue Machine. Shortly after, George Kerr, the Solicitor-General, supposedly attempted to influence a Provincial Court decision. By the time it was straightened out, not only Kerr, but Davis and McMurtry got themselves into modestly malodorous positions as they collectively tried to talk Kerr out of trouble. At almost the same time, John Munro, the Liberal Labour Minister in Ottawa, admitted that he had phoned a provincial judge on behalf of a convicted constituent and he was forced to resign. Kerr, or Davis, or McMurtry or all of them didn't seem to have the sense to do something swiftly in the same style – politicians deep in a hole, as Dennis Healey, the British politician once said – should know when to stop digging. It seemed appropriate that before it was straightened out, someone else should be called in to clear the battlefield – Arthur Maloney was hired. No one seemed to remember that he ought to have been the forgotten man, hiding away somewhere in disgrace.

> *"If the law supposes that," said Mr. Bumble, "the law is a ass – a idiot."*
>
> – Dickens, *Oliver Twist*

Some, of contemplative cast, might say the same of politics.

17

Sixty-Year-Old Smiling Public Man

When Arthur came out of the Ombudsman's office, the legal scene had changed. J.J. Robinette was still around, in a class by himself, very rarely taking criminal cases, and then only for clients from the corporate world. Dave Humphrey was still at it, kidding the juries into giving his clients the benefit of the doubt. But he was to succumb in the late eighties to the Bench where he developed a reputation as a hard judge in criminal cases. It is a reputation of which he is cheekily proud, claiming that his long years as a defence counsel alerted him to every dodge of the criminal mind. And, as he puts it, it is not easy to be sentimental about an accused when they are not paying a fee for the privilege. John Mortimer, the British barrister and writer, claims that the best form of attack for a defence counsel is humour, and if a barrister can get a jury to laugh, there is a good chance of acquittal. Humphrey played that tune with great success in his defence work, and he still has a boisterously lively air about him, but he is now a difficult man to move as he looks down into the prisoners' dock, and his sentences are no laughing matter. He, however, was still around in the late seventies, but many of Arthur's older friends had gone to the Bench.

The Sunday Sun of 1 July 1979 carried an article titled "Meet Toronto's Top Lawyers." It was not entirely accurate, since it contented itself with criminal counsel. Humphrey, Robinette, and Maloney were the old guard. The other four were much younger: Clay Powell, Ed Greenspan, Clayton Ruby, and Earl Levy. Clive Bynoe did not make the list, but he might well have done so, since he was still in practice, respected in the profession and with a substantial following in the criminal world – but not quite a celebrity figure, which is often just a matter of being involved in a case that has public *réclame,* for any number of reasons.

If the various governmental groups still flirted with the idea of using Arthur to give their public commissions stature, the bulk of his practice was, again, criminal. On 12 December 1978, he made his first appearance in court in London at a preliminary hearing for a dentist charged with importing drugs. He was still suffering from his September accident, but he was pleased to be back. "'I'm looking forward to the career ahead of me,' Maloney said as he hobbled into the courthouse on a cane he uses to support a weak ankle he broke in a fall in September." If he had any misgivings, the reception he received on this modest occasion must have heartened him. "Judge G.C. Marshman welcomed Maloney back from his three years as ombudsman. And, throughout the day, lawyers dropped into the courtroom to watch him in action."[1]

There was some insecurity when he returned. Monte Harris was asked to comment upon his performance. "When he was coming out of the Ombudsman's office, he was concerned about building the practice again, and he said to me, 'Well, do you think I'm coming back to where I was? Am I looking okay?"[2] Harris was not the only one who sensed some nervousness. Paul French, had hoped he would choose counsel work with a major firm, but Arthur went back to the kind of loose association that he, in a sense, had invented years previous, when he began to collect students and ex-students around him. He joined French and several other young counsel, most of them trained by him – Mike Wadsworth, Phil Patterson, and later Glenn Hainey, in an office where they worked independently. Hainey, who had stayed on at the Ombudsman's office after Arthur's resignation, came out to be his junior. Neils Ortved saw the change: "He enjoyed himself again. He frankly enjoyed the freedom, without the huge administrative problems of the Ombudsman's office with which he had never felt comfortable. He had a huge ego and he hadn't liked anyone suggesting that what he was doing wasn't right. He knew he was best back practising law."[3]

He displayed some determination to make some money this time, and he avoided, as much as he could, cases where money was scarce. It may well have been a reaction to the years of press nagging about his Ombudsman salary – he was going to show them just how much he really was worth. But it wasn't quite the same as the period immediately before he became Ombudsman. He wasn't always the obvious first name to be considered for important cases. He was still at the top, but no longer alone. If he was the leader of the office, he was no longer the constant centre of energy and high jinks. He used to take care of his young associates, and he still handed off cases to them that he could not, or would not do, but now there was a sense that they were looking after him – and that was to become even more the case, sooner than anyone could have expected, and in an entirely different, sadder way.

There was no sense that Maloney was losing his celebrity, particularly when he was called in to deal with the tag end of the most publicized criminal case of the late seventies in the province. Peter Goddard, the *Sunday Star* "rock and roll" columnist, wrote of it on 22 April 1979:

Who else but Keith Richards could get into – and out of – so many hassles so often? We were standing in front of the Harbour Castle Hilton on a mean, damp February day two years ago. It was the night after the Stones had played the El Mocambo, the weekend after Margaret Trudeau had found herself and a few days after Richard had been charged with possession of heroin for trafficking and possession of coke after a police raid.

In October 1978, Richards had pleaded guilty to the charge of possession, and Lloyd Graburn, the County Court Judge, gave him a suspended sentence on the condition that Richards (and it was presumed the rest of the Rolling Stones) would perform at a benefit concert with the profits going to the Canadian National Institute for the Blind. It looked like a good deal for all concerned – but the politicians knew a better one. Roy McMurtry, who was often accused of having a strong nose for publicity, objected, claiming that the famous performer ought to have been sent to jail, not only as a deterrent, but to show that the rich and famous were not to be treated any better than the *hoi polloi* in righteously indignant Toronto the Good.

There was something in that argument, but there was also something in Graburn's idea that Richards might go free, after a charity had benefitted from his peculiar theatrical endeavours. Despite this, McMurtry's clamour was loud enough to influence the Federal Justice Minister, Otto Lang, into appealing the one-year suspended sentence. The *Star* thought there was some pious hypocrisy about the whole thing. "Justice Graburn's proviso that Richards give a concert to aid the blind, even if unusual, was at least straightforward ... What is not to be applauded is McMurtry's interference in an imaginative and fair sentence or Lang's agreement to appeal it."[4] Richards played fair – when the Justice Department announced that it planned to appeal, it was expected that he and the Rolling Stones would simply forget about touring in Canada, which would hardly have been much of a sacrifice for them. Richards had to be served with the notice of appeal, personally, on Canadian territory, and without his co-operation that could not happen. Surprisingly Richards not only made himself available for service, but announced that he was prepared to do not one, but two concerts.

If Richards was willing to put himself in the hands of the Canadian appeal system, he was not going to do it without the best legal advice. His New York counsel, who had used Austin Cooper at the trial level, now asked for Arthur Maloney. He was chosen, as Jacob Lefkowitz, Richards's American lawyer, said "because he is the best lawyer in Canada."[5] It must have cheered Arthur to see that kind of statement. It was not a difficult case, but it provided considerable work and publicity for Arthur, since the office became a kind of theatrical booking office for the Stones while the chopping and changing involved in putting together a major concert was handled. The legal hush of the office was invaded by constant phone calls, cables, and dozens of importuning letters, asking at the lowest level for tickets, and at the more ambitious level for just a moment of Richards's time to listen to enclosed tapes, as performers and composers in Canada and the United States saw a chance to get to the musician through the simple device of looking up his lawyer in the phone book. When Judge Graburn had suggested, out of the blue, that the Canadian National Institute for the Blind be the beneficiary, the organization was hardly aware of its good luck: "CNIB officials had no idea who the Rolling Stones was when they endorsed Judge Graburn's idea in a telephone call from the judge before the sentencing order, Sanders [the CNIB official] said. 'We assumed he was just another person like the people who come in to entertain the folks at Clarkewood (a CNIB-run residence for elderly blind people). We thought he was just another piano player. We have so many people in and out of here giving concerts for the elderly.'" Richards probably never was told the limits of his fame, but his encounter with Arthur was to prove bracing. Arthur, who only vaguely knew of the Stones before the case, did not let world-class celebrity influence him. He treated Richards as he did all his richer clients – he charged him stiffly, and let him know that he was lucky to have Arthur as counsel. On one occasion, he flew to New York to meet Richards. Richards failed to appear. Maloney finally announced that he would wait overnight, but expected Richards to meet him at 7:30 a.m. the following morning, at breakfast in Arthur's hotel. It was not expected that Richards would obey, but Arthur warned that if he did not, Richards could get himself another lawyer. Just before 8:00 a.m., the next morning, Richards, hiding under a huge hat, strolled into the dining room, was chastised by Arthur for his careless way with appointments, and they got down to business. After that, when Richards phoned in to keep in touch with his case, he always asked for "the Boss," which was the name given to Arthur by the other lawyers in the office. The concerts finally did take place in the rather droll circumstance (a good example of how in the slow-step of the law it was possible to get the cart before the horse) of anticipating the appeal, which was not to be heard until some time after the songs were sung. So Richards had, in fact, fulfilled part of his Graburn penalty prior to it being considered for reversal by the Court of Appeal. On 22 April, the concerts took place in Oshawa, and Arthur presented the CNIB with a cheque for $50,000. In July, he argued the case before the appeal court, which supported Graburn's decision. If it wasn't the highlight of his career legally, it certainly was so in the public sense, since the news of Richards's victory went round the world, albeit at the sophomoric level of evanescent show-business gossip.

It was not, however, the only chance that he got at being back in the papers in 1979. In February, he addressed the Manitoba Law School Foundation in Winnipeg, and there was a long, complimentary article in the *Winnipeg Free Press* (3 February 1979): "He has never been satisfied with the point of view that blindly accepts the law as it is. He holds the view that the law must bear the stamp of the present day – that it must ally itself with the future, not the past; that it must be revised in terms of the needs of each succeeding age." Whenever any changes were suggested, Arthur would be asked to comment, but he was not always on the side of the innovators. In March, he was again at odds with McMurtry, who was proposing a limited form of public defender system, which was common in the United States. Maloney, who ought to have known, feared the influence the bureaucracy might have over counsel in their employ, and he preferred the legal aid system as it stood. "A lawyer's loyalty is divided if his salary is paid by one source and his instructions are provided by another." Maloney saw no good in tinkering with the system that had been put in place in the late sixties. The idea was soon forgotten.

Arthur's ability to recoup was, perhaps, best exemplified by the fact that at the end of the Ombudsman debacle, despite his physical and emotional weariness, he refused a vacation, and immediately went back into practice. But he kept an eye on the Ombudsman. While Donald Morand was being praised by some papers for the quiet modesty with which he took office in early '79, Arthur was still considered the best commentator on matters of ombudsman practice, not only in Ontario, but throughout the country, and occasionally abroad. He never backed down on his argument that Ontario had got a good bargain in the office he had established. In Ottawa, in May 1979, speaking at the Men's Canadian Club, he made the point again:

> "Ontario gets no better value than for the $4.2 million spent yearly by the office of the ombudsman" ... Maloney said the $4.2 million allotted in his last year in office, 1977–78, represented less that 1/35 of one per cent of the provincial budget.
>
> And he recalled Frank Drea, when he was correctional minister, saying the ombudsman's office saved the province $10 million yearly by its mere presence – by defusing potentially costly jail riots and counterbalancing the powers of the prison bureaucrats.[6]

Maloney still had some semi-official standing with the office since he had yet to deliver the official blueprint for the Ombudsman, which he had begun to work on at the start of his tenure. In June, it came out, in typical Maloney style, with lots of publicity and almost six hundred pages of suggestions. Again, he urged the widening of the jurisdiction, especially to deal with municipal institutions, and again, he was unrepentant about the costs. "Obviously an office structured in accordance with these principles cannot be done on the cheap. Indeed, I do not think it an overstatement to say that an ombudsman's office not properly budgeted, not properly staffed *and not properly backed by those who brought it into being* [my italics] amounts to nothing more than a front and a facade." The latter part of the last sentence was the closest that Arthur ever came to publicly suggesting that Bill Davis had let him down.

Neils Ortved was mainly responsible for the blueprint report. There was nothing particularly new in it – it was a refinement on the recommendations that Arthur had been making continually through his time in office. There was, however, a further tinkering with that thorny problem of the complaint from beyond the jurisdiction, and he seems to be suggesting a kind of squatter's right over such: "Concern for the extra-jurisdictional complainant is thus a hallmark of the Ombudsman's office in Ontario and in my view should always continue to be so. Indeed, the principle adopted in Nova Scotia of not only referring out-of-jurisdiction complainants to those who might provide an appropriate remedy to also following up on those referrals to ascertain if there has been a satisfactory resolution of the grievance is a commendable idea for which the office might strive."[7]

It might well have been seen as a bit of mischief making. Certainly Donald Morand seemed satisfied with the present powers, and he often made much of the fact that the public seemed to be getting wiser about the limits of the Ombudsman's jurisdiction. But Maloney's suggestion was true to the original ambitions of the office as he had seen it – helping the bewildered individual to work his way through the corridors of the governmental maze. Like most blueprints, it was not to be entirely followed – in fact, as Michael Zacks has said, it was quite simply ignored. It was not the last time that he spoke on the matter of the Ontario office, or on the ombudsman subject in general, but he had little influence on Morand. From the beginning, Morand kept Maloney at arm's length. Somewhat surprisingly for a man who had been a judge, and therefore trained to come to conclusions only after all the evidence was in, Morand admitted that "I was as critical of this office as anybody before I came in." But he admitted that "I found there was a bigger administrative job here than I anticipated." He slimmed the office, and indulged in his own version of self-congratulation (which Maloney had been chided for practising): "We now have more Indians and fewer chiefs." As the newspaper article reported: "Gone from the ombudsman's downtown Toronto headquarters are the expensive paintings, the exquisite glass pieces and the lavish furniture – replaced by furnishing which could have been advertised in last week's newspaper sales supplement."[8] It was an inverse form of Arthur's version of Lockean "appearance as reality" – a new, more sober, puritan financial rigour expressed in bus-station traditional. Since all those handsome bits and bobs (save for Arthur's considerable personal contribution) had already been paid for, it might seem to be a bit of inverse pretension as well.

Morand started off trying to deal less strenuously with the Select Committee, but even he, bringing the weight of his Supreme Court dignity to the table, found them hard to handle. He did manage to cut the budget back from $4.1 million – he accepted a reduction of $350,000. He wasn't much fun: "The irascible and grandiose Ombudsman Arthur Maloney is gone. The things he said and did were sometimes silly and irritating, but Maloney in full cry was always grand fun to watch."[9]

Arthur hoped for good things from Morand, but in time he found him wanting, particularly in the way in which he led the office away from the centre of public awareness. Dave Rendeiro remembers when Morand was preparing to give way to Dan Hill. Arthur "expressed disappointment with Morand, because he, of course, had put so much effort and energy into making the Ombudsman's office, and then, under Morand, it sort of became very, very quiet – all of a sudden the Ombudsman's office disappeared! When Dr. Hill came in, he approached Arthur, and was receptive to his advice. Maybe Dr. Hill was somewhere in between Mr. Maloney and Mr. Morand. Dr. Hill met with Arthur before he took office, and then, sometimes, after."[10]

In all distresses of our friends
We first consult our private ends,
While nature kindly bent to ease us,
Points out some circumstance to please us.
– Jonathan Swift

Another sign of time passing was the death of John Diefenbaker in August 1979. Through the years Diefenbaker and Maloney had kept up the friendship that had been established at the time of the Camp fight. Diefenbaker had stayed with the Maloneys at the Guelph line farm in the summer of 1978, while preparing to attend the Highland Games at Fergus. There is an amusing picture of the Maloneys and Diefenbaker outside the front door of the Maloney home, with Diefenbaker in full Highland dress, his sporan worn alarmingly high on his stomach, since he had put the straps for the same over his shoulders. Lillian has a letter of thanks, which contains a passage of apology for his maladroit handling of the costume. "The only fly in the ointment was that your beautiful home was used by Trevor Jones to provide his recognized ability as an authority on Highland dress, to put the kilt on me, in reverse!!" Which was probably what Diefenbaker might have expected from a man with a patently Welsh name. Lillian, who has always been idealistic about political leaders, despite her years of experience to the contrary, was slightly disturbed by Mr. Diefenbaker's dismissive and bitter remarks about Pierre Trudeau – not because she was a Liberal, but because she had expected a more statesman-like generosity from the old man.

Whatever Arthur might have felt about the way he had been ignored in office, he retained his respect for the Chief. He was very pleased to be named an honorary pallbearer. Diefenbaker, who, like Arthur, saw himself in operatic terms, had arranged not only to be seen in regal, funereal state in the Parliament buildings in Ottawa, but he had also ordered a long, slow train to carry the bier across the land, stopping in the small cities and towns for the citizens to view his remains. Some, with muted snicker, and some, approvingly, remembered the similar progress of Lincoln's body across the eastern American states in the previous century. The *Ottawa Journal* saw the choice of Arthur as a pallbearer as appropriate, not simply because of his Camp duty, but also because "Arthur Maloney, the Toronto lawyer who became Ontario's first Ombudsman, was a renegade lawyer, unlike the Bay Street enemies of Diefenbaker, but not unlike the Chief." Arthur took his role seriously, and after the lying-in-state in Ottawa, he joined the group of mourners – family, friends, politicians, and reporters who travelled with the body across part of the country. By the time the train left, the idea of displaying the body in an open coffin had to be abandoned for obvious reasons of health and decorum in the late summer, but the rest of the ceremonial practices were observed. Iain Hunter, a young reporter from British Columbia, working for the *Ottawa Citizen* was at the event from start to finish:

> Diefenbaker was lying in the hall, and they had to pull the curtains and stop the public from coming in every once in a while because the flies were gathering – so they pulled the curtains every three or four hours and sprayed everything up and down. Then they opened up and let the people in again. Trudeau had been in the bush, and he arrived with a beard. It was his first public appearance since his defeat. And he looked, and he had a smile on his face. Trudeau admired Diefenbaker, but he was not deeply moved; he was not at all moved.
>
> The coffin was lying open for the better part of two weeks. I was standing at the bottom of the steps at the church, and the guard of honour went up the steps with the coffin and there was a "swish." The body had shifted in the casket, and

the man from the undertakers winced, and muttered, "A repair job." Anyway the ceremony went on, and we were all bussed out to the station, and we got on the train. There were hundreds of people there. I was paid for by the *Citizen.* And I was told by the undertaker that we were not going to have an open coffin from now on; the plan had been to open it on the way west. The train was loaded with people. Some I knew. Some were important. Sean O'Sullivan was on the train. He had been Diefenbaker's protégé, and had just gone into the priesthood. I remember him banging his head and yelling, "Jesus Christ!" I looked surprised and he said, "Oh, oh, I was just checking with the boss." Each time we entered a province, an official group came on, as if they were paying homage.[11]

There was, as might be expected, in the slow progress across the late summer landscape, a good deal of reminiscing, occasional back-biting, and much drinking. The train had not been long out of the station before the battle began over the mysterious trust fund that had been set up for Diefenbaker. It was reportedly still in existence, and in some abundance. Who was to control it, and what was to be done with it became a central of conflict on the train, with contending groups seeking supporters, falling into each other's arms in confrontations of high sincerity, low motives, tears, and too much alcohol. Iain Hunter loved every moment of it:

Oh, it was crazy! There were two groups – Dief trust fund people, and the family executors, and they were parlaying over who had the right to papers, and this trust fund. No one quite knew what it was for. It was constantly referred to as "The Fund." Diefenbaker went to his grave with all these weird tales, which may or may not have been true. Guys like Davie Walker were trying to get hold of these things to suppress them. There were files on enemies – files on Pearson. Files that might become useful sometime. So we had this crazy thing going on where these two factions who both pretended to be the loyalists – and both were, but in different ways. They hated each other because – some of the literary executors were determined to keep everything – they were very much like Diefenbaker.

There was much weeping and wailing about the Chief. Aldred was there, crying about the Chief's reputation. They were all worried about who would be quoted next – to bask in the glory of this guy. They were playing up to the newspaper men. Val Sears [Toronto Star] and I were there, and cottoned on to what was going on. I was writing stories on the quarrels that were going on, blunt and reporterish. Everyone was trying to get their version of the Diefenbaker stories printed. I was constantly being button-holed by these guys, half drunk, trying to tell their stories – there was supposedly money missing from the fund. I don't know where the fund was. I was just interested in colour stories of those silly, old, self-interested bastards.

Hunter was not a man easily impressed by politicians, given his experience of watching them, day after day, at their antics in and out of the Chamber. He had never met Arthur before, and he was impressed by his obvious sense of occasion:

Arthur probably was on the train from the beginning. I sat with him for a while. I didn't know him, and he said that Diefenbaker had inspired him with his feeling for the individual in the mess of provinces and factions. Diefenbaker always spoke of the individual. He talked about Diefenbaker's legal fees when he defended the individuals, and that Diefenbaker always recognized that there were people left behind, particularly in a growing country where people were fighting to get ahead.

It was like an Irish wake on the train, with these groups going up and down, often half drunk, crying and laughing, except that they were crying not only about Dief, but this fight that they were in over the fund – and Arthur didn't seem interested in the quarrel at all.

Maloney was patently touched by the occasion, and his attendance upon the body of his old leader was unmarked by opportunism or political hypocrisy. Hunter has a vivid memory of one thing he said. "I do remember he said, 'I have to be here!' This was an historical thing for him – but he was not involved in the battle going on. He saw it as history – that we were making history!" So Maloney and a small group of mourners rode the rails in singular contemplation of the odd character who had once led them, for a short time, so gloriously – but inevitably, into early disaster. Gord Lomer, in the *Ottawa Journal* (29 August 1979), described the group:

It was a solemn journey, but not without its lasting memories, some of which will be re-enacted in years to come. Martin [Keith Martin], executive assistant to Diefenbaker, Arthur Maloney, the former Ombudsman and Toronto Tory stalwart, and longtime Diefenbaker friend from Prince Albert, Max Carment were everywhere in the railway cars. They came to be known as "the train people," a timely nomenclature. These train people formed a sort of "in" group, which will be known as "The Diefs."

Charles Lynch, who was watching the antics of the wrestling factions, intent on getting the money and the papers, also noticed Arthur Maloney – "sitting above the battle."[12]

The words of a dead man
Are modified in the guts of the living.
– W.H. Auden

18

Time's Winged Chariot Hurrying Near

After a jury address, he would always say, "Well, what do you think?" And I'd never say, "Great, Boss! It was the greatest thing in the world!" Hainey might do that. I'd say, "Well, why didn't you –" and I'd give him a few points. That stayed with me all my time with him. Arthur would laugh at me for never having a good thing to say about his jury addresses! He was a good judge of character; he knew when he could poke away at somebody – the kind of person who could take it, but when someone was fragile, he knew that too. In my articles, we spent a lot of time in the Four Seasons. He was on the wagon half the time, and off it for about the same. He was much easier to get along with when he was drinking, and I used to marvel at his ability to drink and work the next morning. It didn't seem to affect his fineness of thought at all.[1]

One thing that had not changed was the manner he handled students, and the way he chose them. Gordon Meiklejohn joined Maloney and Hainey in the spring of 1979. Hainey was interested in Meiklejohn's academic record, but Arthur was not. Meiklejohn thought his skill as a hockey player was more important to Arthur. His first experience of Arthur's thoroughness occurred almost immediately upon his joining the office.

Arthur had a Jeep Cherokee, and he and I went off to Parry Sound to defend a rape charge. And we went right to the parking lot where it was supposed to have happened. The claim was that it was supposed to have been dark – and it wasn't. He immediately got me to get hold of a photographer, and the pictures were an important part of the defence. He never took anything for granted; he wanted to know all the details. The interesting things was that at the end of it all – and this was truly Arthur Maloney – he left as a friend of the Crown, the judge, the police officers – everybody. He didn't go about the case in a nasty way. He didn't make any enemies, and justice was done, and off he went.

He continued to train his students by letting them do much of the job. He used his students in a manner that is reminiscent of the way solicitors work with barristers in the English system. In most cases, they interviewed the client and the witnesses, as an English solicitor would do, and they were responsible for getting the retainer, organizing the case, and preparing it for trial. Maloney would know what was going on, and would see the client occasionally, but the student put the material together. On the day of trial, Arthur would simply ask who was to be his first witness. "With Arthur, you'd go off to field the phone calls from the Don Jail – and they were always calling – and you'd get a case that you thought was wonderful, and he'd look at it, and if you didn't say the right word, just the right thing within the first two minutes, he'd say, 'Pass it off to so-and-so.' I used to try to figure out what was the word that got him interested in a case." This kind of whimsical decision was not a sign of failing powers; he had always taken cases on the spur of the moment, on whether or not he felt they might be interesting, or involved aspects of the law that he thought he ought to explore, or social questions that he felt he could articulate through the court system.

> He had great depth. You'd tell him of a situation or a point of law, and he'd say, "Well, go back and look at such and such, in 1967, and you'll find this case." And sure enough – he'd been the lawyer. Arthur was not simply a fact man, though he didn't sit down much and discuss strategy. He would just do it, but he knew the criminal law. He'd done a lot of Court of Appeal stuff; he knew what the law was. You had the responsibility to get the case ready, but he would be on top of you, and he would blow his stack if things weren't ready. We often worked on Sundays – out at the farm, and you were part of the family.

Meiklejohn had heard the stories of Arthur's bad habits as a collector of fees, but by the time he got there, things had changed. "There was an almost hard-nosed 'I'm not working for nothing' attitude. Maybe it was the years he put in, but he made it clear that I was to get the money in. He didn't take legal aid cases, usually, but the other lawyers took legal aid referrals from him. He was insulated from the street – he didn't come into contact with the people the way he used to in the early days."

But his natural sympathy for minorities was aroused as Toronto society changed. In 1977, a group had attempted to establish a home for gay youths and young men in Toronto – their application had been turned down. In March 1979, Keith Norton (who at the time had still to reveal his sexual orientation) refused the licence application in his role as Minister of Community and Social Services. In August, the Tri-Aid Charitable Foundation was launched – the tide had turned suddenly, as it sometimes does in social and moral revolutions, and seventeen prominent citizens, including the Mayor, John Sewell, the Very Rev. N. Bruce McLean, the former Moderator of the United Church, and Maloney put their considerable public influence behind the move to protect these young deviants (as they were then considered).

Just before going off on the Diefenbaker train, he had been the guest lecturer at Mount Saint Vincent University in Halifax at the third annual convention of the Canadian Institute for the Administration for Justice (of which he was a founding member). It was appropriate that he spoke to the state of the Bar. He was disturbed by a new, unpleasant aggression developing among the younger counsel, and he felt that the law schools should prepare the students to come to practice in less bellicose temper. Whether such was the case or not in a profession that lives through reasoned quarrels, and has always had its fair share of aggressive practitioners, it was consistent with his tendency to treat the courtroom confrontation as an occasion for civility, although it also ought to be remembered that he could be very rough if angered. More important, however, was his concern with the rumblings in and out of the government, both provincial and federal, about curbing and circumscribing the jury system – he was particularly concerned about the abolition of the Grand Jury system in several provinces.

In early autumn, 1979, the increasing difficulties between the Toronto police and the black community exploded. Mayor Sewell attacked the Metropolitan Toronto Board of Police Commission for its inefficiency and seeming bias in dealing with complaints, especially from the black sector of the city, which was becoming a major social and political force. Everyone remembered that prior to going to the Ombudsman's office, Maloney had reviewed the police complaint procedure. He had recommended an independent civilian review board, an idea which was praised by everyone, save the police, at the time. Nothing had been done to implement the suggestions. The problem continued through the seventies – Mr. Justice Morand had looked at it, and after him, Walter Pitman did the same. They reached the conclusion that Maloney had been right the first time. But nothing happened. Between August 1978 and August 1979, the police had been involved in eight civilian deaths, and their treatment of blacks, in particular, had become a serious social irritant.

Maloney had his fair share of black clients during this time, and was of the opinion that the matter of police misconduct on all questions could only be dealt with, and be seen to be dealt with, by a civilian board. It was, again, a moment of difference from his old friend, Roy McMurtry, whose department would have been involved in any changes in the procedure, and who seemed to be dragging his feet. He was, however, by this time, working on a watered-down version of the civilian board suggested years previous by Maloney. John Downing, a *Sun* columnist, had criticized the proposed changes:

> A caller wants to know why I haven't praised the provincial Tories for bringing in a new method for handling complaints against the Metropolitan police.
>
> I told him that the Tories had handled the issue with all the finesse of a drunken chicken. I was damned if they would get any compliment from me for introducing at the end of 1978, a procedure similar to what lawyer Arthur Maloney recommended five years ago.
>
> Roy McMurtry is lucky that Maloney and Metro Chairman Paul Godfrey are such loyal party members because things would have been much hotter for him recently if they had been Grits.[2]

It was one of the few times that Arthur was accused (if mildly) of playing politics, if only be omission. In his public statements, he still held to the idea of a full civilian board. This kind of comment, and his work in the courts, led to an increasing respect for him among the leaders of minority factions in the city. In June 1979, he had been given the "Eleanor Roosevelt Humanities Award" by the State of Israel Bond organization. In late '79, it was the black community who praised him, if at a somewhat less-socially-prominent level. Al Peabody, a black journalist, set out to ask the black community whom they admired among white, public figures in Toronto. The question was asked, in the main, in Toronto barbershops – Maloney won the poll as the most respected and trusted white man.

He had been a defender of black Canadians faced with racial insult as early as 1974, when he took on Paul Smithers, seventeen, the only negro player in the Mississauga Midget Hockey League, who was charged with manslaughter, arising from a fight during and after a midget hockey game. Speared during the game by a player who, on his way to the penalty box, had yelled, "Let's fight, you stupid nigger!", Smithers confronted the boy after the game, and in the struggle killed him. There was no question that racial insults were regularly hurled at Smithers during hockey games, by the players and the spectators. Maloney argued that they were so offensive that they finally drove Smithers to the frenzy of his fatal conduct. He lost the case, but his frank airing of the subject, with eloquence and compassion, was remembered by the black community as an important comment upon the way society was going sour in parts of Toronto where whites and blacks came into close emotional contact. It was an example of how Maloney would sometimes take a trial beyond its bare facts in ways that had influence in the community.

> Peabody and his crew interviewed about 700 people last spring and an additional 300 in November. About 75 per cent of them were West Indians.
>
> Barber shops were chosen because many West Indians consider the shops to be "sanctuaries or social centres," he explained.
>
> Most people interviewed were in the 18 to 30 age group. The survey was conducted in the Vaughan-Spadina, Bloor-Bathurst, Spadina-Dundas areas, and in Scarborough.[3]

In seventh position in the poll was Roy McMurtry. "Peabody said the attorney-general 'lost a lot of popularity because he's been pussyfooting around about setting up a civilian review board to investigate complaints against the police.'" Arthur must have been amused by that comment, and he was pleased by his own victory. It was some consolation for having to be photographed being congratulated while lying on his back in the Wellesley Hospital. Smiling up at Peabody, who was grasping his hand, Arthur was in the first stages of the fight for his life, although it seemed less serious at the time.

Arthur died of cancer in September 1984, but Lillian and his sisters suspected that the strokes that preceded the discovery of cancer did not cause it, but were, in fact, only outward signs of the more serious disease. Arthur was told, when his cancer was diagnosed, that the disease sometimes hides itself until it is impossible of cure, and often begins some three or four years before it starts to physically discomfit. Not that the first stroke was without frightening incident in itself. Gordon Meiklejohn was there at the beginning:

> We were on a trial down in Kitchener. We were walking through a little mall that is kitty-corner to the court up there, and he just walked into a table and chairs. It wasn't related to anything he'd had to drink or eat. He just physically didn't see them. That was the first one. It was late '79. It was the end of the trial. He was going to a political fund raiser for Chris Speyer who's now the judge down there. He didn't go to the dinner, and he drove home in the Jeep that night to the farm [twenty miles or so east of Kitchener]. He had a tough time driving. He had a devil of a time keeping the Jeep on the road, and he had no idea what it was.

Paul French tells of how Arthur struggled with the little car, "all the cars were tooting their horns at him. He was having difficulty keeping on the right side of the road on the 401." Whatever it was, it seemed to pass, and he and Lillian prepared to go on with their busy social life. They went off to Quebec City for a wedding. He was not feeling well, and in Quebec, he began to feel very dizzy. They went to a doctor, who wanted to put him in hospital, but agreed to let Arthur return to Toronto, if he promised to see his own physician. His doctor sent him for an angiogram. This seemingly innocent test was to be a frightening and macabre experience for Arthur. While it was going on, and the doctor was busily watching the monitor, Arthur felt himself leaving the scene. "'I could feel myself slipping away, and I eventually lost consciousness, but I could feel it! It was the end! I was dying!" His next memory was of coming to consciousness, a day or two later. He looked out the window at the Wellesley; he could see a sign "Rosar-Morrison Funeral Home." "My God, I'm looking down at my own wake!"[4]

So in mid-January 1980 Arthur had the best and the worst kinds of luck: "Former provincial ombudsman Arthur Maloney is the white man most trusted, admired and respected by Metro blacks, says a poll of 1,000 blacks taken by black writer Al Peabody." But he lay in hospital, his mouth twisted and his speech impeded. Lillian took him away to Florida. He had physiotherapy, and gradually got back to work, although one leg never fully recovered and he took to carrying a cane. Despite the stroke, he kept busy through 1980, and as early as late February he was back in the news, representing the former Liberal Cabinet Minister, Bryce Mackasey, who had been appointed Chairman of Air Canada by a falling Liberal administration, and had recently been fired by the new Conservative rulers in Ottawa. Back in the House as MP for Lincoln, there was much speculation over whether he ought to continue to collect his substantial Air Canada pension. He hired Arthur to speak for him. There were signs, however, of Arthur's illness in the fact that the newspaper reports on the matter reveal that Paul French was doing all the talking. In March, however, Arthur was sufficiently fit to be appointed to the Ontario Provincial Court Committee to deal with judges' salaries and benefits, and he worked steadily through the summer and autumn of 1980, although he was in tender shape.

David Rendeiro, whom Arthur took on as a student, in part because he was intrigued by his Portuguese lineage, joined the office as a student in May of 1980. He had made a special arrangement with Arthur to join the office as soon as he finished course work at Queen's, but he was to spend the middle of the summer in Europe, studying international law, before returning in the autumn to take up his articles again. When he joined the office in the late spring, Arthur had just returned to regular work, and he was having a difficult time, physically, and he was often depressed. When Rendeiro returned from his European studies, in the early autumn, Arthur seemed his old self, appearing early in the morning, cheerfully working at full stretch.

In October 1980, he was to take part in a symposium at Ottawa University on "The Future of Criminal Law in Canada," and he was also booked to appear on television, the day previous to the meeting. He went up to Ottawa, and while being driven to the TV station, he had a second attack. "I think I'm having a stroke," he told the law student who was driving him around. "Would you come up with me?" People who saw the broadcast said that they did not notice anything wrong. In 1981, Rendeiro was in Bar Admission, but still kept in contact with the office, and he was amazed how well Arthur coped, "but later on, it caught up with him – one thing after another." Lillian watched him falling apart, and fighting all the way.

> It was a developing process. There were two or perhaps three strokes. After the first stroke Arthur was, to external observers, making a very good comeback. He would talk about what he was able to do, and he was always very optimistic. Another stroke victim, Card Cartwright – Arthur would write to him in his own hand to prove that there was a comeback on a stroke, but I don't think Arthur was ever the same after the first stroke. It took its toll on him and a much greater toll subjectively than any of us appreciated. I think it bothered him a lot.

In the last eighteen months of his life, he insisted on carrying on, although his eyesight and his memory were badly affected – he was still taking cases, some of them of serious proportion, but he was patently unwell. He worked out a system with Paul French and the other lawyers in the office which put him into a role comparable to that of counsel. When he appeared in court (and he insisted upon being there), he always was accompanied by another lawyer who would carry the cross-examinations. His clients were told how much he could do, and how much he would depend upon his juniors, and he took a full part in preparing the case, explaining it to the client, as they went along. But he simply could not take a case on his own. "The same thing in the Court of Appeal. He would go, be there, but he wouldn't argue the case. He would occasionally intrude. He would sometimes ask a question but it had to be in the narrow spectrum of things. The faculties weren't there any more."[5]

There was some gratuitous, dark mutterings in the profession about the spectacle of the crippled, purblind Maloney, being led into court by his young followers. Dennis O'Connor heard of him going into court, surrounded and incapable – "trading on his reputation – but that wasn't the real Arthur Maloney."

Aside from the fact that he would not quit, however sick he was, he could still be useful, as Paul French argues: "The one faculty he retained up until two months of his death was his judgment. I say 'judgment' in a gross sense. We could tell Arthur the pith and substance of a case and he'd give you his gut reaction and his gut reaction was better than anything you'd got from anyone else around. Next day, if you wanted to deal with the same case again, you'd have to go over it because his short term memory had been damaged by the strokes he had suffered. It was an awful handicap for him." Paul French was in an unusual position. He was not simply a former student, but Maloney's nephew, and very close to Arthur, since Matthew, his own son, had not chosen to enter the law, but to go into a good career in computer science. French, a big, handsome man with the finely chiselled features of his mother, Frances, but the broad Irish face of the male Maloneys, is a quiet, restrained man, who in his early middle-age has about him a shy, boyish demeanour – both his parents are possessed of mild, tentative personalities. He knows that he was always distinguished from the other students – he was never encouraged to become one of Arthur's roaring boys. "Let's face it. It was a different relationship. I think that whatever I would ask of Arthur, or whatever I would want of Arthur, or anything Arthur could do for me – I stood at the head of the line. But in terms of camaraderie with for example, Michael [Wadsworth] or Dennis [O'Connor] or Neils [Ortved] – because of who I was – my relationship was a little different. In the end, again because of who I was, I assisted in the managing of his affairs."

This is the saddest story I have ever heard.
– Ford Madox Ford, *The Good Soldier*

Arthur's response to his medical troubles was stubbornly aggressive – he was determined to continue his practice, despite the increasing dependence upon his juniors. For the first time in his career, he set out to bring business into the office by soliciting his political friends, both in the provincial and federal governments. In July 1982, he spoke to his admirer, Frank Drea, the Minister of Community and Social Services, holding himself out to "giving legal counsel for any boards or agencies at any hearing or inquiries." He also approached Nicholas Leluk, the Minister of Correctional Affairs: "I told him I could act as counsel in any hearings before any board, agency, or commission. I explained to him that I was in association with Peter Tetley [who had come to him originally as a student] and I also told him I was well known to the Deputy Minister of Correctional Services, Archie Campbell." He did not stop there. He had some hope of being appointed counsel in an extradition matter if the "Jewish Community would be likely to request an inquiry concerning the handling of the Rocca affair." He met with McMurtry to discuss any possibility of government business that might come his way.

The infamous Nelles case, in which charges were brought against a nurse in the death of several children in the Sick Children's Hospital, might have given him something. "Roy and I discussed the Nelles Affair and he was going to inquire if there was any likelihood of counsel being retained by the Ministry in that matter. We also spoke about the likelihood he would refer government matters to me." It is not the sort of thing that one expects of Arthur, though it is common enough practice for lawyers with political connections to solicit government work.

He was obviously so concerned about building up the practice that he was willing to go beyond party lines. He approached James Fleming, the Minister of State for Multiculturism, having heard of a Federal commission on the matter of Canada's economy. "I spoke to Jim Fleming respecting this and he will recommend that I be considered for some role as one of the counsel before that committee. I told him how my office facilities were such that with the help of Peter Tetley especially I could handle anything like that. He commented on how I had made such a good recovery from my illness of a year ago." Fleming passed his name on to the Hon. Donald S. Macdonald, and to Senator Jack Austin on the chance that they might have some work. It must have been a low moment for Arthur to think that he might be relying on the Liberals to find him a safe, lengthy commission.

Nothing is so dispiriting to witness as the scramble for spoils among the parasites of the political world, and until his illness Arthur had not so demeaned himself, although there were many times when an act of patronage might have been made, if he had wanted such. Patronage is the sometime shady aspect of politics that dares not speak its name, and it is often bestowed in whimsical ways. Aside from those who have done good service, or bought their way into appointments, there are men in high places who have come there not by ever winning an election, but by stolidly losing more than once in ridings in which their party had no chance of winning, but needed someone moderately respectable to run. It takes a peculiarly vain, or masochistic, or insensitive or suicidally loyal kind of personality to commit this futile act, since it usually has to be done more than once, and the sacrificing party knows perfectly well that the task is simply to lose gracefully. But, in the long run, it may bring reward from a party that sooner or later comes into power. Nor is it always necessary to presume that such rewards only come from one's own party. There are many political appointees who, if not entirely dependent upon the kindness of strangers, are, at least, beholden to the opposition for their final reward for loyal service, party notwithstanding. One wily, old stager – a friend of Arthur's – when asked about his luck in picking a plum from the federal government, although he had always been a member of the opposite party, and had never held public office, put it simply in terms of long service to the political game, indicating, with a slow wink, that the adherents of political service are all in the same business and take care of each other, regardless of party affiliation. There is much loyalty among political tradesmen, and a lucky man may be rewarded more than once if his connections remain in centres of power.

It was no mystery to Maloney, who had seen his father and his brother dispensing patronage, and he put a considerable number of jobs about in his short time in Ottawa. It should be said, however, that Arthur had not been interested in the past in searching out government spoils for himself, save for a somewhat desultory try at a Senate appointment in the sixties. He never had to do so. Even after the Ombudsman affair, he was still one of the first names considered when government counsel were needed. By late '82, however – after the strokes, it was no longer the case – for obvious reasons. All he wanted now was a commission or a board which, in the past, he would have turned down as beneath him, as too boring, and paper bound in endless days of meandering, hair-splitting detail. Now, however, he badly needed someplace to sit, with a good fee and a long tenure, if possible. It is sad proof of how sick he was – that he came to such ignoble begging for a place to rest.

Like his father, he seems to have been not quite at the right place at the right time to get to the Senate, and timing is often all that is needed for that particular appointment. In his last two years it came up again, pursued for a few months at the end of '82, and into the early months of '83 with an almost desperate show of determination to get something for all those years of distinguished loyalty and service to the party. The source for all this information on Maloney's attempts to drum up government work is contained in one file of personal memos written to himself, no doubt to protect himself from his fading memory after the strokes. The file also contains the information on his attempts to get into the Senate as quickly as possible at the end of 1982.

No such appointment was made, and it is a somewhat chilling example of how easy it is for the world to pass a man by, however much he was once admired, after he is no longer of any use. and will never be of any use again. By the time he began to press for appointment, he had been assigned to the political *salon des refusés* from which few men return, however much sentimental support they may muster. He did collect a lot of well-wishers – friends, politicians, churchmen, public figures of note. But none was of sufficient power or sufficiently determined to practice what power they had to give him a few months of peace, and the somewhat dubious honour of lolling on the benches of the Upper House, as a final reward for a life well spent in the service of his country. Lesser men got there, but Maloney's failure was, if only in part, an example of how little time he ever really spent at the centre of party politics. It was also an example of that other cruel political truth – refusing to do anything for him was easy enough since it had no real consequences. Maloney, wounded, weary, could mumble, but he could not bite, and his supporters, if prepared to make warm sounds of support and encouragement, would not go any further, however sad they might feel about the long silence that developed after all the promises were made, but came to nothing. No one would fight for Arthur Maloney as he had fought for others.

Of course, he was given sufficiently reasonable excuse to be let down easily. When he began his campaign to get into the Senate, there was talk that two places had been reserved by Trudeau to be filled by Joe Clark, the Conservative leader. It was known that one of those was to go to William Kelly, one of Davis's fund raisers. There was a rumour that Maloney was to have the other one. The *Globe* 18 December 1982, knew all about it:

> Prime Minister Pierre Trudeau is faced with continuing vacancies in the so-called Conservative seats in the Senate. The story around town is that Mr. Trudeau would like Toronto lawyer Arthur Maloney and Big Blue fund-raiser William Kelly to get two of the designated seats.
>
> Nobody would doubt their Conservative credentials, but there is some feeling that Mr. Maloney might not satisfy party leader Joe Clark. A noted Diefenbaker loyalist – "When John Diefenbaker comes in, Arthur Maloney stands up" was his cry – Mr. Maloney has not always shared Mr. Clark's view of the party.
>
> The practice of designating Conservative seats was started by Mr. Trudeau to maintain some semblance of an opposition in the Senate. When filling vacancies caused by the death or retirement of the few Tories in the Upper House, he has agreed to do it after consulting with the Tory leader about worthy Conservatives.[6]

Maloney busily and quickly called in all his friends to support the rumour, insofar as it was in his favour. As early as 22 October 1982, Bishop Carter had jumped past the Conservatives and Joe Clark in a letter to Prime Minister Trudeau. While it is usually thought that such appointments come from some kind of spontaneous groundswell of mutual intent among those who have the ear of the appointers, the file reveals that Arthur was carrying on his own campaign to get into the Senate, and he not only solicits support, but takes advice on how to proceed further:

> I spoke to his excellency Bishop Alex Carter this morning in North Bay. He is also strongly in support of my appointment. He suggested I contact Chief Justice Jerome of the Federal Court to confirm that I would have his support too. He

says he has already spoken to Jerome. Jerome was well disposed towards the idea.

Mr. Maloney spoke to Chief Justice Jerome in Ottawa today.

The list of supporters grew in both the Conservative and Liberal ranks. McMurtry suggested a talk with Lowell Murray, and several other Senators. His Excellency Bishop Wall offered to speak to both Clark and Trudeau.

In early November, Maloney spoke to Clark. Prior to that, the rumour of Arthur's position seemed very strong. But Clark, in a telephone conversation with Arthur, made it clear that such was not true. He suggested that Arthur might be best served if he could get Senator Joseph Sullivan, who was eighty, to resign. There was a rumour that Sullivan was thinking just that. "He is strongly of the view that if word could be got to Sullivan and if he were to resign there would be no problem." But in the memo on the conversation with Clark, there is no mention of any specific list of nominees, nor that Arthur having any place of priority. Clark claimed he was to get one seat for the Senator Grosart vacancy, and no more.

Maloney was not deterred. He kept chasing supporters. In late November, while in Ottawa working on the Amway case, he managed to get around to see Mark McGuigan, the Minister of Justice, who also agreed to support him. He also spoke to Jim Fleming, Robert Kaplan, the Solicitor General, and to Bert Raphael of the Canadian Committee on Soviet Jewry. He saw several others, both in and out of politics, despite the fact that he had been told that he was not on the list that Clark had given to Trudeau earlier in the year. Unless Trudeau rejected that list, he could not hope to be put on it, in any position, even if Clark wanted to do so; or so Clark had told him. What he seemed to be doing was going behind Clark's back in order to open up the contest, not only by talking to Conservatives and Liberals in Ottawa, but going further:

I called Jim McGrath and spoke to him in Ottawa yesterday and he advised me that he had not personally heard anything further re the Senate. He urged me, however, to call Brian Mulroney in Montreal, that Brian was expecting to hear from me. Accordingly I called Brian last night and he informed me he had found favourable reaction to the Senate possibility from Jim Coutts and he also told me he had been in contact with Roy and that Roy seemed to be of course strongly supportive of the idea. It was as a result of my conversation with Jim McGrath that I phoned Mulroney and got this information. Mulroney told me that there had been a meeting in the last few weeks which I believe was held in Europe and that Mr. Coutts was present at this meeting and related the very favourable reaction to the idea had been expressed [*sic*] by Coutts and also

Coutts related that the P.M. was strongly sympathetic to this idea.

Apparently Coutts was of the view that the Senate was heavily over-loaded with Liberals, that the appointment of a few well regarded P.C.'s might now be in order.

The most touching support came from his brother, Father Henry, whose own celebrity as a cleric with political connections was such that he was able to get to the men in power quickly. On 16 December, he had an appointment with Joe Clark specifically to argue Arthur's case, and Clark explained, at some length, how the process worked. Again Clark urged an approach to Senator Sullivan, and it was evident to Father Henry that Arthur was not on any short list in Trudeau's possession. On the following day, he got in to see Trudeau: "I had a conversation with Mr. Trudeau with regard to the appointment of an Irish Catholic Conservative Senator from Toronto and that I was speaking to him on behalf of my brother Arthur. His words were: 'I have had several presentations on behalf of Arthur including the Cardinal.' He smiled and shook hands with me. I told him I would be praying for him at the Christmas Mass."[7] The Father was not finished yet. He had been told by Clark that the Ontario Premier had some influence in the matter, and on 25 January 1983, he arranged to see Bill Davis. Davis thought that Father Henry was there to speak about problems in Bancroft. "Father Maloney said no this was on a personal family matter about Arthur and the possibility of Arthur's appointment and Premier Davis said he would certainly support Arthur's nomination to the Senate he said Arthur has a lot of service to give and he has also given great service [*sic*]."

In late December, Clark, who had obviously gotten some idea of how busily Arthur was working around and about him, and upset by the *Globe* story, wrote directly to him. Clark was only going to get one seat – that from which Allister Grosart had resigned a year before. The list in Trudeau's office did not contain Arthur's name, and that list had been prepared with the full knowledge of Bill Davis. Clark asked Arthur to publicly refute the claim that they were at odds. Shortly after William Kelly was appointed to the Senate.

Arthur still did not give up. He managed to get Senator Sullivan to admit that he was thinking of retiring, but not before the next session of Parliament. Now, the importuning of figures presumed to have power went on with the future Sullivan retirement as the goal. The last memo on the matter was written on 25 March 1983, and it indicates a suspicion of where the weak spot was, despite denials to the contrary:

I spoke to John Munro at the Benchers' Luncheon today at Osgoode Hall. He is very strongly supportive of the appointment to the Senate – The Prime Minister is too. He told me that many of his colleagues are supportive of the idea that I go to the Senate. The big stumbling block is to make sure that I am on the list of Conservative candidates recommended by Joe Clark to the Prime Minister.

Margaret Godin recalls the time:

I remember the family saying that somebody was asking Mr. Trudeau to appoint Arthur to the Senate, and I said, 'What does Arthur think about it?' And they said, "Well, I suppose he would think it a nice quiet ending to a political career." – When he started to be sick, I think.

The most notorious case of his last years was the Amway Corporation tax battle in which Arthur represented one of the Amway executives, and which was to go on after Arthur was able to take an active part in the swings and roundabouts of legal complication and endless negotiation. He made a good fee out of it, often without doing much; as was his way with large corporations, he billed high, and regularly, even when not much was being achieved. The case was to be the cause of a serious falling-out with Dave Humphrey. Humphrey prefers the quarrel to be seen as a minor incident, caused more by Arthur's illness than any serious differences of opinion. "Anyway, I did not have a falling out with my friend, Arthur Maloney. I had a falling out with a shell of the man, unfortunately, that he was at the end. It was so sad, Jesus! It was so sad. It was really, unbelievably sad! And the guts that he had to try to carry on! Never crying for himself, but trying to bull it through."

It would not have occurred in the old days, and was precipitated by a question that would never have arisen in the relationship between Maloney and Humphrey in the past. They had worked together several times, and there had never been any question as to who was the senior man – it was an unvoiced assumption that Arthur came first. In the Amway case, however, it was Humphrey who had been hired to take on the company defence, and who suggested that Arthur come on as the counsel for one of the executives who was charged individually. After months of wrangling Humphrey complained about the constant intrusion of the American lawyer, and, as a result, Humphrey was taken off the case by Amway. He was to return later to represent the owners in setting up the guilty plea that was to confine the conviction to the corporation at a smart fine of $25 million, but was to let the individual participants go free. Arthur took exception to Humphrey making the settlement without consulting him, although he was, by that time, so ill that he knew very little about the matter.

Arrangements were set up that they would put an indictment in the Supreme Court and I would go along and plead guilty on behalf of the owners. Maloney heard that and he phoned me up and wanted me to come down and see him. I went down with a young lawyer from my office. And he berated me – "And I got you on this case ..." I said, "Arthur, I got you on the case." "Well," he said, "I don't think this is ethical – behind my back!" And it was a complete misperception. And I said, "Arthur, if we are going to talk about ethics, how much have you billed them and how much do you know about the case? Don't talk ethics to me, Arthur. I'm really sorry that you feel this way. I'm not doing anything behind your back. You're acting for Dale Discher, against whom the charge will be withdrawn. I'm mandated to act for the owners." He was really berating me, and I said, "Well, look Arthur, I'm awfully sorry – I can't just abide this attitude."

Humphrey walked out and went on with the arrangement for the guilty plea. In court, a representative from Arthur's office appeared to speak on behalf of Discher. Humphrey informed him that there was nothing to say since the charges against the executives were separate and were being dealt with in Ottawa. The deal was such that when Humphrey turned over the $25 million cheque and pleaded guilty, the Ottawa court, on the next day, would withdraw the charges against the individuals. Maloney objected to this, wanting to delay the disposition of the case to a later date when it would be convenient for him to get to Ottawa. This caused everyone to be upset, and further words flew between the Humphrey and Maloney offices.

The two musketeers of the law never quite reconciled. They met a very few times in the corridors of the courts, and in the narrow conjunction of streets around Osgoode Hall that constitute the battle grounds of trial lawyers in downtown Toronto, but it was always a grudging grunt of recognition – if it got any further, it could turn bellicose.

He would say, "I understand that people are saying that I'm incapacitated – no person that was loyal to me would say anything like that!" He couldn't read; he was walking badly with a cane. His memory was shot. I just decided it was better for me to stay out of his way. First of all, I hated to see him like that – he just wasn't going to give up. It was just wrenching to see him that way, and the unfairness of it all! Here was a guy who had been so goddam charitable, and most importantly – and maybe this is one reason why I'm a flaming atheist – a guy who served his God so well, and had been such a living example of Catholicism, and the unfairness of the thing was almost more than anybody could bear.

There was at least one moment of humour in the struggle to keep his end up in the Amway affair. In the period when Humphrey was off the job, the American clients and their lawyers were determined to find out what was going on in Canada, and they asked Arthur to come to Washington to meet them. Arthur knew better than anyone how limited was his grasp of the case, and he asked Phil Patterson, who had been associated with Humphrey on the file, and had been fired with him, to go with Arthur to meet the Americans. Patterson was reluctant to do so, but went as a favour to Arthur. They arranged the presentation in such a way that Patterson was to do most of the work. During the meeting, the Amway people and the American lawyers wanted Arthur to do the talking, and they made attempt after attempt to get Arthur to address the specifics of the case, while Arthur airily frustrated them, despite their insistence that they wanted him to speak to the matter, by calling upon Patterson to answer their queries. However they put their questions to involve him, Arthur always managed to work his answer around in generalities which Patterson would flesh out with detail. They left the meeting no wiser than when they came in as to how much Arthur really knew about what was going on, although his patently ravaged physical state must have given them some suspicion that he was not entirely in control of himself, or their very complicated case.

The most amusing, and in some way touching part of the trip came after Maloney and Patterson had managed to escape the Amway meeting. Arthur wanted to see the John Kennedy grave. Lillian was with them, and the three of them travelled to Arlington Cemetery in the limousine that Arthur had hired for use in Washington. As they drove towards the memorial, a school bus was unloading children at the entrance to the site. As the huge black car rolled to a stop before the grave, the whole class suddenly was transfixed by the sight of this aged man, in dark sunglasses, carrying a cane, as he was being helped out of the car. Arthur immediately sensed their interest, and as if by some subliminal arrangement, the children presumed that this mysterious man must be of some moment. In mutual, if inchoate regard, the whole group suddenly turned their small cameras on him – Arthur turned to them, assumed a posture of majestic dignity and posed – it was one of his last acts of ego.

It was, perhaps, his finest hour in the Amway case, if irrelevant to it. The case was certainly not one of his finer moments at the Bar, for reasons that were obvious. Humphrey is rueful about what had happened. In a mildly amusing way, he talks about being sorry that he had to deal alone, at the end, with the Amway people, since in assessing a final bill for settling the case, he quoted a figure of some substance, based upon what the American lawyer was getting. He asked for the same amount, but when the cheque came, it was in Canadian money! "If Arthur had been around, that would have never happened!" It was one of the few times that Arthur was complimented for getting fees right, even if, on this occasion, he didn't get the chance to do so.

There is a way in which the Amway people got their money's worth from Arthur, even if he did very little work. French defends his determination to stay on the case, and his value thereto: "Don't forget that Arthur was popular. If you had him acting for you, you had that goodwill which, let's face it, in criminal cases is sometimes 90 percent – it may be all that you have going for you." French knew that there was some laughing going on about Arthur refusing to quit, and he is unrepentant in defending his uncle:

> Even in the last months, you could still bounce things off him, and I still think that there were individuals around whose *derrières* were saved because of Arthur's sense of how to deal with something; not only did he have the sense, he had the *entrée*. If Arthur phoned, whoever was at the other end would pick up the phone and take it ... There were several cases where that saved the day. He knew what had to be done and he could get the door opened to get the mechanics dealt with.

The strokes had crippled him, and seriously affected his sight and memory, but they did not kill him. One day he came home and quietly told Lillian, "I went to the doctor's today. I've got a dull, little ache in my side." Lillian talked to the doctor; he put the situation bleakly. The doctors operated, but the cancer had spread. From that moment on the matter was closed, although everyone tried to make the best of it. Arthur continued to go into the office on an irregular basis until July 1984. Two tumors were found in the spine, and he took radiation treatment. He was often very ill, but he would pull himself together, and pretend to be in control of the situation. He developed a bemusing way of faking short-term memory which his doctor told Paul French was not uncommon with patients in his condition, and he had a wry way of mocking his predicament. By the late summer, French was taking care of the tag ends of the practice, and dealing with Arthur's financial affairs, in anticipation of the inevitable.

> It was a question of managing his resources. What came in, went out – straight Grade Eight accounting – and there were other sorts of physical problems. I would explain to Arthur that he had to do this or had to do that, and he would just say, "Oh, yes, Paul. Yes, Paul." It was never really sinking in, so I arranged this meeting one day with Lillian, because I felt that Lillian would be on side, and I wanted Arthur and Lillian to know what I was doing, and what the situation was, and so I bought this white board – so that if I put it there, Arthur could

hear it, and actually see it. So on the appointed day, I brought in this huge white board – the thing was about seven feet by six feet. I had my black magic marker and my sheet with my figures. Arthur turned himself sideways to face the board. He was not looking forward to this; he knew we'd prepared a couple of days in advance. So finally he faces the white board – then pulls out his sunglasses – black, black sunglasses – there was no way anybody could see through those things, and he puts them on and says, "Proceed, Paul." [Paul laughing] It was so typical of Arthur. He just didn't want to hear that nonsense – that was, in the end, my relationship with him.

Well, he never was much interested in money.

Everyone did the best they could in that last summer. Arthur still was thinking about cases, when he could think of anything, given his constant illness, and the concussive after-effects of the therapy. He had always loved the theatre at Stratford; had always spent time when his children were home, preparing them for the plays. Lillian and the family did the best they could.

We went to Stratford to see *Julius Caesar* with the children that summer. He died in September. It was July, and it was a long play. We had a dinner at the church restaurant. I think Nell was with us. He said, "I think I'll go to the car. Martha, would you walk to the car with me? I'll listen to some nice music. You go ahead and have your dinner."

After that he got thinner and thinner, and went down hill, but he'd still go out and walk around the farm. People from the office would call him.

Dave Rendeiro had become a close personal friend of Martha, and he was at the farm regularly through the last days. Most of Arthur's old students and friends, knowing he was dying, left Arthur and the family alone. Arthur complained to Rendeiro about his friends abandoning him, but almost all of them, when speaking of Arthur's last months, admitted that they would have liked to see him, but thought it improper to intrude – an example of that fumbling insecurity of male friendship that often withdraws when most needed. Rendeiro spent a lot of time with Arthur. Rendeiro, a thoughtful, gentle man, remembers him tenderly, and with some formality. He always spoke of Arthur as "Mr. Maloney." "Mr. Maloney was not only a mentor to me, but I got to know him personally. Since he died, I haven't found a mentor. He was a great loss to me."

By August, the whole family had gathered. Matthew had come home from the States to stay at the house, as did Martha. Nell was there. Arthur steadily got worse. Three days before he died, Paul French was still trying to clear up estate matters. An officious bank official, who knew the situation, insisted upon Arthur's signature on a minor document. French was furious. "So I went back to the farm. This was three days before he died. And I asked Arthur to sign these things for me. He was very weak and very thin, and I did not appreciate that he was completely blind, but he said, 'Just show me where to sign.' So I helped his hand and he signed. But he bluffed it, you know. He would never say, 'I can't do it! Show me where and take my hand.'" Just before the end, he found it difficult to swallow, and there was some suspicion that he had suffered another stroke. He went into hospital in Guelph. It wasn't a stroke – the cancer was spreading to the brain. Two days previous, the signs were clearly there of a new, frightening confusion.

I was reading to him from the *Globe*, and he was teasing me about "lying in bed here and having my wife read me things I'm interested in" – and I looked over and he was asleep. Later he was going to take a shower, and told me so. Then he called out, "Lillian, where's the bathroom?" The bathroom was across the hall, but he had wandered down the hall. He came back, sat on the edge of the bed, and said, "My God! When is this going to pass? I'm no good to anybody. I'm becoming a burden to you!" He never complained. He had morphine, but he hardly ever took it. He'd tease, if I asked him about his pain. "Not as much as Christ's." And then he'd laugh.

He slipped into a coma, and three days later, he died. A grand funeral service was held in Toronto, and all the important people were there in a kind of reprise of his Ombudsman installation. He was buried in the Mount Hope Cemetery in Toronto. Something happened that Paul French found odd, and he spoke of it later with Gerry Donnelly, Arthur's last faithful secretary, who had served him in the law, followed him to the Ombudsman's office, and back into the law again.

On the day that Arthur was buried, we went to the cemetery. It had been a clear day, but the moment we drove into the cemetery – the moment we drove in – this incredible fine mist fell. I've never seen it before and I've never seen it since. It was a rain that was so fine – as if someone was kissing your hand. Then when the time came for the casket to be dropped, it stopped – just like that. When everybody entered their automobiles, it started again, and as the cars left the cemetery, it stopped. It was the most incredible thing! And I spoke about it to Gerry and she described it as "the tears of the angels."

Epilogue

THE LAST OF THE TRIBUNES

No one, including Arthur Edwin Martin Maloney, would disagree that there are more profound scholars of the criminal law in Canada than he. But as a trial strategist and courtroom tactician, Arthur Maloney is probably the best defence counsel around.[1]

There was never any question about Arthur's skill in the courtroom, and his reputation remained intact, save for the unfortunate few months at the end when he ought not to have been in the public arena, but would not stop trying. That was understandable, given his character. Yet so much has been made of his trial prowess that it is often forgotten that he was an excellent appeal lawyer, and in the minds of some of his contemporaries the difference lay not so much in a limited ability to work at the appeal level, as in his decision to spend most of his time in trial confrontation, which he often admitted he simply liked better. On the matter of his ability to argue law at the trial level, Clive Bynoe has no reservations:

The belief that he depended upon others to prepare his cases is utter nonsense! Certainly he depended upon his students, and juniors, given the amount of work he did, but Maloney had a store of law that he didn't have to look up. He used to edit cases for the Criminal Law reports, and he was an editor of the Criminal Reports. It was just that he found the research of law boring, unless it was to be put into action. I remember a civil case in which Canada Packers was involved. A very substantial case. He got the brief a day or two before, and he was a prodigious worker – when he made his mind up to work, everything else was irrelevant. He won that case in amazing fashion! He had a great recollection of cases and when he did research, he did it very quickly. It was true that he would get bored with detail. He would say, "just give me the outline; that's all that I need to know." He was never one for repetition or superficial detail, unless, of course, that was a key to the case.[2]

Pat LeSage, while still a very young Crown, had several occasions to see Arthur impose his own style on a trial, whatever the Crown or the judge might have in mind to the contrary. Maloney was perfectly happy to reveal his defence, not only to the Crown, but to the judge, and LeSage saw it as an asset for both sides, since it allowed the case to unfold logically and efficiently.

In fact, not only did you know what his defence was, he worked on you to get you to accede to it; he would, at the outset, as comment to the presiding judge, say, "Your Lordship, just so you will know how this case is likely to unfold, Mr. LeSage and I have discussed this case and the issue is –" It would have been considered improper if he had said these things to the jury ... they just happened to be sitting there and heard it. He would identify what the defence was, early on. Then there wasn't quite the disclosure there is now. I tried to tell him, and defence in those days didn't tell much – but Arthur usually would speak to the Crown before a trial ... All the trials I had with Arthur, there was never any acrimony.

Aside from his general attempt to choose the ground for confrontation in a civilized manner, Arthur never attempted to impose his formidable reputation on LeSage. LeSage, however, knew that if law was needed, Arthur would have it easily at hand. He rarely would quote law, preferring to put his positions forward with logic and common sense, "but if he was pressed, he knew what the legal authority was for his argument. He surprised me on more than one occasion by coming up with cases I certainly had never heard of, but which were established. I think he had an excellent legal mind – not everyone would agree with that; he didn't expose it as a legal mind, but in persuasive argument. He had a great knack of explaining his position that was consonant with the law, but without ever making any reference to the law."

As his cases show, Arthur's greatest skill lay in taking the facts of a case as he found them, and turning them in his hands into a way of looking that made the charge against his client less tenable, and on occasion, legally unconvincing. LeSage saw him do this over and over again, and was as appreciative of his skills as the man on the losing end could be, and somewhat more so, since he remembers his confrontations with Arthur as part of a wider experience of professional and personal friendship.

Juries are not deciding law – they are deciding fact. So his ability to sway a jury was legitimate. It was his duty to bring the jury to find the facts in his client's favour. Very often the facts are not in dispute; the position you advocate is the more likely interpretation of the facts. The facts are not in dispute, but having regard to these facts, it is not logical to presume that this person would have reason to – for instance – use that degree of force to protect himself – or if using drugs, could he form the intent – or given the facts of the surrounding situation, could he form the intent to murder – or whatever it was.

To watch Arthur – he didn't ask a lot of high risk questions; he knew when to stop, and he had a way with his charm and persuasiveness. The intimacy began with the witnesses. He would try to get the witnesses to agree with his position. Even if it was to agree that it was a nice day, and the sun was shining – to get the witness to take it easy. There was rarely any antagonism between Arthur and a witness, unless it was difficult – and then he might take a strong position, but even then he didn't want to antagonize the jury or the judge by picking a fight with somebody with whom they might have some sympathy.

He always had that Ottawa Valley accent that was charming. I never saw him use sarcasm, in the sense of belittling anyone. I found him very careful in his rapport with a jury. In part it was his eloquence, and in part, the impression of commitment to the verdict of 'not guilty.' He would never say it was his opinion, but there was this air of commitment. I found him very persuasive – in fact, I followed him in many jury addresses, and I would always start off by telling the jury what a pleasure it was to follow him, and how wonderful his jury addresses were, and how convincing and persuasive he was – and I meant it.[3]

Keith Hoilett who had seen him in the magistrates' courts, before joining him in the Ombudsman's office, recognized a professionalism that belies the suggestion that he was a catch-as-catch-can counsel. The fact that Maloney took great care even at the lowest level of the judicial system says something of his professionalism. He was particularly careful after conviction to prepare his argument as to sentence: "A lot of lawyers never assigned what I regard as the important, the appropriate regard to the sentencing procedure in a criminal trial ... As a general rule, Arthur always had letters from employers, priests, friends – and sometimes, you would wonder if the accused was there for canonization or for sentence, but that was an aspect he never ignored. It was his way of saying, 'He's in trouble today, but there are some people who value him.' He really served his client well."[4]

Hoilett's comment upon the care with which he surrounded his convicted clients with social concern, and particularly, his perception of what Arthur was saying to the Bench: "He's in trouble today, but there are some people who value him," leads to the further and perhaps more important point of Arthur Maloney's service, not simply to his clients, or to the Bar, but to society as he saw it. Stephen Traviss saw it many times when Arthur fought for lawyers who had done stupid things, and had ruined their lives. Traviss recognized the Christian humanist in Maloney in his belief that man was capable, however debased, of redemption, not only in the spiritual, but also in the social sense. "He felt very passionately about the rights of the accused. He was a reformer. There was a restless quality about him – but it was a positive thing, since something always came of his dissatisfaction in accepting the supposed inevitable."[5]

He wasn't, however, fatuously committed to spilling criminals on to the streets. He knew when they could use a sharp bit of punishment. On once occasion, Monte Harris accompanied him to a sentencing of a young client before Fred Thompson, the magistrate. Maloney requested a suspended sentence, and Thompson agreed. On the way out, Harris congratulated him on getting a good result, but Maloney was clearly not happy. Harris was puzzled, until Maloney explained that his client, at the early stages of a criminal career, would have been better served if they had appeared before Tupper Bigelow, who would have surely put him in the reformatory for a few months.

From early in his career, it was recognized both in and out of the profession that however haphazardly Arthur Maloney had fallen into the criminal law (as he claimed), it was his natural role, and he was often asked to speak publicly about the duties of the criminal lawyer. Among his papers, on half sheets prepared for public use, is an address, hand-corrected in ink, dated "February 8, 1955" and titled *MY RIGHT TO DEFEND A CLIENT WHOM I KNOW TO BE GUILTY*. He is unrepentant.

> In the course of my professional career, I have often acted in the defence of persons whom I believed to be guilty, and on a considerable number of occasions, of persons, whom I knew to be guilty. Quite frequently I have witnessed the acquittal of such persons. You will be prompt to ask me how I felt about this, and I will be prompt to tell you that I felt fully justified about my participation in such matter, and experienced feelings of very real satisfaction.

It was not, however, for Arthur, simply a matter of professional triumph in exercising his skills against the odds. In part it was a matter of his duty as a counsel, but more significantly it was a matter of his duty to society: "The best interests of Society are furthered and the proper administration of justice is maintained in the defence of the guilty, with the single qualification that I do not stoop to use improper or dishonest means." He knows this is difficult for a layman to understand. No-one is "guilty" in the legal sense of anything, until the legal system has exhausted all avenues of investigation under the rules of law to prove him or her so. One may be clearly revealed in a socially reprehensible act and may, indeed, be of the personal opinion that one has broken the law, but neither the unstructured opinion of society or of the individual, however well-informed, is sufficient to deem a person guilty. Maloney well understood why that is so: "This is a salutary rule of our jurisprudence that was designed to allay the apprehensions of those who were concerned about the proper safeguards for the rights of the innocent under the law. The fact that in its application the guilty have been and continue to be freed time and time again, does not warrant any temporary or permanent suspension of the rule." What is, perhaps, most significant in this address, which goes on to show the way in which the law has, on many occasions, in many jurisdictions, protected the innocent from conviction in its rigorous demand for safeguards, is the way in which Maloney characterizes his role in the continual battle for justice, not simply as a good job well done in the interest of all, but as something else."I have suggested to you during the course of this address that it has been my privilege during my professional career to defend the guilty and to prevent such persons from being improperly convicted – to see to it that such persons were tried according to law – to thwart any efforts to deny them justice – all that – I say – *has been a privilege*." [italics mine] It is that peculiar awareness of the nature of what he is doing that reveals Arthur Maloney as a creative thinker about the law. Most lawyers can easily, and convincingly argue for the necessity of the rules of jurisprudence to protect the innocent, ruefully accepting as a result that some of the guilty are also likely to be allowed to run free. It takes an entirely different sensibility to see further into the proposition that the guilty must be accorded the same protection – that their sometime escapes through the complications of the legal rules are not simply necessary evils, but a further, positive accomplishment of the system. More to the point is his admission that for him it is a privilege.

In December 1955, Arthur was one of the two counsel who appeared on behalf of Wilbert Coffin in the Supreme Court of Canada, and had argued against the use of a mixed rather than a unilingual jury at the trial level. They had argued that the mixed jury really was two juries, one which understood French and one which understood English, and that Coffin, who did not understand French, was, in effect, tried before two separate juries. The majority opinion on the Court rejected the argument that Coffin had, therefore, not received a fair trial, although Mr. Justice Cartwright, Arthur's old friend from his student days, dissented, believing that the selection of the mixed jury invalidated Coffin's right to a fair trial. There were several other points of law, and points of fact argued at the time, all in vain – Coffin was executed on the 10 February 1956.

The question of whether Coffin was guilty or had been treated fairly remained a public issue, and as a result of continuing public interest, and the work of the journalist Jacques Hébert, who published two books on the trial in 1958 and 1963, the Quebec government in the mid-sixties ordered a judicial inquiry with Mr. Justice Roger Brossard heading the commission. Arthur Maloney took part in that inquiry, and Roy McMurtry accompanied him as his counsel. Sometime during the hearing, McMurtry heard something that convinced him that Coffin was, in fact, responsible for the deaths of the American hunters. On the way back to Toronto, McMurtry mentioned what he had heard to Arthur, and Arthur made it clear that he, too, was of the opinion that Coffin did the killings – but that was no reason why he should have desisted from fighting so hard for Coffin at appeal, and he was still prepared to argue that he should not have been convicted. It was not a matter of what Coffin had done – it was a matter of Coffin being wrongly convicted, given the way in which the trial had been conducted. As a private citizen he despised the homicidal act, but as a barrister, he didn't, in a sense, care that Coffin had killed – what he cared about was that Coffin had, in turn, been killed as a result of an unfair trial. Aside from his deep aversion to the death penalty, he could not accept Coffin's conviction simply because he was convinced that Coffin had done the act. Coffin was entitled to be fairly tried, and had that been done, he might either have been convicted or might have walked free – either result would have satisfied Maloney.

It is this peculiar ability to face down the most obvious responses of social indignation and moral hypocrisies that make his work and his comments upon not only the criminal, but the social world, so different from many of his contemporaries. He is, however conservative his upbringing, his politics, his profession, often out there alone, determined to break through the carapace of established social barriers to the contemplation of a new kind of awareness of the complication of human endeavour and conduct. It is, in part, what his friends and colleagues are attempting to articulate when they comment upon his tendency to occasionally break rules, to reject the usual Pavlovian posturings of respect and acceptance of the way things are, which was suggested in the introduction to this study.

It could be a personal matter, as it was on one occasion, when he came upon a judge who went too far in using his position of superiority to abuse him. G. Arthur Martin tells a story of Arthur having difficulty getting an adjournment in open court, and being assailed with a more than usual amount of gratuitous spleen. (Abuse is a common element in the process of getting adjournments, particularly if busy counsel are involved, since they usually are juggling several cases at the same time, and often find themselves caught up in the problem of temporarily begging off more than one in several different courts. One Maloney student was of the opinion that after working with Arthur, his finest skill was in getting adjournments without falling into deep depression every morning as the court lists were called up.) After the public encounter, Arthur followed the judge into his chambers, and once the door was closed, proclaimed to the astonished man, "You are the rudest judge I have ever appeared before, and not only that, you are the ugliest!" Martin thought that was improper, since Arthur had engaged in personalizing a legal difficulty. But it was typical Arthur – to beard the bully in his den, and bloody his nose.

Dave Humphrey tells of one occasion when Arthur managed to publicly chastise a judge, while giving a lesson in why the jury is important in the administration of justice. It was his old nemesis Frank Donnelly on the Bench:

> He was defending a fellow called "One Eyed" Connelly. Frank Donnelly was presiding, an Irish Roman Catholic. They hated each other. An irascible, nasty judge – charming out of court. So Donnelly was interfering and Arthur was addressing the jury, "You know, Members of the Jury, if we wanted to, we could have been tried by a judge alone, but we didn't want that – we wanted a jury. Why did we not want to be tried by a judge alone? Because a judge alone is a captive of his own personal biases – prejudices. No, we didn't want to be tried by a judge alone. Another reason why we didn't want to be tried by a judge alone is because of his very limited experience of life. You, Members of the Jury, bring a wealth of such experience. And that is why the jury verdict is always correct." He should have said "is always just." Well, Donnelly jumped in, "What's your authority for that, Mr. Maloney?" And Arthur said, "Truth and justice, and I'll thank you not to interrupt my jury address, and I'll promise you I will not interrupt yours!"[6]

It was not, however, simply a matter of taking care of himself in court, but of a constant vigilance about the way human beings were taken into the court system and pulverized by it. He saw the jury as one way in which the individual was given a chance against the odds, and he saw the rules that hedged around the powers of the state as another aspect of that frail protection of the individual. The lawyer was the individual best able to use the rules and the jury to protect that individual, and he knew, and was extremely sensitive to the constant attempts to intrude upon those safeguards. As things stood, he was not pleased with the situation. He often spoke of the huge apparatus of the state that confronted the accused. In an address to the Law Society of Alberta in Edmonton on 11 February 1966, he described the nature of the foe.

> In the first place let us remind ourselves of what a prosecution really is. Even the title by which our prosecutions are conducted inspires awe. It is "Our Lady the

Queen versus a named member of our society." The awe inspiring style of cause, as you well know, is not a misnomer. It is a very apt description of the opposing parties in a criminal proceeding in Canada. On the side of Her Majesty are skilled, trained police officers who have conducted detailed investigations and lengthy interviews of witnesses, particulars of which invariably are incorporated into careful summaries and statements, have made sketches, taken photographs, and have brought to bear all the latest scientific advances to aid them in their enquiries. All this is then delivered to a trained lawyer who acts as counsel for the prosecution. In the event the prosecution is dissatisfied with an acquittal it has power to appeal on a question of law – a power which I regret to see being exercised in far too many cases in recent years, and a power which is not allowed in most other jurisdictions since it would violate the double jeopardy rule. For this purpose it can order costly transcripts of evidence in a trial that might have lasted several weeks. The funds, in other words, available to the prosecution are literally speaking, inexhaustible.

He was suspicious of the way in which the law was used to enforce aspects of public morality which were sometimes questionable, particularly in a changing society. His attitude to minor drug convictions, for instance, is as worthy of consideration today as it was when it was made, almost twenty years ago. His opposition to mixing morality and criminal law was constant. The law against marijuana, he said, "symbolizes the contempt for the law and its institutions that is engendered by our persistent and fruitless attempts to enforce morality by proclaiming laws."[7]

During the seventies and eighties, as the crime figures rose in Toronto and in Ontario at large, with a resulting increase in the cases coming into the courts, there was much rumbling about ways to speed things up. The suggestion was made that, perhaps, the jury should be eliminated in civil actions. More alarming, however, was the suggestion that it should be curtailed in criminal actions, and that various other limitations should be imposed. Maloney was quick to realize that the "improvements" all fell on aspects of the system that favoured the rights of the accused.

From early in his career, he had fought to protect the jury and its role, particularly in the criminal justice system. On 14 February 1956, in an address to the Ontario Subsection of the Administration of Criminal Justice of the Canadian Bar Association, he discussed the problem of anticipating the possibility of an unsympathetic judge influencing the jury, and in his comments, made his opinion of the role of the jury evident:

When you expect that the defence and its theory will not be treated by the trial judge as sympathetically as you hope, the following would be perfectly proper and, it seems to me, appropriate language:

"I often wonder whether juries realize the supremacy of their power in a criminal case and the reason they are given that power. When a juror is sworn to try a case he becomes stamped with a mark that remains indelibly upon him until he has discharged his duties in the case. This is a mark of a judge. It confers on you all the dignity and all the authority that goes with that distinguished office. As judges there rests upon you, and you alone, the awful and final responsibility of deciding whether the accused man at the bar is to be convicted or to go free.

"The power of final decision being yours and yours alone, the roles of the rest of us in this proceeding are relatively unimportant ... Finally, it is the duty of the trial judge to review the facts in order to assist you and while not his duty, it is his privilege to express an opinion on the facts ... But here, gentlemen of the jury, is where the supremacy of your power manifests itself. You not only may, you must – you are bound in conscience by the oath you took – to discard and cast to the four winds my submissions, my friend's submissions [i.e. the Crown's] and the opinion on the facts of his lordship, if what I say, or any of us say, is not in accord with your own view of the facts formed after a conscientious review of the evidence. This is because, as I have already stated, on you alone rests the awful and final responsibility of determining the grave issue of my client's guilt or innocence."[8]

Arthur always believed not only in the value of the jury system, but of the duty of the Bar to defend it against its detractors, and those who would circumscribe its powers, either by attempting to change it, or by defining it too narrowly. In the seventies, when the suggestion was being mooted that the jury was no longer valuable, he led the fight to stop the rot:

I find there are a great many who do not comprehend the function of a jury in our system. The late Henry Bull, Q.C., would sometimes, in addressing a jury, say to them "You must approach your task without feeling or emotion – as mathematicians might approach a mathematical problem." When I was engaged in a contest with that very skilful adversary I would either anticipate his approach in my address if I went first or deal with it in my reply where I did not call evidence and admonish the jury that, that is exactly what they must not do. *In their deliberations they should bring into play every part and fibre of their being; a juror has no obligation to take a surgeon's scalpel, then excise his heart and place it in a pickle jar until he has agreed upon his verdict.* [italics mine]

Mr. C.A. Harvey, Q.C., a sometime Vinerian scholar of Oxford University and a Past President of the Pegasus Club was in 1958 the author of *The Advocate's Devil*. At page 4 he says,

"It is one of the prime functions of a jury to dilute logic with mercy. It was juries who mitigated the barbarity of the criminal law of a century ago, which enjoined the death penalty for the theft of anything worth more than forty shillings, by resolutely and perversely finding that the most expensive objects did not have that value. In modern times they have constantly saved prisoners from the gallows by bringing in verdicts of manslaughter when the only logical choice was between Not Guilty and Guilty of Murder."

I have always believed it is part of our role as advocates to defend the jury system. Of all the creations of imperfect man none has done more to preserve his freedom and save him harmless from the vast apparatus of the state than the jury.[9]

A significant aspect of this argument was his support of the proposition that the jury was not to be circumscribed by "reason," as Henry Bull and many others would have wished, but had the obligation to "dilute justice with mercy, to act perversely, and against logic." The heart as well as the head had a role in Arthur's idea of the ideal jury. It is not surprising, then, to find him, in his 1957 address, arguing that a defence counsel should become involved emotionally with his client's cause:

Juries are quick to detect any lack in a defence counsel of the qualities of earnestness and sincerity they expect from someone who is advocating a serious cause. These qualities are not successfully feigned. I agree that you should not go to jail with your client, *but I have some difficulty in understanding the temperament of a counsel who does not acquire some feeling for the client he represents and the cause he is advancing. To that extent you must identify yourself with your client; in this sense you are in truth your client's "alter ego."*[10] [italics mine]

By the early seventies, Arthur was sufficiently exercised by the pressure to change the rules in the criminal trial to complain that, in fact, the state had already too much power over the individual accused. Not only did it have a formidable apparatus with which to investigate and prepare a case against the individual, but it also could spare no expense in pursuing the accused, even after the case had been adjudicated at the trial level. He spoke, as he had in his 1966 address to the Law Society of Alberta, of the high incidence of appeals by the Crown.

In my early days as a lawyer – in the 1940s – the exercise by the Crown of its right to appeal either acquittals by juries or by judges sitting alone or sentence was a very rare occurrence. In the last fifteen years the incidence of Crown appeals has increased in Ontario to a very marked degree. The other provinces appear to be following this rather dubious example.

I deprecate the too frequent use of this power by the state against the citizen – especially one who has been acquitted by a jury.

> First, it does violence to the Jury System but further it is unfair that a citizen should be tried a second time for mistakes for which he was not personally responsible.[11]

In 1972, when the Canada Law Reform Commission proposed that judges be given the power to limit the number of witnesses, and to compel spouses to testify, he was quick to respond: "I don't know how much some of these things alarm you but they do alarm me." Appearing on a panel of lawyers, discussing the proposed changes, he made his point of view obvious:

> I can't imagine anything more devastating to the marital relationship than compelling a wife to testify against her husband.
>
> In our country, statistics show that of the number of persons who are arrested and brought to trial in indictable cases, approximately 90 per cent are found guilty either because they are convicted or because they plead guilty. There doesn't seem to be much need for improvement in the percentage of success enjoyed by the prosecutor.[12]

When Mr. Justice Edson Haines suggested that the right of silence be taken away from an accused, Maloney was particularly alarmed. There were quite enough impediments put in the way of the defence counsel as the rules stood. He had always spoken out against the rule that deprived a defence counsel of his right to address the jury after the Crown, if the defence put in any kind of defence. And he was not happy that an accused, who did choose to testify, could have his previous record revealed, seeing it as an unfair impediment put in the way of defence counsel who needed his client's testimony, but feared the revelation of his criminal record. "Once a witness, the accused can be subject to a factual cross-examination of his previous record of convictions. The fact that the jury must be told by the trial judge that the record is not relevant to anything except his credibility, *is a pious bit of nonsense* [italics mine] as we all well know."[13]

The idea that an accused should be forced to testify was the ultimate insult to Maloney. He rejected, out of hand, Haines's acceptance of the argument that only the guilty would refuse to speak of a criminal matter. For Maloney, the innocent might well be equally reluctant to do so, particularly if the cause in question might involve collateral matters that the innocent wished to keep to himself. "Furthermore there is always present the danger that an innocent man knowing he can be forced to take the witness box in his own defence will confess and plead guilty to a crime he did not commit. Even now many accused plead guilty without benefit of counsel's advice." An unpleasant or inamicable or inarticulate accused might be prejudiced, and the accused with a record would be undoubtedly compromised. "The whole concept of a fair trial, the very root of the rule against self incrimination is the law's respect for the basic dignity of man. This right and other rules have created, in turn, a respect for our legal process – a respect that would soon be lost if we deny to an accused whom we believe to be guilty the rights that create a fair trial."[14]

Maloney's entire career at the Bar was accompanied by this interest in the social nature of the criminal law. If he left the making of new law, in the main, to other counsel, he was constantly vigilant to the dangers of intrusion upon the rights of the individual caught up in the great machine of criminal justice, and he fought publicly against the machine becoming any more powerful than it already was. There are two further elements in his social comment upon the criminal justice system. He was always of the opinion that anyone caught up in the disaster of criminal conviction deserved another chance, and he was painfully aware of the fact that many of his clients came with blighted lives, both as children and adults. In his defence of one of the Kingston rioters in 1971, he made a poignant comment in his praise of the way in which Mr. Justice William Henderson had dealt with his client: "In the case of my client ... the background of deprivation, impoverished in every conceivable particular, not just in terms of money but in terms of every other basic decency that most of us enjoy over the periods of our lives, to be confronted by a person in authority such as yourself who treated him, perhaps for the first time he was so treated by a person in that position, with such a deep sense of humanity, will have its salutary effect, I know, on him."[15] It did not matter to Maloney that the client might fail in the future to live up to this experience. What was important is that even the despicable facts of the Kingston riot murders did not preclude his client from being treated as a human being. His blasted personal life, which had been so frightful from an early age, should be considered as some reason for his outrageously savage conduct. He was an animal, in part, because he had been treated as an animal. What moved Arthur was the fact that Mr. Justice Henderson understood, as Arthur always did, that human beings bear only so much responsibility for their anti-social behaviour – what society has done to them, must also be considered.

When you retained Arthur Maloney, you got his soul ... when we did the Kingston Pen riots, his client was Bobbie Robidoux, who had a very unfortunate background ... he was a psychopathic killer, but Arthur took a real interest in the kid and bought him nice clothing to come to court in, and Robidoux said to my client, "If I were Arthur Maloney's son, I wouldn't be sitting in this fucking pen

– I'd be sitting in Parliament!" There are very few lawyers who would warm to Robidoux and my client, but Maloney could see something in that guy – some spark of humanity. It was that Catholic faith – of course, Arthur was a very religious person. He genuinely believed that Bobbie Robidoux was a child of humanity ... Maloney was a lot like Jesus Christ breaking bread with a prostitute. He would treat her with the same dignity and respect as he would treat the Queen Mother, and I don't know whether that's because of his religious views, or that he was just a plain, goddam humanitarian. As Arthur Martin once said, "Arthur Maloney was a humanitarian long before all the do-gooders became professional." That was his life style.

– Dave Humphrey

With cheerful semblance and sweet majesty;
That every wretch, pining and pale before,
Beholding him, plucks comfort from his looks.
A largesse universal like the sun
His liberal eye doth give to every one,
Thawing cold fear, that mean and gentle all,
Behold, as may unworthiness define,
A little touch of Harry in the night.

– Shakespeare

He enjoyed pomp and pageantry. Well, it's like the time he was getting ready to receive his Honorary Doctorate, and there was an urgent phone call for Arthur Maloney. And he goes to the phone and it's some bootlegger from North Bay – the police have shot his dog, and he has to get hold of Arthur. So Arthur commiserated with him, and just so the gathering wouldn't think it was something silly, he said, "And they killed him, did they? Well, I'll look into this when I get back." As if it was a murder case or something equally important.

– Dave Humphrey

Arthur was the most idealistic person I met in terms of the law. There wasn't a kid in first-year law school whose eyes were shining with the hope of making a better world who could match Arthur. To the day he died he was like that ... I can't recall Arthur, drunk or sober, ever doing anything ungentlemanly. He really was a gentleman.

– Bob Johnstone

I think he did more for the young criminal bar than anybody I have ever heard of. He brought people along, and he included you. He influenced them – pricked their social conscience – the capital punishment – the Roberts thing, when the mental defective got 24 years for arson – he set up sub-committees, always organizing something.

– B. Clive Bynoe

Arthur was fabulous with emotional defences. He could always draw on Shakespeare – on what made the human being tick ... A gentleman from Chicago had come to Toronto. He was unfamiliar with our cross-walk system, and he went through a cross-walk, and struck an infant, a three-year-old boy, and flung him across into the other lane of traffic. An oncoming vehicle, someone driving a pick-up truck saw something on the roadway that he thought was just some refuse – a bag of garbage – and, of course, just ran over it, and afterwards, when he stopped, realized that it was a child ... There were two things remarkable about the case. It was a dangerous driving charge against the American. Arthur was a great master of the courtroom. The first witnesses at the trial were the parents of the child. Arthur stood up and said to the judge that it was not necessary to call these people. He was quite prepared, in front of the jury, to admit whatever it was they were going to give in their evidence – with the view of sparing them the torment of giving evidence. You know, from the point of view of trial tactics, it was quite remarkable. He admitted that which was going to be proven in any event, but it looked so bloody good in front of the jury that he was being so very gracious and magnanimous.

But the other thing was quite as remarkable: his address to the jury. I don't think I have a hard heart, but my role as a student for Arthur was to take notes – write like hell – and I remember as Arthur's jury speech was going on, I could hear this noise – part of your role with Arthur was to deal with the clients – so you learned that you were to control the clients, and so I heard this noise, and, you know, if the client was speaking out loud – whatever – you would stand up and go over and tell him to be quiet. In this case, I turned round. This poor man – he had no criminal record. He was an innocent fellow, about fifty years old – a family man. He had never encountered the cross-walk system before. He was just tormented by the death of this child. There was no evidence of speed, alcohol. Just a decent guy driving along, and he didn't see or appreciate what was happening. In the middle of Arthur's speech, I hear this noise. I turn around. There he is – in the middle of Arthur's speech – in the prisoner's box, bawling his head off. He's just totally broken down, crying. So I didn't know what the hell to do, and I'm looking around to see if it's distracting Arthur – and I started to look at the jury – two of the jurors were crying uncontrollably. Both of them, men, crying – just weeping, and I look up at the judge. It's obvious that the judge is totally taken up by this scene – transfixed. So I just had to keep my head down.

Of course, the jury was out for no more than half an hour, and came back with a "not guilty" verdict. Which is as it should have been. But it was the remarkable passion that he could bring to a jury speech. It was quite fabulous.

– Paul French

He was always someone I could call upon. He used to coach me at his home, and have me listen to records of Shakespeare. He used to give me hell all the time, but it was always in good spirit.

– Monte Harris

At the end of my articles, I wanted to go into criminal work, but Arthur was adamant that I should not do that. I should not get myself in the situation that he was in. Not with regret, but I still think that Arthur appreciated that criminal law had its limitations. And I think, in his heart of hearts, he knew that it required a special kind of person. Really the only cases I feel comfortable in are criminal cases. He didn't mind admitting that there was where he felt most comfortable – his hero was Mr. Robinette, and Mr. Robinette's ability to move effortlessly from civil to criminal to appeal work with ease. Although I think he was happiest doing criminal.

– Neils Ortved

I always thought those were the golden days at the Bar. [When he, Martin, Maloney and Dubin were handling the major cases.] Each would help the other to the extent that you could. You could accept their word on anything; you knew that they would never disclose a confidence, and you practised with a sense of security dealing with them.

– J. J. Robinette

He wasn't a glad-hander. He was approachable. He was genuinely interested in people. He loved to be loved. He liked recognition, but that's not what this was. He was interested, and curious, in a sense, about people – remarkable that way. He respected institutions, and enjoyed his associations with the leaders at the Bar, and he had a touch of disdain for the pompous or financially successful.

– Dennis O'Connor

"Well, Arthur, do you think that there is anything wrong with the judge's charge?" And he said, "Absolutely, the judge neglected to put it to the jury." "What's that, Arthur?" "The judge failed to apprise the jury of their age-old right to bring in a perverse verdict!"

– Bob Johnstone

It's a rule of God's Providence that we succeed by failure.

– Cardinal Newman

Appendices

JURY ADDRESSES

The addresses printed here were taken from copies of the original trial transcripts. There has been some minor correction of obvious typographical errors, but no attempt has been made to correct the text. It is, as a result, sometimes awkward and grammatically incorrect, but illustrates the loose oral style which Maloney chose to use when addressing a jury. It is, of course, also possible that some of the errors may well be the responsibility of the court reporter, but it is quite impossible to distinguish such errors from those made by Maloney.

APPENDIX A: THE *BLETA* CASE
Address (Mr. Maloney)

ADDRESS TO THE JURY BY THE DEFENSE

MR. MALONEY: May it please Your Lordship and ladies and gentlemen of the jury: we have now arrived at the very final stages of the case of Her Majesty the Queen against Karafil Bleta. The evidence has all been given; you have had an opportunity to observe the witnesses who presented it and the course that is now taken in the trial is this: I speak to you first on behalf of the accused Karafil Bleta and when I conclude my remarks I am followed by my learned friend Mr. Klein, Q.C., who will make such submissions to you as he sees fit on behalf of the prosecution. And when we both have finished His Lordship, the Trial Judge, will instruct you as to the law that applies to the case and express such opinions on the facts as he may choose to do.

I speak first because the rules that govern the conduct of criminal trials require that I should for the reason that this accused exercised the fundamental basic right of every person accused of a crime to go into the witness box and testify in his own defense and to call witnesses to give evidence in support of his defense. Once an accused person does that, under our law – under our system of criminal procedure – once he calls evidence himself or in his own defense, his counsel loses the right to speak last to the jury. Somebody has to speak and that is the way the problem is resolved. Since Bleta took the stand and since he called witnesses in his defense, I speak first to you and my friend Mr. Klein speaks last and I have no right of reply to what he says. His conduct of the trial has, as I am sure you have observed from beginning to end, has been characterized by very conspicuous fairness and I have no doubt that this spirit of fairness will continue in the remarks he makes to you. If there are things that are said to which I should like to reply, I will have no opportunity so to do because the rules preclude me from doing so.

You were selected as the judges of the facts in this case. Every one of you, when you were brought forward and sworn on the Bible to sit as a juror in this case, became marked with the indelible stamp of a judge with all the authority of that office, with all the privileges of that office, and you remained stamped as judges until you have concluded your deliberations in the case. You are the judges of the facts in this case and in every ultimate sense you are the person who determines the future life and destiny of this accused – nobody else – that is your obligation, nobody else's. Your role in this trial – and it is the role of a jury in any criminal trial – is one of the most absolute supremacy. Your role far transcends in importance mine, my friend's, and My Lord's, the presiding Trial Judge. The reason for that is because you have the ultimate obligation, as I say, of deciding what will become of Karafil Bleta, deciding what the future destiny of a fellow human being will be. Since you have that rather terrific power right in your own hands, it follows that your position in this proceeding is one of very considerable supremacy.

I can make my submissions to you on the facts from the point of view of the defense; my learned friend can make his submissions to you on the facts from the point of view of the Crown and in due course My Lord, the Trial Judge, will tell you what the law is that is applicable and by those instructions you are bound and then, if he chooses, he may or may not express some opinion of the facts, all of us being careful to remind you that you are the ultimate judges of the facts and if what I say on the facts is not in accord with your view, or my friend, or if any opinion that might be expressed from the Bench is not in accord with your own, then you not only have a right, you have an obligation under your oath to disregard it because it is your view of the facts formulated in the light of the instructions you will be given and on the basis of the evidence you have heard, that must prevail. Each one of you is a judge, each one of you has a separate obligation and each one of you must be separately convinced beyond a reasonable doubt to the point of moral certainty before this accused can be convicted and each one of you must unanimously concur in saying to yourself, "We are satisfied beyond a reasonable doubt of the guilt of the offense charged" before there could be a conviction. Failing the ability of jurors like yourselves to unanimously concur in that conclusion, we end up, unfortunately, sometimes with disagreements. This often has to be but our law says that you must separately, you must separately be satisfied beyond a reasonable doubt and come back unanimously with a verdict one way or another if you can or with a disagreement to report to the Court if you can't. It is a state of affairs that nobody encourages.

The accused is before you in an indictment which says this:

> The jurors for our lady the Queen present that Karafil Bleta on or about the 4th day of January, in the year 1963, at the Municipality of Metropolitan Toronto, in the County of York, murdered one Hairedin Gafi and thereby committed non-capital murder, contrary to the Criminal Code.

He is not charged with capital murder, he is charged with non-capital murder, the second most serious crime in the catalogue of criminality that a man could be compelled to face in a criminal court. That is the charge – non-capital murder – the unlawful killing of another person in circumstances that the Crown alleges amount to non-capital murder.

What is the issue here? Sometimes in homicide cases the jurors have the first obligation of deciding, "Well, did the accused even do the deed that brought about the death of the deceased?" Sometimes that issue fails to be determined on circumstantial evidence. Sometimes you don't know whether it was the accused did it or not. Sometimes in cases of this sort the defense of the accused, if it is warranted, would be a defense of alibi, that he didn't even do the deed. There is no such issue before you at all in this case. As you obviously already had made clear to you, the accused did the deed, he wielded the knife that stabbed into the neck of Gafi that caused his death. We start off with that and it is from that starting point that we pass judgment on the issue of whether or not he was guilty of any crime.

The Criminal Code, Section 201, defines murder as follows:

> Culpable homicide is murder where the person who causes the death of a human being (i) means to cause his death, or (ii) means to cause him bodily harm that he knows is likely to cause his death, and is reckless whether death ensues or not.

Those are the contingent elements of the crime of non-capital murder. The accused must intend to kill or, failing that, must intend to cause a bodily harm that he knows is likely to cause death. So that you immediately start off with the realization that not every homicide is punished by the criminal law, that there may be circumstances in which one man may cause the death of another that does not amount to non-capital murder, that does not amount to manslaughter, they amount to no crime at all.

I said a little while ago that each one of you has to be separately satisfied beyond a reasonable doubt before a verdict of guilt of anything could be arrived at because under this system of law that governs you and me, and under whose protection we all live, every person under that system of law is presumed to be innocent of any crime with which he may be charged and that presumption of innocence remains like a cloak wrapped around him until evidence is brought forward that satisfies two women and ten men beyond a reasonable doubt to the point of moral sureness that the offense charged has been proven or that some other offense included within it has been proven. In other words, Karafil Bleta ever since 4:30 or 5:00 o'clock, or whatever it was, on January 4th, 1963, when he was taken into the custody of the law and charged with the offense of murder, was presumed to be innocent of that, presumed to be innocent of the crime with which he is charged and he stays so marked with that presumption of innocence ever since, every hour of this trial right up until the very last instant of it. He is presumed to be innocent of the crime charged and he stays that way unless and until you twelve ladies and gentlemen, after due deliberation, can say to yourself, "We are, each one of us separately, satisfied beyond a reasonable doubt to the point of moral certainty that he is guilty." That is a pretty hard state of mind in any case for a juror to come to I suggest to you. It has a heavy onus of proof but a wise one evolved over the centuries for the protection of fellow citizens unlike the system that prevails in some other jurisdictions where the onus of proving innocence is on the accused. Under our law, it is the other way round. The onus of establishing guilt of the crime charged, or of any crime legally included within it, rests solely and squarely on the prosecution.

Well, we know the charge against him, we know the issue that is involved, we know that he stabbed Gafi, we know about the burden of proof, we know about presumption of innocence. Where do we go from there? What is the defense to this charge?

I made some notes of the evidence of Dr. Stokes because it is really in the framework of his evidence that the conduct of Bleta becomes explained. What does he say in effect? He says that the accused was suffering from a severe trauma or blow to the head. He called it a "moderate to severe blow to the head" in medical terms. This, he said, brought about a state of clouding of the consciousness in consequence of which Bleta behaved in a manner that was devoid of rational control, of rational control of his brain, and it was accompanied by a patchy type of amnesia that he talked about, of confusion, a tendency to confabulate, to fill in the amnesic gaps by whatever information he learned from others or by his own imagination and surmise, not capable, in the opinion of the doctor, of forming any intent to do anything whatever, not capable of forming any rational conclusion. His actions were not the voluntary actions of a rational man, that is that he was an automaton and his conduct and behavior on January the 4th, as a result of a blow to the head, was automatic behavior and his mental condition could best be likened or could be likened to the condition of a sleepwalker.

What does that mean? It so happens that you and I, and all of us here in Canada, live under a system of law that is sufficiently civilized to recognize that men shall not be treated as criminals, convicted as criminals, punished as criminals and sent to prison as criminals unless their mind accompanies their actions and unless the actions in which they engage are the voluntary actions of rational men. Our law is that civilized and that is the law that applies to this case. What is it then? The theory of the defense, as stated by the doctor, is that Karafil Bleta was an automaton whose behavior was automatic, whose actions were not the voluntary actions of a rational man, and as a result of the blow he received to the head he was incapable of forming any intent whatever let alone the prohibited intents that are in the Code. He was for all practical purposes incapable of committing a crime in the interval between the time of the blow to the head and the time he regained something of his judgment, I think somewhere in the Police Station. It all hinges really, doesn't it, on Dr. Stokes' evidence? And bear this in mind, this man remains stamped with that presumption of innocence until you say otherwise.

You may say to yourself, "Well, we have listened to Dr. Stokes. He may well be right. We don't know." Well, then, you are in a state of reasonable doubt. Dr. Stokes may well, as I submit he should have, convinced every one of you of the correctness of his opinion but he may not have. We are all inclined, or have a tendency to be our own lawyers and our own psychiatrists and our own doctors. It is a temptation we should perhaps avoid in this case particularly but even if you are so inclined, even if you do say to yourself, "Well, with all the respect we have for Dr. Stokes, we are still not sure that what he said by way of opinion was right." Don't you see, then, you still have a doubt – and the doubt of a reasonable person – and you must acquit him.

Who is Dr. Stokes? He is obviously a professional man of very considerable background and experience. He has been at work for quite a while – The Toronto Psychiatric Hospital – a witness, I presume right in that box, on a number of past occasions. He has certainly been a witness before called not just as a witness for the defense but called as a witness for the Crown whose integrity is vouched for in those circumstances by both the defense and the Crown. No one would doubt his integrity, his professional experience or reliability. You remember the very last thing he said? I said to him, "Doctor, you would be the first to concede you are not infallible but in your own mind have you any doubt whatever about the correctness of the opinion you have expressed in this case?" And what did he say, "None. None. Absolutely none."

Well, you realize that if this accused were to be convicted of any crime whatever, in the light of what Dr. Stokes has said, it would be tantamount to each one of your saying to yourself, "I am satisfied beyond a reasonable doubt that Dr. Stokes expressed an opinion that is wrong." That is what it means. It is as simple as that. He has expressed an opinion. You are the triers of the facts. You are entitled to disregard any opinion. I would think you would be very loathe to set yourself up as your own specialist in the field of psychiatry and cast aside the considered opinion of an honest, reputable man of integrity. But that is what you would have to do. You would really have to say to yourselves, "We have considered his evidence and we have come to the conclusion that we are satisfied beyond a reasonable doubt, we are morally sure that that opinion isn't right." And, frankly, with the greatest respect and without usurping a single one of your functions, I submit to you just how could you possibly do it, really, in view of the weight that I submit must clearly be attached to that evidence.

If you and I were to walk out of this City Hall tonight and suffer a severe blow to our head the first thing we would hope to happen to us would be that somebody would get us into the care of somebody like Dr. Stokes and that is what happened here. He saw Bleta, he examined him, he diagnosed his problem. He says this man was an automaton, his behavior was automatic, he is not capable of forming any intention whatever, he is incapable of committing a crime when he is in that condition on January 4th. He has got some pretty solid facts – even for us laymen in his field – he has got some pretty solid facts to support his opinion and these are facts that don't depend on Bleta at all. Most of them, if not all of them. First of all, he has got the evidence of that most shocking blow to the head. He said in his evidence, the doctor did, to a layman this would be a very severe blow. Well, it sure was. To a medical man, in medical terminology, "moderate to severe."

You heard the evidence of Mrs. DeGeer, you heard the evidence of Mrs. Trimble. Can't you just reenact that moment when that man's skull cracked against the concrete with the kind of severity that caused them to wonder in amazement how he could ever get up? You start off with that. And, remember, this was probably only seconds before the jabbing with the knife into the man because you will remember Officer Bond said when he drove along in his car the two figures burst out of the crowd.

Was it he who said that? No, that was the school principal. But the Officer said he saw them standing and so they were to fight and he went and parked his car and by this time the accused was right over in the vicinity of where he was. In other words, the stabbing was all over, the whole thing was less than a minute. So don't forget that. This colossal blow to the skull of this man was within probably seconds of the stabbing.

Now, we have got a number of witnesses. It is like every other incident. I suppose if you and I suddenly went out on the street and an accident took place and we were all brought back and separately wrote down our observations of what occurred and how long it took for this and that to happen, we would all come up with something different in the details but in the general outline we would all be agreed. But here you start off, then, with that frightful blow to the head and you have the evidence of the man across the street, Mr. Rosenfarb, who saw the fight obviously at an earlier stage, if this short little episode can be divided into stages. He saw the accused knocked to the ground, he saw Gafi beat him around the head with his fists; and you have the evidence of Mrs. DeGeer and Mrs. Trimble again who said when he did get up, after this blow, he didn't seem to have any balance – the accused didn't – he staggered like a man who was drunk and we all know he doesn't even drink. He was staggering, and the doctor says this is very significant. You remember one of the ladies said he was confused and dazed. She said, "He had a look in his eyes that made it appear to me he was not even in this world." This all fits in with what the doctor says. Then they describe him going over, raising his arm and bringing down the knife and that is the end of Mr. Gafi. And after that the accused starts to walk in a zig zag fashion without any reason whatever, sometimes on the sidewalk, sometimes on the road still in the throes of this clouded state of consciousness in which he is an automaton and doesn't know what he is doing or what he has done, doesn't know where he is. And you have the evidence of Officer Kiekebelt. Here is the Officer of the Law who comes along to take him into the custody of the law and he searches him, throws his arms up while he puts his hands in his pocket and retrieves the knife and the scabbard. He says, "The fellow didn't even seem to be conscious I was there. He was in a daze." What more could you have? What more could have to confirm the medical opinion to your satisfaction and mind as laymen in this sort of thing given by all these thoroughly independent people who have nothing either for or against this accused?

Then you have the accused's own evidence. He said, "I remember up to a point and the last thing I remember" – in effect this is what he says, I don't purport to quote his verbatim – "the last thing I remember is when I put my arm on the wrist, the right wrist of Gafi, and then I don't remember anything again until I am in a police station with a police man." And do you remember what the doctor said was particularly significant about that? Here is Karafil Bleta, quite a low I.Q. – what was he, in the lower ten per cent of the population? – and he says in effect, he doesn't remember from an instant that is just an instance before the blow to the head and his recollection comes back after he is in the police station. What was significant about that to the doctor was that even if Bleta were trying to make up a story of amnesia he would have started by saying, "I don't remember anything from the blow to the head." Bleta, with the low I.Q., not really able to deceive anybody, certainly an expert medical man who is trained to find out this sort of thing. He gives an account of his amnesia that is normally compatible with medical understanding of this sort of thing. It just upholds the validity of the amnesia that he tells us about.

You have got the statement that he was questioned about that he made at the police station to the police, full of gaps, confusion, bewilderment. Don't forget that was made that evening probably an hour and a half after the incident itself. Just what the doctor would expect to find. Everything fits in to his diagnosis. In other words, the observations of the lay people on the street as to what was done to him, the behavior of Bleta himself, the beclouded, bewilderment of his mind, they are all part of the medical pattern that led inevitably to the conclusion that he was an automaton.

The doctor commented on his bewilderment. Right in the witness box it was there. You could see it for yourself; the history of headaches ever since, a history that may flag him until the day he dies. This accused man has no more recollection of having stabbed Gafi than a man in the moon. Don't you remember in the statement to the police he said, "About that murder. I didn't murder anyone." He wouldn't believe the police when they said, "But you did kill somebody." "No." Wouldn't even believe his little wife when she said, "People say you killed him." And he didn't believe it until a friend told him the next morning in court, "Yes, it is true." And still no matter how he gropes and searches within the fathoms and recesses of his mind he can't conjure up any concept or picture of himself having done that. To this day he doesn't realize it is done.

I thought it was very significant, when the doctor was giving evidence – My Lord really got to the root of the case when he said to the doctor, "It may be that we would not believe the accused's statement of two knives being in the possession of the deceased man." And then His

Lordship went on to say, "But, doctor, even though we may not believe that, is your evidence such that you say, as an opinion, that the state of mind of the accused caused him to believe that this is how it happened?" The Doctor said, "Yes, exactly." This accused is bewildered, confused, confabulating, trying to mix fact with fiction sincerely believing what he tells you. And in all that he is in direct compatibility with the medical belief of his case.

You may well say to yourself, "I just can't see it. I can see Gafi with one knife, I can see Bleta with another but I can't see it happening the way Bleta told us." And you may be quite right. I don't know, I wasn't there. All I know is that I accept the doctor's opinion that he believes this is how it happened. Remember this. This disaster that happened on January 4th happened as a result of a blow to the head. It wasn't a blow to the head that was inflicted because Bleta went out and got drunk and staggered into something and fell smashing against the pavement. It was a blow to the head that he never dreamed would occur to him and that he was absolutely blameless for and the most unfortunate thing about it all is that this unfortunate man Gafi was the author of his own misfortune right from the beginning to the end. It was he who inflicted that blow that drove Bleta to the concrete, it was the concrete that administered the injury to the brain that led to the death of Gafi. That is why I said a little while ago our criminal law is civilized. It doesn't punish and condemn people like you or me or Bleta whose minds do not accompany what otherwise might be criminal actions.

Who is Bleta? Forty years of age, born in a country far from here of a respected family highly regarded in a little community, a little farming community in Albania; goes over to a refugee camp in Greece, highly regarded there; off to Munich to the United States Labour Service, highly regarded there; off to Canada and he arrives here without a penny, with nothing, no knowledge of our language, no knowledge of our customs, with nothing of the worldly goods. What does he do? By sheer force of his persistence of hard work he builds up a family, three little children, a wife; acquires four properties, works like a slave to pay off the mortgages, and all this with quite a low I.Q.

Evidence has been given of his previous character – and this isn't a red herring, this is all perfectly permissible and the law says it is very important – because Karafil Bleta's good character wasn't built up in a day. It was built up day after day, month after month, year after year over all the years of his life and we have traced it right back to his little village and we have brought him right up here to Toronto and he is a man who by virtue of his behavior, by virtue of his conduct, by virtue of his way of life, has established himself in the esteem of the communities in which he has lived and in law is not likely, not likely to have done it with the intent alleged that it says he did. It would be unthinkable, in my respectful submission to you, that a man like Bleta, in a state of mind of which he is not himself the author, not brought about even indirectly by his own fault, that he could here be condemned and that everything he worked for, lived for, and strove for, for the forty years of his life could have been cracked in ruins with his head on January 4th last. And it is as simple as that, that is what happened to him could happen to you, to me or to any human being we know of comparable respectability. There was no crime and the act was committed, in my respectful submission to you, by no criminal.

I have not attacked Gafi. His Lordship expressed rightly when he said the other day that we are all in a difficult position where we are discussing the reputation of a man who is deceased and can't defend himself. All we know is this: from the evidence we have heard he certainly was a strange and inscrutable man. His behavior was certainly peculiar. He said he was trying to get more money off Bleta – he had already got some – he said he would leave Bleta alone only if Bleta would do what he told him to do; he was seen to spit on him in the restaurant; wielding a knife was not something of which he was afraid, apparently, nor a practice to which he was unaccustomed. He certainly broke up the home of Alickolli; he threatened to do the same to the home of Bleta. What he did in the way of letters, he wrote back to Albania, was absolutely inexcusable. Can't you imagine how frustrating that would be? Here was a man who was doing his best in his new country, who had acquired a wife. You could tell from the attitude and demeanour of that pathetic little lady in the witness box there was a band of love between the two of them that this fellow Gafi couldn't hope to pray upon and can't you imagine the feelings it must have created at the Bleta household that these lies and slanders were being written back to Albania to people who couldn't possibly know if they were true or false? Well, these things give you an insight into the mental processes, anyway, of this man Gafi, the sort of person he was.

His Lordship in due course will charge you. You will be instructed that you may bring in a verdict of "guilty as charged". Probably open to you to bring in a verdict of guilty of manslaughter or not guilty at all? Manslaughter. If Dr. Stokes' evidence is right Karafil Bleta is guilty of nothing, not a thing in the eyes of the criminal law. Don't compromise and say, "Well, we don't really think he is guilty of anything at all – we agree with the opinion of Dr. Stokes – but he stabbed a man." That is not judicial behavior, that would not really be in conformity with the pledge you took when you became jurors, compromise of that sort has no place in your deliberations, because go back to what I said a moment ago. If Dr. Stokes' opinion is right, he is guilty of nothing at all, not a thing.

His Lordship will tell you the law of self defense, the law of provocation and that sort of thing, your rights in regard to manslaughter. These are matters that he must leave with you but remember what I said; the opinion of Dr. Stokes, if valid, says that the conduct of Bleta was not a crime at all and that he is entitled – if that is so – he is entitled after the four or five months he spent out at the local bastile, to walk out of this courtroom with you and me and all of us tonight and back to his home and to his properties and to his children. And so I submit that is what your verdict should be. Thank you.

Appendix B: The *Esposito* Case

ADDRESS BY MR. MALONEY

MR. MALONEY: May it please your lordship and gentlemen of the jury: The case of our lady the Queen and Raffaele Esposito has now drawn to its close, and there passes from me to you the awful responsibility of seeing to it that the rights of this accused man under the law are vigilantly protected. That is your duty. For four long months or more he has waited in the custody of the law, and has lived in expectation of this day. If someone were to falsely accuse you of any single thing and failed to bring forth any concrete single piece of evidence to support it, you would say, "I have nothing to answer," and I submit I have nothing to answer here today. If our law directed that this accused or any other should be called upon to demonstrate his innocence – and the law does not do that – but if it should, I should say to you today, I am entitled to an acquittal because the accused man has demonstrated his innocence. The law, I say, looks upon accused persons which much more favour. The law does not require me to demonstrate his innocence. The law is this instead, the law presumes that he is innocent until he is proved to be guilty. Day after day as he came into this room, day after day, as you heard the witnesses who testified from that box before you, he sat before you an innocent man, and he is still an innocent man until his guilt has been proved beyond a reasonable doubt. There, I submit, is where the Crown's case fails. Not only has he demonstrated his innocence, but you cannot possibly say to yourselves as twelve men that you are satisfied beyond a reasonable doubt of his guilt. I am inclined to be apologetic almost for even mentioning the question of reasonable doubt because to me there is no room for doubt here. By the Crown's own witnesses, he is less suspect than many of the others, and by the Crown's own witnesses the impossibility of the commission of this crime by him has been demonstrated. Notwithstanding that, it is my duty to discuss, as my friend did, the question of reasonable doubt with you twelve men.

The doctrine of reasonable doubt is a sacred and a salutary doubt that evolved in the development of our law over centuries of experience. It is a doctrine that was not designed solely for his protection, or for any other accused person with whose circumstances you may have in the past become associated. It was designed for the protection of every citizen of this country. It was designed for your protection, and for mine. It was designed for the protection of everyone you know, everyone you hold dear, everyone for whom you have a high regard, and the day that any juryman relaxes to the slightest fraction of a degree the doctrine of reasonable doubt, a very grievous situation would have developed indeed. A reasonable doubt means moral certainty. In other words, gentlemen of the jury, you must be able to say to yourselves, "We are morally sure that Raffaele Esposito committed the crime with which he is charged." It is not enough to act on what you think; it is not enough to act on what you feel; it is not enough to act on what you heard; it is not enough to act on what you suspect; you have got to act on moral assurance. To act on anything less is a violation of your oath, and a serious violation of the very law of God. I picked you twelve men to be our judges – men from all walks of life in this district, from all callings of life. Each one of you has a sacred duty to perform here. Each one of you is charged with the responsibility, separately and individually, of giving me the benefit of every reasonable doubt you entertain. Each one of you must be able to say to himself, "I am morally sure of the guilt of this accused man on the basis not of what I think, suspect, or feel, but on the basis solely of what I have heard under oath from the witnesses who testified before me during the last few days." The supremacy of your power, of the power of any jury in a criminal case, is not often known to all of you. Your power is supreme. There is a good reason why you should have such power in any criminal case. There is an especially good reason why you should have such power in a murder case. I can perform my duty here and leave this room with a free conscience no matter what your verdict, for I have performed it to the best of my ability, with whatever limitations there may be. My friend can leave this room with a free conscience and can say, "I am not a party to his conviction; I did my duty. I brought out all the evidence that we had." My Lord can leave this room with a free conscience, and say, "I am not responsible for a conviction. I did my duty. I told them the law." We act like Pontius Pilate. You twelve men have all the responsibility. Upon you conscience is this verdict going to lie. Upon your conscience will be the life of that accused man if you mistakenly convict him of murder. You cannot consider the consequences of your verdict, if you are otherwise satisfied beyond a reasonable doubt, in any criminal case, but you must consider the consequence of your verdict in this case, if you carelessly, mistakenly, improperly, render a verdict of guilty. In the ordinary affairs of life when you and I make a mistake in reference to our fellow man, we can compensate him in some way, in dollars and cents. If you make a mistake in the case of Our Lady the Queen and Raffaele Esposito, you will never compensate him because he dies if you find him guilty of murder.

The case against this accused man, or what is purported to be the case against this man is what has been described to you by my friend and will again be described to you by my Lord, is one of circumstantial evidence. Circumstantial evidence, as it will be described to you in a short while by my Lord, is this – it must not only be consistent with his guilt; it must be inconsistent with any other rational conclusion than that he is the guilty person. Apply that test to every single item of evidence you have heard in the witness box. Give me the benefit of every reasonable doubt. I am entitled to demand that you do both if you discharge the duty you assumed when you took your oath. Do those things and there will be but one verdict in this case, and it will be – Not Guilty.

I am going at this stage to give you a brief outline, as I recall them, of the facts that have been adduced in evidence here. I shall have occasion after that to refer in somewhat more detail, but as briefly as I can, to separate individual items which were mentioned during the trial.

Before I do that, I ask you to try and recall in your own minds the general lay-out of the area. You will recall, to the east we have the Lakehead; to the west, we have Kelly, Larson, James, and Mack – sections with whose names you became familiar during the course of the trial. From the Lakehead to the Linco the C.N.R. and the C.P.R. travel almost side by side, and from the Lakehead to Linco, in addition, the Trans-Canada Highway travels beside the C.P.R., but when we arrive at Linco, the tracks and the highway then begin to diverge, and when we get to Kelly, in relation to the C.P.R. and to the Trans-Canada highway, we are just south of Savanne, a distance of about six miles, one witness said.

Access to Kelly from Savanne is available by one and possibly two trails, not uncommonly used by trappers, and obviously a means of escape for anyone who had perpetrated such a crime as this at Kelly.

On Saturday June 19th of this year, Mr. Clark, the engineer on an extra, arrived at Kelly for a meet, and on his arrival he found the Kopplin premises in flames. He arrived there, you will recall, at ten after five. At that stage the main building or the dwelling house was furiously burning, and flames had just begun to pierce through the roof. The fire in the building to the rear – I think it was the wood shed – had apparently just begun shortly before his arrival. He, as you will recall, with Mr.

Lacharite and Mr. Lyons, had the terrible experience of being the first human beings to discover the terrible sight – the body of this poor lady, and ultimately the body of her children the following day – three people who had a right to live – three people for whom someone should be required to pay – not anybody – the man who did it. The body is found badly beaten on the head, with wounds, and horrible burns, and sadistically trussed up with rope. All those things are discovered by Mr. Clark and his companions. The doctor subsequently decides that this poor lady's death came about by the blows to her head. I will deal later with the time of death, or what the evidence says as to that point; but for the time being let me revert to the movements of the accused. The accused was seen in Kelly, not at five o'clock, not at four o'clock, not at three o'clock, not at two o'clock – at ten o'clock; he was seen in the vicinity of Kelly about fifteen hundred feet west, proceeding back towards the west to Larson. He is seen at that time by Wallie, the road master – no blood, nothing on him, perfectly natural, except he is red in the face and nervous, according to Wallie. I will develop that in a little while. Peter Koczkur was so embarrassed at driving the speeder that he practically asked me not to ask him how he got to Linco. Esposito had good reason to feel nervous because not only is he going to involve himself in a little difficulty, but he had been given the permission of the foreman. The accused has an explanation as to why he was in Kelly. That explanation is evidence before you. The evidence before you is the evidence that was given by Mintenko, the constable who interviewed him on the Monday morning – nothing to hide – "sure, I was in Kelly on Saturday morning. I was going to go to James. I got a sore stomach. I was going to ask the fellows in James to get me some groceries. I got a sore stomach, and I came back. After I had stayed around the bunk house for awhile, I went out in a boat, and I was there after the local went through, and I came back around seven." That is the accused's explanation – when first confronted with this being on Monday morning by Constable Mintenko. Nothing to hide, no lie about it. He did not say, "No, I was not in Kelly." He said, "Sure, I was in Kelly" – the reply of a truthful man, the reply of a man who had nothing to hide. There was one rather noble thing in the version that he gave to Mintenko. He volunteered "I did not have permission to go." His first instinct was to protect the foreman who had given him permission really to take the speeder. That is the explanation the accused man gives constable Mintenko as to why he had been in Kelly, and when he had been in Kelly is corroborated by the evidence of other witnesses. The night before, according to Mr. Kuryliuw, his foreman, he asked permission to use the speeder the following day for the purpose of going to James. Would Raffaele Esposito have told the foreman on Friday that he was going to take a route that would bring him through

Kelly, would Raffaele Esposito have set out on the Saturday morning in full view of all the witnesses who saw him go down the track east towards Kelly if his mind were filled with the intent which is alleged by my friend? Do you suppose that he would have behaved in that open manner if it was his intention to go down and have any relationship whatever with the lady down there? The very openness of his conduct negatives any suggestion that he had any evil intent in his mind when he set out, or at any later time.

That brings me to the remark that my friend mentioned – the remark that Tiano, Borrelli, and Rossi said that he had made the previous Thursday. For the time being this is all I say: three different witnesses give three different versions of what the accused man is supposed to have said. First of all, you will have to say to yourselves, Was anything of that nature said at all? Secondly, if you come to the conclusion that something of that nature was discussed, you will have to say what was said; and in determining what to believe or not to believe in relation to that item of evidence, do not forget one very important thing. Two of the men who seek to establish that the accused stated that he intended to go to Kelly are Rossi and Tiano – two witnesses who otherwise would be strongly suspected of the thing themselves. That is significant. Bear in mind that each one of them, excluded from the court room, gives a different version, and bear in mind that Rossi, contrary to what my friend suggested, was mad at this accused. He swore in the witness box that he was not, but then we confronted him with what he had sworn to under oath just a few weeks ago, and he said then that he was so mad at him that he was not even speaking to him; and finally and most important of all, in determining the credibility of these men, remember this – "Did you ever talk sex in the railway? No. Did you ever hear anyone talk about it on the railway? No." – one by one – every time they answered No to that question, you know as well as I do that they told a lie, – you know. In that respect, as I shall point out to you later, I am entitled to call upon your knowledge of human nature, your knowledge of human behaviour, your knowledge of the behaviour of a group of men working at that section, and when you call upon your human experience and your knowledge of human nature, you will agree with me that every time they said No to that question, every one of them was a liar, and yet you are being asked to find that this accused made that remark on that kind of evidence. Bear in mind that you must be satisfied beyond a reasonable doubt that it was made, because I am entitled to the benefit of the doubt in regard to every single issue of fact that exists in the entire case. I am entitled to the benefit of the doubt there as well as on all the other facts in this case. Apply that text, and you will not have much trouble in dismissing that evidence from your mind. The insignificance of any such remark becomes obvious anyway when you consider certain other matters – very vital and important matters. Assume he had said it, and assume that he told the truth – so what? He was leaving Kelly at ten o'clock, and you have no alternative but to conclude that that lady was alive and well at eleven-thirty because Hedwig Kopplin would not have been lying in a pool of blood in her chicken run at eleven-thirty and her little boy playing with the little dog as he was – they would be out in front doing that? The dog would have been whimpering and running all over the place. You have no alternative but to conclude that she was alive and well at eleven-thirty, and once you come to that conclusion, the so-called remark of Thursday is of no consequence whatever. It means nothing. How much later was she proved to have been alive? The little boy is seen in the window again at two-fifteen. Why would the little boy be out in front playing with the little dog and then be seen in the house if not because she called him in for lunch. What proof is there that it was lunch? – the contents of this lady's stomach disclosed that she had peas. All those things compel you to conclude that she was alive and well, and nothing was wrong long after ten o'clock.

For the time being, let us go back to Larson awaiting the accused's return after he had been seen proceeding home by the speeder at ten o'clock. He arrives there at eleven-fifteen or so. Nothing abnormal about his behaviour, no blood, no attempt to conceal anything. He stayed around the bunk, and his movements fully accounted for until two o'clock or thereabouts, and then he is seen to go out with a gun as though to hunt, and walk off in the opposite direction altogether, and go west of his bunk house, a direction farthest removed from this poor lady's place. Then there is the next event that you should remember – at three o'clock two young men suddenly form the idea that they will go east towards Kelly, two young men who know just as well as Esposito that Mrs. Kopplin is alone suddenly decide they will go east towards Kelly, and they walk down the track east towards Kelly until, as they say, they turned off to go into an abandoned bush camp that a forest ranger at Savanne swore that he was almost positive did not exist. What is the next event? Who comes back first? The accused man is seen to come back from the west, from the west, a half mile west of his bunk house, and with his gun. What does he do? Does he run away when he sees somebody? Does he try to hide? No, he comes up to them, and shakes hands with one of them, and no scratch marks then, no blood then, wearing the very jacket that has been filed as an exhibit, and not a spot on it in any way, and then the other two young men about whose testimony I will have more to say in a moment, they come back, according to their evidence, about eight o'clock. On Saturday or Sunday he was seen to cook some eggs. Well, I will have more to say about the eggs in a moment, but when I talk about them then it will be to tell you what you know and what I hope you know ought to be done with them. Brown eggs, – that technically the people in the chicken business used to describe them, and that little Rossi used to describe them, although he frankly admitted that Inspector Craig asked him if they were brown eggs.

Then there was the examination made of his clothing, and all this clothing was produced, and I will have more to say about that as we go along. Before I deal with some of the items in somewhat greater detail, it may be well to remind you of the history of this unusual case. Forget that Raffaele Esposito is the accused. Imagine that it is someone you know; imagine that it is someone you believe to be perfectly innocent, and listen to the history of the case of our lady the Queen and Raffaele Esposito. He is arrested on the night of June 21st, and improperly and illegally held in custody for a week, with the full sanction and authority of people who are supposed to be experienced officers of the law, and then he is charged with murder, and then there is a preliminary hearing held in August, and we hear just a little evidence, and then we go down to Toronto and a judge down there says – in layman's language – "produce further evidence or let him go." Inspector Craig knows that. Erickson knows that. They all know that. What happened? What kind of evidence do we hear about next? A little bit more at the second preliminary hearing, and finally, at the trial, after it is well in progress, and as the going does not look too good, we hear a little bit more. We hear about scratches. Do not forget the history of this case. That is not the way to conduct a murder case. You may have some concern about the administration of justice in the Lakehead and in the District of Thunder Bay, and if you have, do not forget the history of this case.

There are, as I said before, a few items of which I wish to make specific mention. One, the time of this poor lady's death. No one has been very much help to us there. Doctor Allin says she died on Saturday sometime. That is about all he can say. As I indicated a moment ago, she must have been alive at eleven-thirty, or there cannot be any other possible explanation of the conduct of the little boy and the dog. She had lunch – the little boy remained inside, and was seen looking out at the local, and he would know about the local, and he would hear it come along, and his looking out the window was just a repetition of his day after day behaviour. That suggests pretty strongly that still nothing was wrong. Something happened after that; when, we do not know. When, we will never know; or how, we will never know. That is what mystifies me about this case. If you close your eyes, and you ask, how was it done; where was it done; when was it done; why was it done – you cannot answer any of them; and yet you are being asked to hang a man, and you cannot answer a single question I put to you, not a single one. All we know then is that she was clearly alive at eleven-thirty, and in all probability was alive at two-fifteen. According to Doctor Allin, there is evidence that she was alive when the burns were inflicted. Perhaps you could derive some help if you could establish the time of the fire. That is almost impossible to do. Suffice it to say that she came to her death sometime after two-fifteen and sometime before ten after five when her body was discovered in these perfectly terrible circumstances by Joseph Clark.

I want to address myself to this so-called process of elimination that the Crown used, allegedly to establish this man's complicity in this most terrible crime. The Crown says, we will find out every one else who might have done it, and we will eliminate them, and that will prove by a process of elimination that the accused must have done it, and so they take all the possible suspects. They take Rossi, first of all, and Lylak, and the Crown says, Well, they did not do it; they told you then they went down the track to an abandoned bush camp. Who says so? Did you see them go there? Did I? Did my friend? They said so; what else do you think they would say? Do not forget what I mentioned briefly a little while ago – in giving you various people as possible suspects, I am not for a moment suggesting that they are guilty. I have no right to do that, because I have nothing but suspicion against them, but all I ask is that I be given the same consideration. Do not forget that at three o'clock Rossi and Lylak, having suddenly formed the intention to go to an abandoned bush camp, set out east towards Kelly. How long did it take as they travelled down the track? Rossi says an hour, and Lylak says half an hour. How long did it take from the track to the bush where the abandoned camp was? Rossi says two hours; Lylak says one hour. How long did it take once you got into the bush? An hour, says Rossi; an hour, says Lylak. How long back to the track from the bush? Two hours, says Rossi; one hour, says Lylak. How long from the track back to Larson? One hour, says Rossi; half an hour, says Lylak – seven hours in all, says Rossi. "I should have been back home at ten o'clock, but I was back home at eight." Four hours in all, says Lylak. "I should have been back at seven." He was back at eight. Do not forget that when you are considering whether or not the Crown has eliminated all possible suspects. Once you establish that this lady was alive at eleven-thirty, as I submit she clearly was, Esposito is less suspect than anyone else in the vicinity, because he is the only one seen to walk away from Larson. Two other men are seen to walk right down in the direction of the lady's house. What search was made by the investigating officers for the abandoned camp? None. What search was made for the lake? None. What search for a boat? None. What search to show they had fired their guns? None.

When Dante Rossi and Lylak told them that version of their conduct, why was an investigation not made to prove its truth or falsity. When Esposito told them that he had gone out in a boat in the lake, what did they do? They went to find out if there was a lake, – and there was. They went to find out if there was a boat – and there was. They did not tell that evidence until I dragged it out of them.

Once you establish that this lady was alive at eleven-thirty, there is less evidence against him than against a whole legion of other people. You may think when you consider the nature of the perfectly horrible injuries to this poor lady, that one man could not have done it. A healthy lady, well nourished, faced with a sadistic attacker who has obviously planned to kill her, knowing that she must summon up all her strength and resist him. How could he tie her if he was alone unless he had knocked her out before, and if he had, why tie her? Who had her while the ropes were tied? Examine the injuries to her head – two different types of instruments – I do not know whether two men did it. That rather suggests to me that two men might well have done it; and finally, with those two men as possible suspects, do not forget this – they were a matter of only a few miles from the scene of the crime once they get into that bush, if they did go into the bush.

You will remember the fire was burning furiously. You will remember there was smoke. They said they saw it but they thought it was a train. They must have thought, – some train causing that kind of smoke? They knew that was the only dwelling in the vicinity. If they saw the smoke, why didn't they go down to help? They did not go.

Who is the other possible suspect that the Crown supposedly has eliminated? – Tiano. Has he been eliminated? On June 15th, 1953, Mrs. Hedwig Kopplin sends a letter to her husband in which, among other things, she said to him, "I have dreamed about you. Come and get me. There is something I must tell you about Vince." What explanation does Vince give? This is why Mrs. Kopplin wrote to her husband; this is what she wanted to tell her husband about me – this is what she thought was so important that she put it in her letter – "I went up one day to buy a rooster, and I said, 'Two dollars for a rooster.'" Do you believe for one single moment that is the reason why Mrs. Kopplin wanted to confide some secret to her husband? What was so secret about that? What did she have to tell him? What had Tiano done? You do not know; I do not know; my friend does not know; we will never know. This is important in considering this possibility – the husband's original plan was to return to Kelly on June 19th. That plan was changed. He communicated with his wife, and said, I will not be able to come on the 19th. I am going to come instead on the 25th – six days later – the following Friday. Anyone who had a single solitary reason for getting rid of Mrs. Kopplin before her husband returned, this was his last chance – a week-end, when everyone else had gone away. This was his last chance because every day in the following week would be a work day. But we are told he is not a suspect. He went to town. He stayed at the Princess Hotel. He did not come back until Sunday. Who said so? Did you see him in town? Did I? Did my friend? He said so; Borrelli said so; and Kuryliw said so. Where is the register from the hotel, and even if that is produced, why did they check out at eight o'clock in the morning. If they bought a case of beer, where is the slip from the brewers' store? He is not a suspect. Why? That is what I would like to know. Why isn't he a suspect? All this independent evidence available to confirm his alleged alibi, and not produced – no beer slip, nothing like that – just his own statement, and the statement of the young fellow Borrelli, and obviously under the influence of an older man. Do not forget, too, that he had the key to his lady's house. Do not forget that, and do not forget that he denied knowing that he had the key. He said, "If I had the key, I did not know it." Kopplin did not tell us that. Kopplin did say, "The key was in an envelope when I gave it to him."

Finally, in the possibility of these gentlemen as suspects – an examination of the private organs of this poor lady disclosed two sperm – 250 million in an ordinary male ejaculation – and Dr. Allin, when asked if that could have been deposited in her vagina on June 15th, said, "It becomes more probable."

I am not accusing anyone of the murder here. I have no right to. I have not got enough evidence against them, but I have more reason to be suspicious of the three men I have mentioned so far than of the accused.

Beatty, the tramp – such a weird sight had never been seen in these parts before. He is seen right at Kelly on Sunday, right at the scene of the crime. He is allowed to plead guilty of vagrancy because he was not able to give a satisfactory account of himself. No, he is not a suspect because we have a witness who saw him at a place called Mack at twenty to seven on Saturday night. I do not want to know where he was then. I want to know where he was on Saturday afternoon, and you do not know that any better than I do, and neither does my friend. Beatty is not a suspect. He has been eliminated. What about the Indian trappers? They called one, who says that he did not do it, but adds to the confusion by saying that there are four or five others in the area. Who are they? What did they look like? How big are they? How old are they? You do not know anything more about them than I do, nor does my friend. Where were they on June 19th? What about the lumber project just twelve miles east. How many men are working there? We do not know. A lot of men? – I cannot tell you. Old men? – I don't know. Young men? – I don't know. Men with criminal records? – I do not know – nor do you. Where were they on Saturday June 19th. And finally, what about all these male passengers on the local that went through Kelly that afternoon as the train slowed down? My friend says that he eliminated all the men on the extra gang, that they could not have done it. Why? He said, "I called the foreman. I paid them all their wages for that day, so they must have worked." The foreman did not check them that day; the time checker did; and the only witness who knows whether they all worked that day is not called as a witness at all, and so when my friend says, "I have eliminated everyone else who could have done it," you and I know that is not right. There are perhaps hundreds of others who have not been eliminated, and who could never be eliminated, and some of them are men against whom greater suspicion attaches for the reasons I have already suggested then against this accused man. Having mentioned these additional suspects whose movements have not been accounted for, let me remind you again – I am entitled to the benefit of the doubt.

Now, let us get along to some of the specific items I spoke about. This so-called statement that was made on Thursday; remember what I have already told you; three different men give three different versions of what was said, two being strongly suspect themselves, one of them admittedly hostile to my client, and tried to lie about that in the witness box. Bear in mind all that, and in determining whether you believe them at all, do not forget to bear in mind that they lied when they told me that they never talked about women or about sex, and bear in mind that we had to hear their evidence through the medium of an interpreter. Put all those things together. Would you hang a man when you do not even know what he said, and what you are told that he said was not even in English, and they seek to convey it to you through an interpreter. I am entitled to the benefit of the doubt. Whether this statement was made is of no consequence. For reasons I have already given, the intention could not possibly have been carried out. I told you a little while ago that Doctor Allin said that there would be about 250 million sperm in an ordinary male ejaculation, – and none on the accused man's clothing, and none on the deceased lady's slip; none on the ground; none on her body. Whoever violated that lady did not violate her person on Saturday. That could not be, and I ask you to so find. Assuming you find that any such expression was made or used, I said a little while ago I was entitled to call upon your knowledge of human nature, the knowledge you have of human experience, gentlemen, and if you were to hand every man you know who expressed a desire to fornicate with some woman who is subsequently murdered, you will hang a great many men, and you know that as well as I do. My friend says his presence at

Kelly at ten o'clock in the morning is an incriminating piece of evidence. Why? The road master went through Kelly at ten o'clock in the morning, and nobody said it was incriminating for him. Why was it so incriminating for the accused man to be there? When he was asked if he had been there, he did not say No. He said, Yes, I was there. He said, I got sick at the stomach, and as I will mention later, he has a bad stomach, and you know he has a bad stomach; the evidence proves that he has, and he is pumping a hand car, and he said, I originally intended to go to James, and I turned back. I was going to order some groceries at my friends. Who are his friends? They are Tiano and Borrelli. They told him on Thursday that they planned to go to town. We often plan on Thursday to go some place and change our mind before the day arrived. He was entitled to assume that they might have had a change of heart, so he said, I went to see my friends. They live in a bunk house, which is shown on exhibit two. The approach to it is by mean of a board walk. He finds they are not in. He goes back. He goes back to Larson from whence he came. If he had gone to the scene of the crime, the earth from his boots would have come from the scene of the crime, and Doctor Allin says it did not correspond, and the reason it did not correspond was because he was not even there, and the reason there was no earth on his boots from the scene of the crime is because he was not anywhere near the scene of the crime and did not walk on any of the earth nearby. There is nothing suspicious. There is nothing any more suspicious about his being at Kelly than about Mr Wallie; no suspicion attaches there. Bear in mind that if it was his intention to have intercourse with this lady, bear in mind what I said a little while ago – would he announce his plan to go to her house to his foreman; would he go in broad daylight so everybody could see him? All these things are suggestive strongly of an innocent mind, and do not forget, at the risk of boring you with a repetition of it, – she was alive and well at eleven-thirty; and do not forget, and this is very important – that when this Italian immigrant who speaks but broken English – simple and illiterate, and he cannot read or write – when he is confronted with this knowledge by all the authority of the law, as vested in constable Mintenko, he said, "I was at Kelly" – nothing to hide – and then somebody said he spoke to the foreman after the police had left, and he said, "The police think I murdered that woman," and he is crying. Why shouldn't he cry? "Didn't you see me at Larson," and the foreman said, "I did not see you at Larson except in the morning." Why all the fuss about that? It is all true. My friend apparently did not attach much importance to that, because he did not mention it.

Now, let us come to the rope. Let us come to the rope. I mention that piece of evidence for one very good reason – it is to invite you to disregard it. On the hands and around the neck of this poor lady is found rope that corresponds with rope that can be found and that admittedly is kept in every bunk house from the Lakehead to Sioux Lookout. What does that prove? – nothing. But here is something very very sinister about the evidence of the rope. Here is something that you, charged with the proper administration of justice in the Lakehead, should not forget – we were not told that the police had investigated the grocery store in the Lakehead and Kakabeka Falls. We were not told that the police had found out that this was a common type of rope. We were not told that the police had found out that this rope was kept by every section hand from the Lakehead all the way up the line. We dragged that out. If this man had been before you without a lawyer, you would have been left with the impression clearly that rope was found on her body that corresponded and was similar to rope in his possession. Think of the damaging effect that would have had on your minds, and yet the investigating officers knew all the time when they tried to create that impression – they knew nothing whatever of any importance attached to the rope. That is a sinister piece of business indeed. I hope I never see anything like that happen, never in the experience I will have as a lawyer. Nothing turns on the rope. Shown to Doctor Ward Smith, he said, "Show them to an expert." There is only one expert in Canada, and we are told it was not shown to him at all.

Now, let us come to the egg shells. Remember the first preliminary hearing in August; remember the judge in Toronto; remember the second preliminary hearing in October. I never once heard that egg shells had the slightest connection with the case. What are you entitled to think, when you hear about egg shells for the first time after a judge at Toronto says, Produce more evidence against this man or let him go. What are you entitled to think? You and I know and think it. What is the evidence about the egg shells? It is alleged, first of all, that on Saturday or Sunday, the accused man was seen to cook some eggs for his lunch. Rossi says that. Bear in mind, it is always Rossi. It is always Rossi who strives to tell the strongest tale against us, and do not forget the significance of that. On Saturday or Sunday he says the accused man cooked himself some eggs. On June 21st the accused man is arrested. June 22nd goes by, and so does the 23rd, the 24th, and the 25th, and so on, all the way down the line to the 29th, when Rossi brings Inspector Craig to the dump, and on the top of the dump he finds some egg shells – eight days later – ten days after the 19th, – at a time when the accused man was in the custody of the law, at a time when Rossi was the only one who occupied that bunk house, at a time when every-one in Larson had access to that dump, and if I had known what the evidence of the eggs was going to be, I would have asked his Lordship not to have allowed you to hear it, and I will ask him to tell you to disregard it now. That is the least suspicious piece of evidence I have ever heard of in a criminal case of any kind; and lo and behold, they fly up Doctor Smith all the way from Toronto to hold up an egg and to hold up the egg shells, and say, "In my opinion, gentlemen, they are similar," and he does not know any more about eggs than you do. The only man who knows less about chickens than Doctor Smith is myself, because he never accused a rooster of laying an egg. Suppose he did have brown eggs, if you call them brown; I don't; they are white to me. Suppose he was seen to cook the eggs. We have the evidence of Doctor Allin, who is also an ornithologist, who tells us of three or four or five different types of birds that lay eggs up in this type of community, and would have been laying eggs around the time that this happened – brown eggs. Rossi did not take out a ruler like Doctor Allin did, and measure the egg shells. Even if Rossi is telling the truth, all he can say is "I saw a man with egg shells that were brown."

Then, do not forget the scratch marks. Rossi saw the accused on June 19th at eleven-fifteen in the morning. Lylak saw the accused at about that time. Romanchuk saw the accused on Saturday when he came back from the hunt. Louis Koczkur saw the accused on Saturday afternoon when he came back from the hunt. No suggestion of scratch marks. Preliminary hearing Number One – never mentioned – what are you entitled to think when you hear about scratch marks for the first time after the judge in Toronto says, Produce further evidence against the man or let him go. What are you entitled to think? Well, think it.

Constable Mimtenko gave evidence late in the course of the trial. He sees the accused man in his bunk on Monday June 21st, early in the morning, and he says, I observed three scratch marks. What could have been more important evidence if it were true. So we say, Mr. Mintenko, show me the notes you made about it, and he did not make any notes – none. Why didn't they take a picture of the accused? Why didn't they have Doctor Allin examine him? He examined everything else – rocks, boulders, pieces of wood, pants, shirt. I suggest to you there never were any scratches. To me that is a very serious state of affairs. Now we come –

HIS LORDSHIP: Do you suppose you could finish in ten minutes?

MR. MALONEY: Well, just give me about fifteen minutes –

HIS LORDSHIP: I would rather that you did finish now. You have covered this pretty well.

MR. MALONEY: Well, I am not putting that in writing, but I will do my very best – in regard to the scratch marks, we asked Doctor Allin if he examined beneath the finger nails of this deceased lady. No evidence whatever of scrapings that one would expect to find there from a woman who was clawing her attacker in order to ward him off. Doctor Allin examined all these various items of clothing. In regard to the two pairs of pants which were said to have been found in the bunk house, he said, I found spots but so small that I just had enough to enable me to make a little bit of a test that enabled me to say it could have been a whole lot of things. What a terrific contribution that was to the issue of the guilt or innocence of Raffaelo Esposito? He found a little bit of a stain on two pairs of pants, and nobody suggested the accused was wearing every type of clothing that he owned on the 19th of June, and the two items of clothing that he is proved to have been wearing are the dungaree jacket and the shirt; and in regard to the dungaree jacket, there is nothing on it. In regard to the shirt, he admitted under cross-examination and not before that he saw a little spot of blood on the collar of the shirt that was consistent with being the blood of a mosquito. Now, it strikes me we do not need any expert here to tell you whether clothes look as if they had been recently washed. In the first place, no one saw the accused wash his clothes, and yet everybody saw him when he came back in the morning, and when he came back in the evening; and, in the second place, the shirt that looked as if it had been recently washed had been on his back for a week in the local jail. So any opinion of Doctor Allin that they had been recently washed must be subject to the fact that his shirt was not recently washed at all. It strikes me that this woman's attacker must have been splattered with blood, just splattered with blood, right from head to foot; she was lying right in a lake of blood. The evidence of Doctor Allin as to the search made of this man's clothing is the strongest proof there is of this man's innocence.

Then constable Mintenko added a bit or two. He said, When I came to see him on Monday morning he looked nervous, and he said his shirt was going like that, in and out, and he pulled it in and out. Did you ever hear of a shirt going that way in all your life? I never have; and then he put his hand against his heart, and it was palpitating wildly. I think Constable Mintenko must have been reading some book of Edgar Allan Poe. I think he let his imagination get carried away with himself. The important thing about constable Mintenko's evidence is this; The first opportunity the police officers had to tell the accused and to ask him about his whereabouts, he tells them. He tells them. I dismiss this evidence about the accused man being ill and having missed some work. It is perfectly ridiculous. There is plenty of evidence that he had stomach trouble. The Crown proved that he had stomach trouble through its own witness. He was a regular purchaser of pills for his stomach. He complained of it all the time, and he planned to have an operation if the doctor recommended it, but preferred to go back to Italy where it would be cheaper to have it done. It is always a sort of a weak case when they bring out a lot of little items one by one, that mean nothing, as all of these items mean nothing, in my respectful submission to you. Do not forget the important evidence of the gravel on the boots. Doctor Allin, at the request of Inspector Craig, examined earth from the scene of the crime. Doctor Allin examined earth from the boots of the accused, and they do not correspond. Do not forget that. That is a vital piece of evidence from the point of view of the defence. They do not correspond. I have also reminded you of the importance of the evidence about the little boy being alive at eleven-thirty. You know what that means as well as I do – that the little boy's mother was alive and well, too. I have also reminded you of the importance of this fact – that when first confronted with Mintenko's question, he told him where he had been, and he made a more detailed statement to Inspector Craig. He was questioned on Monday. He was questioned on Tuesday, and Inspector Craig admitted he made a detailed account of his movements on the Tuesday. The law prohibits me from introducing into evidence what my client said to the Inspector. The law is that my client's statement at that time can only be introduced in evidence if the Crown counsel chooses to put it in evidence. It is not my fault that that statement is not before you. Bear in mind, too, that on the strength of what the accused man said, they checked the lake, and they checked the boat, and found the statement to Mintenko was true. Do not forget, as I have already reminded you, the appearance of the accused when seen on his return from Kelly in the morning, and when seen in the evening at a quarter to seven. No soot on his clothing or face, as there ought to have been if he were coming from a conflagration of this sort, and no blood, and nothing at all, and no effort to conceal himself; he shakes hands with his friends; no marks on his clothing or body, and no evidence of any scratches on his leg, or no evidence of any bites as one would expect if a man were attacking a lady in the presence of her dog. All those things are absent; and do not forget when once questioned by the police, he did not attempt to flee. He stayed right in his bunk house. Is that what a guilty man would have done, or would he have tried to take to the bush – an illiterate Italian D.P. – frightened by the authority of the law? Isn't that what he would have done if he were guilty? He stuck to his guns, and stayed at home. His foreman said that he was a quiet, hard-working man. Do not forget that his crime was committed by a sadistic man. I repeat, that it is my submission that the accused man in this case has demonstrated his innocence. He may demonstrated it could not have been done by him. A theory has been put forward to you by my friend, and having put the theory before you, what evidence has he offered to support it? None. How could he have done it? It was not done in the morning. How could he have done it in the afternoon? He could not have gone down the track; Rossi and Lylak were on the track, and they saw no one. He could not have gone through the bush because the Crown called witness after witness to prove that that was impossible, that you cannot go through the bush.

This man has demonstrated his innocence. I am the first to admit that a terrible crime was committed in this district on the 19th day of June last. Three people had their lives snuffed out who had a right to live – a husband bereaved of everything he holds dear. I shudder with revulsion when I think of it, and so does he. Hang the man who did it, and not the man who did not.

As I conclude, I say to you, if there is anything I have overlooked in my summation to you which I should have mentioned, if I have been guilty of the slightest dereliction of my duty to this man, the slightest negligence in my performance of it, I must assume the whole responsibility. It would be an awful thing to send to the gallows a man who did not commit this crime, a terrible thing indeed, and it will prey on your minds for the rest of your life. Go back then to your jury room. Remember the facts as I have outlined them. Remember that the evidence must be consistent with his guilt and inconsistent with any other rational conclusion. Act not on what you think, act not on what you may feel, act only on what you are morally sure. Do that and you will come back to this room with but one verdict, and in very short order – Not Guilty.

Notes

CHAPTER 1 THE FIGURES IN THE CARPET

1 Sean O'Sullivan, *Both My Houses: From Politics to Priesthood* (Toronto: Key Porter Books, 1986), 234

CHAPTER 2 IN THE VALLEY

1 John French interview, Ottawa, 10 Apr. 90
2 Tom Edmondstone interview, Renfrew, Ont., 20 Apr. 91
3 Nell Maloney interview, Ottawa, 24 Apr. 90
4 John French interview, Ottawa, 22 May 91
5 Nell Maloney interview, Ottawa, 22 May 91
6 Frances French interview, Ottawa, 24 Apr. 90
7 Anna Lyons interview, Ottawa, 10 Apr. 90
8 Margaret Godin interview, Toronto, 9 Mar. 91
9 Nell Maloney, *supra* note 3
10 Nell Maloney, *supra* note 5
11 Lillian Maloney interview, "Rockwood" on the Guelph line, 21 Apr. 90
12 Anna Lyons interview, Ottawa, 22 May 91
13 Frances French, *supra* note 6
14 Nell Maloney, *supra* note 3
15 Lillian Maloney, *supra* note 11
16 Margaret Godin, *supra* note 8
17 Frances French, supra note 6
18 Frances French interview, Ottawa, 24 Apr. 90
19 Letter from Arthur Maloney to Mrs. M.J. Maloney, Montreal, postmark, 18 Aug. 30
20 Letter from Mrs. Maloney to Arthur Maloney, Eganville, 21 Oct. 38
21 Letter from James Maloney to Arthur Maloney, Renfrew, 6 Jun. 40
22 Letter from Anne Cillis to the *Ottawa Citizen*, 31 Jul 73
23 Mrs. Jake Dunlap interview, Ottawa, 19 Apr. 91
24 Cillis letter, *supra* note 22
25 French, *supra* note 4

26 Edmondstone, *supra* note 2
27 Letter from "Sandy" to Arthur Maloney, Regina, Saskatchewan, 7 Feb. 62
28 Dalton Camp, *Gentlemen, Players & Politicians* (Toronto: McClelland and Stewart Ltd., 1970), 243
29 Edmondstone, *supra* note 2
30 Mr. Justice Frank Dunlap interview, Kingston, 18 Mar 91
31 Edmondstone, *supra* note 2
32 Lillian Maloney interview, "Rockwood" on the Guelph line, 11 Feb 91

CHAPTER 3 EARLY YEARS

1 Mr. Justice Frank Dunlap interview, Kingston, 21 Mar. 91
2 Mr. Justice Frank Dunlap interview, Kingston, 19 Mar. 91
3 Frank Dunlap, *supra* note 1
4 Arthur Maloney file, Upper Canada Law Society Archives, Osgoode Hall, Toronto
5 Osgoode file, letter from Arthur Maloney to Mr. Earl Smith, Secretary, The Law Society of Upper Canada, 6 May 42
6 Osgoode file, *supra* note 5
7 Osgoode file, letter from the Chairman, Legal Education Committee to J.A. Maloney, Esq., Renfrew, Ontario, 7 Oct. 42
8 Osgoode file, letter from Arthur Maloney to the Secretary, The Law Society of Upper Canada, 1 Sep. 43
9 Osgoode file, letter from R. H. Greer, K.C. to J. Shirley Denison, Esq., K.C., 11 Sep. 43
10 Royal York testimonial dinner address, 1979
11 Ibid.
12 Ibid.
13 Mr. Justice G. Arthur Martin interview, Toronto, 1 Dec. 90
14 Ibid.
15 Mr. Justice Charles Dubin, Court of Appeal offices, Toronto, 15 Oct. 1991
16 J.J. Robinette interview, Toronto, 12 Feb. 91
17 Martin, *supra* note 13
18 *The Toronto Daily Star*, 15 May 47
19 Lillian Maloney interview, "Rockwood" on the Guelph line, 11 Feb. 91
20 Lillian Maloney interview, "Rockwood" on the Guelph line, 22 Jan. 91
21 Lillian Maloney, *supra* note 19
22 Lillian Maloney, *supra* note 19

CHAPTER 4 SERIOUS BUSINESS: SUCHAN AND JACKSON

1 Frank Dunlap interview, Kingston, 18 Mar. 91
2 Douglas Crane interview, Toronto, 8 Mar. 91

3 Bob Johnstone interview, Toronto, 5 Apr. 91
4 Frank Dunlap interview, Kingston, 21 Mar. 91
5 B. Clive Bynoe interview, Toronto, 21 Apr. 90
6 Crane, *supra* note 2
7 Judge Monte Harris interview, Toronto, 6 Feb. 90
8 Jake Dunlap interview, Ottawa, 19 Apr. 91
9 Mr. Justice G. Arthur Martin interview, Toronto, 1 Dec. 90
10 Paul French interview, Toronto, 29 May 91

CHAPTER 5 BROWN EGGS AND MURDER

1 John Craig, trial transcript, *Esposito*, 536–7
2 Craig, cross-examination, *Esposito*, 543–4
3 Dante Rossi, examination-in-chief, *Esposito*, 214
4 Vincenzo Tiano, cross-examination, *Esposito*, 172
5 Walter Koczkur, cross-examination, *Esposito*, 144
6 Peter Kuryliw, cross-examination, *Esposito*, 250–1
7 Ward Smith, cross-examination, *Esposito*, 358–9
8 Craig, cross-examination, *Esposito*, 538–45
9 Arthur Maloney, jury address, *Esposito*, 619–20
10 Rossi, cross-examination, *Esposito*, 214
11 Rossi, examination-in-chief, *Esposito*, 204
12 Craig, examination-in-chief, *Esposito*, 534
13 Craig, cross-examination, *Esposito*, 547–8
14 Smith, cross-examination, *Esposito*, 349–52
15 Dr. Albert E. Allin, examination-in-chief, *Esposito*, 446–50
16 Allin, cross-examination, *Esposito*, 450–6
17 Maloney, jury address, *Esposito*, 620–2
18 R. MacKinnon, cross-examination, *Esposito*, 30–4
19 Rossi, cross-examination, *Esposito*, 229–31
20 Con. Douglas Forbes, cross-examination, *Esposito*, 490–1
21 Frank Henry Kailik, cross-examination, *Esposito*, 526–7
22 Maloney, jury address, *Esposito*, 609–16

CHAPTER 6 THE FIFTIES AND POLITICS

1 Mr. Justice John O'Driscoll interview, Toronto, 6 Apr. 90
2 Bob Johnstone interview, Toronto, 5 Apr. 91
3 Glenn Hainey interview, Toronto, 30 Nov. 90
4 Mike Starr interview, Oshawa, Ontario, 6 Apr. 91
5 Johnstone interview, Toronto, 5 Apr. 91
6 Peter Oliver, *Unlikely Tory: The Life and Politics of Allen Grossman* (Toronto: Lester Orpen Dennys, 1985), 144

7 Ibid.
8 Ralph McCreath interview, Toronto, 17 Oct. 91
9 Starr interview, *supra* note 4
10 Jerry Wilk interview, Parkdale, 27 Mar. 91
11 Arthur Maloney, address to the Young Progressive Conservatives Association, Parkdale, 20 Jun. 56
12 Arthur Maloney, undated speech, Parkdale election file

CHAPTER 7 WAITING FOR DIEFENBAKER

1 Michael Starr interview, Oshawa, 6 Apr. 91
2 Ralph McCreath interview, Toronto, 17 Oct. 91
3 Bob Johnstone interview, Toronto, 5 Apr. 91
4 Jack Horner, *My Own Brand* (Edmonton: Hurtig Publishers Ltd., 1980), 37
5 Mr. Justice Pat LeSage interview, Toronto, 17 Nov. 90
6 Frank McGee interview, Toronto, 29 May 91
7 Peter Stursberg, *Diefenbaker: Leadership Gained, 1956–62* (Toronto: University of Toronto Press, 1975), 184
8 Jake Dunlap interview, Ottawa, 19 Apr. 91
9 Jerry Wilk interview, 27 Mar. 91
10 George Karmanin interview, Toronto, 24 May 91
11 George Nagy interview, Toronto, 29 May 91
12 Judge Monte Harris interview, Toronto, 13 Feb. 91
13 McCreath, *supra* note 2
14 Douglas Crane interview, Toronto, 8 Mar. 91
15 Henry Hodowany interview, Toronto, 9 Oct. 91
16 Johnstone, *supra* note 3
17 Lillian Maloney interview, "Rockwood" on the Guelph line, 11 Feb. 91.
18 Letter from Arthur Maloney to The Reverend Sister Martin of the Sacred Heart, D'Youville College, Buffalo, New York, 9 Jul. 62
19 Letter from Senator Joseph A. Sullivan to Arthur Maloney, 19 Jul. 62
20 Glenn Hainey interview, Toronto, 30 Nov. 91
21 Eric Murray interview, Toronto, 9 Oct. 91
22 John Diefenbaker, *One Canada: Memoirs of the Right Honourable John G. Diefenbaker: The Tumultuous Years, 1962 to 1967* (Toronto: Macmillan, 1977), 178–9
23 Lillian Maloney interview, "Rockwood" on the Guelph line, 22 Jan. 91.
24 Mr. Justice W.D. Roach, *Report of the Honourable Mr. Justice Roach As a Commissioner Appointed under The Public Inquiries Act by Letters Patent Dated December 11, 1969*, 219
25 Ibid., 225

CHAPTER 8 MURDER ON THE RUN

1 John McGuire, trial transcript, *Bleta*, 42–51
2 Ibid., 58
3 Dr. Chester McLean, *Bleta*, 30
4 Rustem Kaziu, *Bleta*, 78–9
5 Eleanor May Trimble, *Bleta*, 89
6 Ibid., 90
7 Ibid., 92
8 Trimble, *Bleta*, 94
9 Ibid., 98–9
10 Ibid., 102
11 Ibid., 103
12 Ibid., 104
13 Mazie DeGeer, *Bleta*, 109
14 Ibid., 114
15 Sidney Coles, *Bleta*, 137
16 Philip Rosenfarb, *Bleta*, 148
17 Charles Bond, *Bleta*,159
18 Ibid., 169–70
19 Norman Hobson, *Bleta*, 181–3
20 Ibid., 185
21 Kiekebelt, *Bleta*, 203
22 Alexander Golab, *Bleta*, 215–16
23 Arthur Maloney, *Bleta*, 232
24 Ibid., 233–4
25 Arthur Klein, *Bleta*, 236–7
26 Maloney, *Bleta*, 240
27 Ibid., 244–5
28 Mr. Justice Aylen, *Bleta*, 245
29 Ibid., 248
30 Ibid., 250
31 Ibid., 252
32 Ibid., 293
33 Klein, *Bleta*, 354
34 Dr. Ronald Stokes, *Bleta*, 415
35 Ibid., 440
36 Ibid., 442
37 *Bleta*, 442
38 *Bleta*, 457
39 *Bleta*, 458
40 Klein, *Bleta*, 475
41 Maloney, *Bleta*, 477

42 Ibid., 478
43 Ibid., 479
44 Ibid.
45 Ibid.
46 Ibid.
47 Marcel Proust, *The Past Recaptured* (New York: Vintage Books, 1971), 164
48 *Regina v. Bleta, CCC,* 1964, Vol. 2, 191
49 *Bleta v. The Queen, CCC,* 1965, Vol. 1, 2
50 Chief Justice D. Porter, *supra* note 461, 192
51 *Supra* note 491, 1
52 *The Toronto Daily Star,* 2 Jun. 64

CHAPTER 9 COMING TO THE RESCUE

1 *The Telegram,* Toronto, 21 Jul. 62
2 Ibid.
3 Roy McMurtry interview, Toronto, 7 Apr. 90
4 G. Arthur Martin interview, Toronto, 1 Dec. 90
5 Frank McGee interview, Toronto, 29 May 91
6 Bob Johnstone interview, Toronto, 5 Apr. 91
7 George Karmanin interview, Toronto, 24 May 91
8 Doug Crane interview, Toronto, 8 Mar. 91
9 Eric Murray interview, Toronto, 17 Oct. 91
10 Stephen Traviss interview, Osgoode Hall, Toronto, 16 Nov. 90
11 Maloney, McCorkell trial transcript, 1706–9
12 Ibid., 1714
13 Ibid., 1719
14 Ibid., 1722–3
15 Ibid., 1731
16 Ibid., 1732
17 Neils Ortved interview, Toronto, 5 Feb. 91
18 Mike Starr interview, Oshawa, 6 Apr. 91
19 Peter C. Newman, *The Distemper of Our Times: Canadian Politics in Transition: 1963–1968* (Toronto: McClelland and Stewart, 1968), 136
20 Ralph McCreath interview, Toronto, 17 Oct. 91
21 McMurtry, *supra* note 3
22 Jack Horner, *My Own Brand* (Edmonton: Hurtig Publishers, 1980), 75
23 McMurtry, *supra* note 3
24 Pat LeSage interview, Toronto, 17 Nov. 90
25 Tom Edmondstone interview, Renfrew, 20 Apr. 91
26 Starr, *supra* note 18

CHAPTER 10 MURDER, A WOMAN SCORNED, AND THE NEW CRITICISM

1 W. Neils Ortved, "The Defence of Gary Staples," in *Advocacy in Court*, ed. Franklin R. Moskoff, Q.C. (Toronto: Canada Law Book, 1987), 1–23
2 Ibid., 9
3 Ibid., 8–9
4 Ibid., 1
5 Arthur Maloney, jury address, *Staples*, 1420
6 Ibid., 1420–1
7 Ibid., 1421–2
8 Ibid., 1429–30
9 Christine Kates, *Her Majesty the Queen vs. Gary Staples – Arthur Maloney, 1972* (Toronto: Osgoode Law Society unpublished paper, 1972), 54
10 Maloney, *supra* note 5, 1401–2
11 Ibid., 1413–14
12 Ibid., 1414–15
13 Ibid., 1425

CHAPTER 11 SIXTY THOUSAND A YEAR, A CAR, AND A DRIVER

1 Pat LeSage interview, Toronto, 17 Nov. 90
2 Paul French interview, Toronto, 29 May 91
3 Neils Ortved interview, Toronto, 5 Feb. 91
4 Roy McMurtry interview, Toronto, 7 Apr. 90
5 Doug Crane interview, Toronto, 8 Mar. 91
6 Stephen Traviss interview, Toronto, 16 Nov. 90
7 Clive Bynoe interview, Toronto, 21 Apr. 90
8 Crane, *supra* note 5
9 Bob Johnstone interview, Toronto, 5 Apr. 91.
10 Bynoe, *supra* note 7
11 Ortved, *supra* note 3
12 Phil Patterson interview, Toronto, 17 Nov. 90
13 Michael Zacks interview, Toronto, 4 Oct. 91

CHAPTER 12 CULTURE AND THE CIVIL SERVICE

1 Michael Zacks interview, Toronto, 4 Oct. 91
2 Lillian Maloney interview, "Rockwood" on the Guelph line, 22 Jan. 91
3 Glenn Hainey interview, Toronto, 30 Nov. 90
4 Zacks, *supra* note 1
5 Arthur Maloney, address to the Second International Ombudsman Conference, Jerusalem, Israel, 27 Oct. 80, 17
6 Ibid.

7 Ibid.
8 John Loftis interview, Kingston, 29 Apr. 90
9 Keith Hoilett interview, Toronto, 17 Oct. 91
10 Phil Patterson interview, Toronto, 17 Nov. 90
11 Loftis, *supra* note 8
12 Zacks, *supra* note 1

CHAPTER 13 THE CHILDREN'S CRUSADE MEETS REALITY IN NORTH PICKERING

1 Glenn Hainey interview, Toronto, 30 Nov. 90
2 Ibid.
3 Keith Hoilett interview, Toronto, 17 Oct. 91
4 The Hon. John R. Rhodes, Minister of Housing, Statement to the Select Committee, undated, 4
5 Letter from Hon. John R. Rhodes, Minister of Housing, to Arthur Maloney, 7 Jul. 76
6 Michael Zacks interview, Toronto, 4 Oct 91
7 Hainey, *supra* note 1
8 Rhodes, *supra* note 4, 17
9 Harold Greer, *The Brantford Expositor*, 25 Aug. 76
10 Harold Greer, "Queen's Park Report" in *The Brockville Recorder and Times*, 12 Oct. 76
11 Hainey, *supra* note 1
12 Eric Murray interview, Toronto, 17 Oct. 91
13 Roy McMurtry interview, Toronto, 7 Apr. 90
14 Letter from Arthur Maloney to Premier Davis, 12 Nov. 76
15 Letter of resignation from David Humphrey to the Lt. Governor of Ontario, 15 Apr. 77
16 Letter from Ian Scott, Q.C. to Mr. Donnelly, Chairman of the Commission, 17 May 77

CHAPTER 14 CIRCLING THE WAGONS

1 Bob Johnstone interview, Toronto, 5 Apr. 91
2 Harold Greer, *St. Catharines Standard*, 20 Jan. 77
3 *The Bancroft Times*, 19 Oct. 77
4 *Sunday Star*, 11 Dec. 77
5 Memo from Alice Murray to Arthur Maloney, 23 Mar. 77
6 *Sunday Star*, *supra* note 4
7 *The Toronto Star*, 11 Dec. 77

CHAPTER 15 THE MONSTER IN THE COMMITTEE ROOM AND KITTY BAR THE DOOR

1 Memo from Neils Ortved to Arthur Maloney: re 1st Meeting of *The Select Committee on Guidelines*, 5 Nov. 75, 2–3
2 Arthur Maloney, remarks to *The Select Committee on Guidelines*, 13 Nov. 75, 3–4
3 *First Annual Report 1975–1976*, 572–3
4 Phil Patterson interview, Toronto, 17 Nov. 90
5 Letter from Arthur Maloney to James Renwick, 18 Mar. 77, secs. 7 & 8
6 Ombudsman Office Memorandum, *Role and Function of the Select Committee on the Ombudsman*, unattributed, Maloney Select Committee file
7 Memo from Brian Goodman to Arthur Maloney, 5 Dec. 77, 8
8 P.D. Lawlor, MPP, *Hansard*, 2nd Session, 31st Parliament, 5 Jun 78, No. 78, 313–14
9 Claire Hoy, *The Toronto Sun*, 15 Dec. 77
10 *The Toronto Daily Star*, 17 Dec. 77
11 *News Reports Re The Select Committee and the Office of the Ombudsman*, 29 Aug. 78, 1–2
12 Eric Murray interview, Toronto, 17 Oct. 91
13 J. Dickson, *Re British Columbia Development Corp. et al. And Friedmann et al.*, 14 *D.L.R.* (4th), 141
14 Murray, *supra* note 12

CHAPTER 16 RUNNING ON EMPTY

1 Gary Dunford, *The Sunday Sun*, 22 Jan. 78
2 Arthur Maloney, Crime Report, 10 Feb. 78, A8
3 Maloney resignation file
4 Memo from John Beaufoy to Arthur Maloney, 24 Jul. 78
5 *News Reports re Mr. Maloney's resignation*, Maloney resignation file, 15 Aug. 78, 16
6 Phil Patterson interview, Toronto, 17 Nov. 90
7 Lillian Maloney interview, "Rockwood" on the Guelph line, 22 Jan. 91
8 Eric Murray interview, Toronto, 9 Oct. 91
9 Letter from Tony O'Donohue to Arthur Maloney, 18 Aug. 78
10 Letter from Bill Johnson to Arthur Maloney, 30 Aug. 78
11 Gordon Meiklejohn interview, Toronto, 8 Oct. 91
12 Jonathan Manthorpe, *Kitchener-Waterloo Record*, 16 Oct. 78

CHAPTER 17 SIXTY-YEAR-OLD SMILING PUBLIC MAN

1 *Oshawa Times*, 12 Dec. 78
2 Monte Harris interview, Toronto, 13 Feb. 91
3 Neils Ortved interview, Toronto, 5 Feb. 91
4 *The Toronto Daily Star*, 21 Mar. 79
5 *Kitchener-Waterloo Record*, 16 Jan. 79
6 *The Ottawa Journal*, 9 May 79
7 Arthur Maloney, *Blueprint for the Office of the Ombudsman in Ontario*, 378–9
8 *London Evening Free Press*, 8 Jun. 79
9 Jonathan Manthorpe, *Kitchener-Waterloo Record*, 14 Jul. 79
10 David Rendeiro interview, Toronto, 9 Oct. 91
11 Iain Hunter interview, Ottawa, 15 Mar. 91
12 Charles Lynch, *Montreal Gazette*, 22 Aug. 79

CHAPTER 18 TIME'S WINGED CHARIOT HURRYING NEAR

1 Gordon Meiklejohn interview, Toronto, 8 Oct. 91
2 John Downing, *Toronto Sun*, 18 Dec. 79
3 *The Toronto Daily Star*, 14 Jan. 80
4 Pat LeSage interview, Toronto, 17 Nov. 90
5 Paul French interview, Toronto, 29 May 91
6 *The Globe and Mail*, 18 Dec. 82
7 Father Henry Maloney, memo dictated over the telephone, 18 Dec. 82, Maloney Senate file

EPILOGUE THE LAST OF THE TRIBUNES

1 Rae Corelli, *The Toronto Star*, 16 May 74
2 B. Clive Bynoe interview, Toronto, 21 Apr. 90
3 Mr. Justice Pat LeSage interview, Toronto, 17 Nov. 90.
4 His Honour Keith Hoilett interview, Toronto, 17 Oct. 91.
5 Stephen Traviss interview, Toronto, 16 Nov. 90
6 Dave Humphrey interview, Toronto, 3 Oct. 91. There is a further comment upon the "One Eyed Connolly" case in an address that Arthur made to The Advocates' Society in 1974: "When you gather to hear a talk on the Role of the Advocate you are entitled to hear from someone more eminent than myself. I was reminded a few years ago of what rung on the ladder I belonged to. It was a case involving the defence of a Bay Street character popularly known as 'One Eyed Connolly,' now deceased. Dave Humphrey, Q.C., and I acted together in the matter although for different accused. Now it came to pass that 'One Eye' was found not guilty on all counts but one but alas was sentenced as though this were not the case – at

least according to my biased view of the matter. The case against 'One Eye' had been investigated by a police officer who had pursued the investigation with unrelenting zeal, much to the annoyance of Connolly. Connolly left to serve his sentence. Not too long afterwards the enterprising police officer got into trouble himself and came to me to defend him. His arrest and the charge got much notoriety. Before his case came to trial 'One Eye' Connolly was given a week-end pass and unannounced he dropped into the office to pay his respects. He said: 'I read where you're defending that (expletive deleted).' I acknowledged I was. He said: 'I'll never figure out why he'd come to you' – All during the trial he'd say 'Why the hell did you hire Maloney. Everybody knows that Humphrey is the best lawyer in Canada.'"

7 Corelli, *supra* note 1

8 Arthur Maloney, "Addressing the Jury in Criminal Cases," in *The Canadian Bar Review*, Vol. xxxv, Apr. 1957, No. 4, 381–2

9 Arthur Maloney, *Notes of Address Delivered by Arthur Maloney, Q.C., at the Fall Convention of The Advocates Society, 1974, entitled "The Role of the Advocate,"* 3–4

10 Maloney, *supra* note 8, 375

11 Arthur Maloney, *Notes of Address Delivered by Arthur Maloney, Q.C. to a Luncheon Meeting of The Confederation Club in Ottawa at the El Mirador Hotel on Thursday, April 24, 1975*, 9

12 Rae Corelli, *The Toronto Star*, 6 Nov. 72

13 Arthur Maloney, "Law Enforcement and The Citizen's Liberty," Address to the joint Annual Meeting of the Law Society of Alberta and the Alberta Branch of The Canadian Bar Association held at Edmonton, 11 February 1966, *The Canadian Bar Journal*, June 1966, 174

14 Arthur Maloney, "The Right to Remain Silent," undated manuscript, 8–10

15 Scott Young, *The Globe and Mail*, 16 Dec. 71

Index